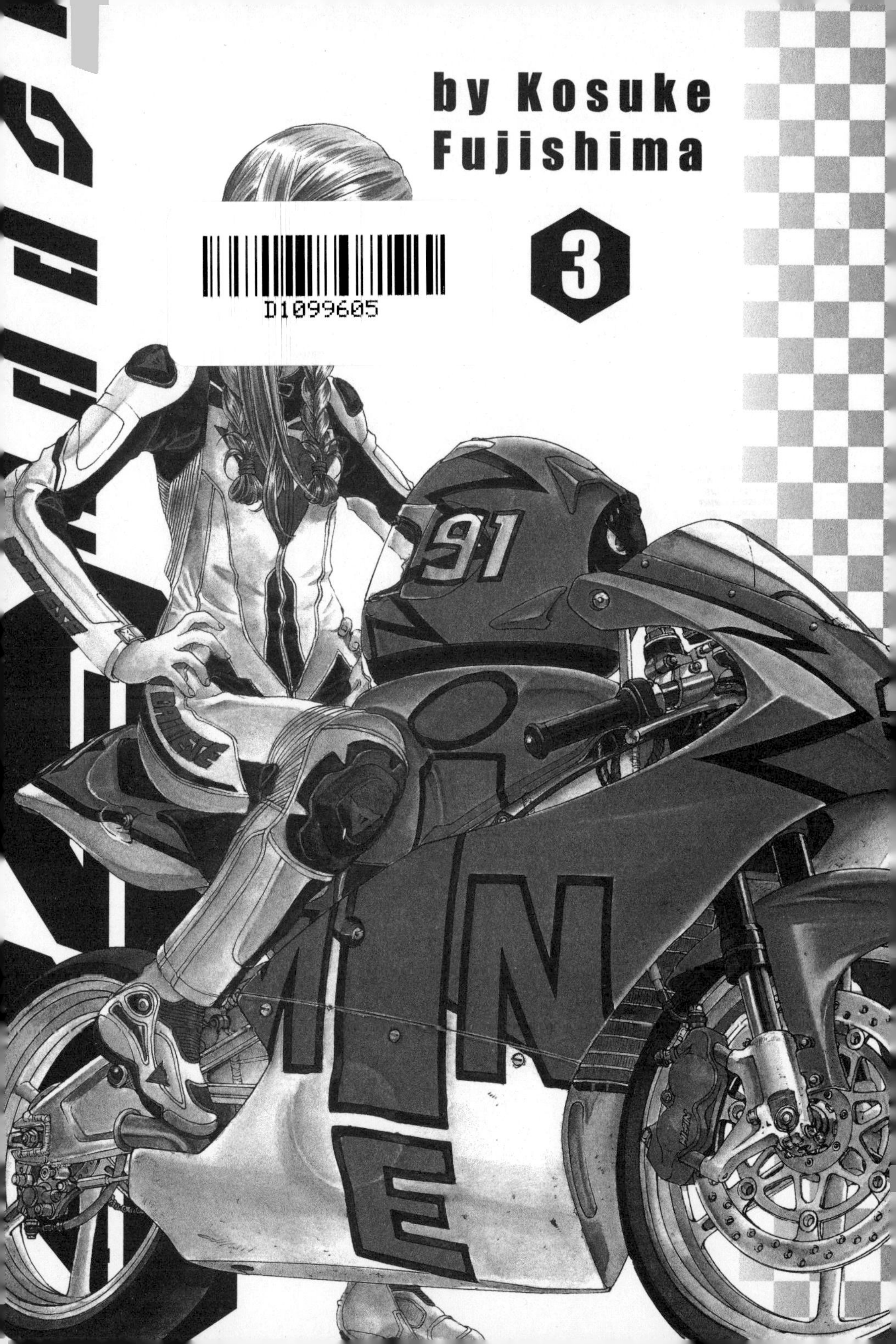
by Kosuke
Fujishima
3
91

[TOPPU GP]

Presented by

Kosuke Fujishima

Lap 15:

ACCELERATION BATTLE

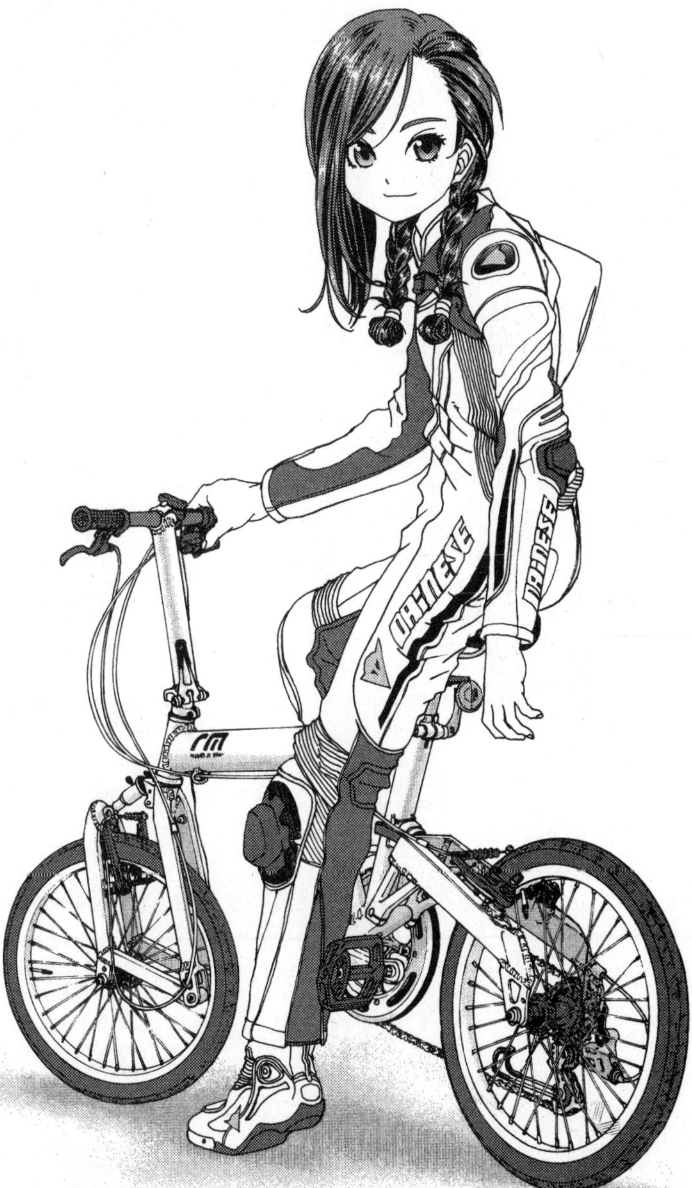

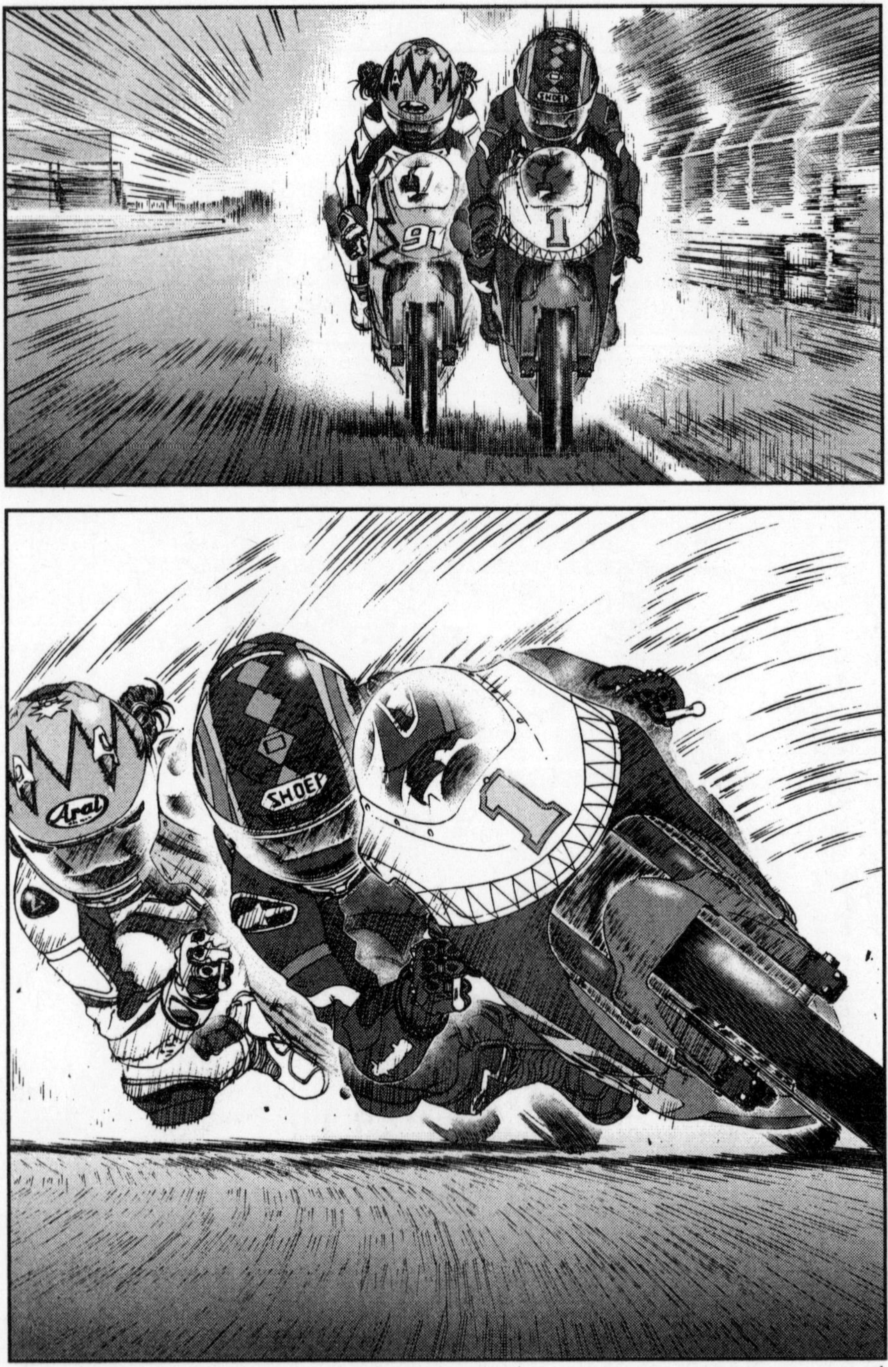
SHOEI
91
1
Arai
SHOEI
1

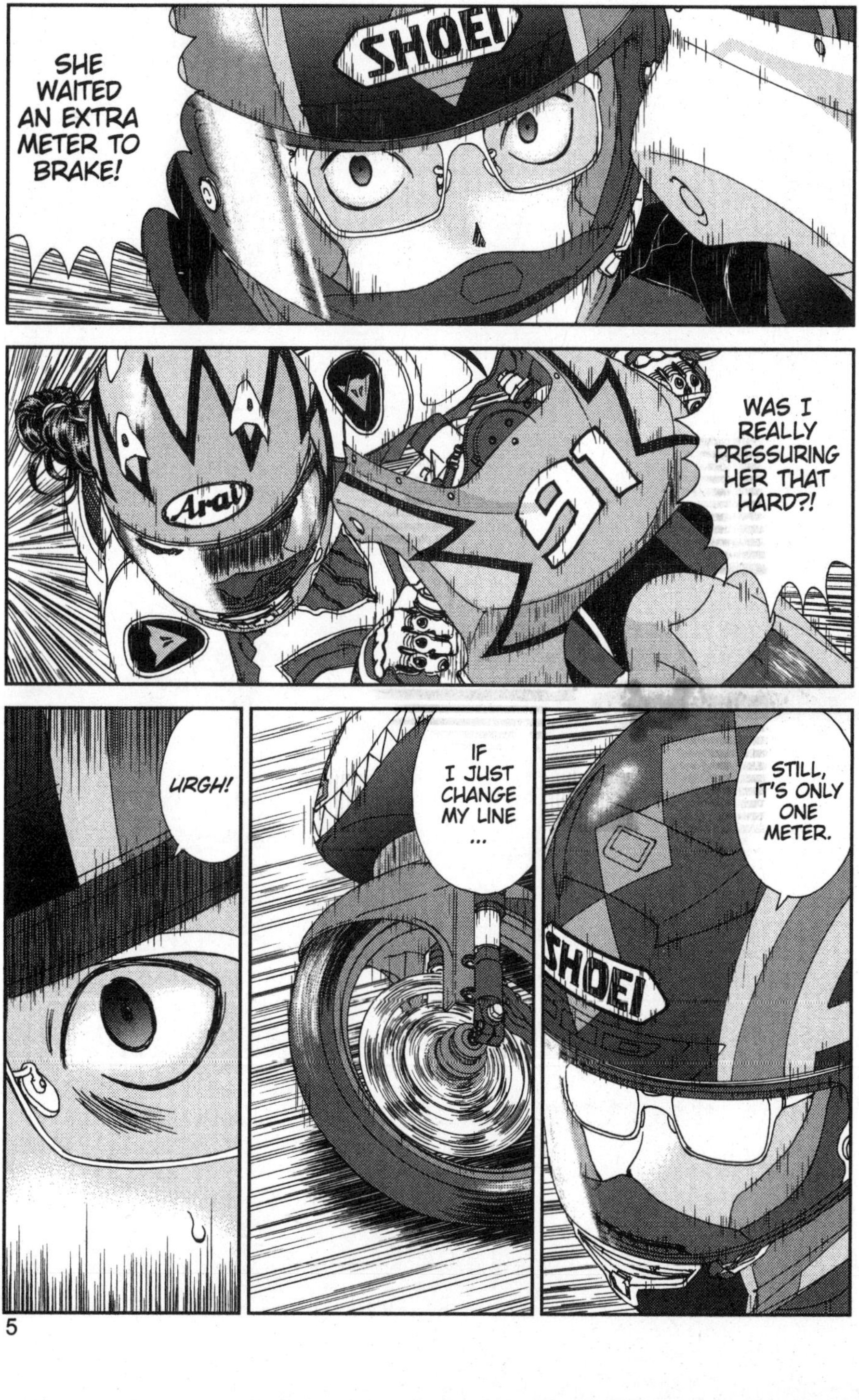
SHE WAITED AN EXTRA METER TO BRAKE!
SHOEI
WAS I REALLY PRESSURING HER THAT HARD?!
Arai
91
STILL, IT'S ONLY ONE METER.
SHOEI
IF I JUST CHANGE MY LINE ...
URGH!

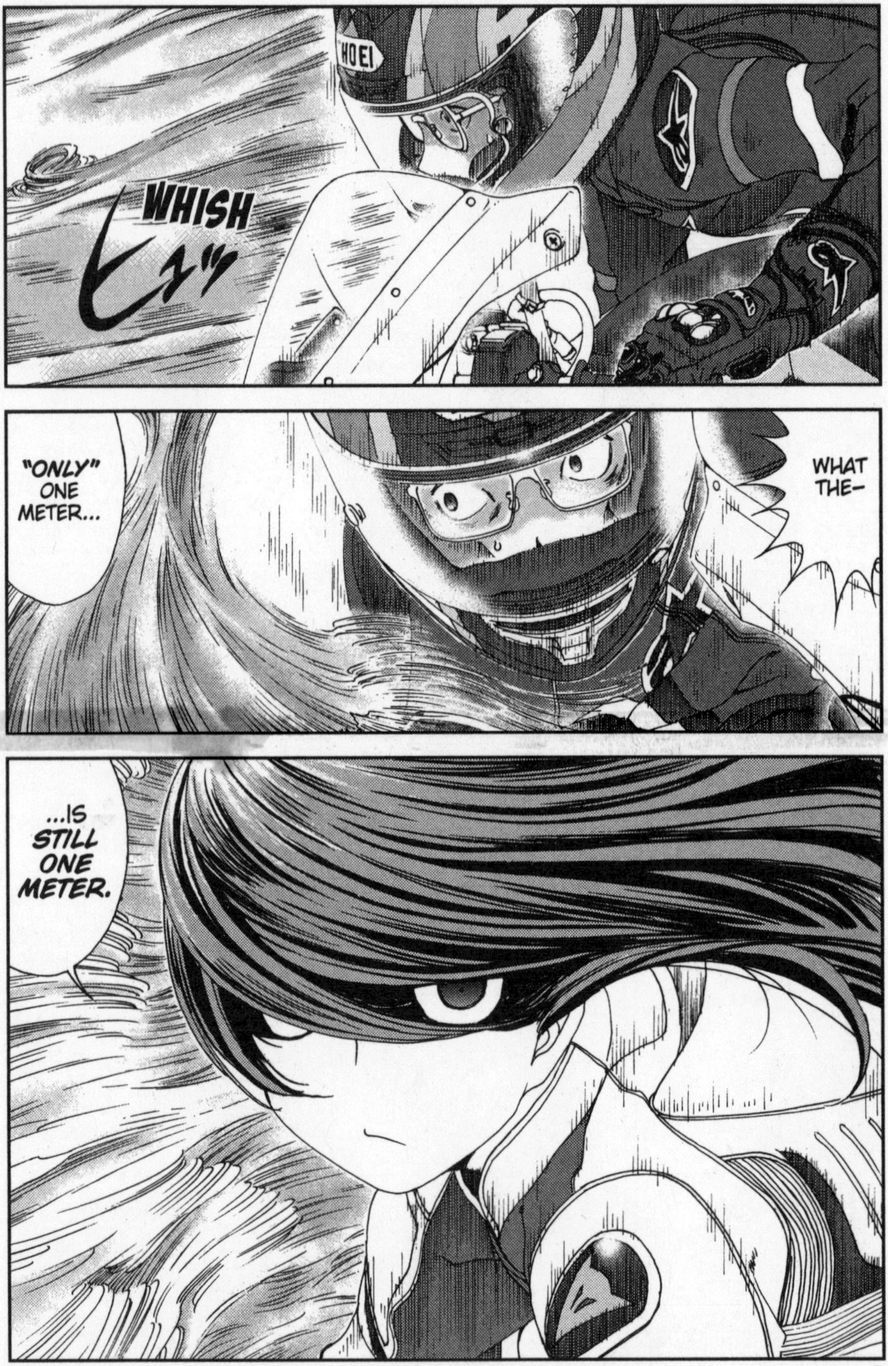
WHISH
ヒュッ
WHAT THE-
"ONLY" ONE METER...
...IS STILL ONE METER.

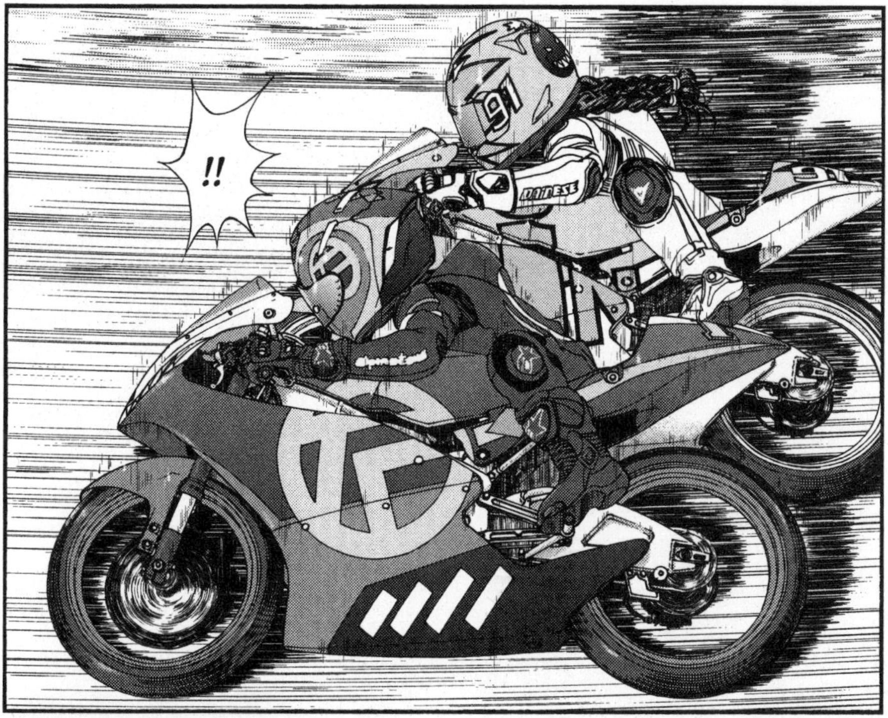
!!

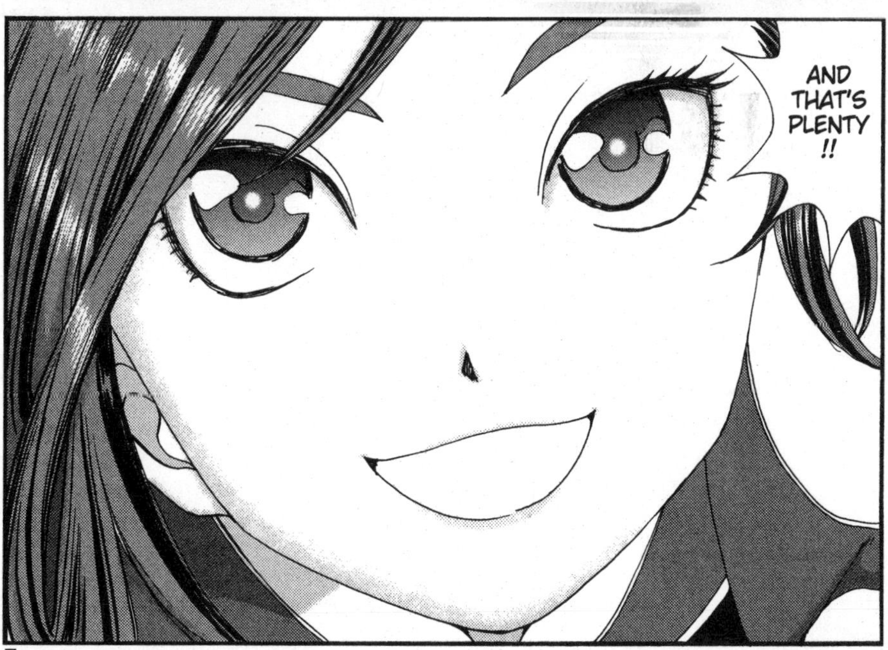
AND THAT'S PLENTY !!

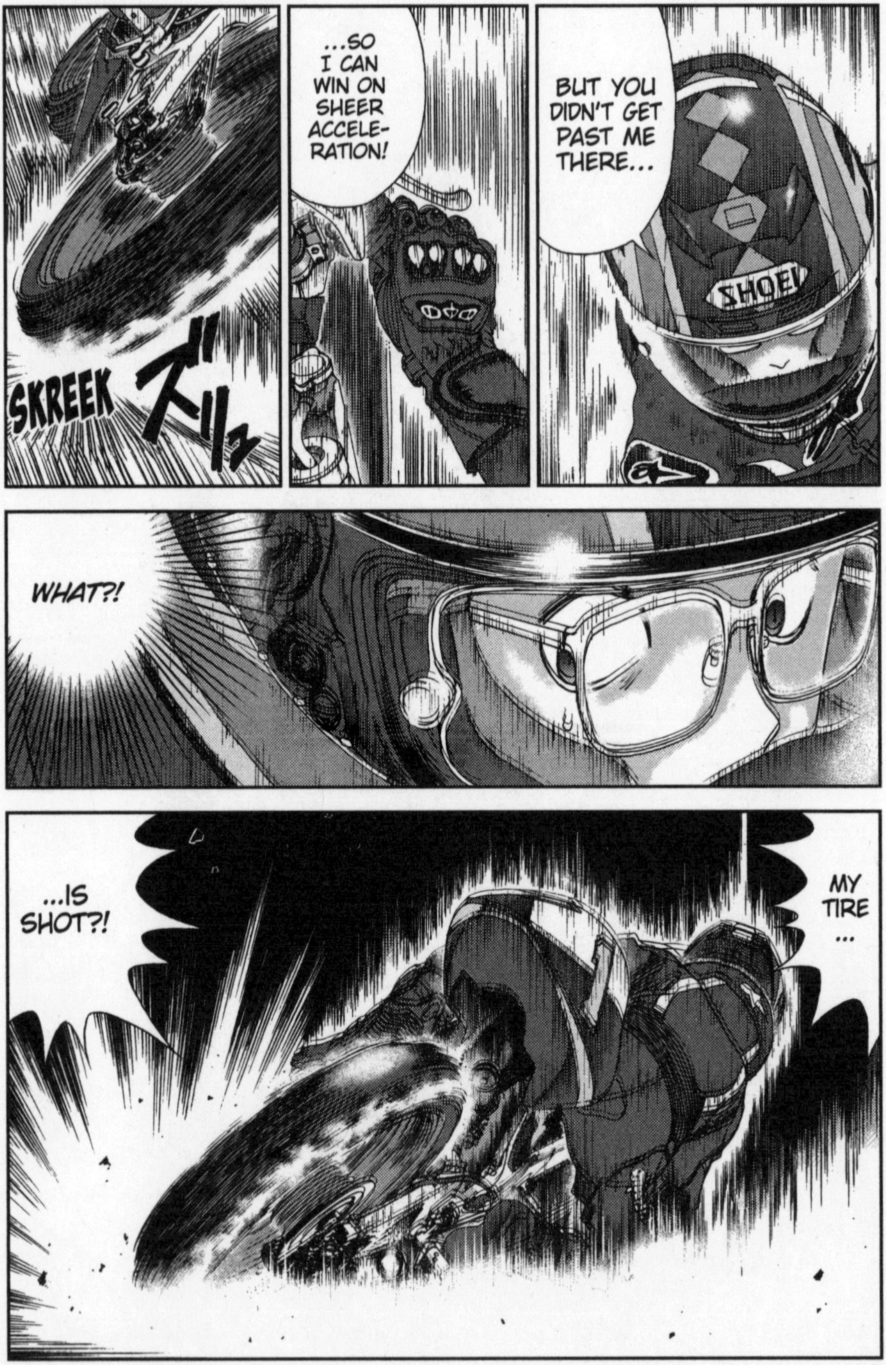
BUT YOU DIDN'T GET PAST ME THERE...
...SO I CAN WIN ON SHEER ACCELE-RATION!
SKREEK
WHAT?!
MY TIRE ...
...IS SHOT?!

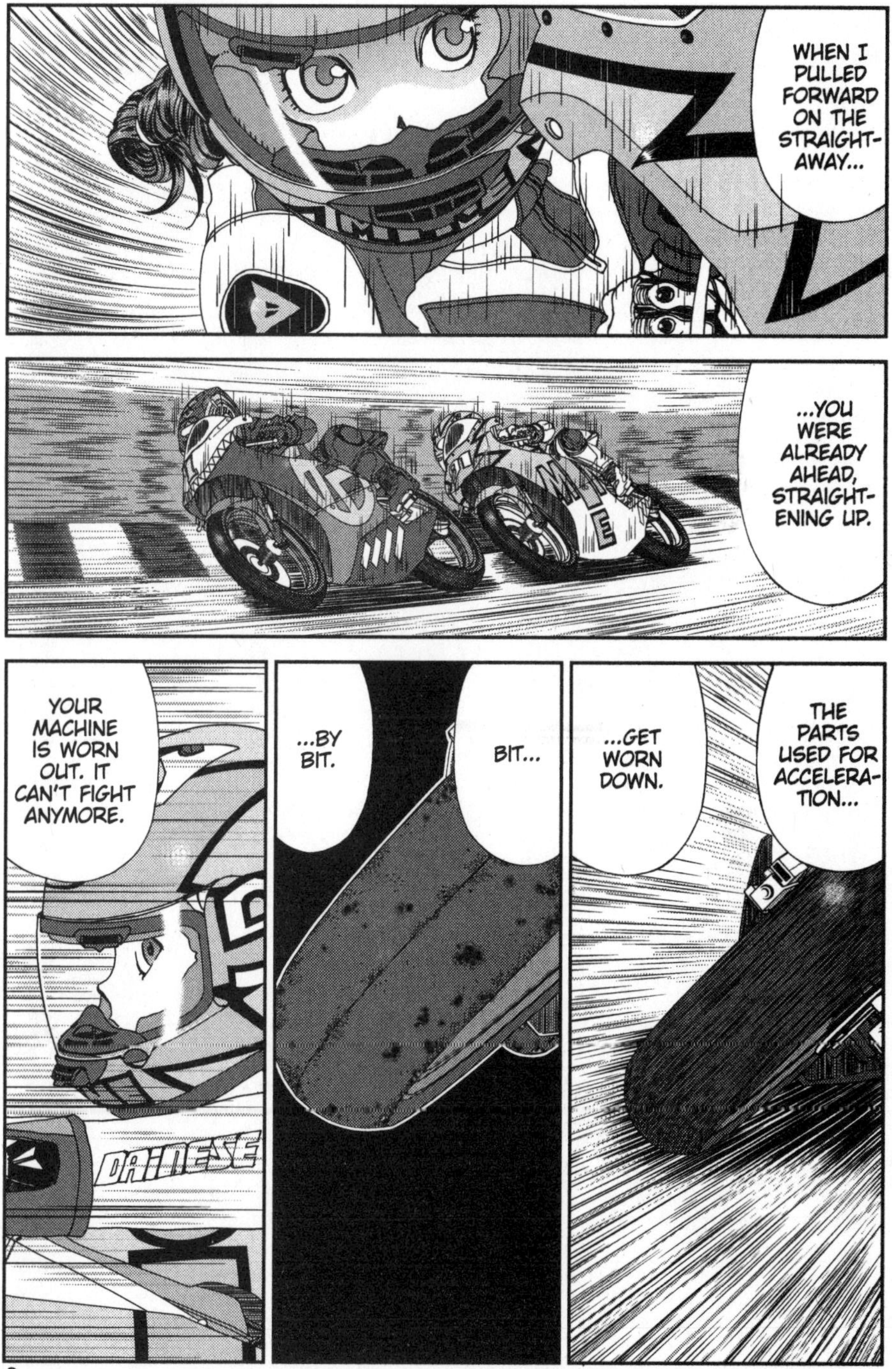
WHEN I PULLED FORWARD ON THE STRAIGHT-AWAY...
...YOU WERE ALREADY AHEAD, STRAIGHT-ENING UP.
THE PARTS USED FOR ACCELERA-TION...
...GET WORN DOWN.
BIT...
...BY BIT.
YOUR MACHINE IS WORN OUT. IT CAN'T FIGHT ANYMORE.
DAINESE

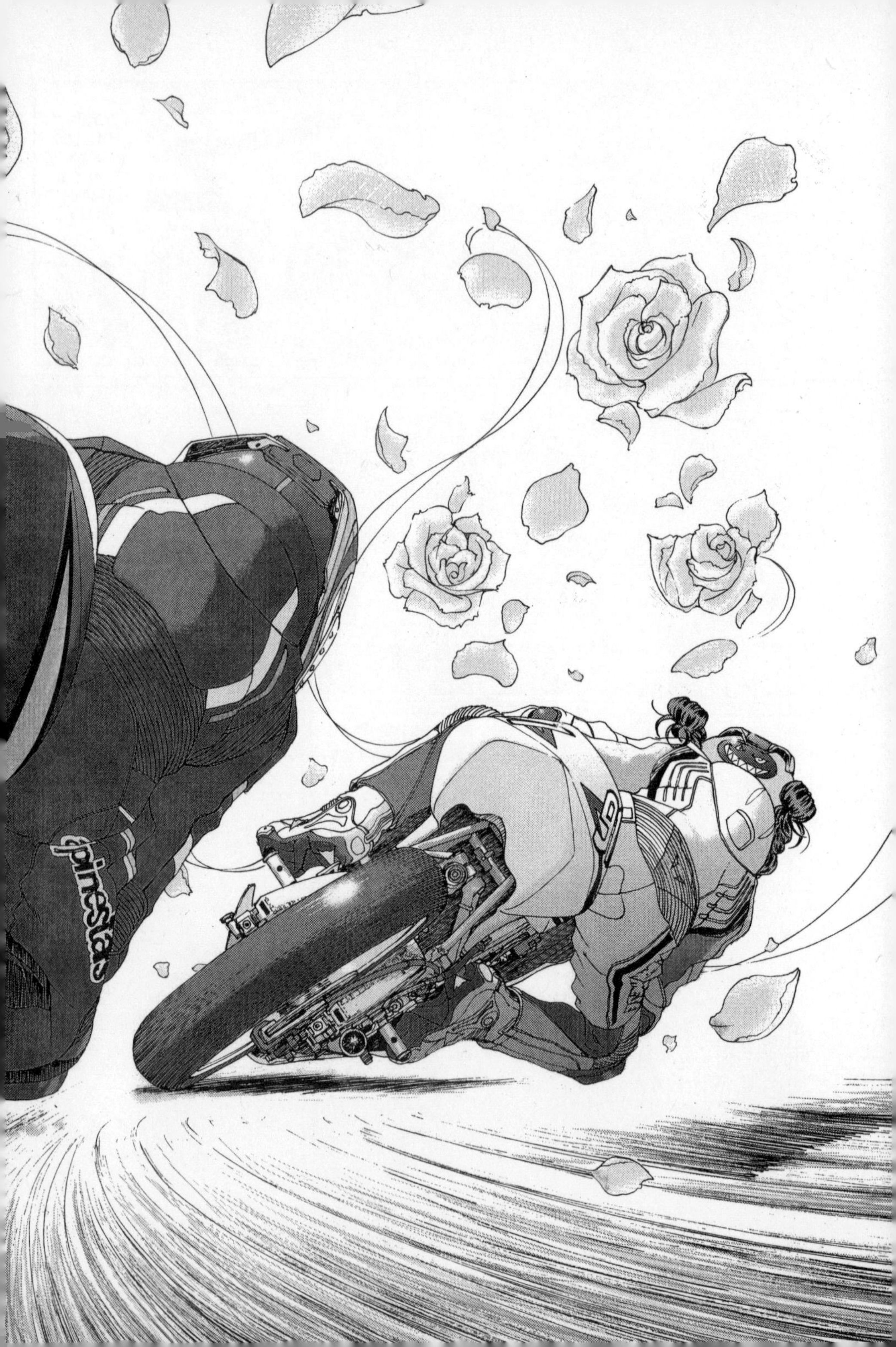
alpinestars

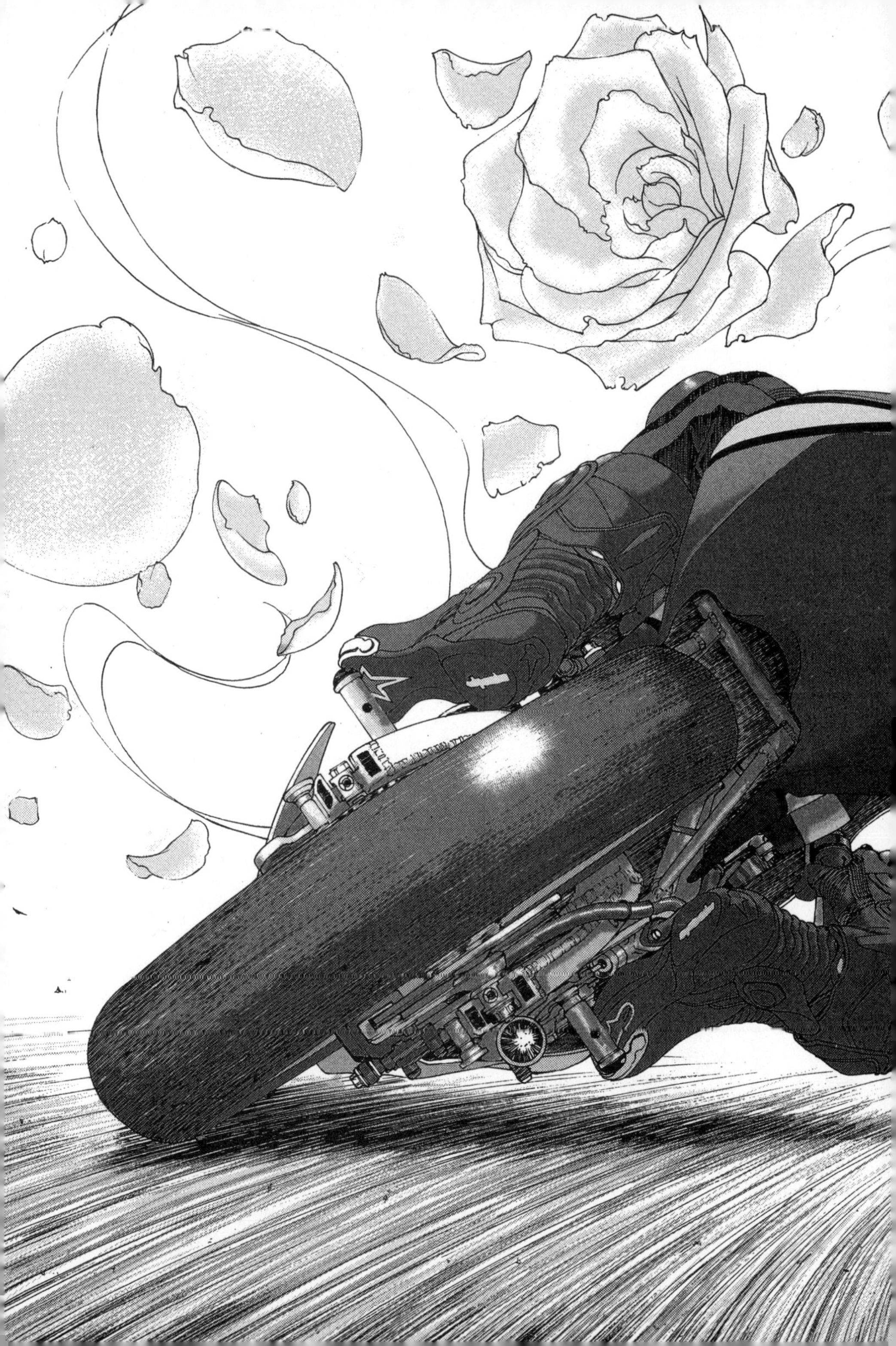

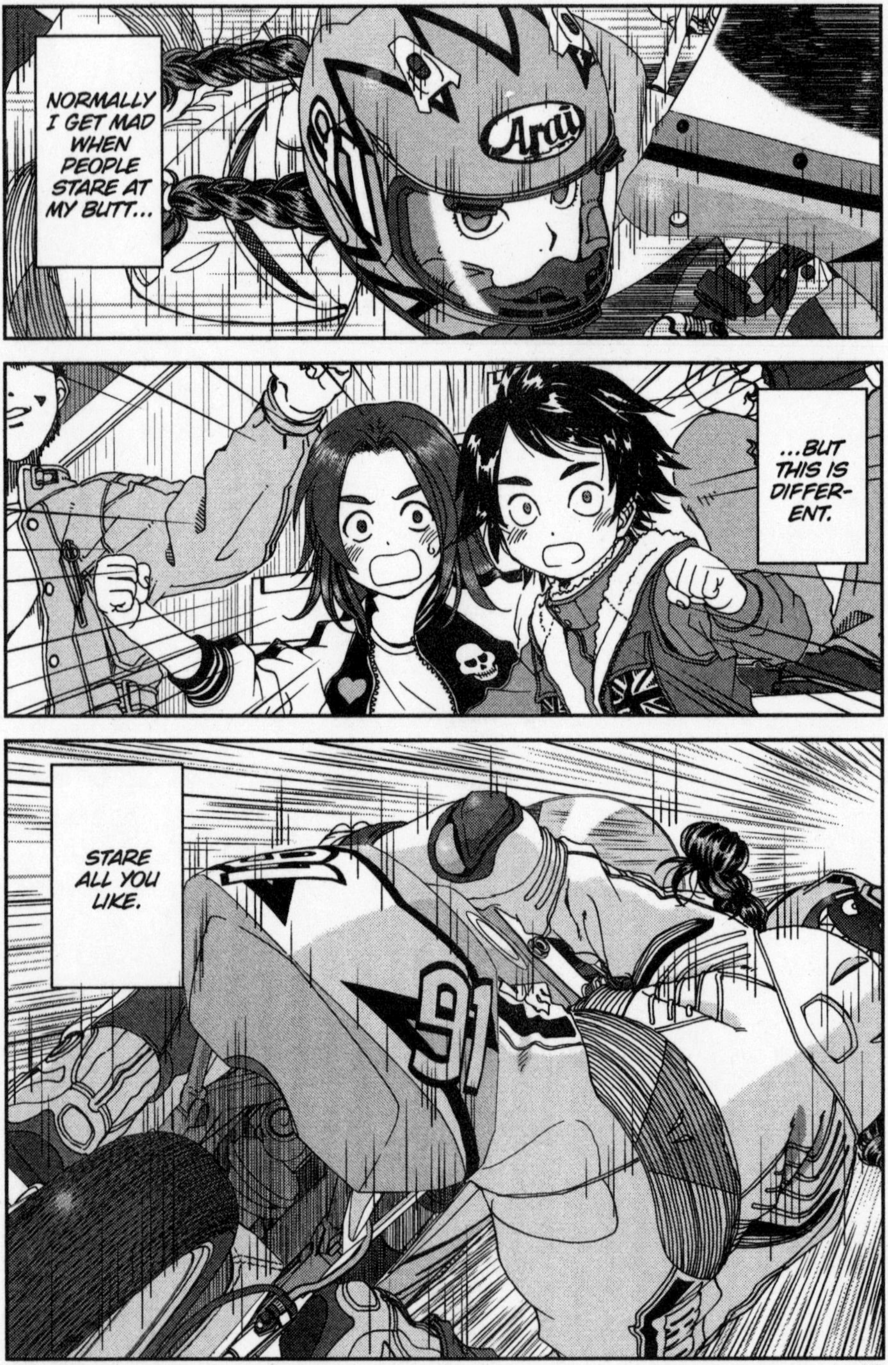
NORMALLY I GET MAD WHEN PEOPLE STARE AT MY BUTT...
...BUT THIS IS DIFFER-ENT.
STARE ALL YOU LIKE.

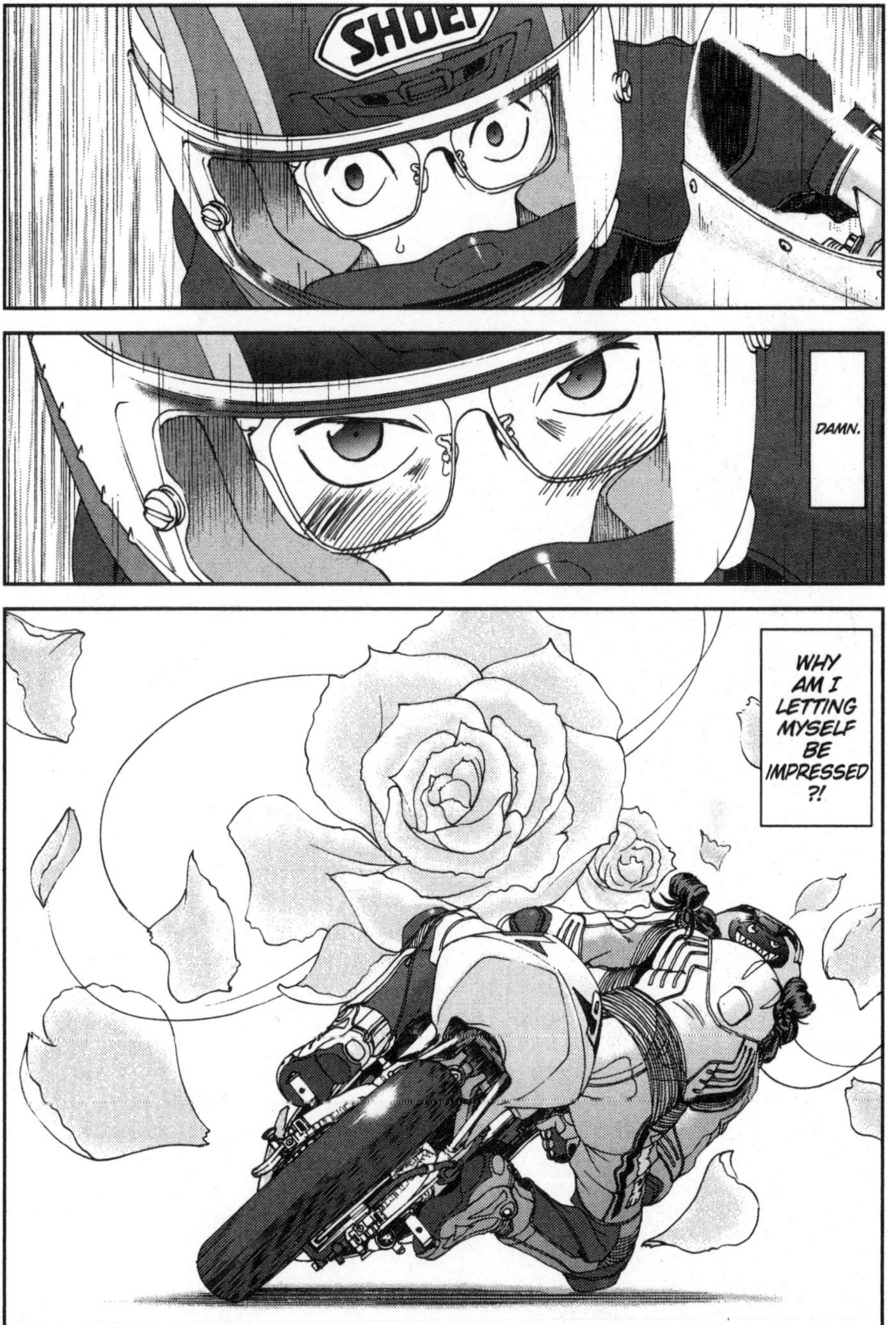
SHOEI
DAMN.
WHY AM I LETTING MYSELF BE IMPRESSED?!

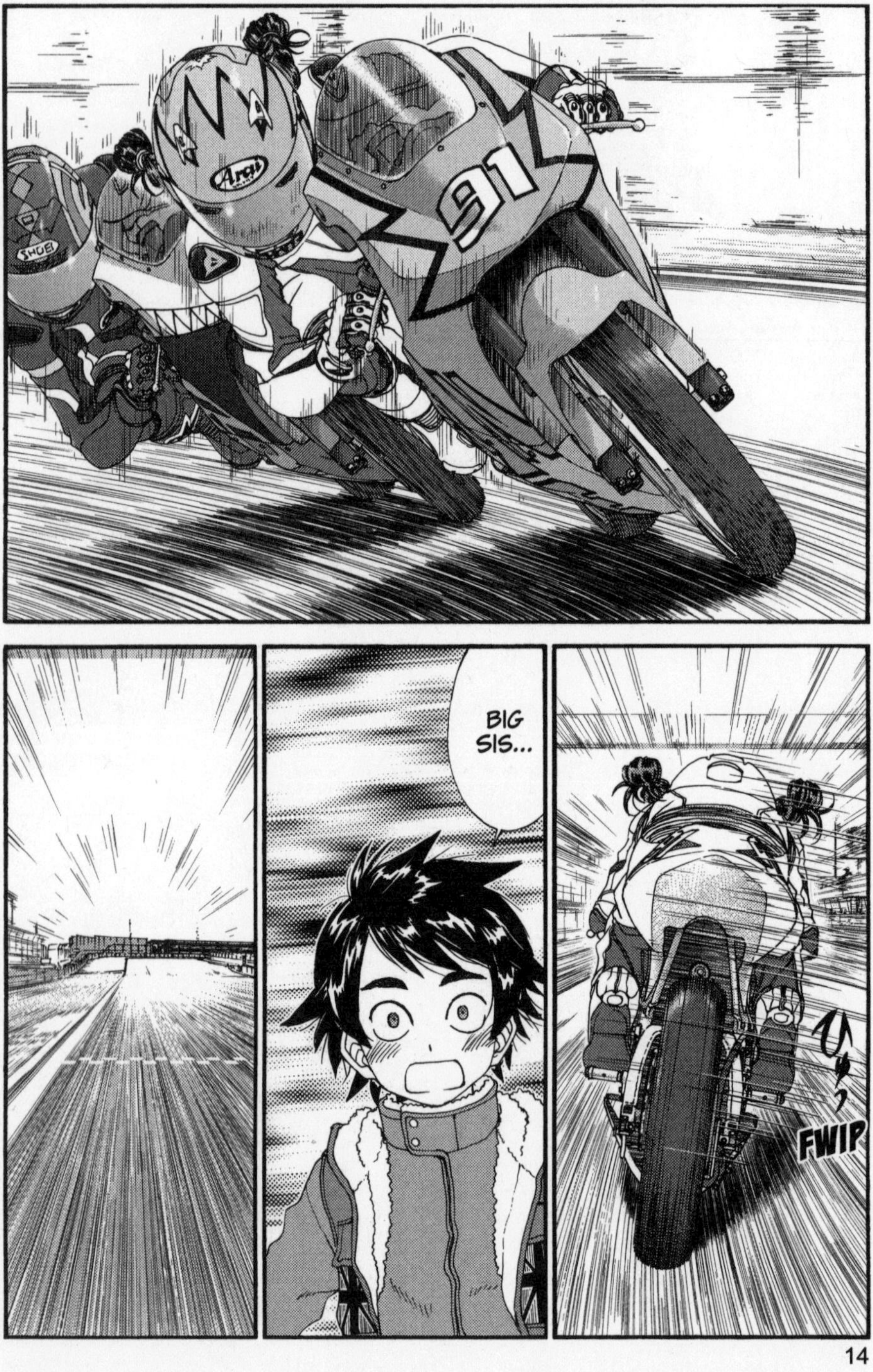
BIG SIS...
FWIP

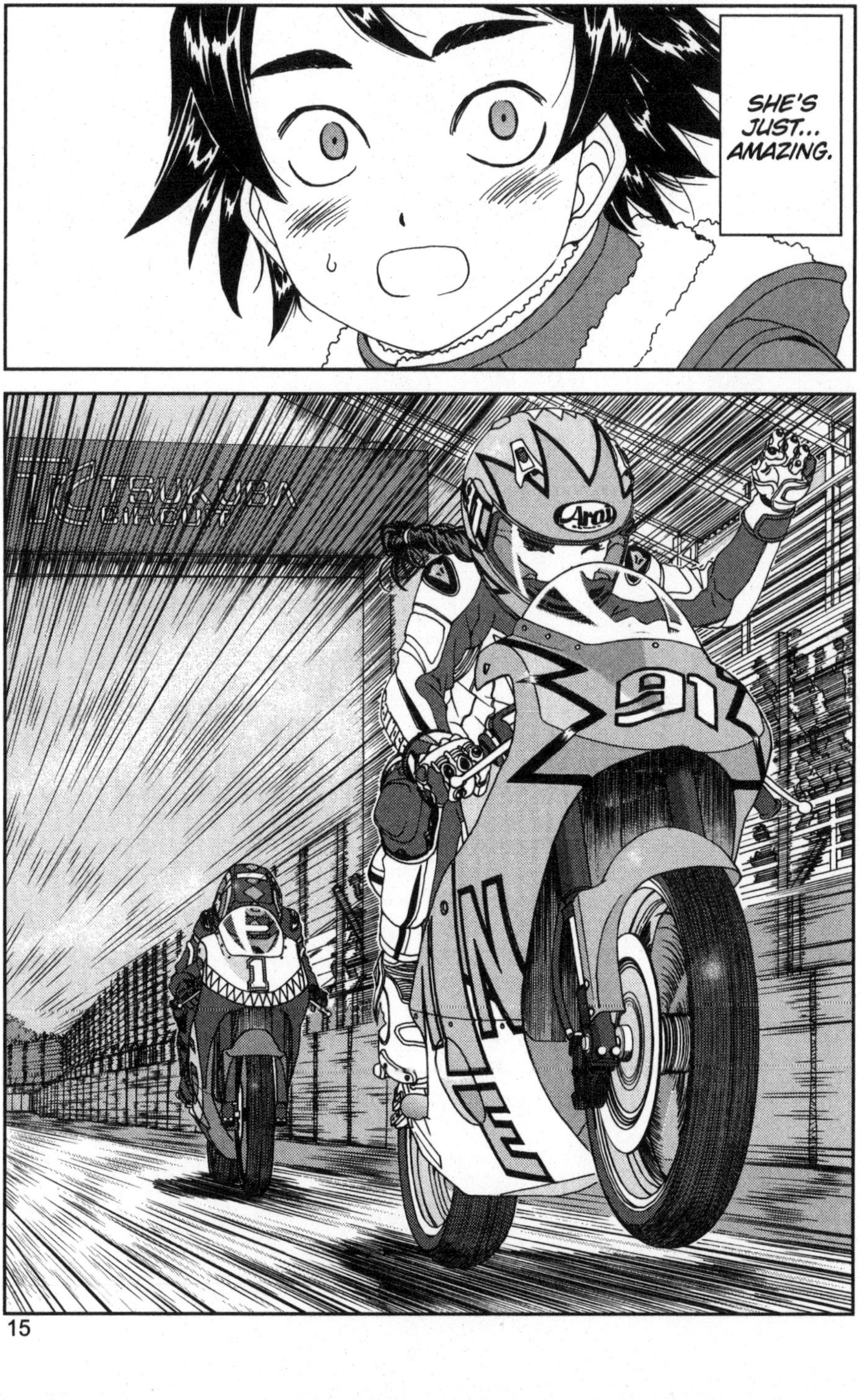
SHE'S JUST... AMAZING.
TSUKUBA
Arai

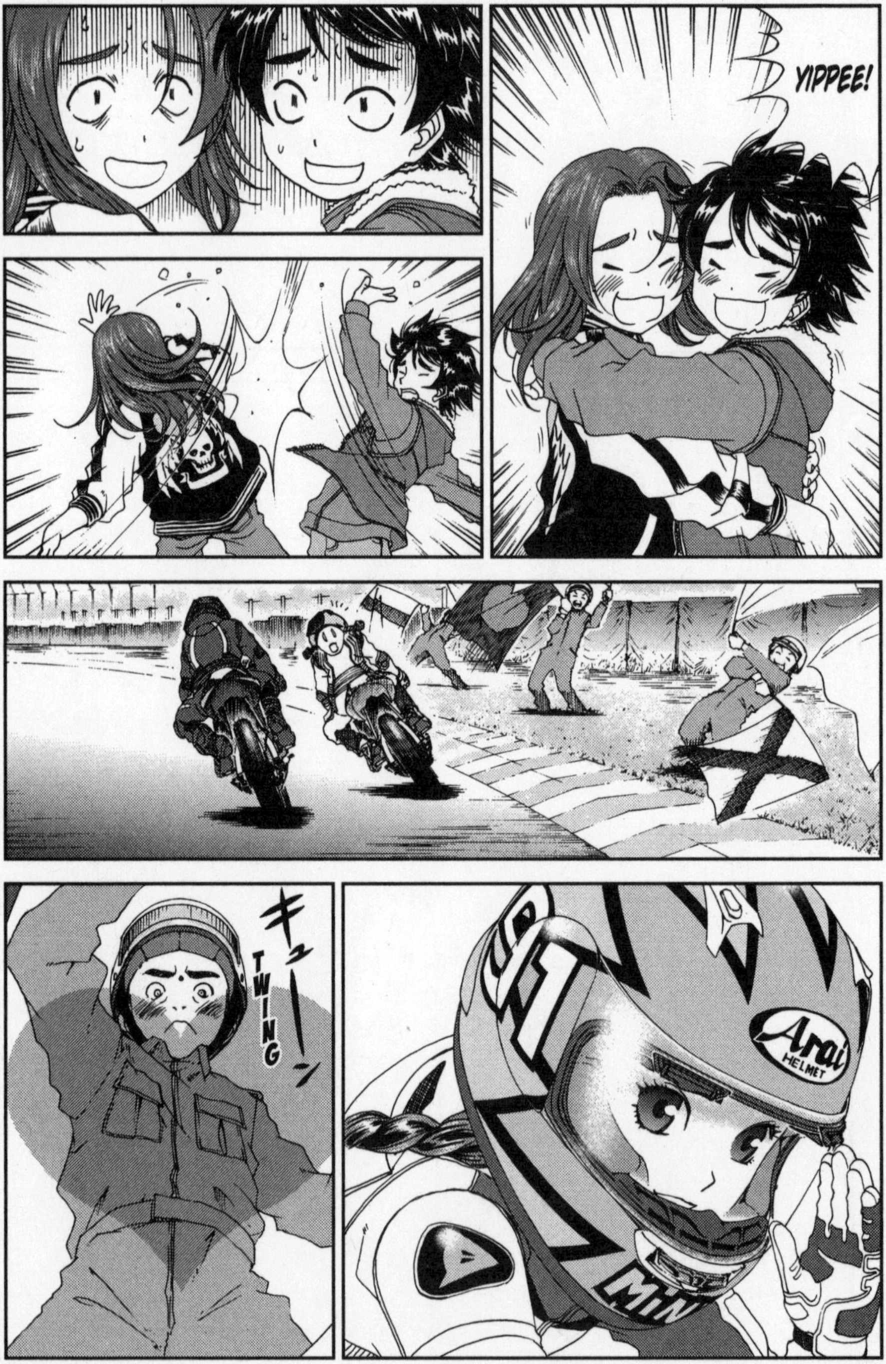
YIPPEE!
キュー
TWING
Arai
HELMET

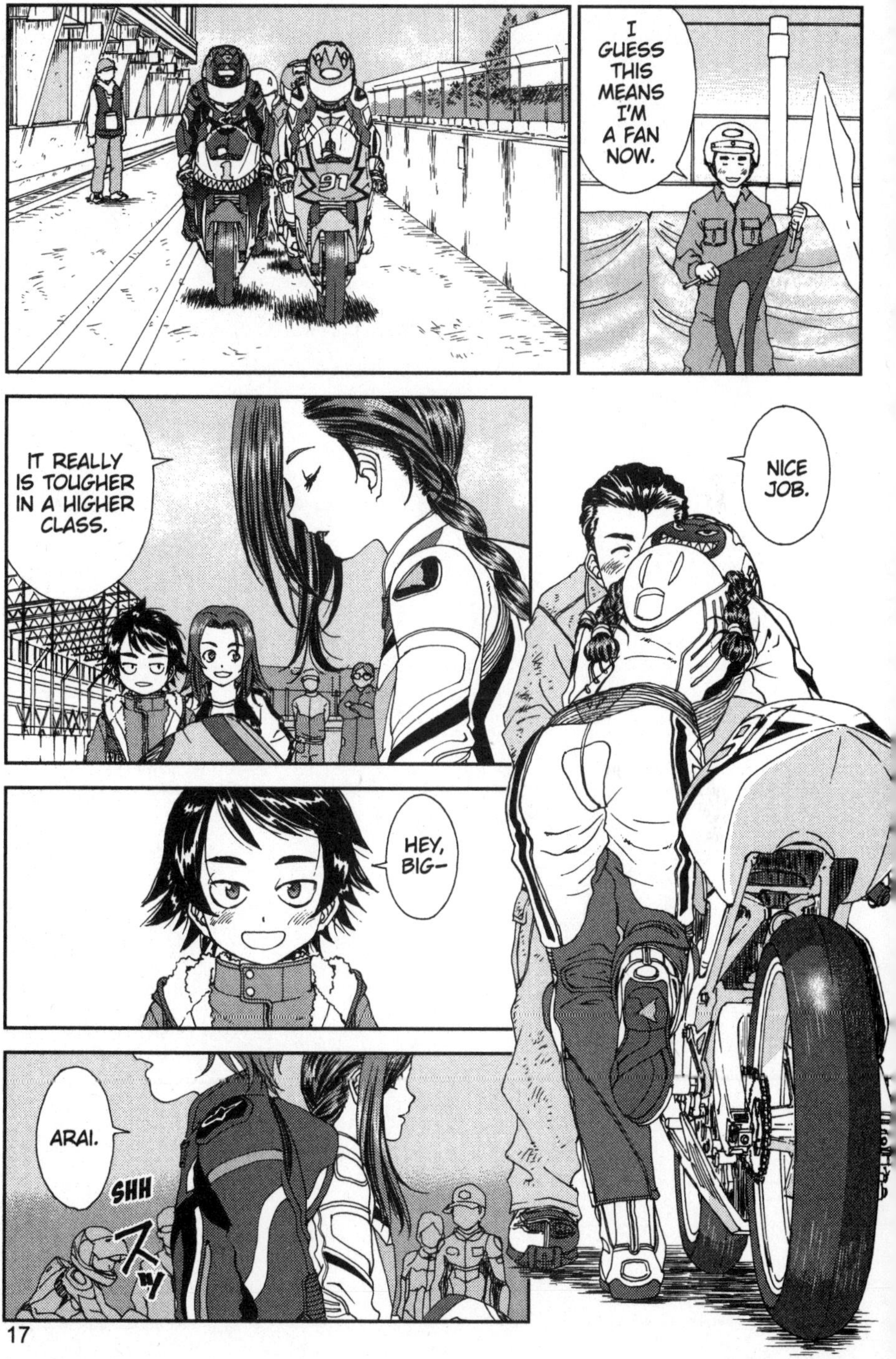
I GUESS THIS MEANS I'M A FAN NOW.
NICE JOB.
IT REALLY IS TOUGHER IN A HIGHER CLASS.
HEY, BIG-
ARAI.
SHH

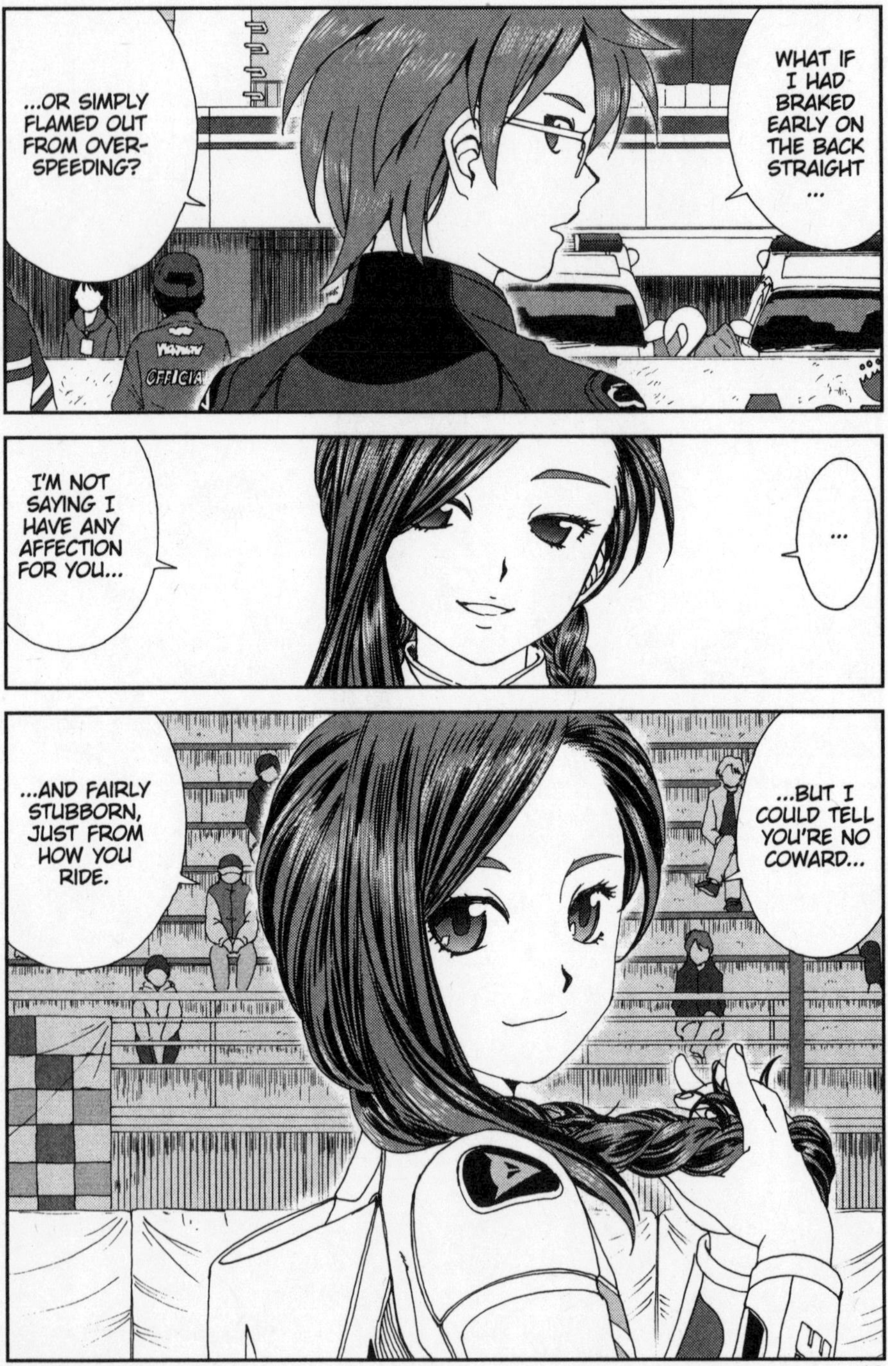
WHAT IF I HAD BRAKED EARLY ON THE BACK STRAIGHT ...
...OR SIMPLY FLAMED OUT FROM OVER-SPEEDING?
OFFICIA
...
I'M NOT SAYING I HAVE ANY AFFECTION FOR YOU...
...BUT I COULD TELL YOU'RE NO COWARD...
...AND FAIRLY STUBBORN, JUST FROM HOW YOU RIDE.

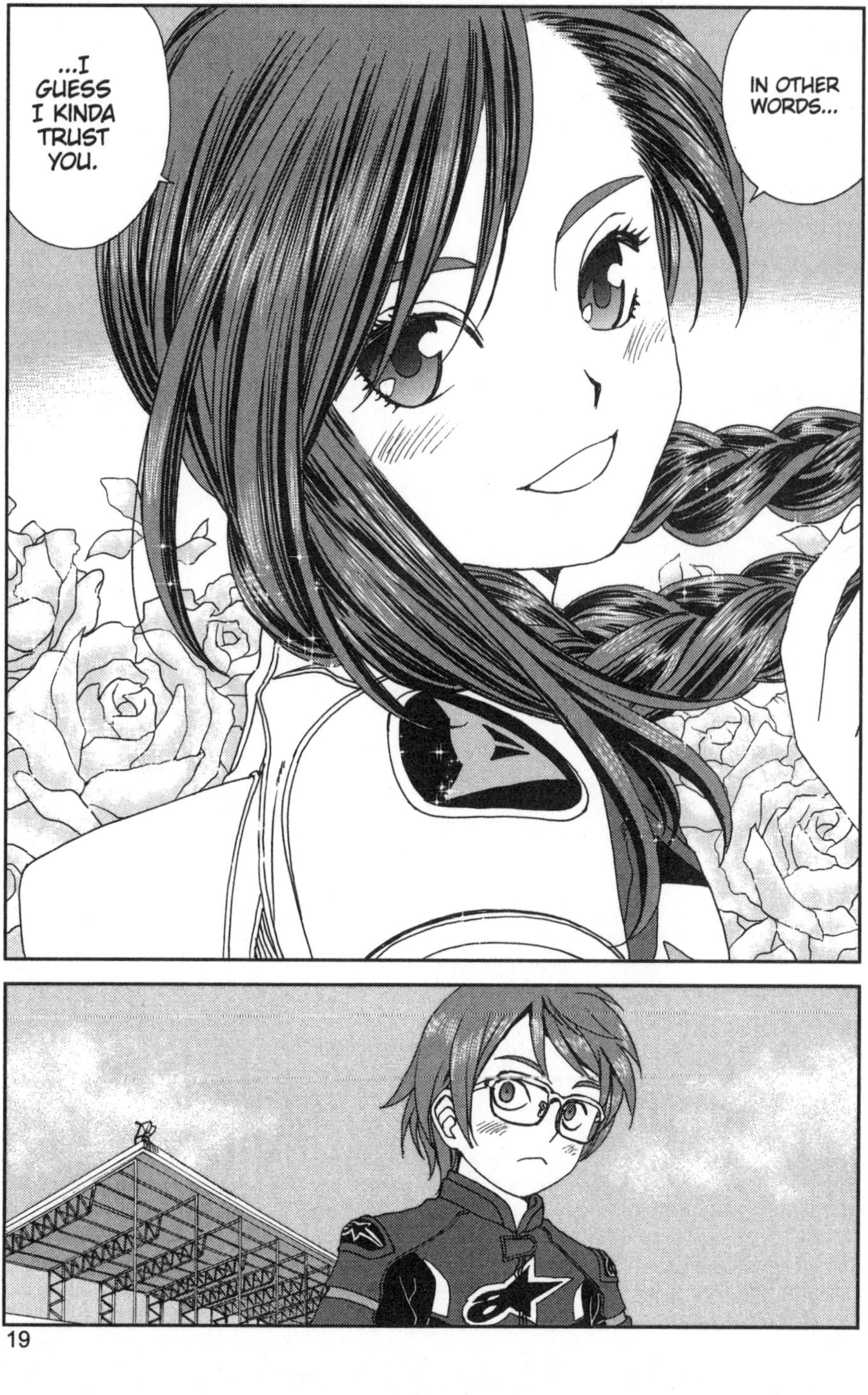
IN OTHER WORDS...
...I GUESS I KINDA TRUST YOU.

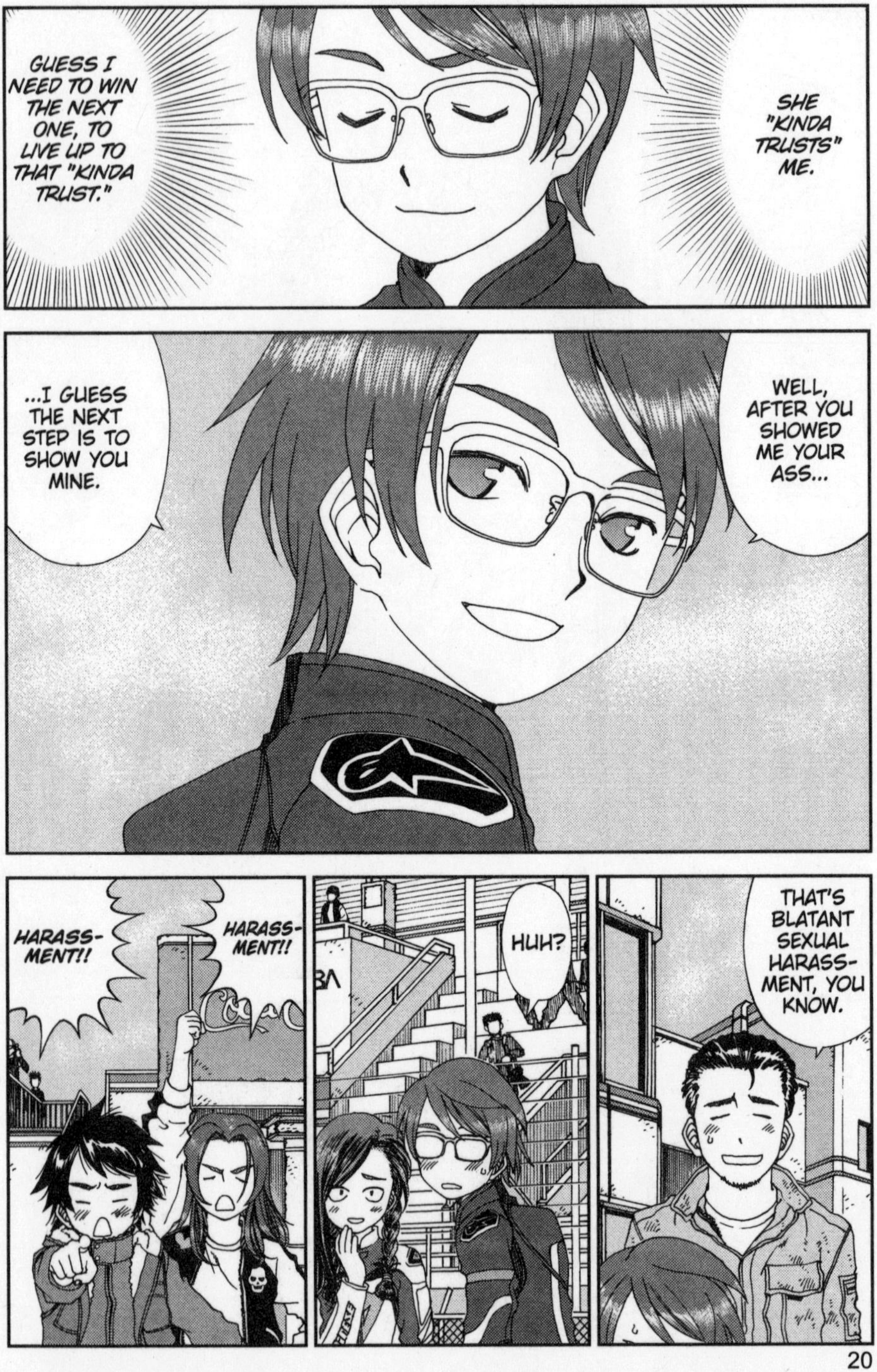

SHE "KINDA TRUSTS" ME.
GUESS I NEED TO WIN THE NEXT ONE, TO LIVE UP TO THAT "KINDA TRUST."
WELL, AFTER YOU SHOWED ME YOUR ASS...
...I GUESS THE NEXT STEP IS TO SHOW YOU MINE.
THAT'S BLATANT SEXUAL HARASS-MENT, YOU KNOW.
HUH?
HARASS-MENT!!
HARASS-MENT!!

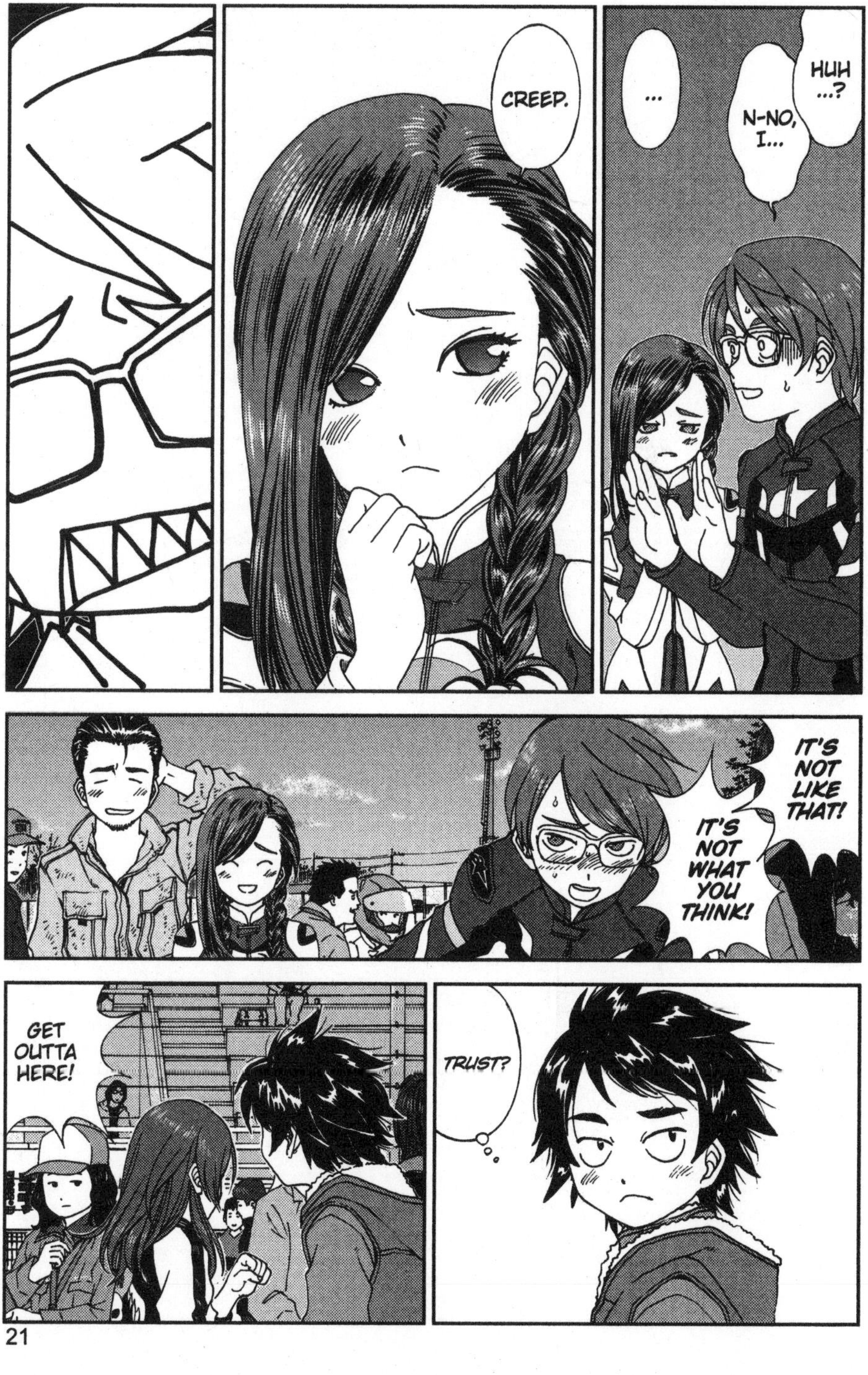

HUH ...?
N-NO, I...
...
CREEP.
IT'S NOT LIKE THAT!
IT'S NOT WHAT YOU THINK!
TRUST?
GET OUTTA HERE!

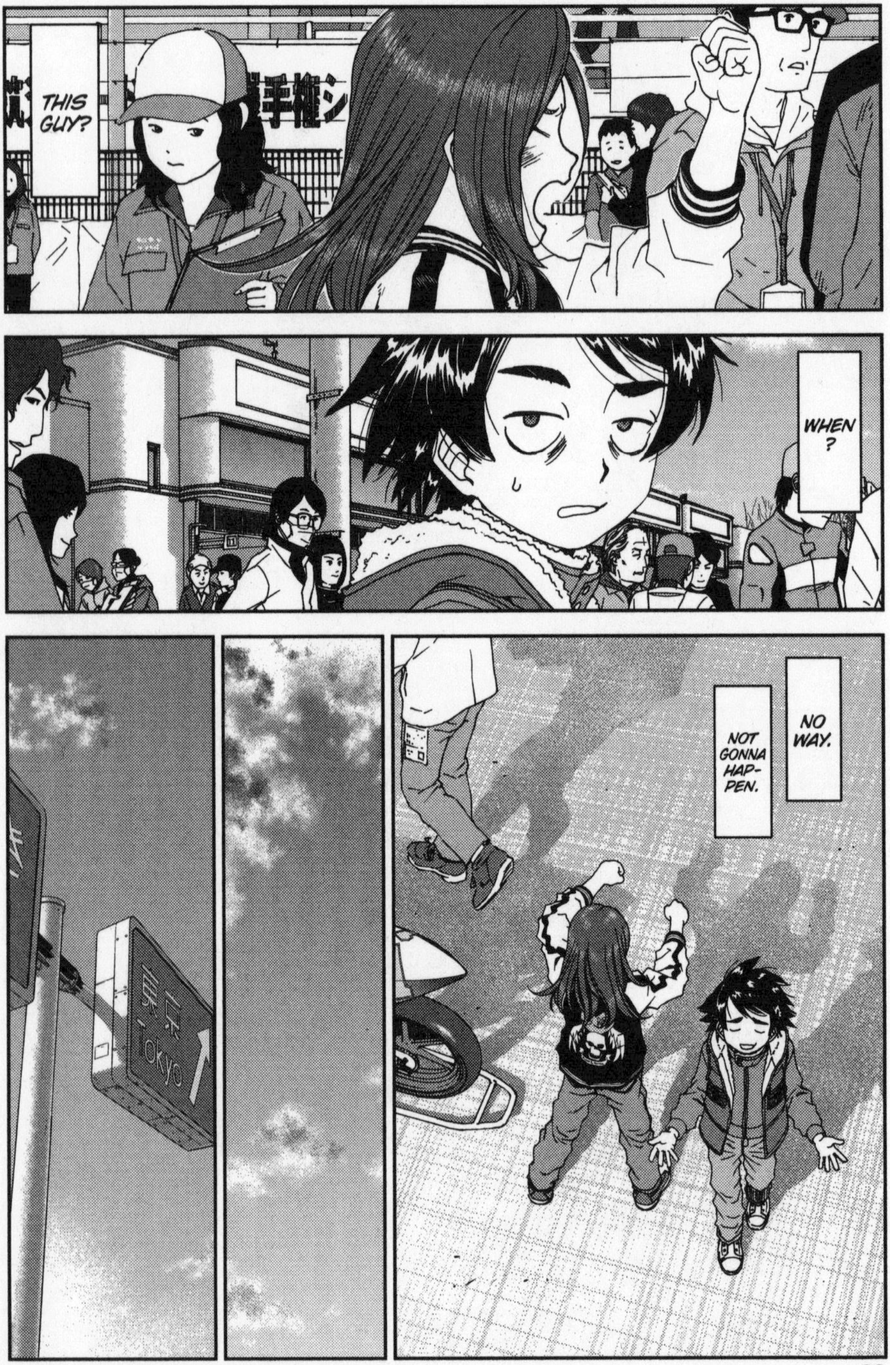
THIS GUY?
WHEN ?
NO WAY.
NOT GONNA HAP-PEN.
東京
Tokyo

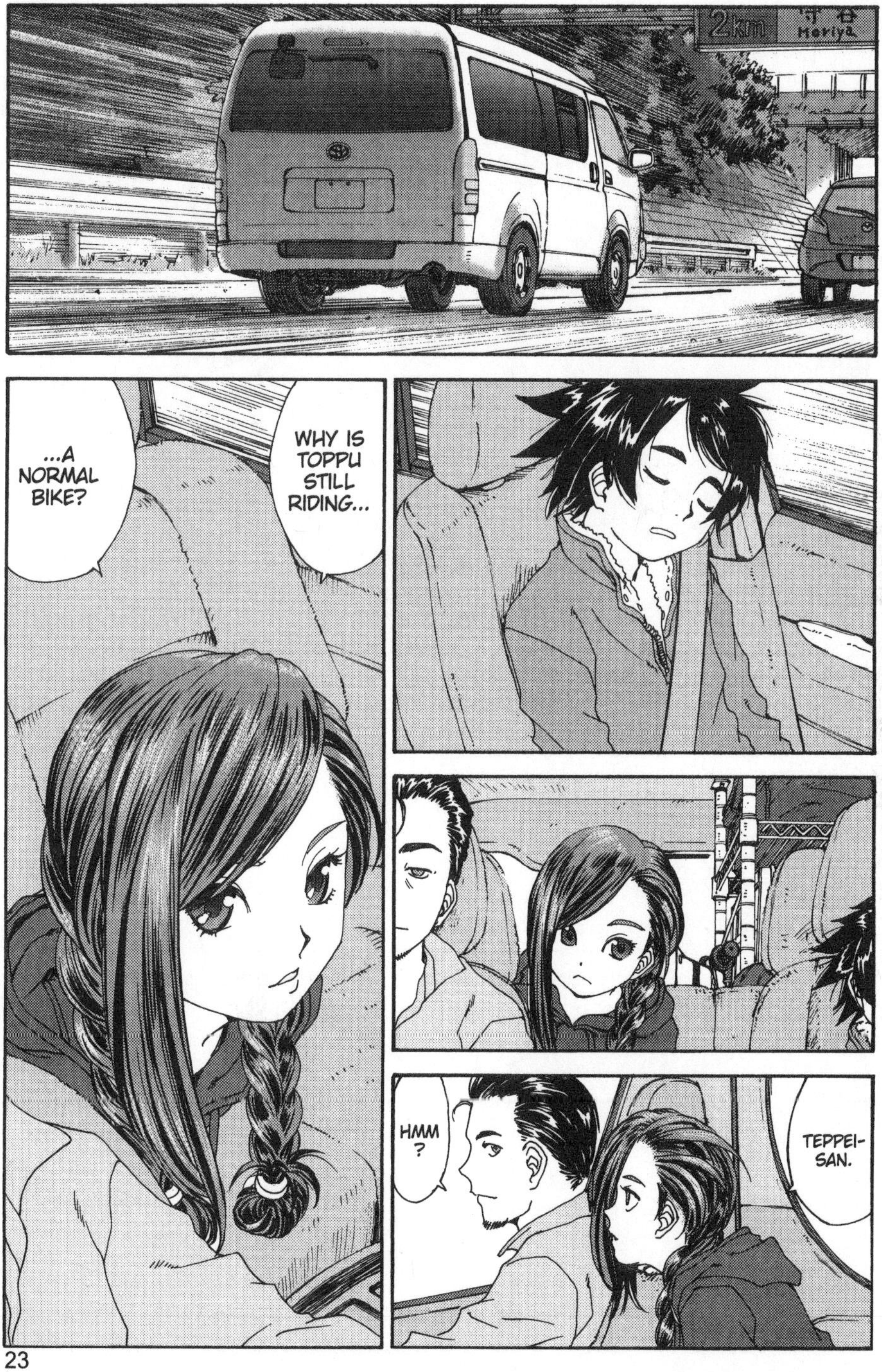
2km
Moriya
WHY IS TOPPU STILL RIDING...
...A NORMAL BIKE?
TEPPEI-SAN.
HMM ?

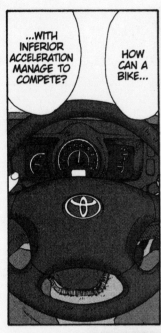

WELL ...
I THINK YOU SHOWED HIM WHY IN TODAY'S RACE.
HUH?
HOW CAN A BIKE...
...WITH INFERIOR ACCELERATION MANAGE TO COMPETE?
YOU USE YOUR WEAPONS TO THE BEST OF YOUR ABILITY ...
...TO ERASE YOUR OPPONENT'S ADVANTAGE.
YUP.
NO TWO RACES ARE EVER IDENTICAL.

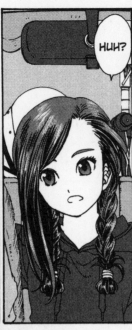

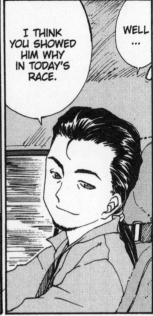

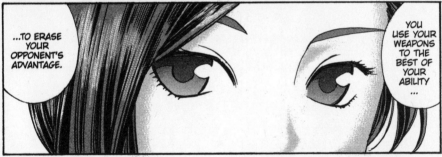

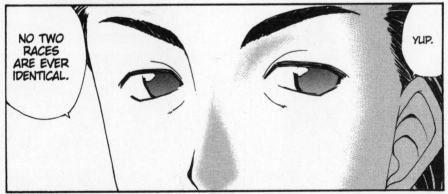

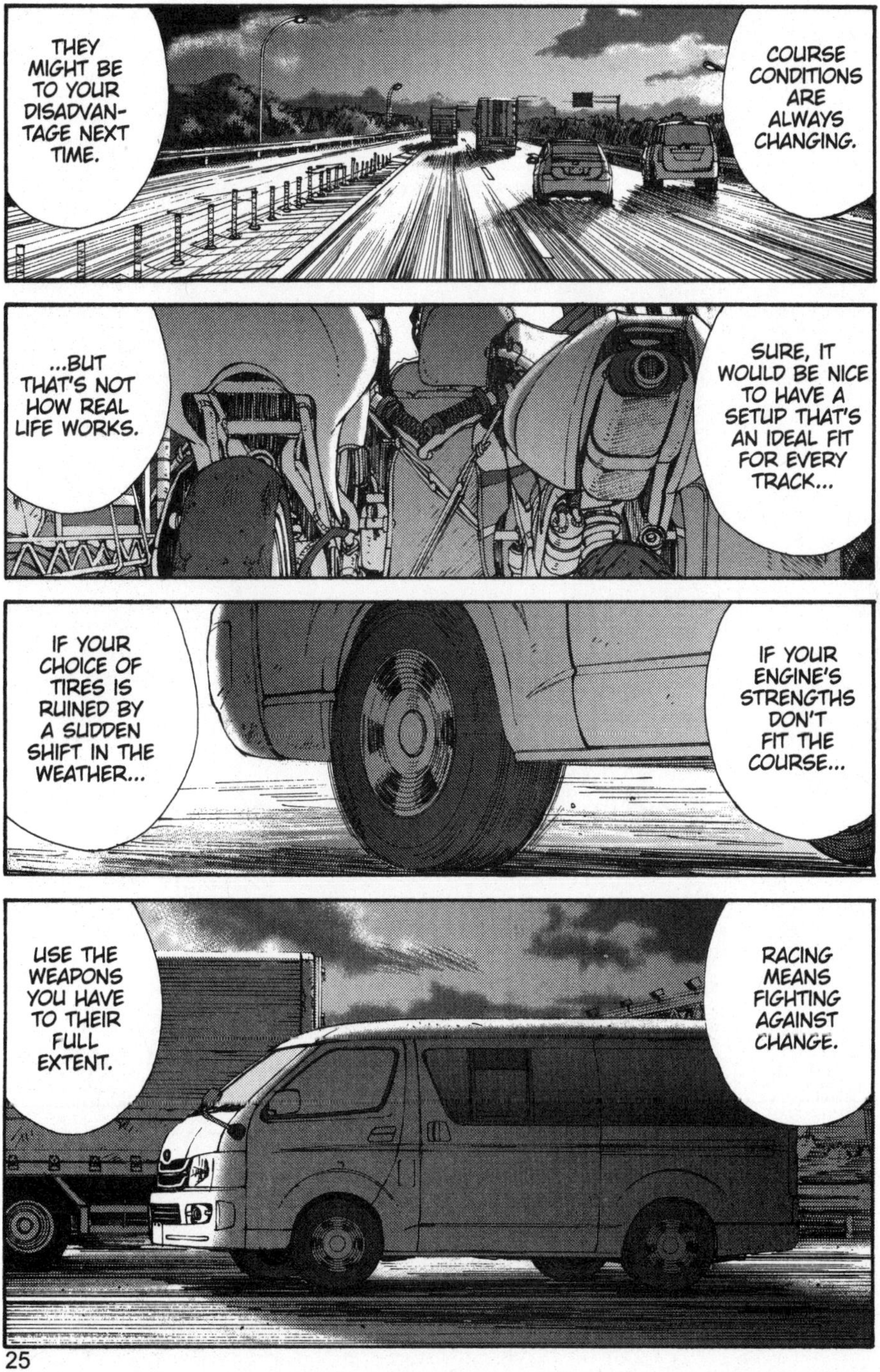
COURSE CONDITIONS ARE ALWAYS CHANGING.
THEY MIGHT BE TO YOUR DISADVAN-TAGE NEXT TIME.
SURE, IT WOULD BE NICE TO HAVE A SETUP THAT'S AN IDEAL FIT FOR EVERY TRACK...
...BUT THAT'S NOT HOW REAL LIFE WORKS.
IF YOUR ENGINE'S STRENGTHS DON'T FIT THE COURSE...
IF YOUR CHOICE OF TIRES IS RUINED BY A SUDDEN SHIFT IN THE WEATHER...
RACING MEANS FIGHTING AGAINST CHANGE.
USE THE WEAPONS YOU HAVE TO THEIR FULL EXTENT.

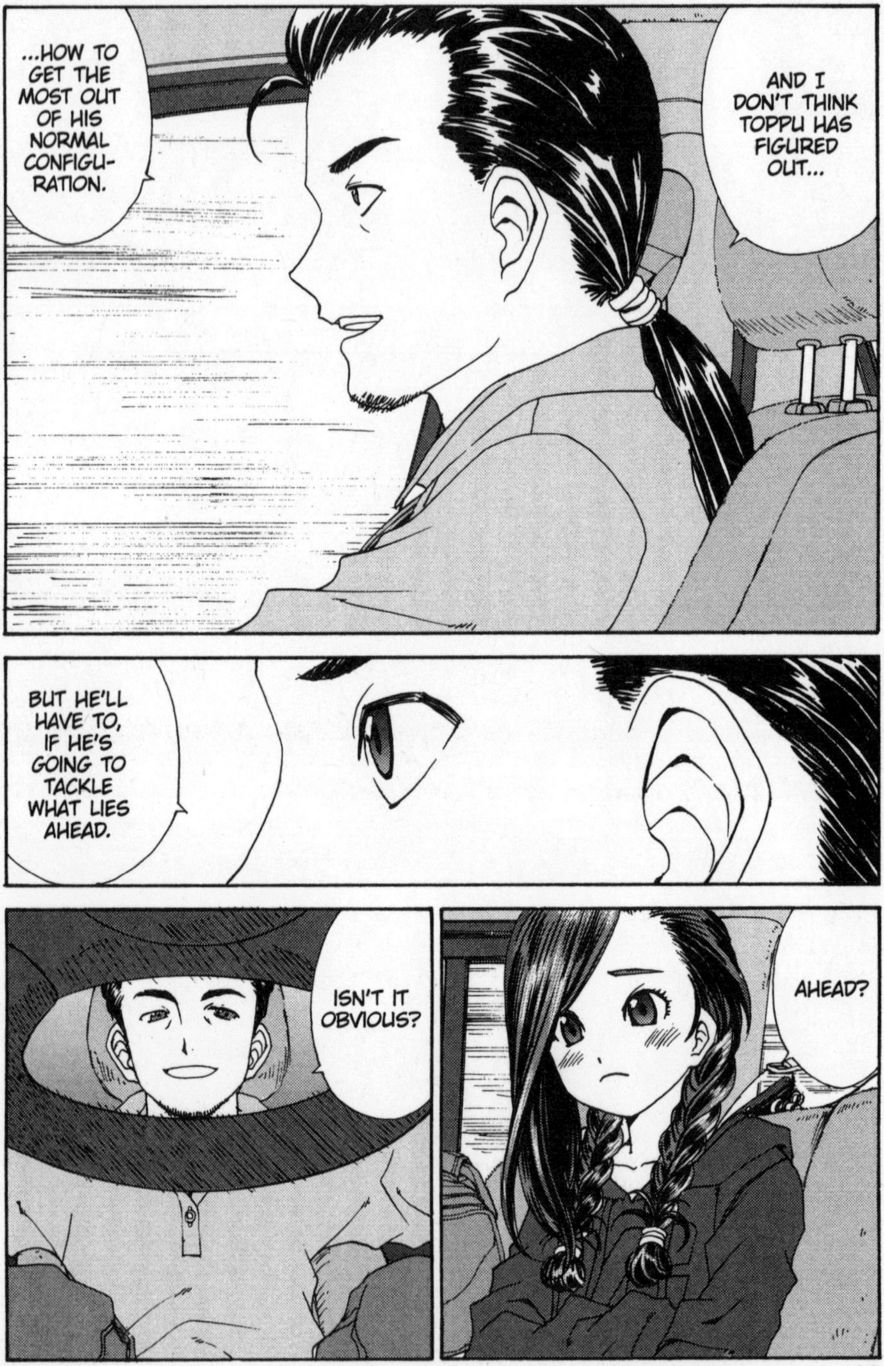
AND I DON'T THINK TOPPU HAS FIGURED OUT...
...HOW TO GET THE MOST OUT OF HIS NORMAL CONFIGU-RATION.
BUT HE'LL HAVE TO, IF HE'S GOING TO TACKLE WHAT LIES AHEAD.
AHEAD?
ISN'T IT OBVIOUS?

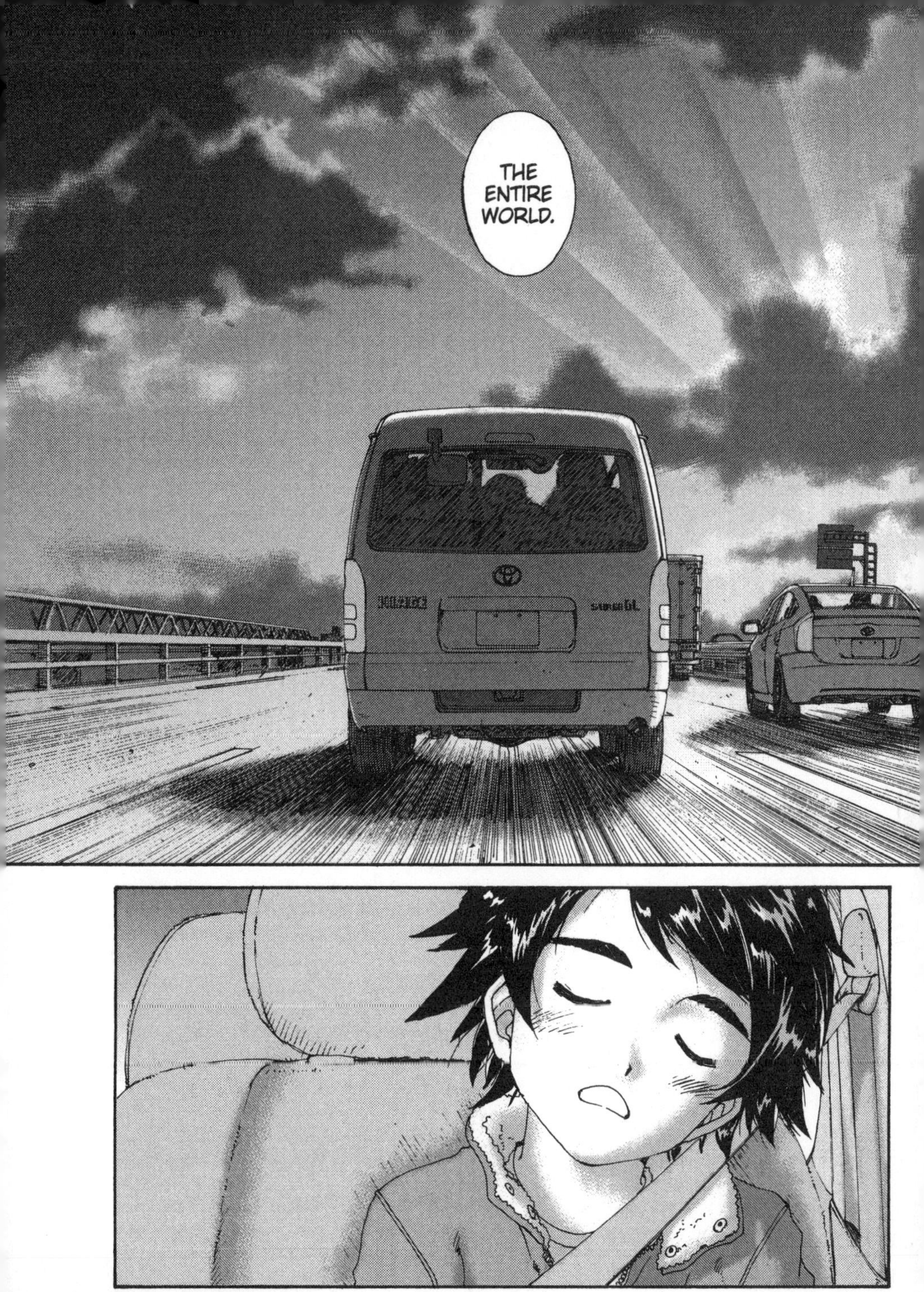
THE ENTIRE WORLD.

Lap 15: end

Toppu GP

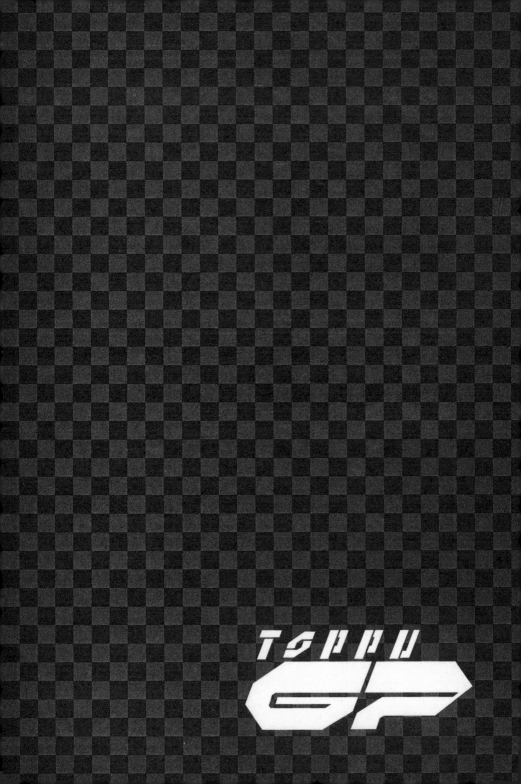

Lap 16:
DESIRE TO WIN

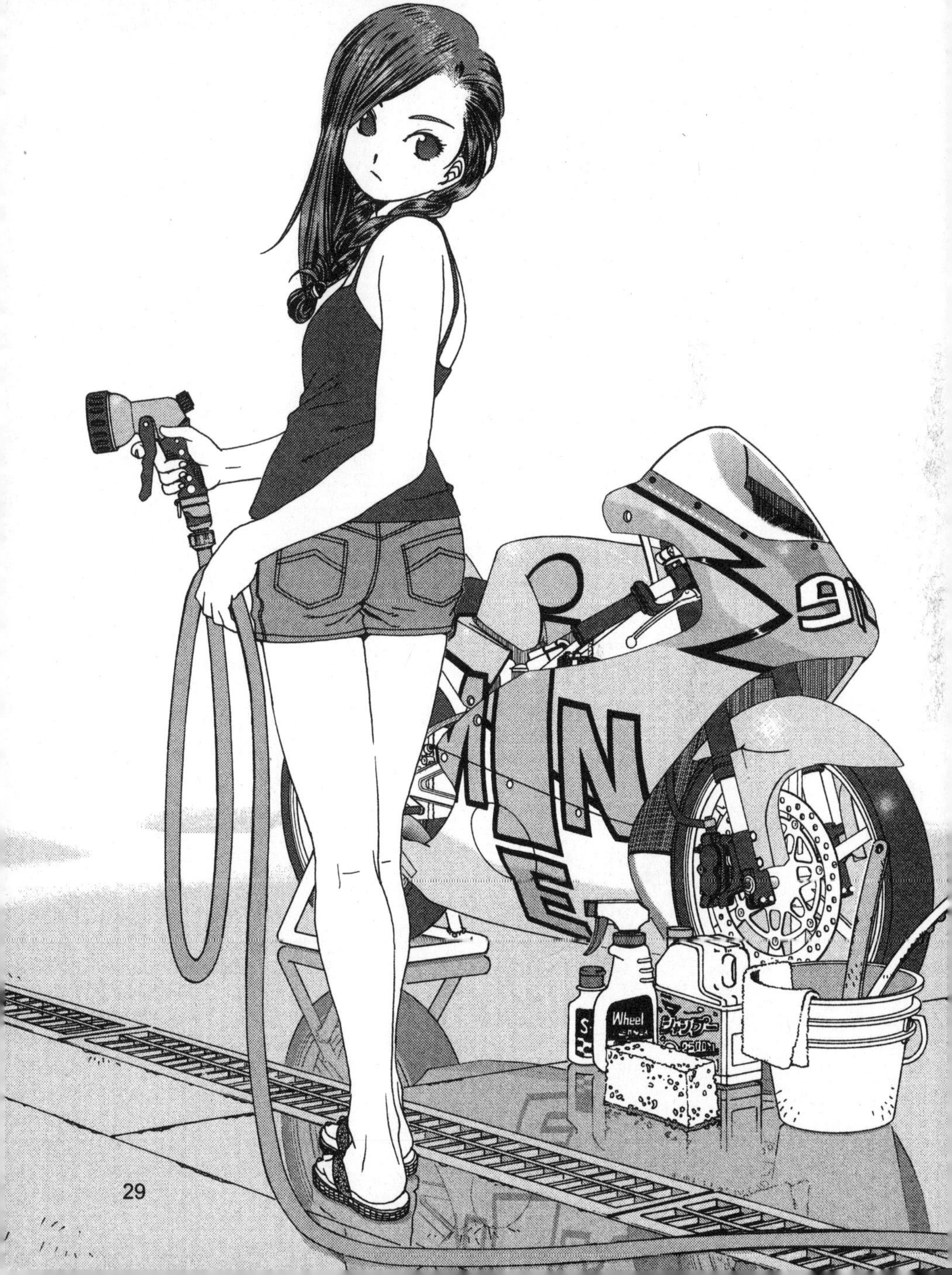
Wheel
シャンプー

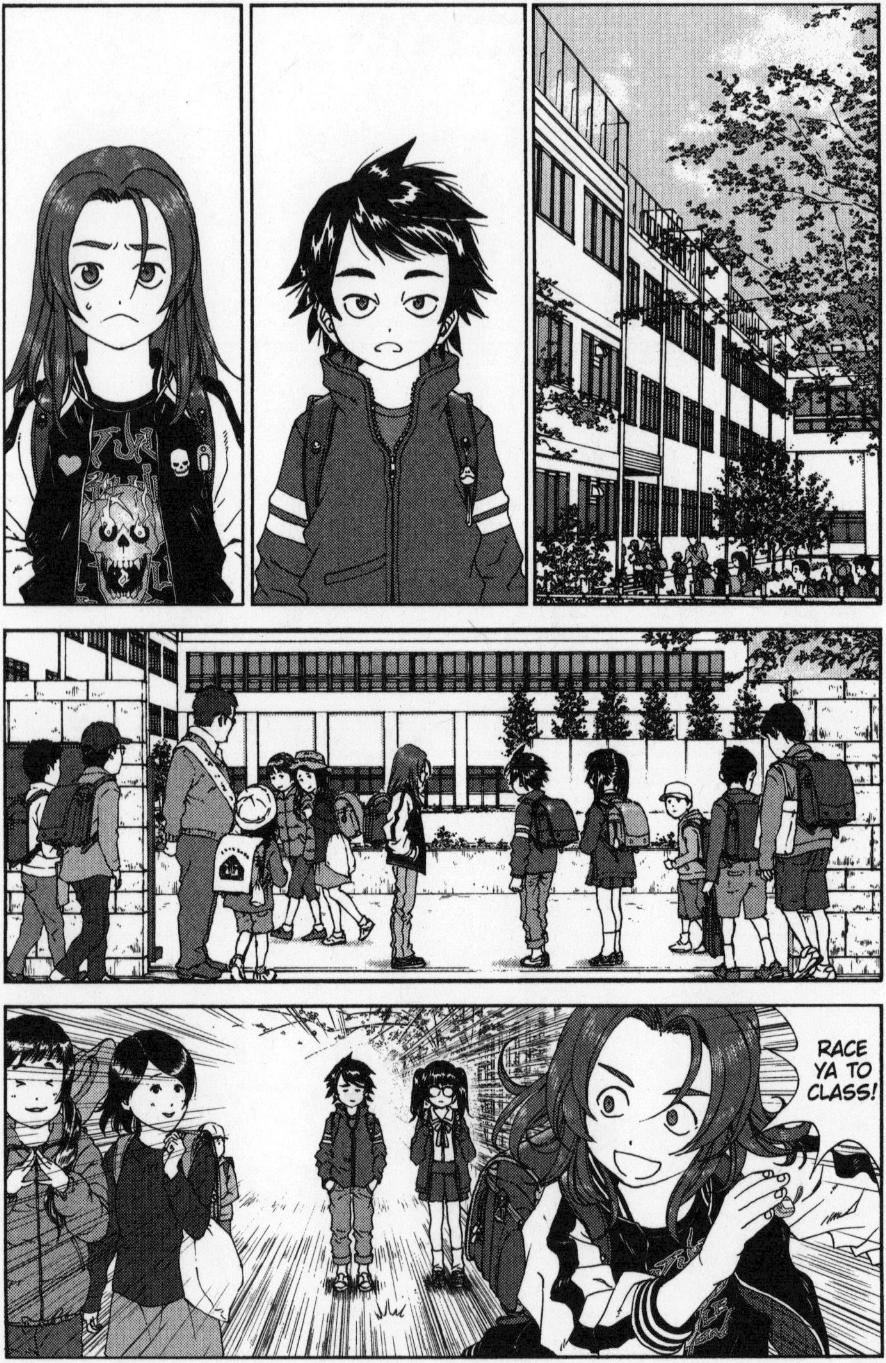
RACE YA TO CLASS!

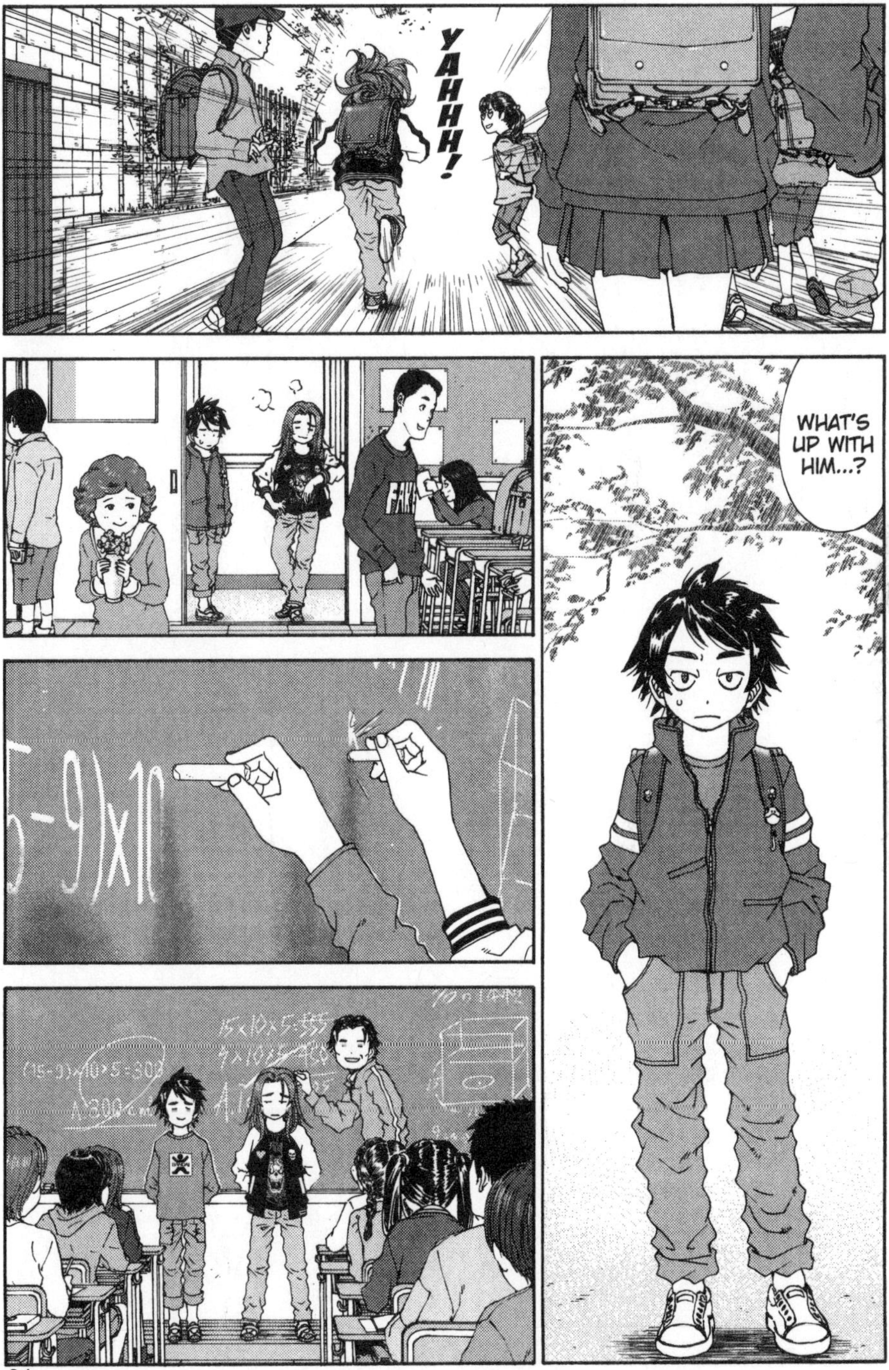
YAHHHH!
WHAT'S UP WITH HIM...?

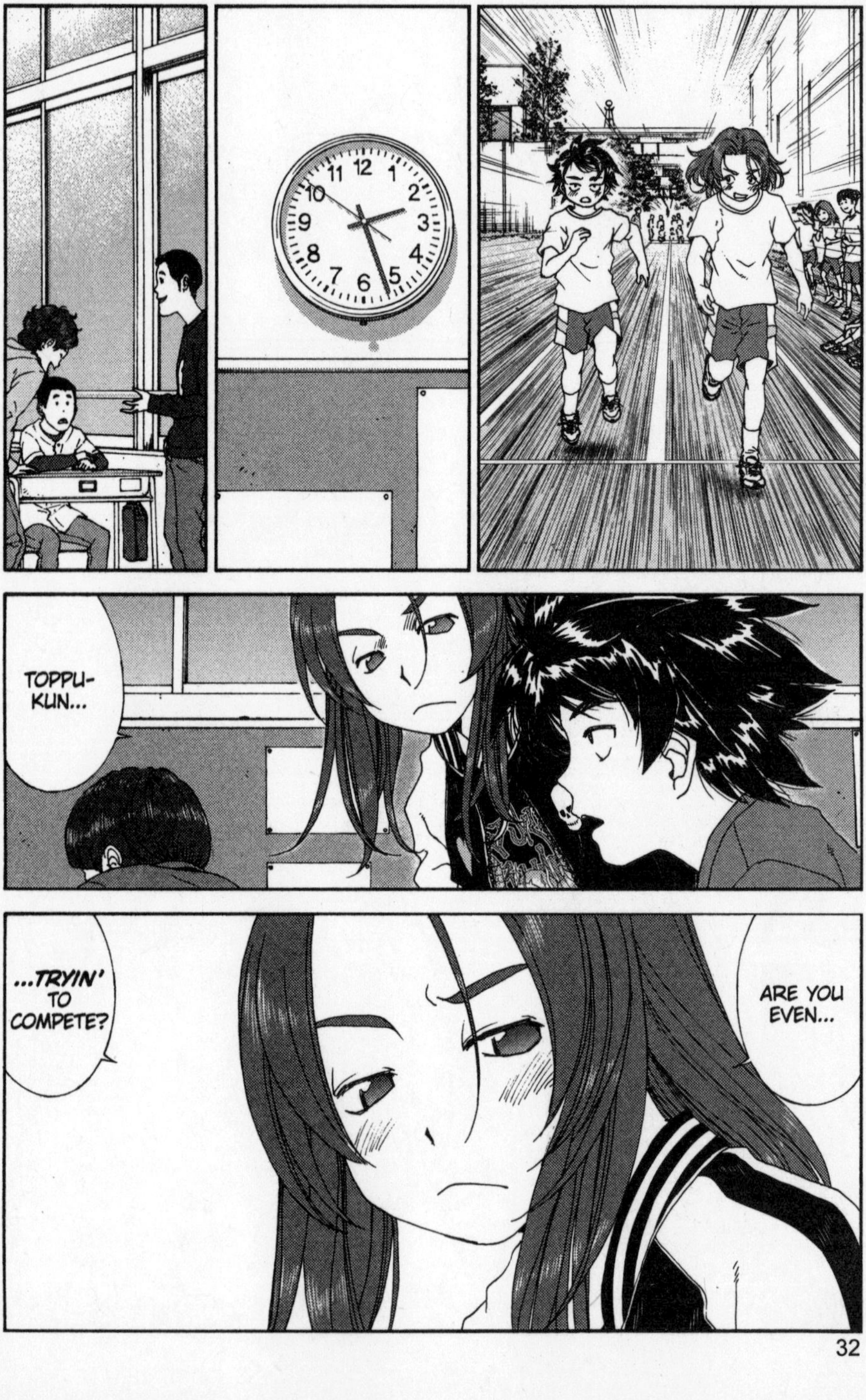
TOPPU-KUN...
ARE YOU EVEN...
...TRYIN' TO COMPETE?

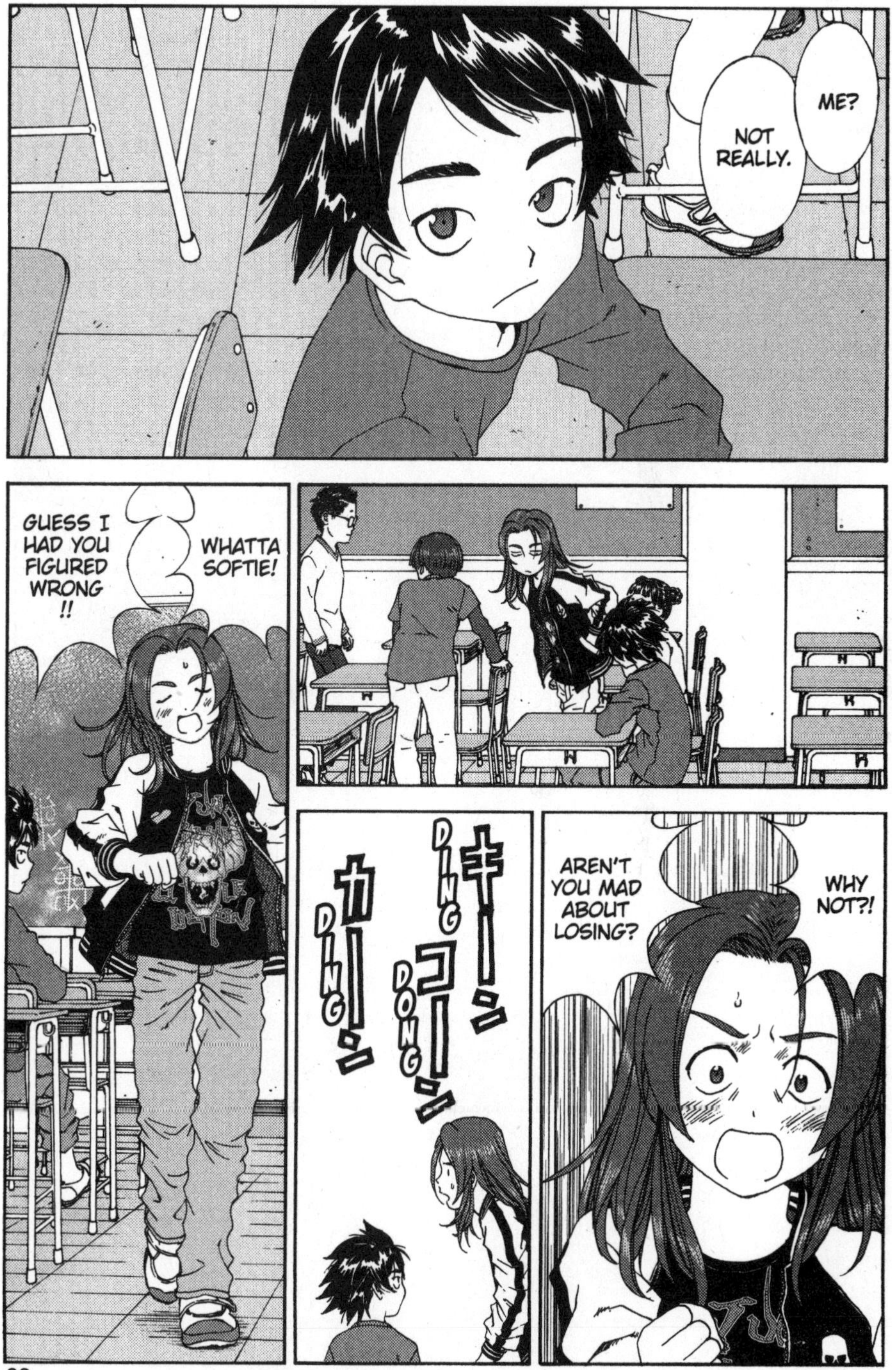

ME?
NOT REALLY.
WHY NOT?!
AREN'T YOU MAD ABOUT LOSING?
キーン
DING
コーン
DONG
カーン
DING
WHATTA SOFTIE!
GUESS I HAD YOU FIGURED WRONG !!

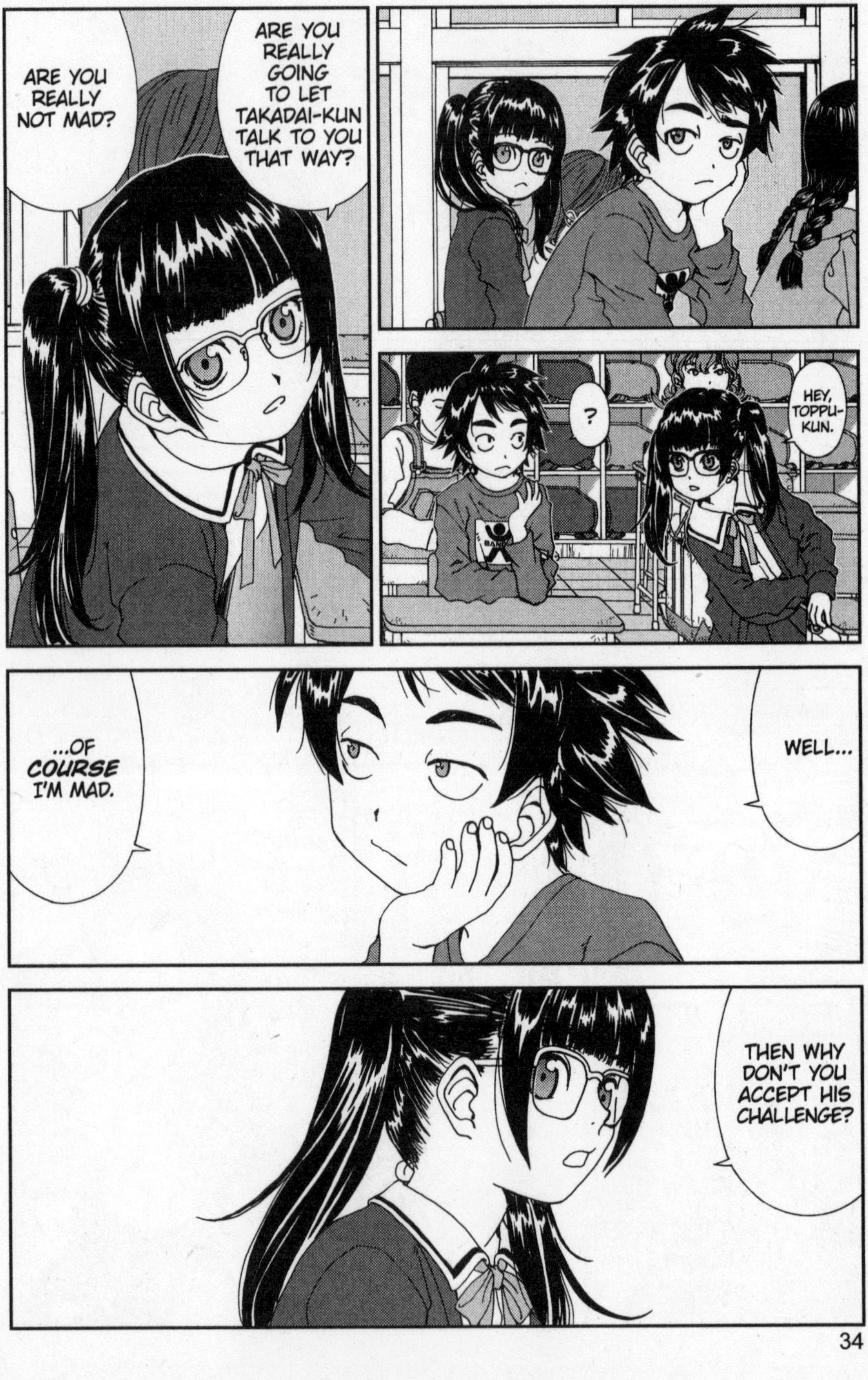
HEY, TOPPU-KUN.
?
ARE YOU REALLY GOING TO LET TAKADAI-KUN TALK TO YOU THAT WAY?
ARE YOU REALLY NOT MAD?
WELL...
...OF COURSE I'M MAD.
THEN WHY DON'T YOU ACCEPT HIS CHALLENGE?

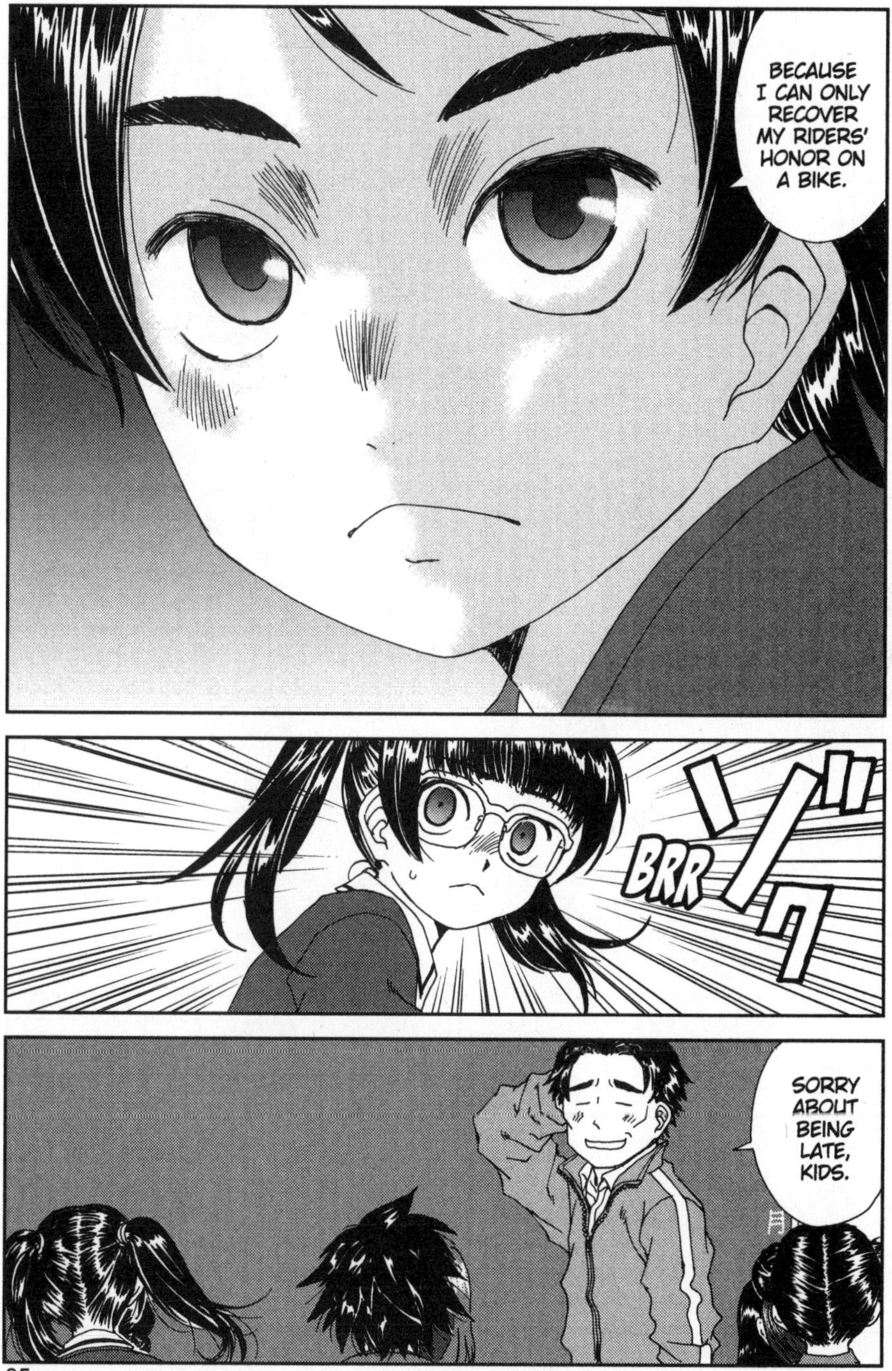
BECAUSE I CAN ONLY RECOVER MY RIDERS' HONOR ON A BIKE.
ゾク
BRR
SORRY ABOUT BEING LATE, KIDS.

YOU'RE DIFFERENT THAN USUAL WHEN YOU TALK ABOUT MOTORCYCLES.

...

...IS DEADLY SERIOUS.

TOPPU-KUN...

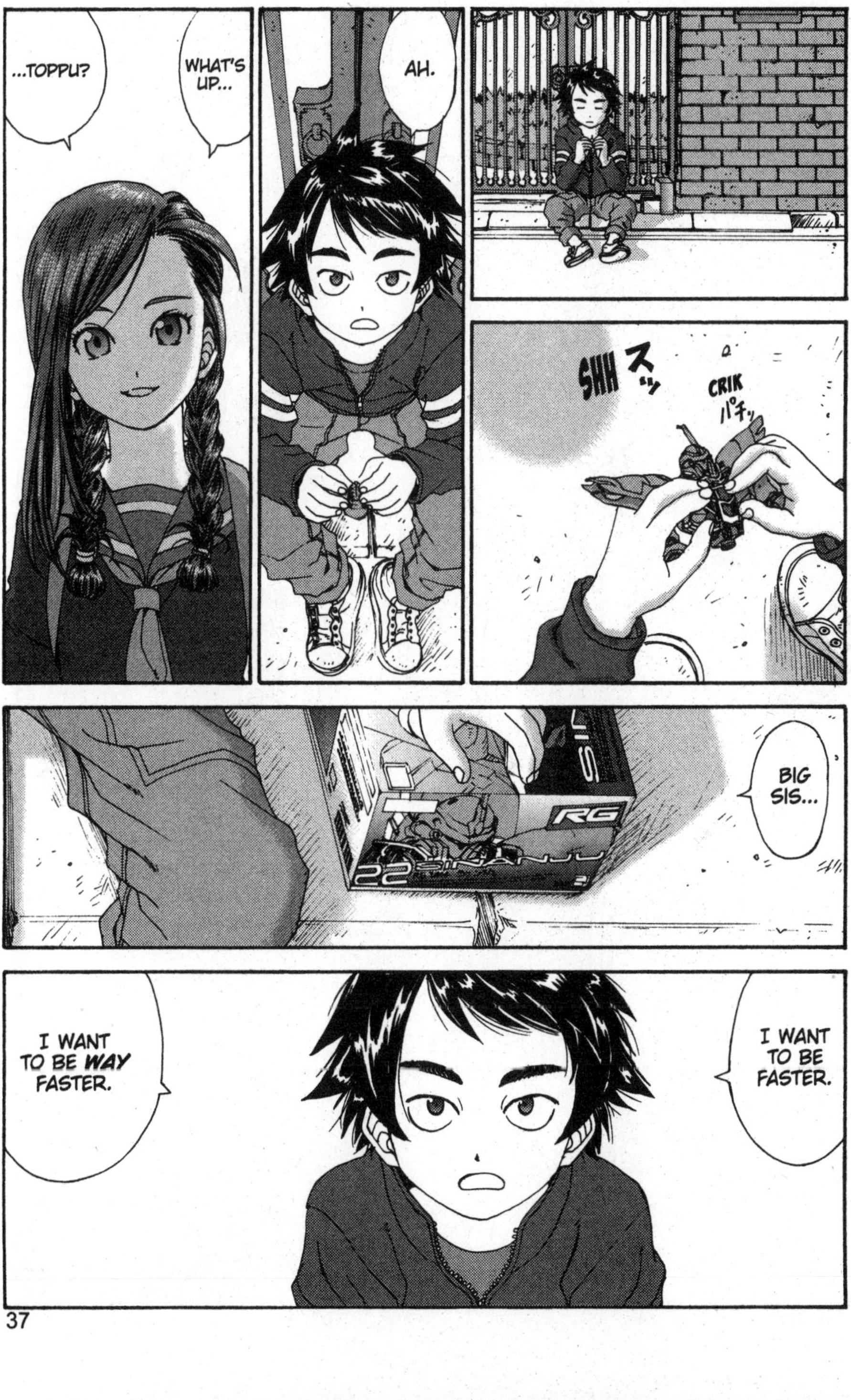
AH.
WHAT'S UP...
...TOPPU?
SHH
CRIK
BIG SIS...
I WANT TO BE FASTER.
I WANT TO BE WAY FASTER.

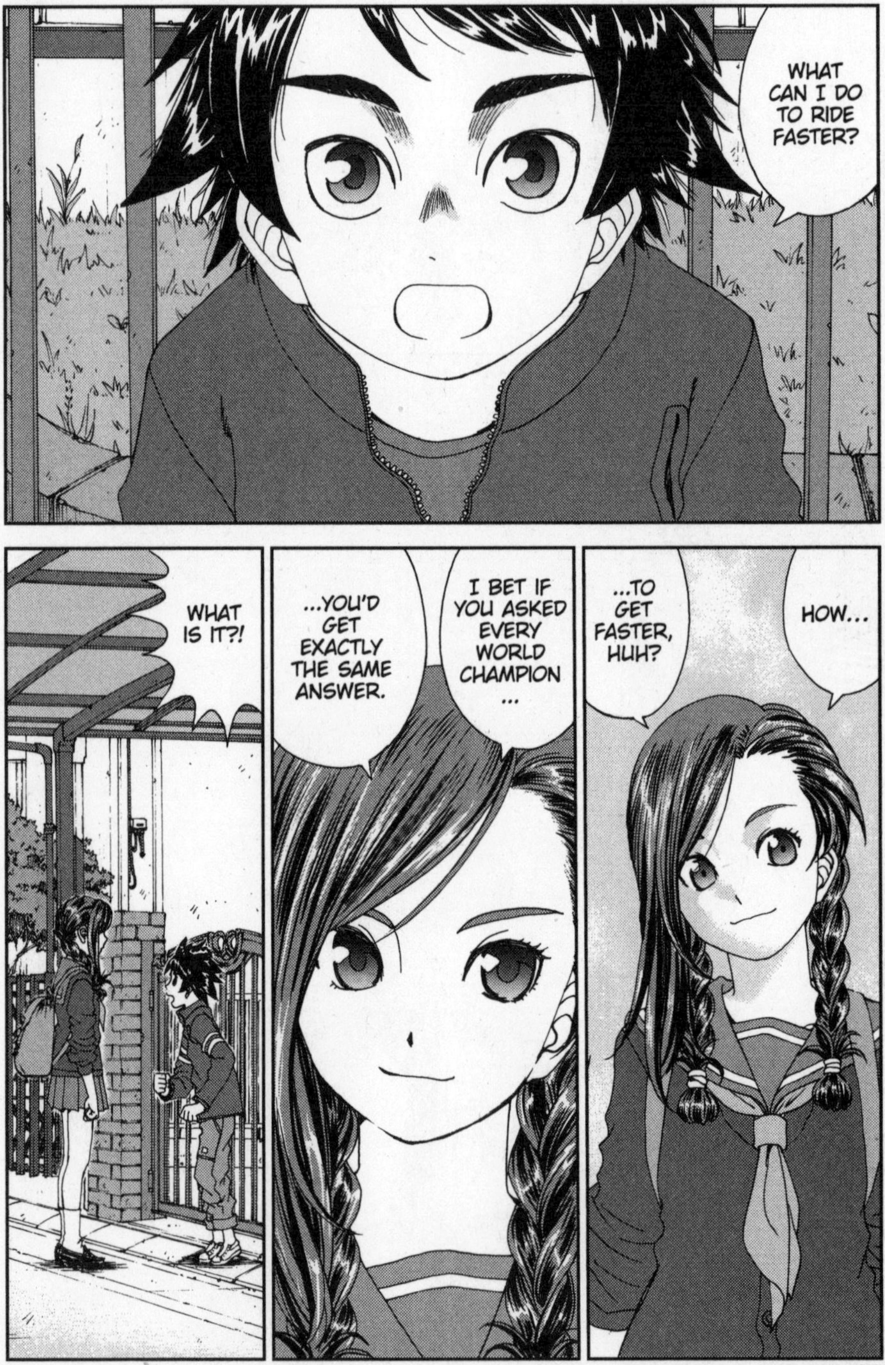
WHAT CAN I DO TO RIDE FASTER?
HOW...
...TO GET FASTER, HUH?
I BET IF YOU ASKED EVERY WORLD CHAMPION ...
...YOU'D GET EXACTLY THE SAME ANSWER.
WHAT IS IT?!

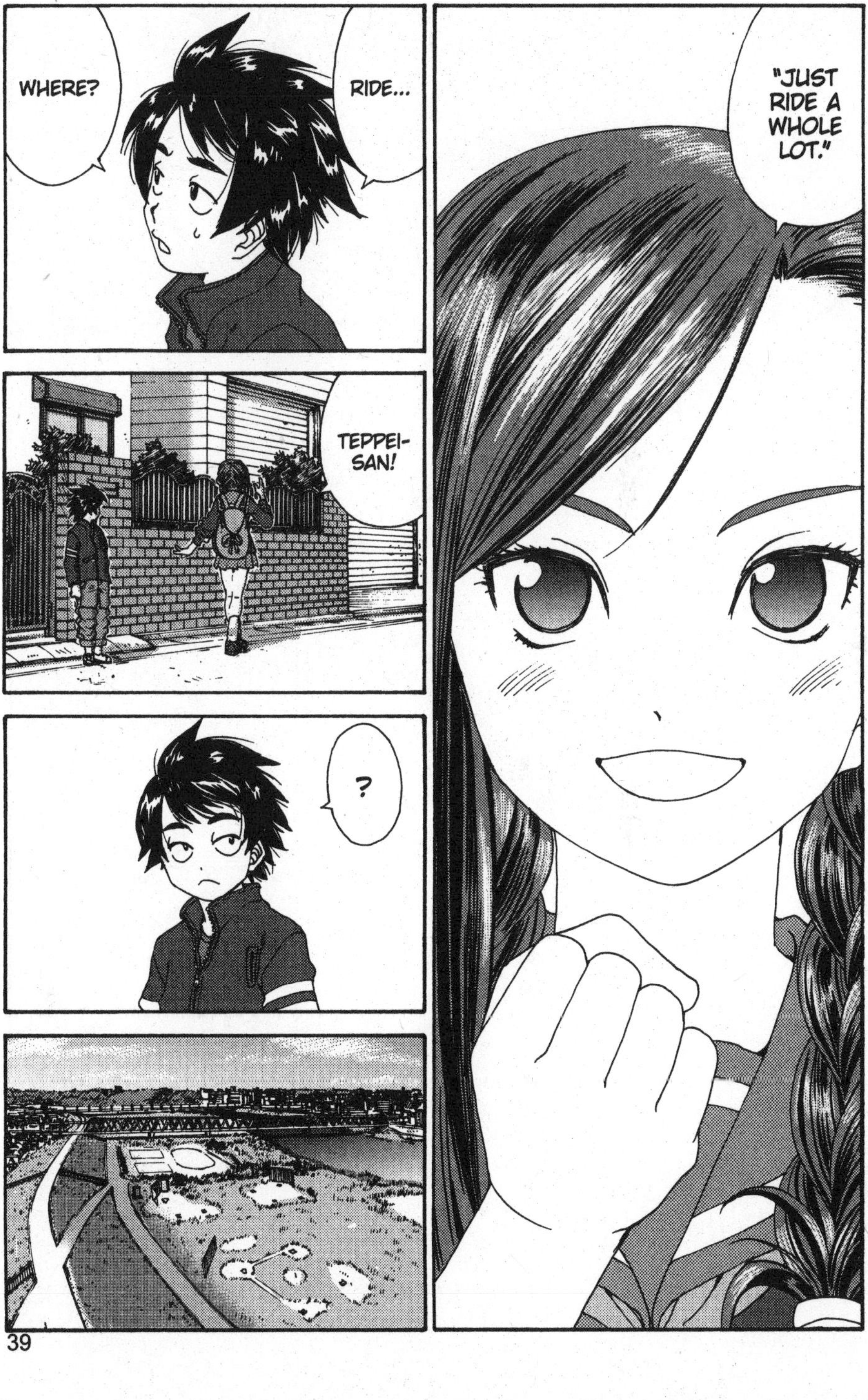
"JUST RIDE A WHOLE LOT."
RIDE...
WHERE?
TEPPEI-SAN!
?

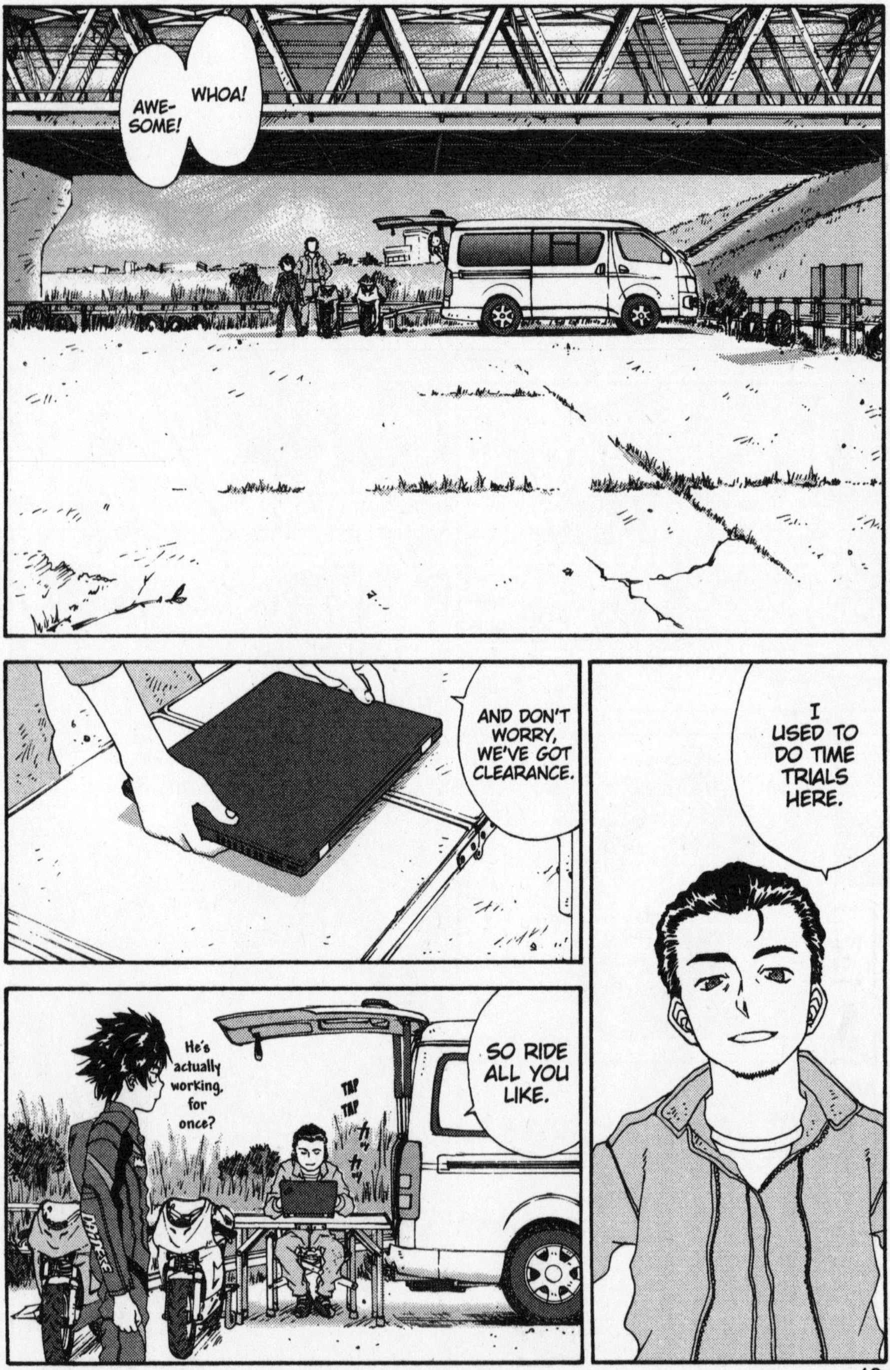
WHOA!
AWE-SOME!
I USED TO DO TIME TRIALS HERE.
AND DON'T WORRY, WE'VE GOT CLEARANCE.
SO RIDE ALL YOU LIKE.
TAP TAP
He's actually working, for once?

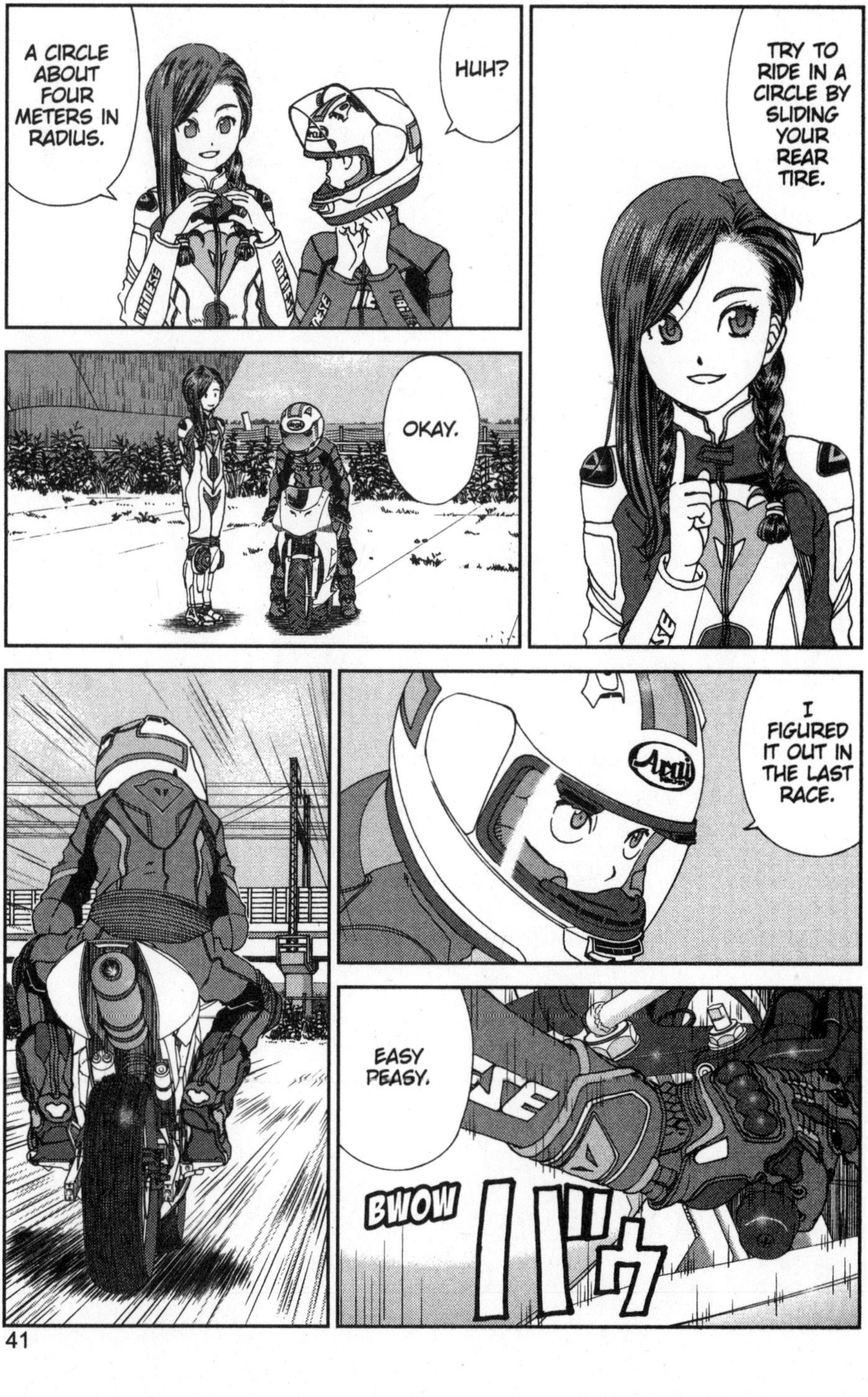
TRY TO RIDE IN A CIRCLE BY SLIDING YOUR REAR TIRE.
HUH?
A CIRCLE ABOUT FOUR METERS IN RADIUS.
OKAY.
I FIGURED IT OUT IN THE LAST RACE.
EASY PEASY.
BWOW
ドゥ

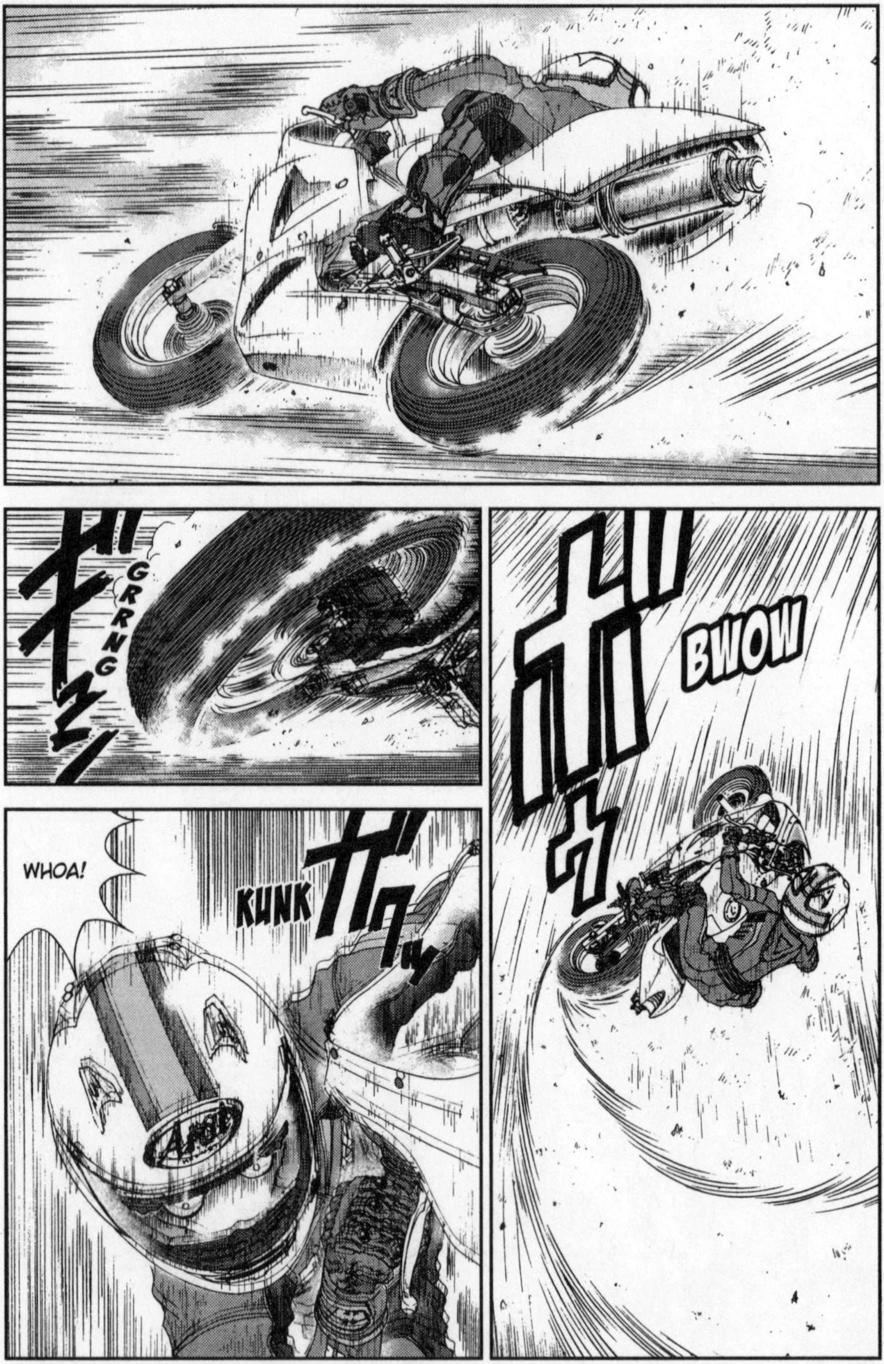

GRRNG
BWOW
WHOA!
KUNK

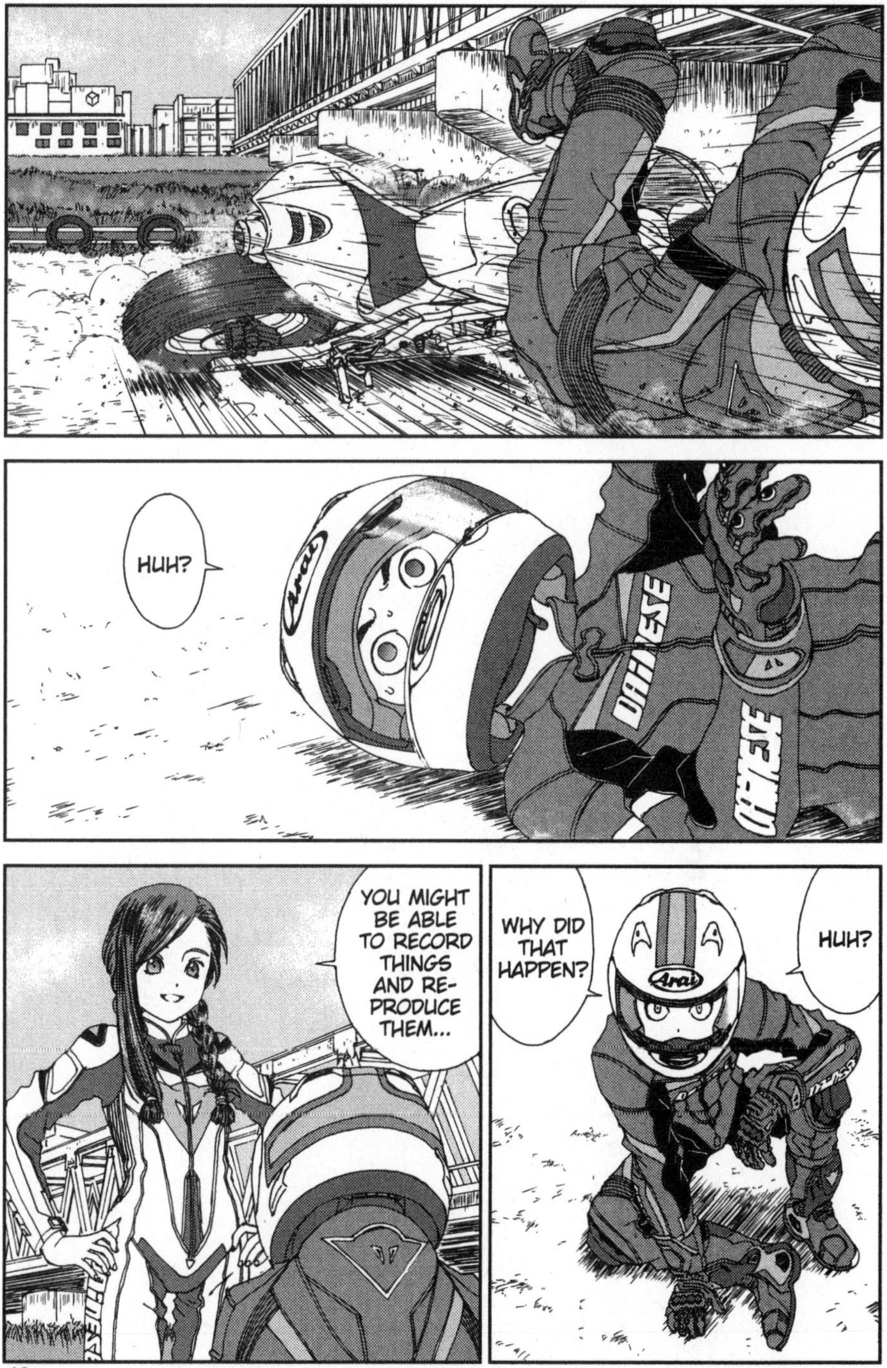
HUH?
HUH?
WHY DID THAT HAPPEN?
YOU MIGHT BE ABLE TO RECORD THINGS AND RE-PRODUCE THEM...

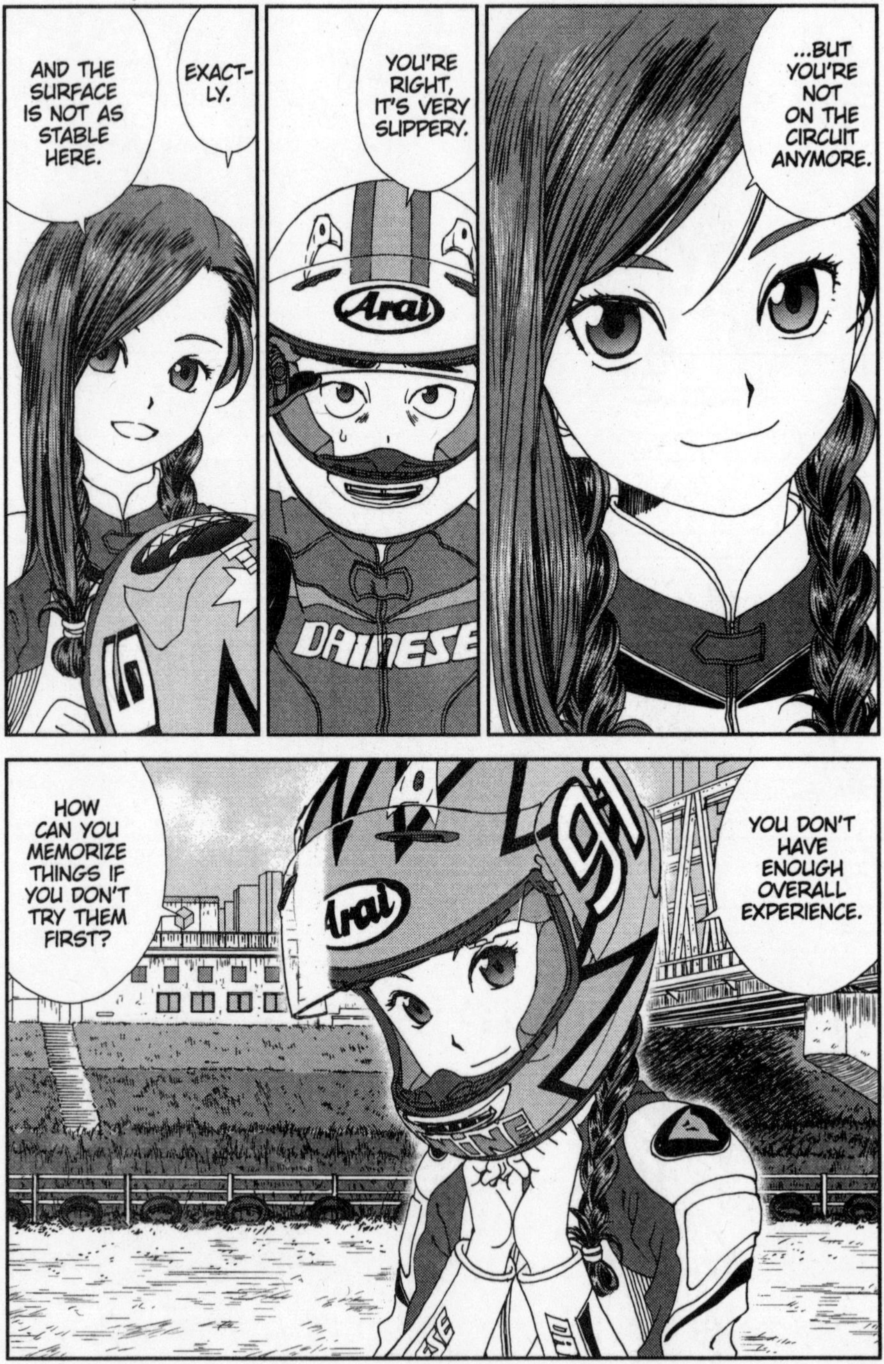
...BUT YOU'RE NOT ON THE CIRCUIT ANYMORE.
YOU'RE RIGHT, IT'S VERY SLIPPERY.
EXACT-LY.
AND THE SURFACE IS NOT AS STABLE HERE.
YOU DON'T HAVE ENOUGH OVERALL EXPERIENCE.
HOW CAN YOU MEMORIZE THINGS IF YOU DON'T TRY THEM FIRST?

I'LL SHOW YOU HOW TO DO IT!!
ギュル
GRUNG
MPH
FFT
KWIK

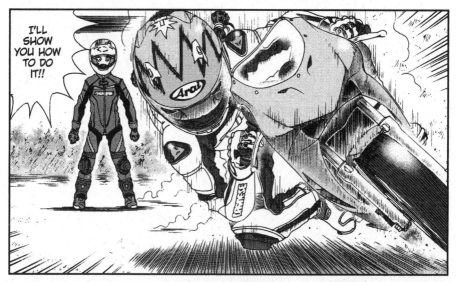

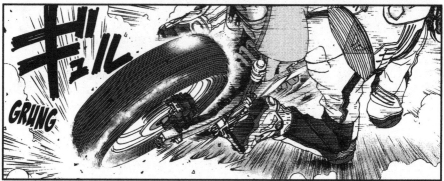

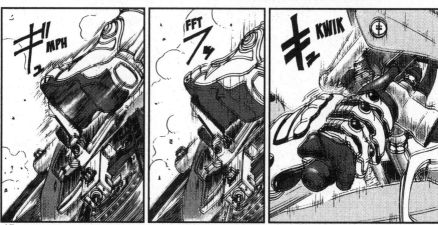

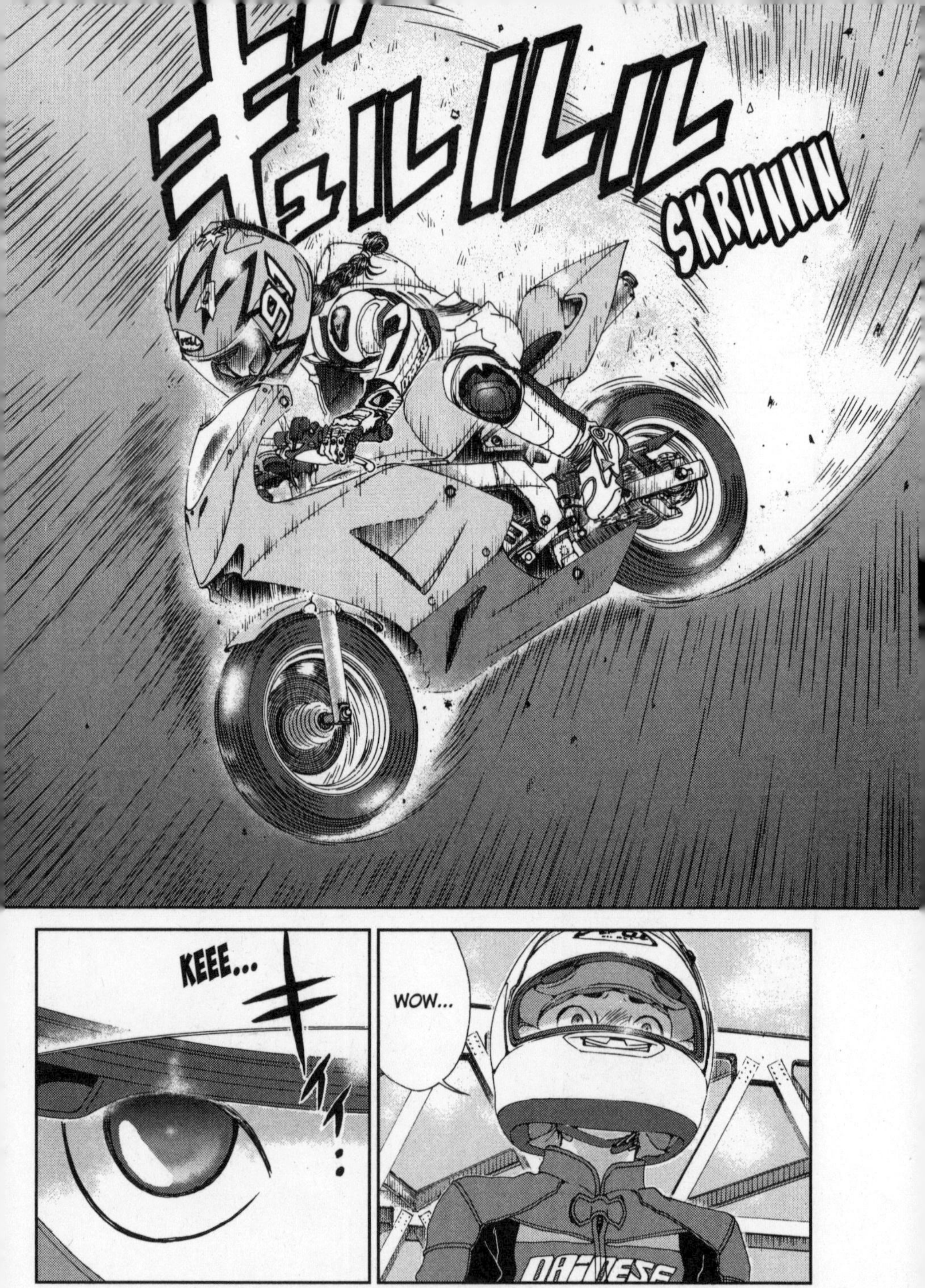
SKRUNNN
WOW...
KEEE...

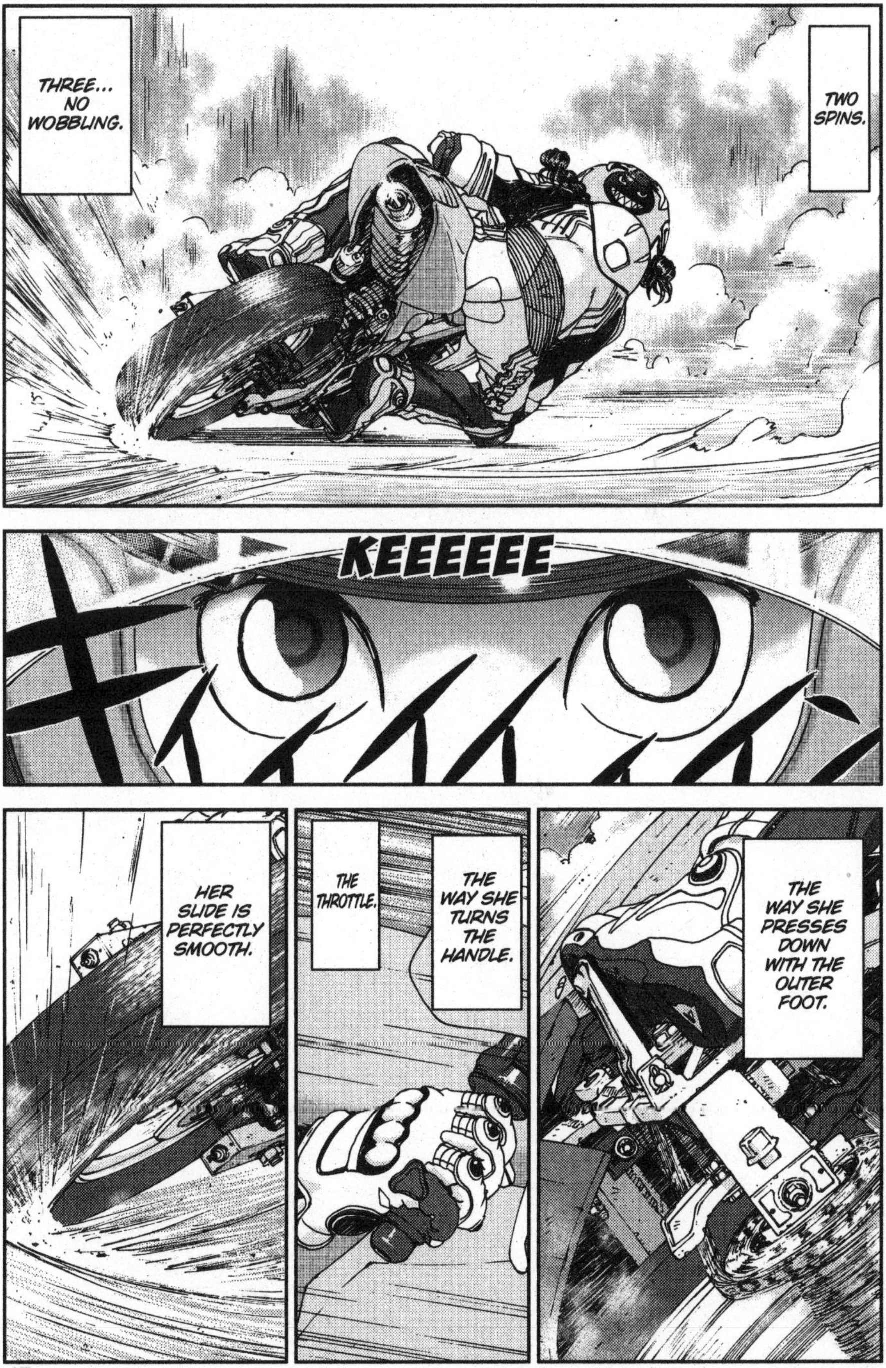
TWO SPINS.
THREE... NO WOBBLING.
KEEEEEE
THE WAY SHE PRESSES DOWN WITH THE OUTER FOOT.
THE WAY SHE TURNS THE HANDLE.
THE THROTTLE.
HER SLIDE IS PERFECTLY SMOOTH.

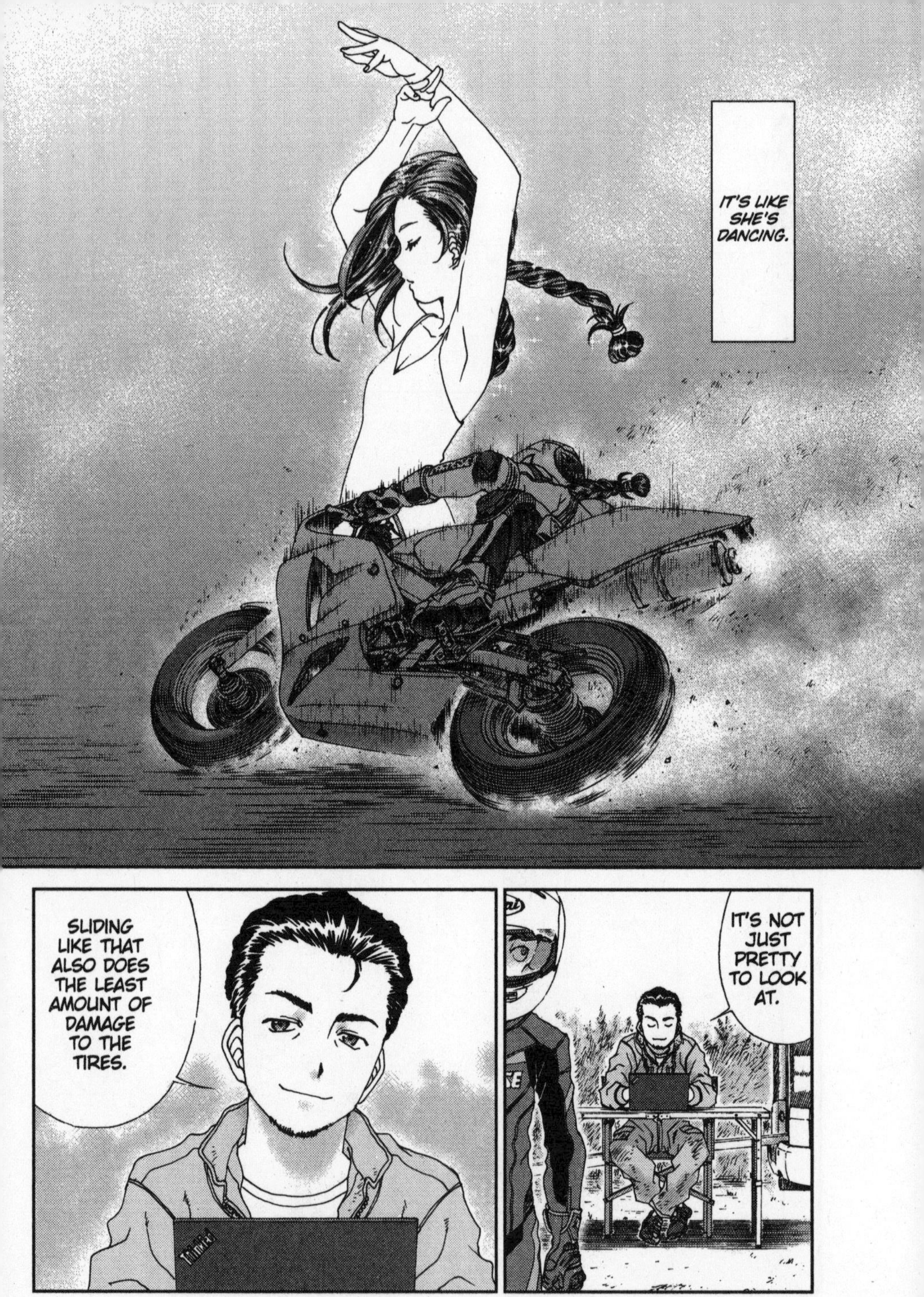
IT'S LIKE SHE'S DANCING.
IT'S NOT JUST PRETTY TO LOOK AT.
SLIDING LIKE THAT ALSO DOES THE LEAST AMOUNT OF DAMAGE TO THE TIRES.

I WANT...

...WITH HER.

I WISH I COULD RIDE...

...AND WIN.

...TO RIDE AGAINST HER...

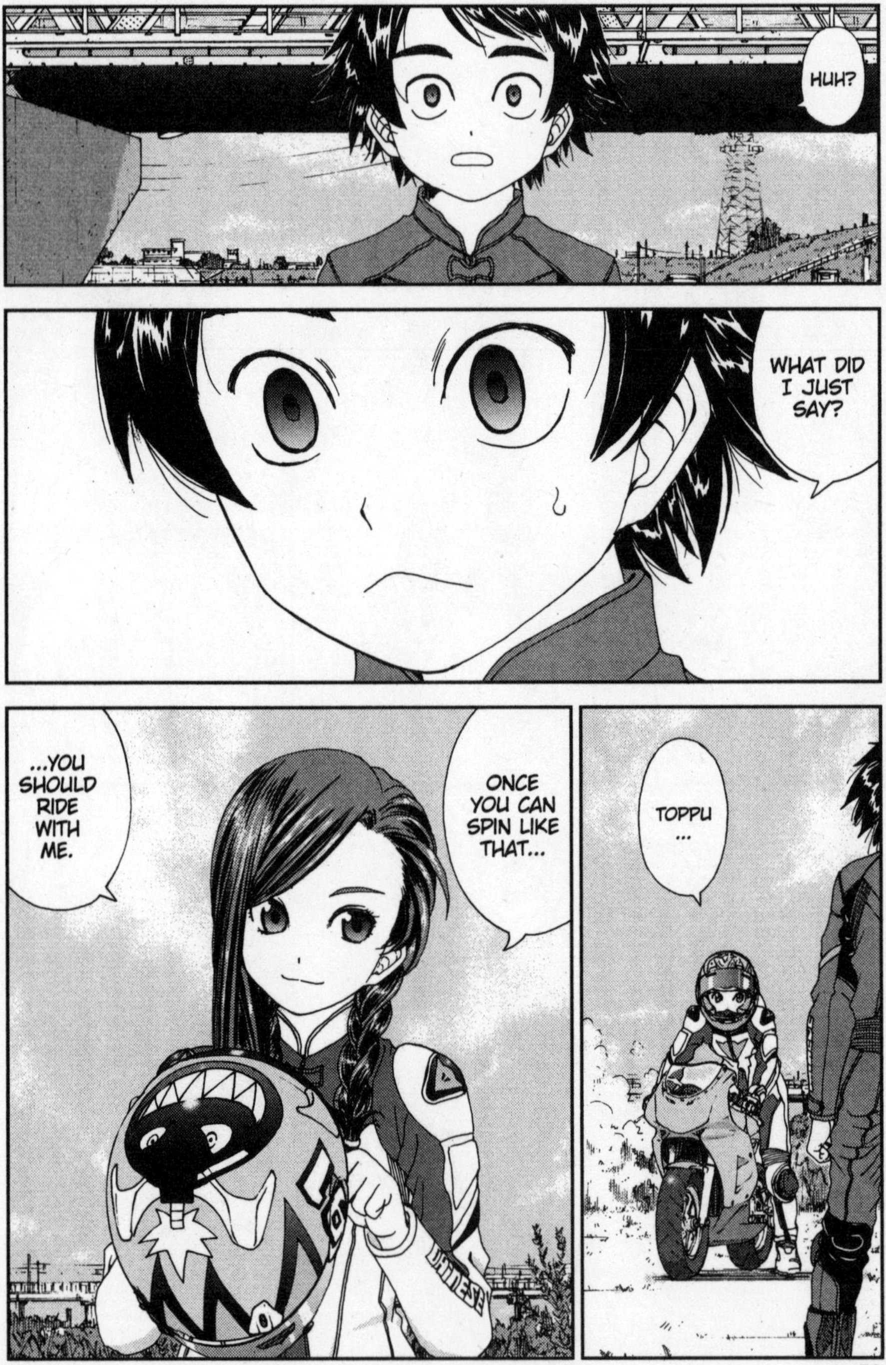
HUH?
WHAT DID I JUST SAY?
TOPPU ...
ONCE YOU CAN SPIN LIKE THAT...
...YOU SHOULD RIDE WITH ME.

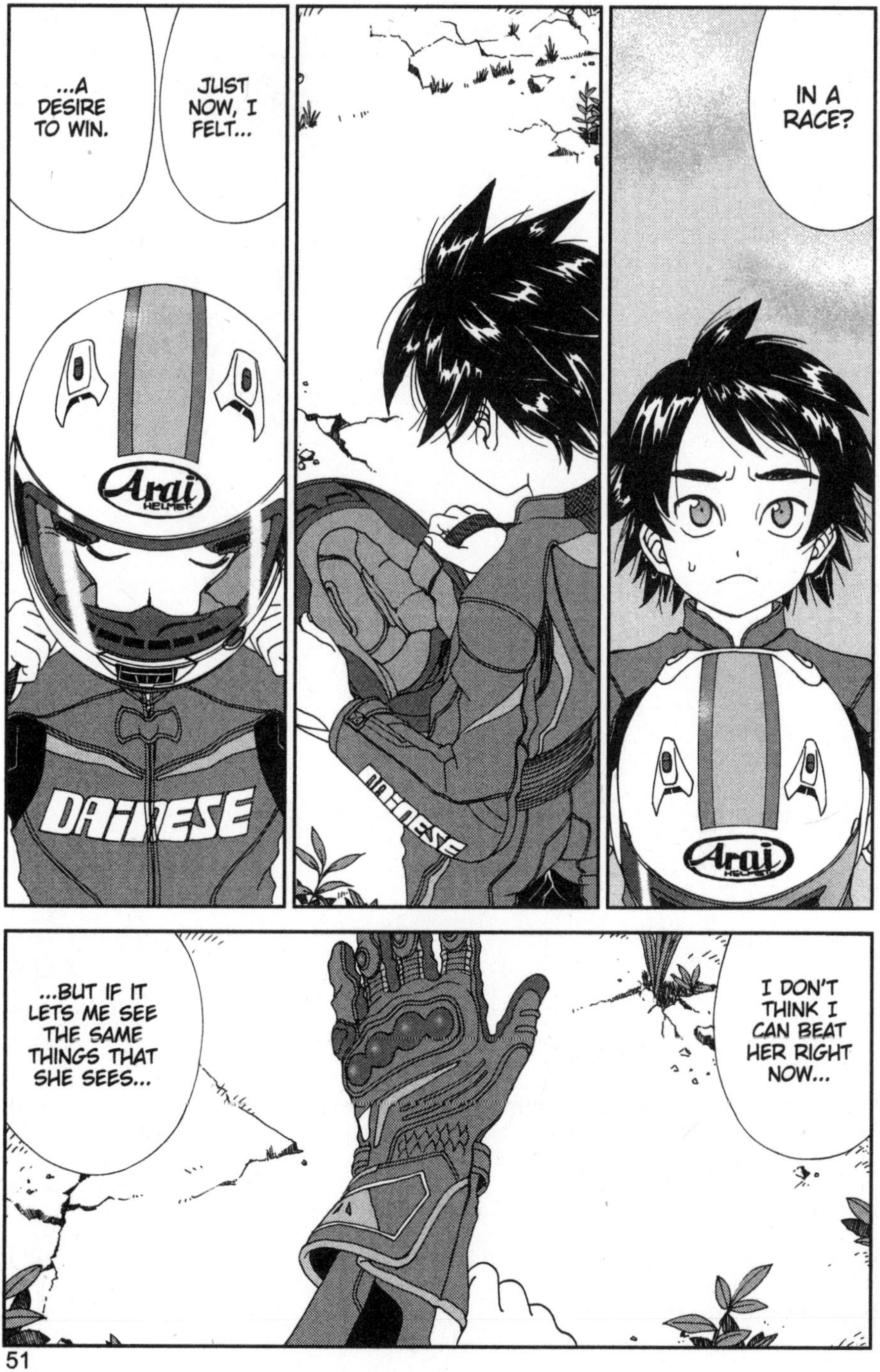
IN A RACE?
JUST NOW, I FELT...
...A DESIRE TO WIN.
I DON'T THINK I CAN BEAT HER RIGHT NOW...
...BUT IF IT LETS ME SEE THE SAME THINGS THAT SHE SEES...

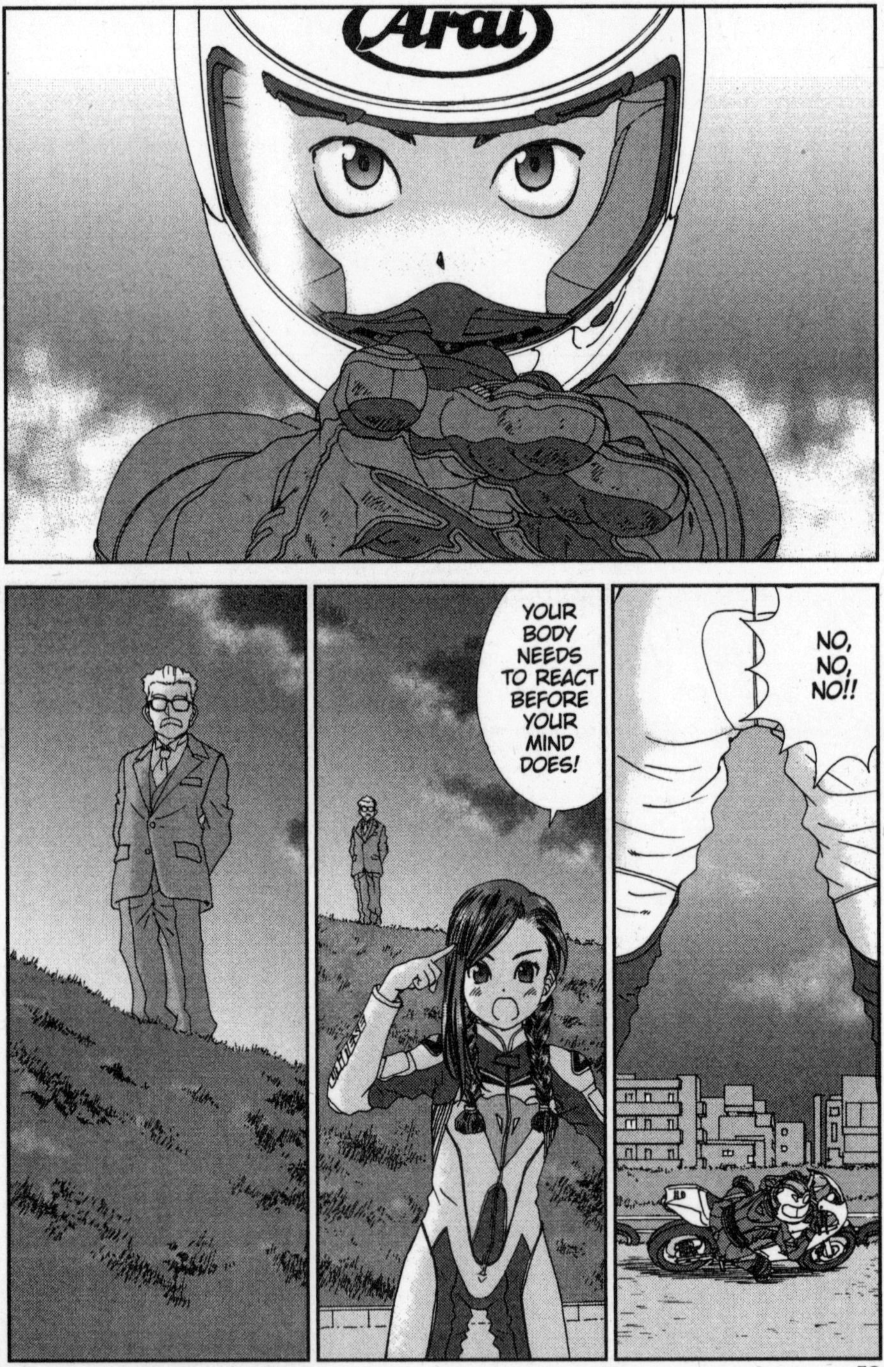

Arai
YOUR BODY NEEDS TO REACT BEFORE YOUR MIND DOES!
NO, NO, NO!!

Lap 16: end

Arai

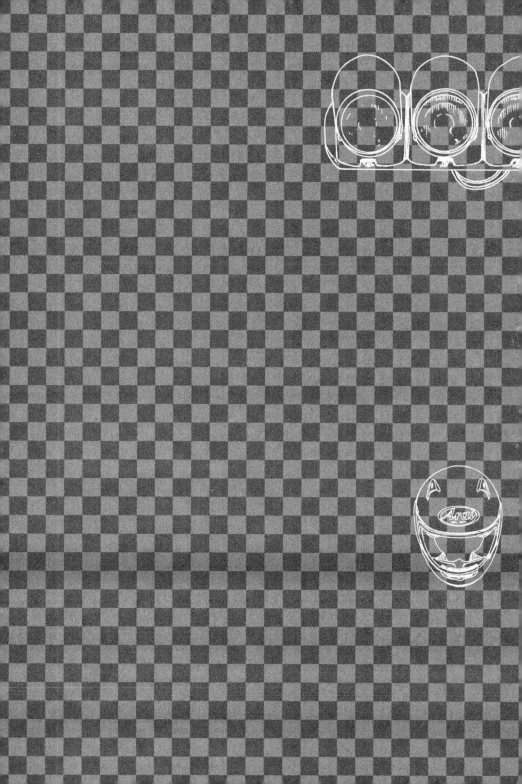

Toppu GP

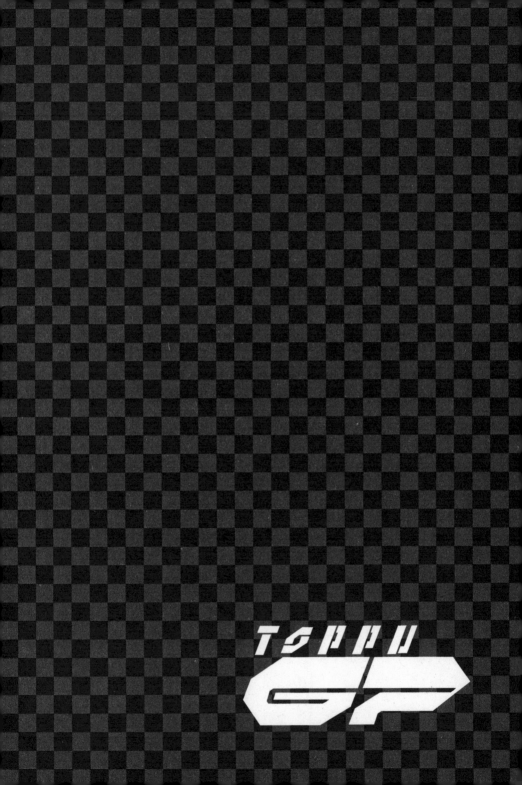

Lap 17:
SPIN, SPIN, SPIN

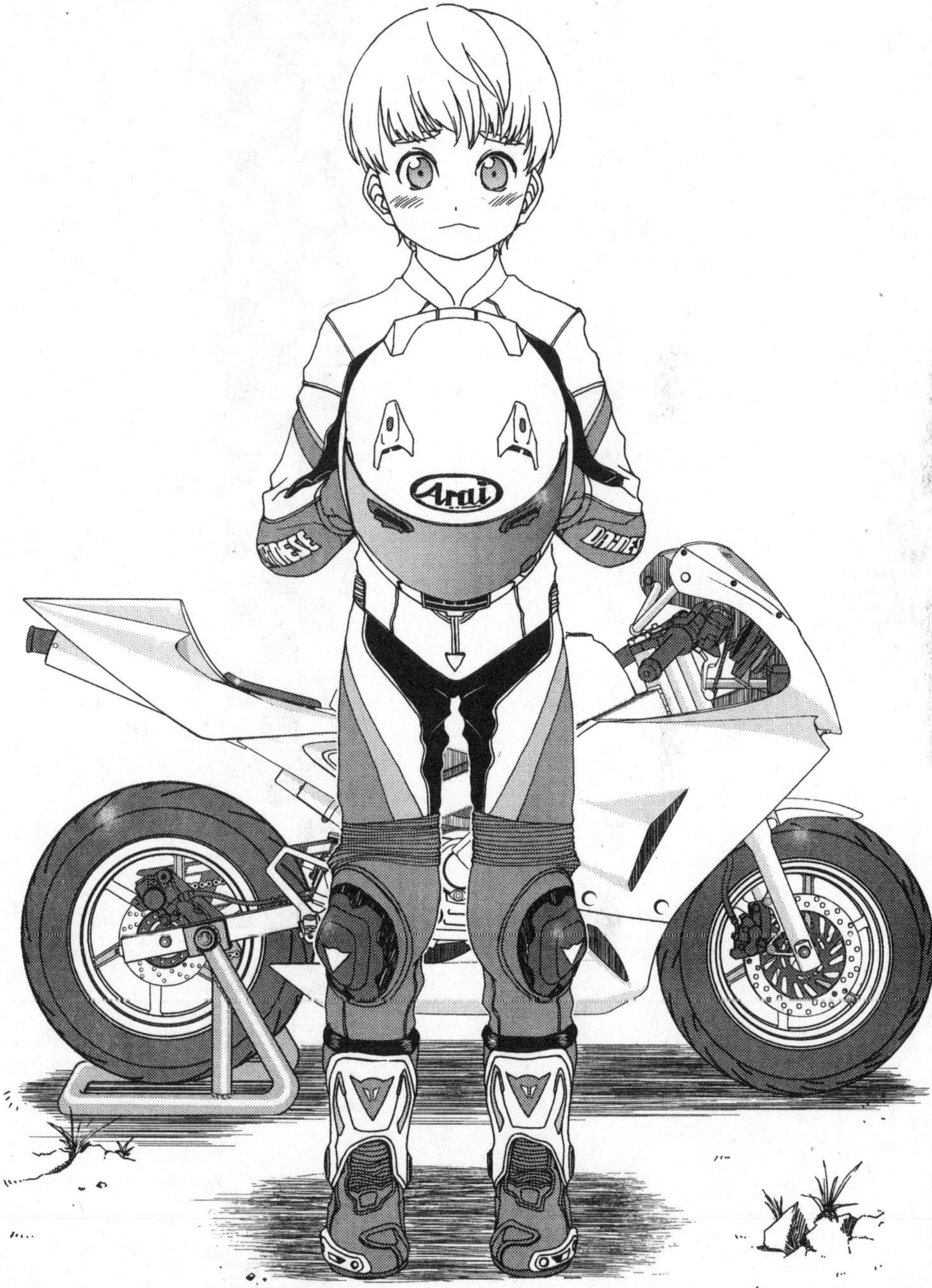
Arai

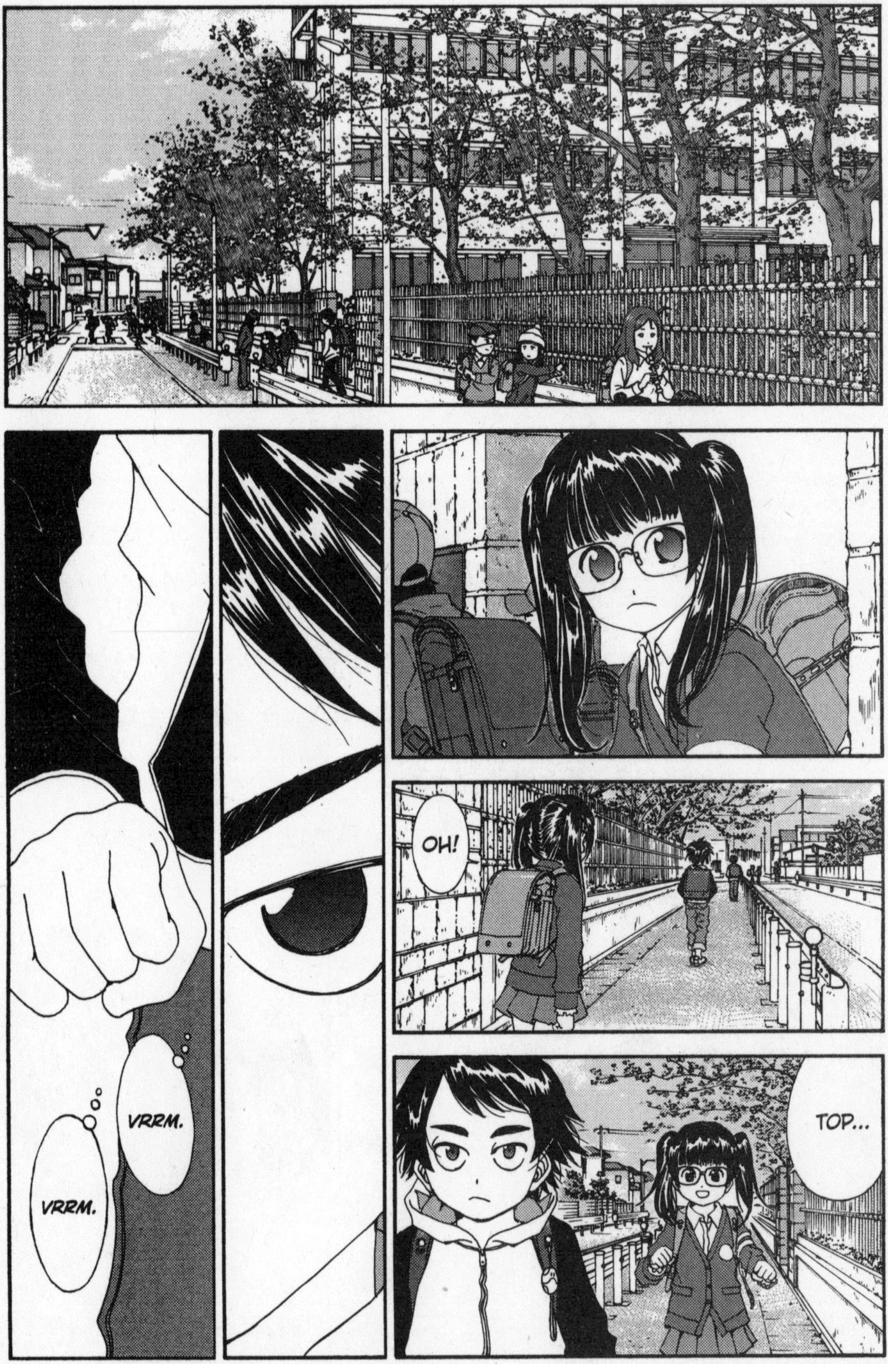
OH!
TOP...
VRRM.
VRRM.

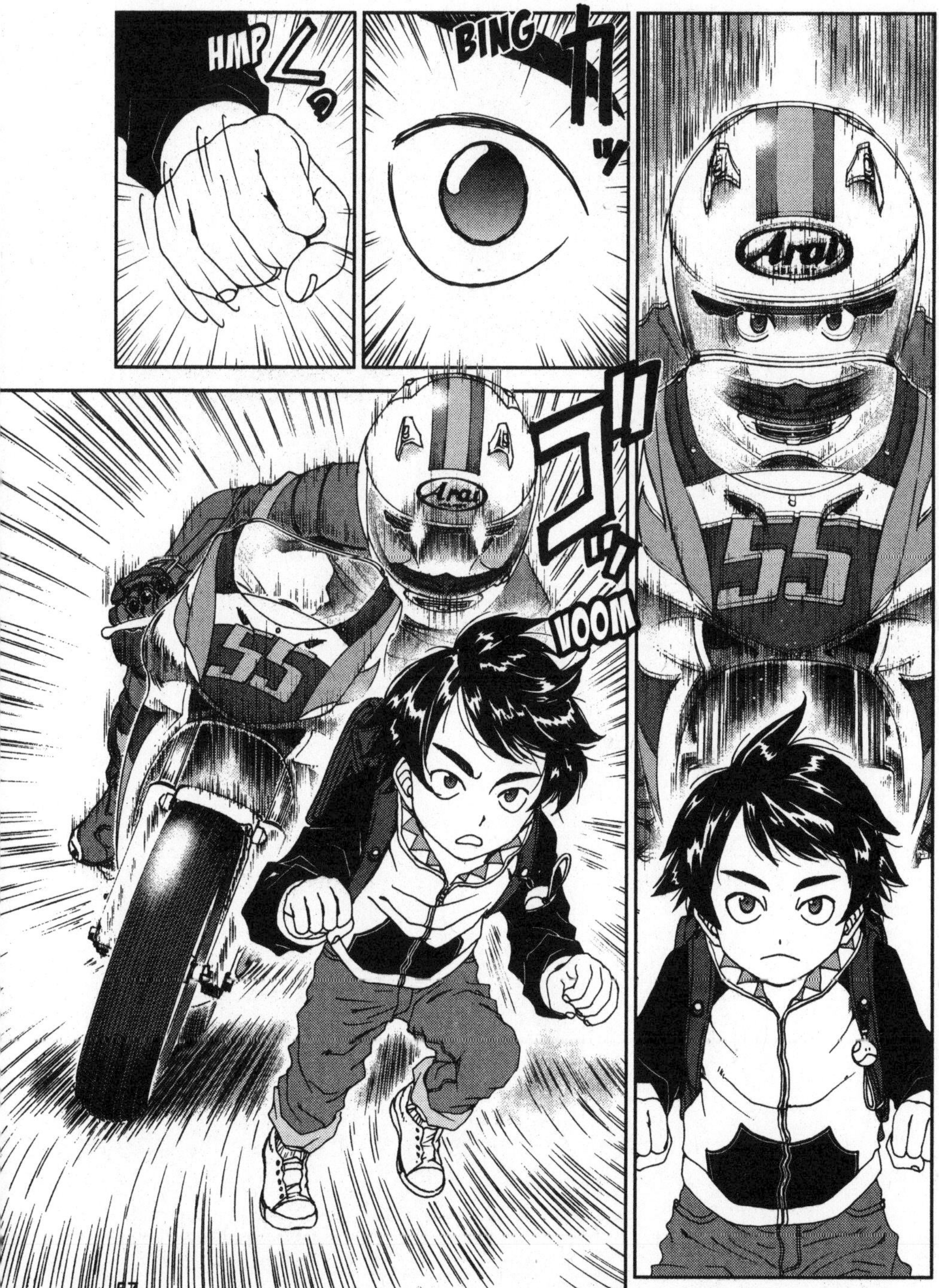

HMP
BING
VOOM

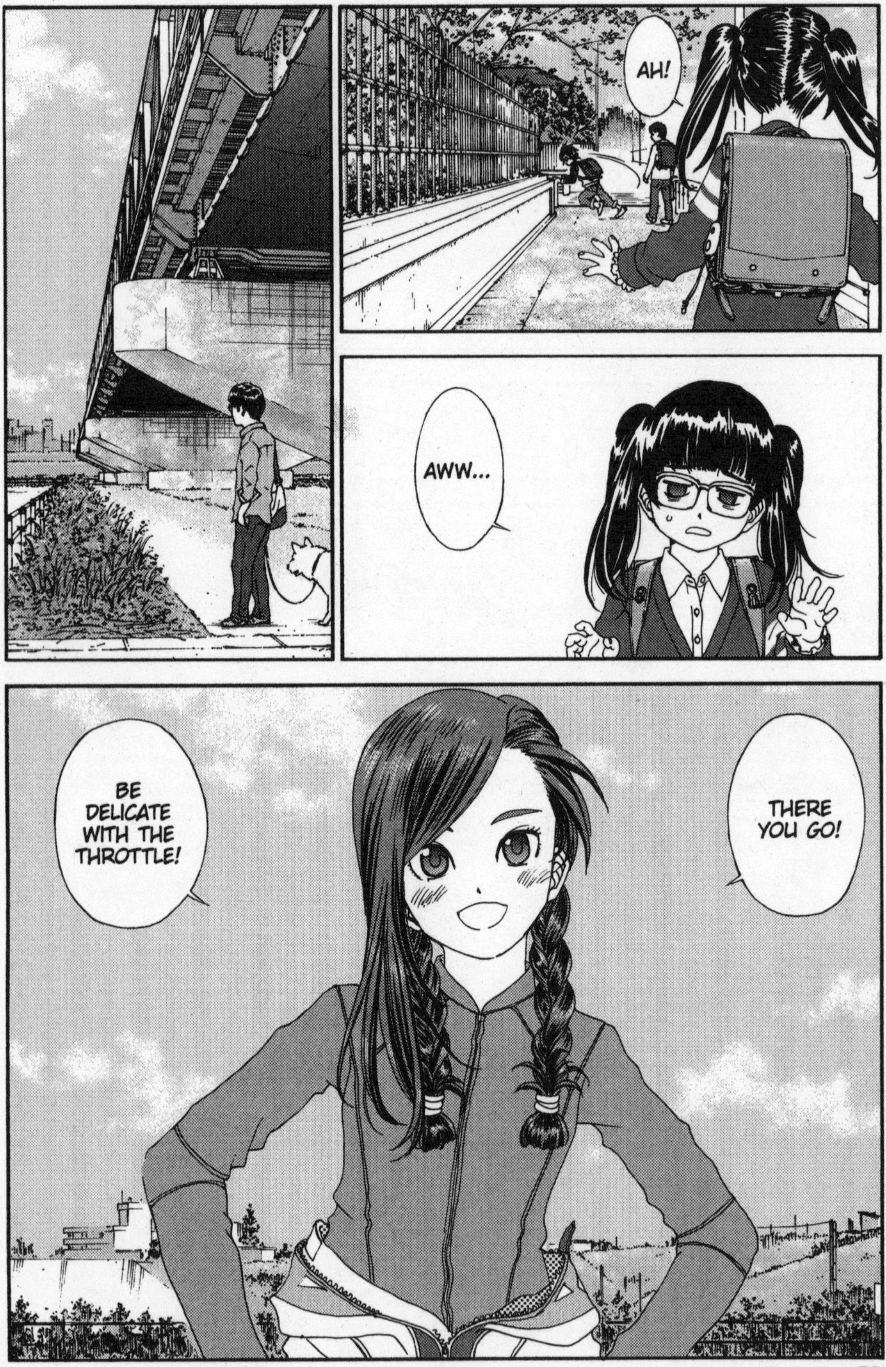
AH!
AWW...
THERE YOU GO!
BE DELICATE WITH THE THROTTLE!

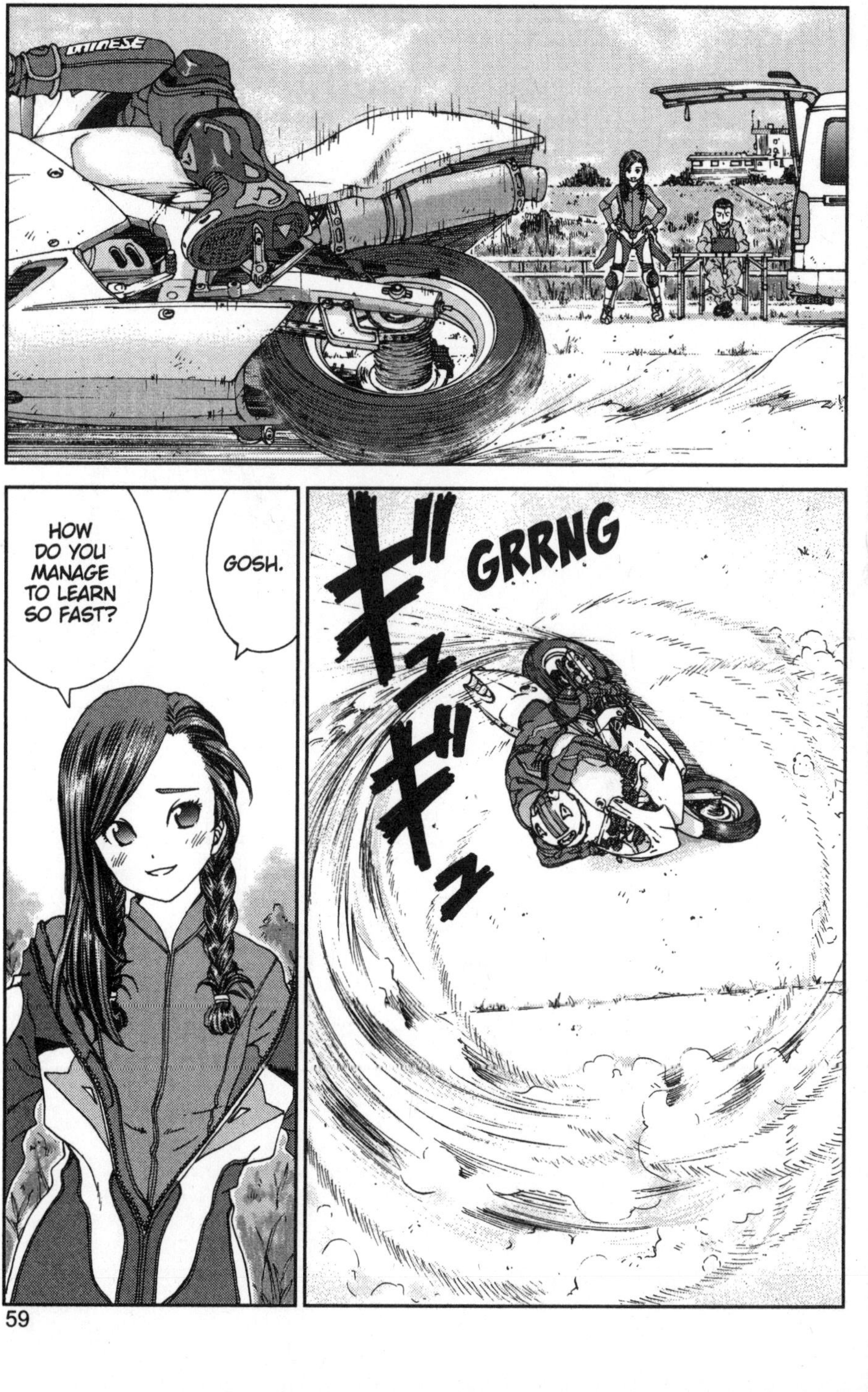
GRRNG
GOSH.
HOW DO YOU MANAGE TO LEARN SO FAST?

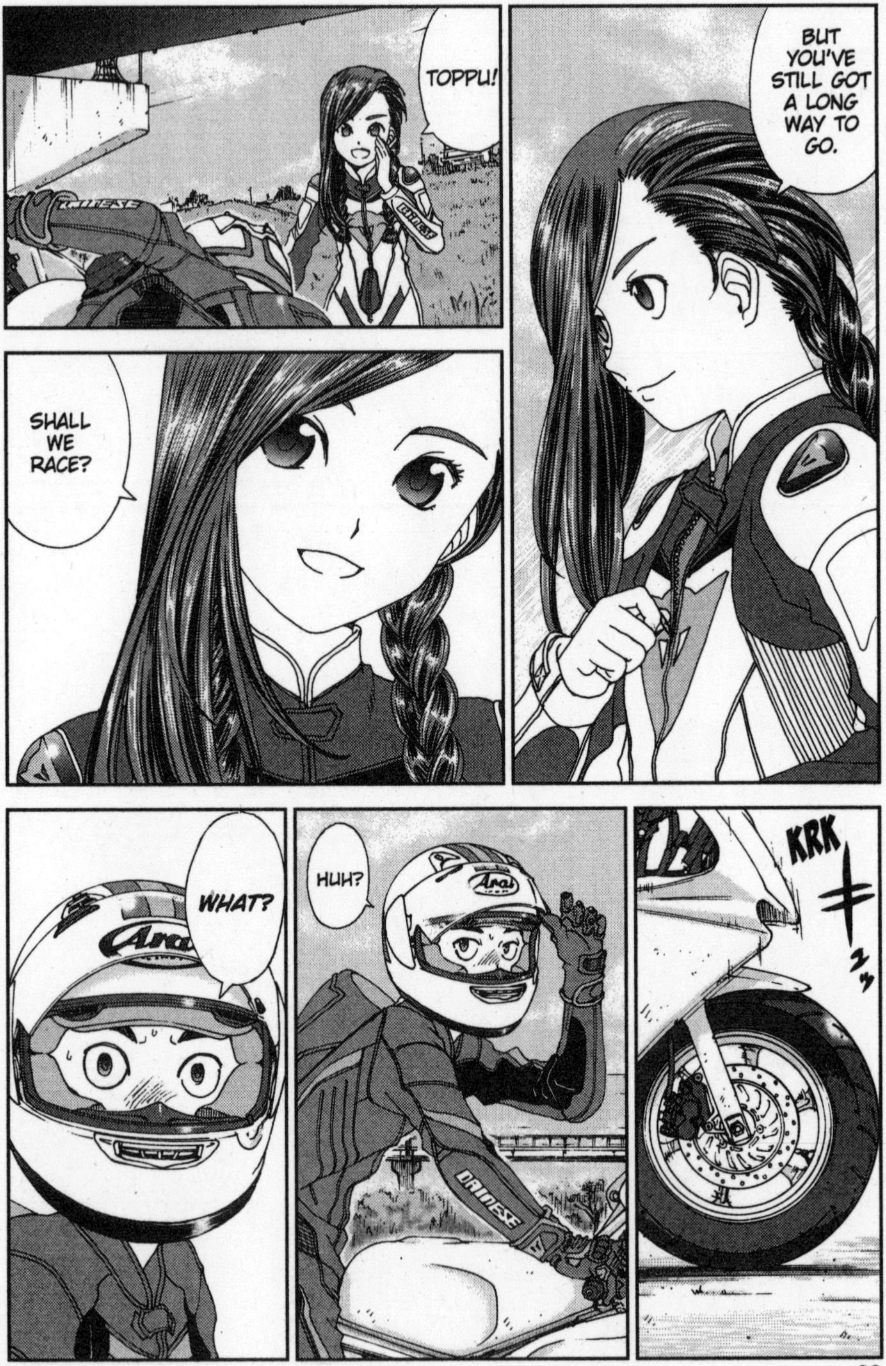
TOPPU!
BUT YOU'VE STILL GOT A LONG WAY TO GO.
SHALL WE RACE?
KRK
HUH?
WHAT?

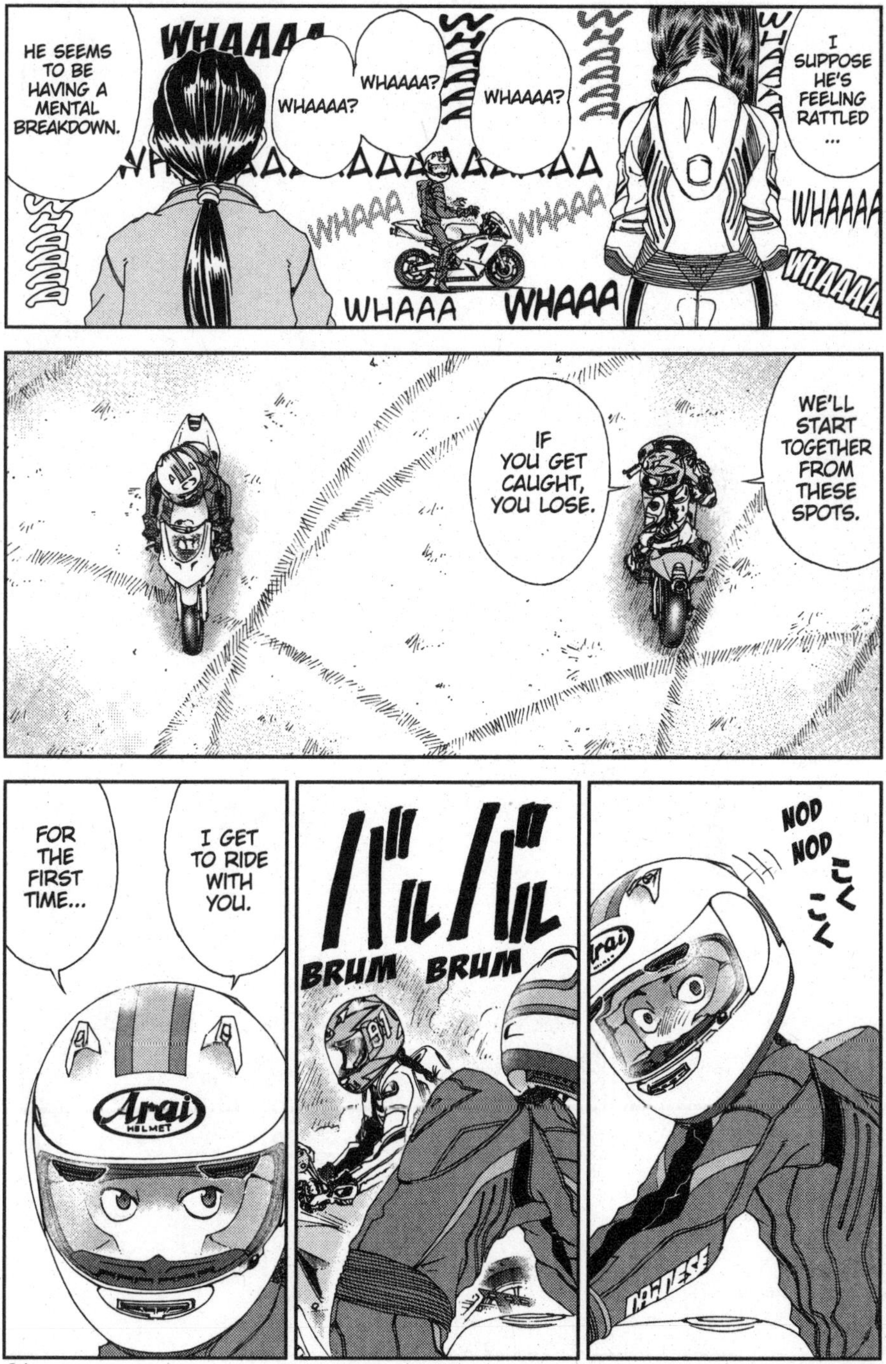
I SUPPOSE HE'S FEELING RATTLED ...
WHAAAA
WHAAAA?
WHAAAA?
WHAAAA?
HE SEEMS TO BE HAVING A MENTAL BREAKDOWN.
WHAAA
WHAAA
WHAAA
WHAAA
WE'LL START TOGETHER FROM THESE SPOTS.
IF YOU GET CAUGHT, YOU LOSE.
NOD NOD
バルバル
BRUM BRUM
I GET TO RIDE WITH YOU.
FOR THE FIRST TIME...

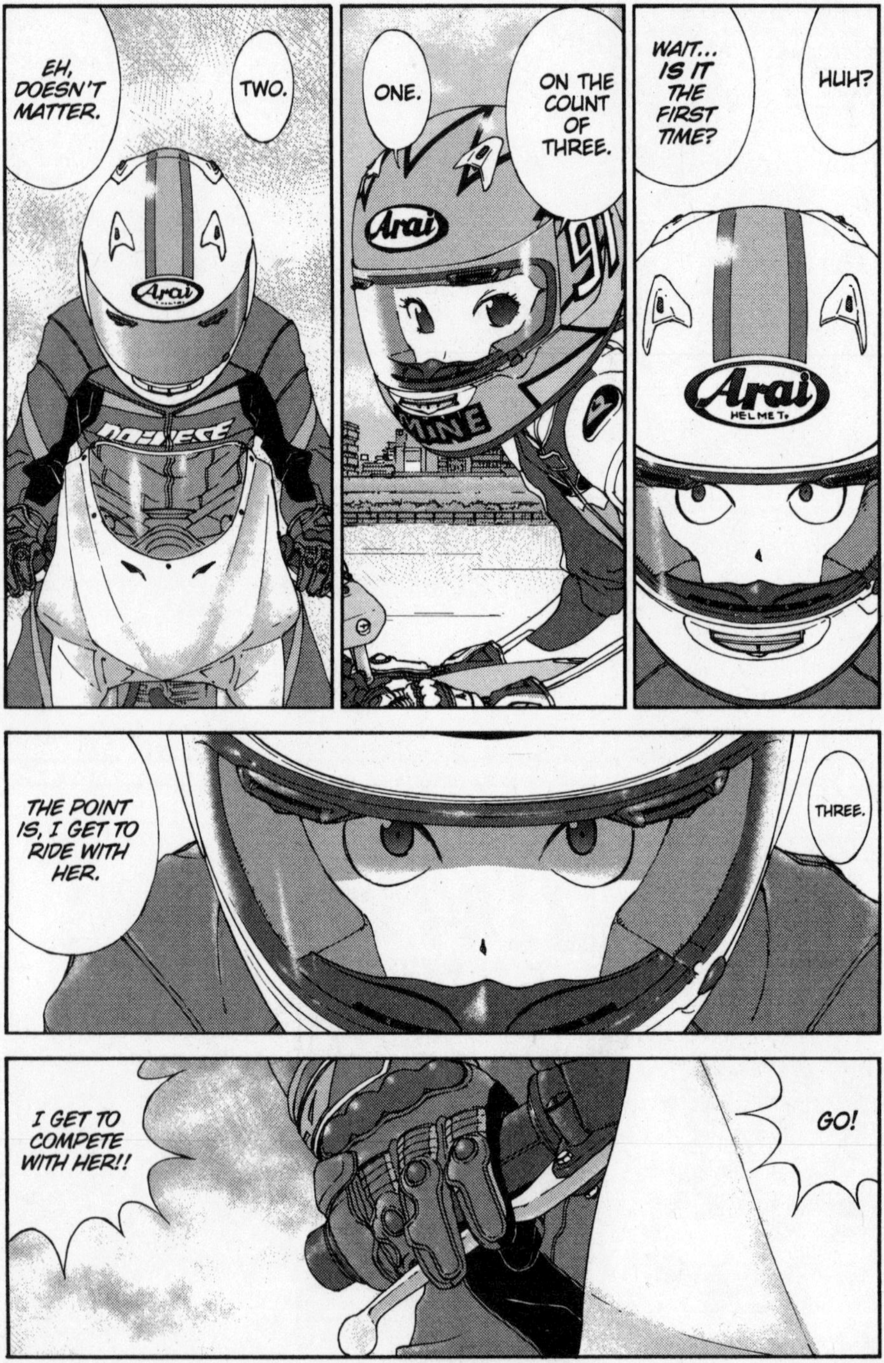
HUH?
WAIT... IS IT THE FIRST TIME?
ON THE COUNT OF THREE.
ONE.
TWO.
EH, DOESN'T MATTER.
THREE.
THE POINT IS, I GET TO RIDE WITH HER.
GO!
I GET TO COMPETE WITH HER!!

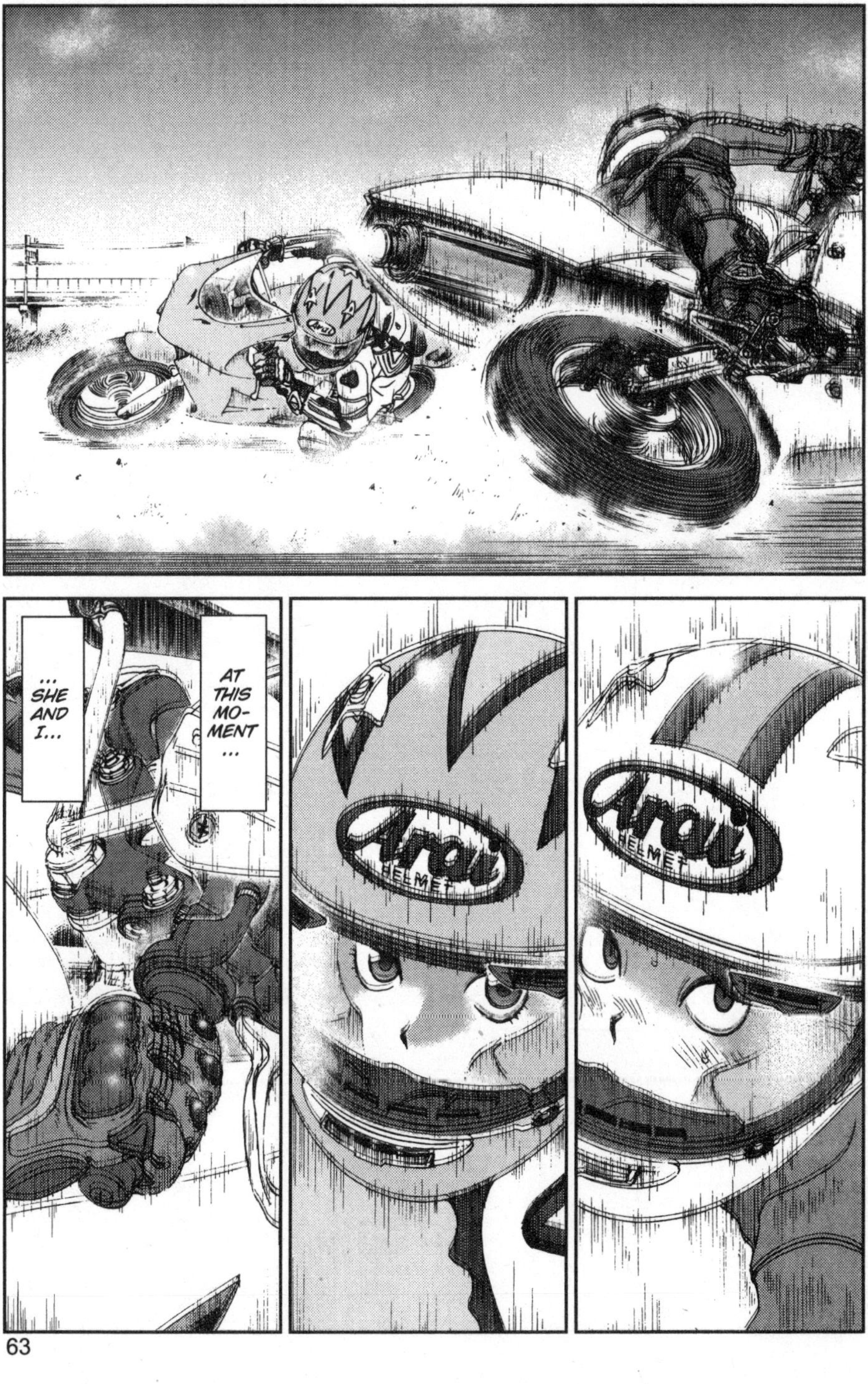
AT THIS MO-MENT...
...SHE AND I...
Arai HELMET
Arai HELMET

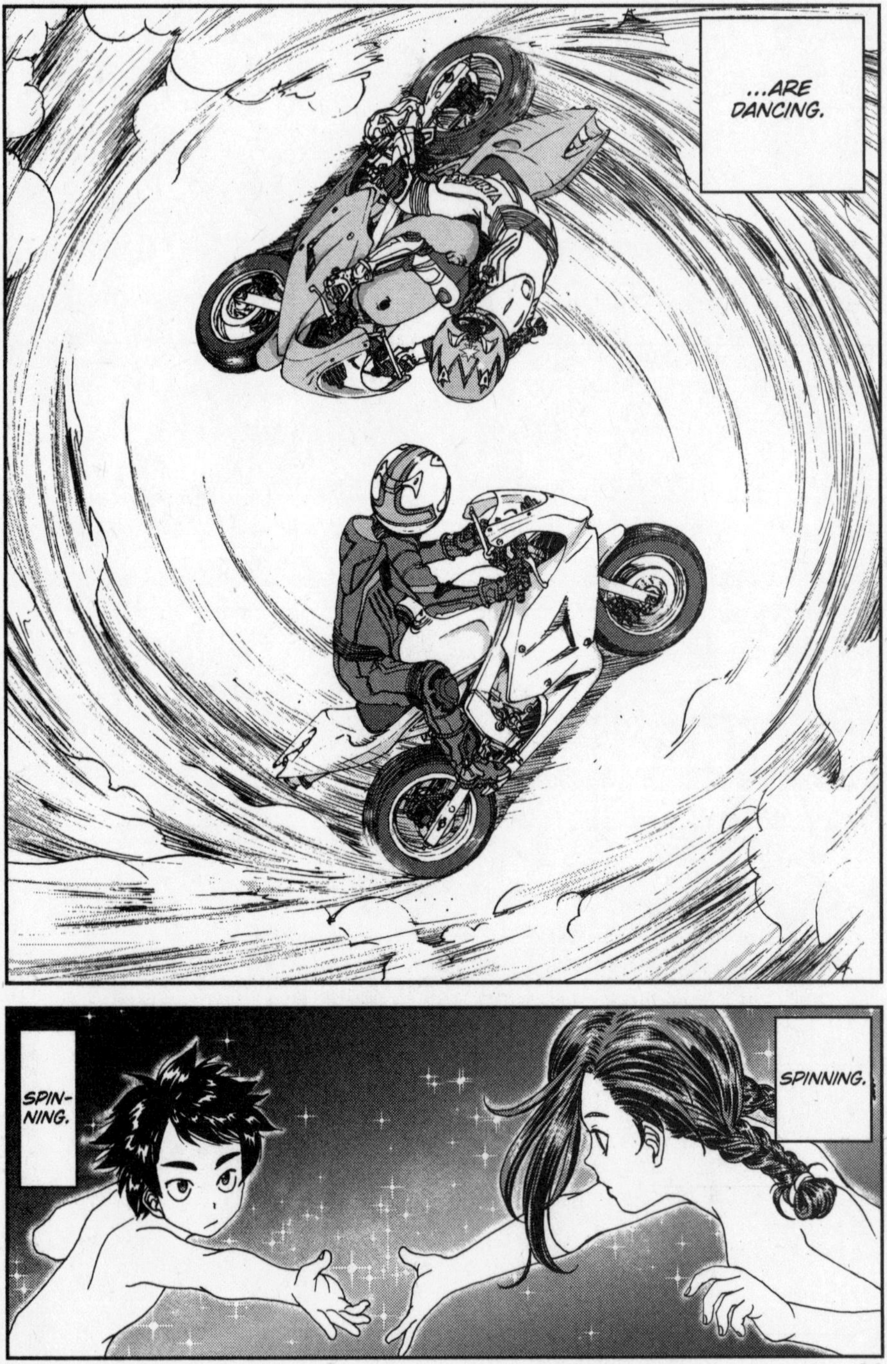
...ARE DANCING.
SPINNING.
SPIN-NING.

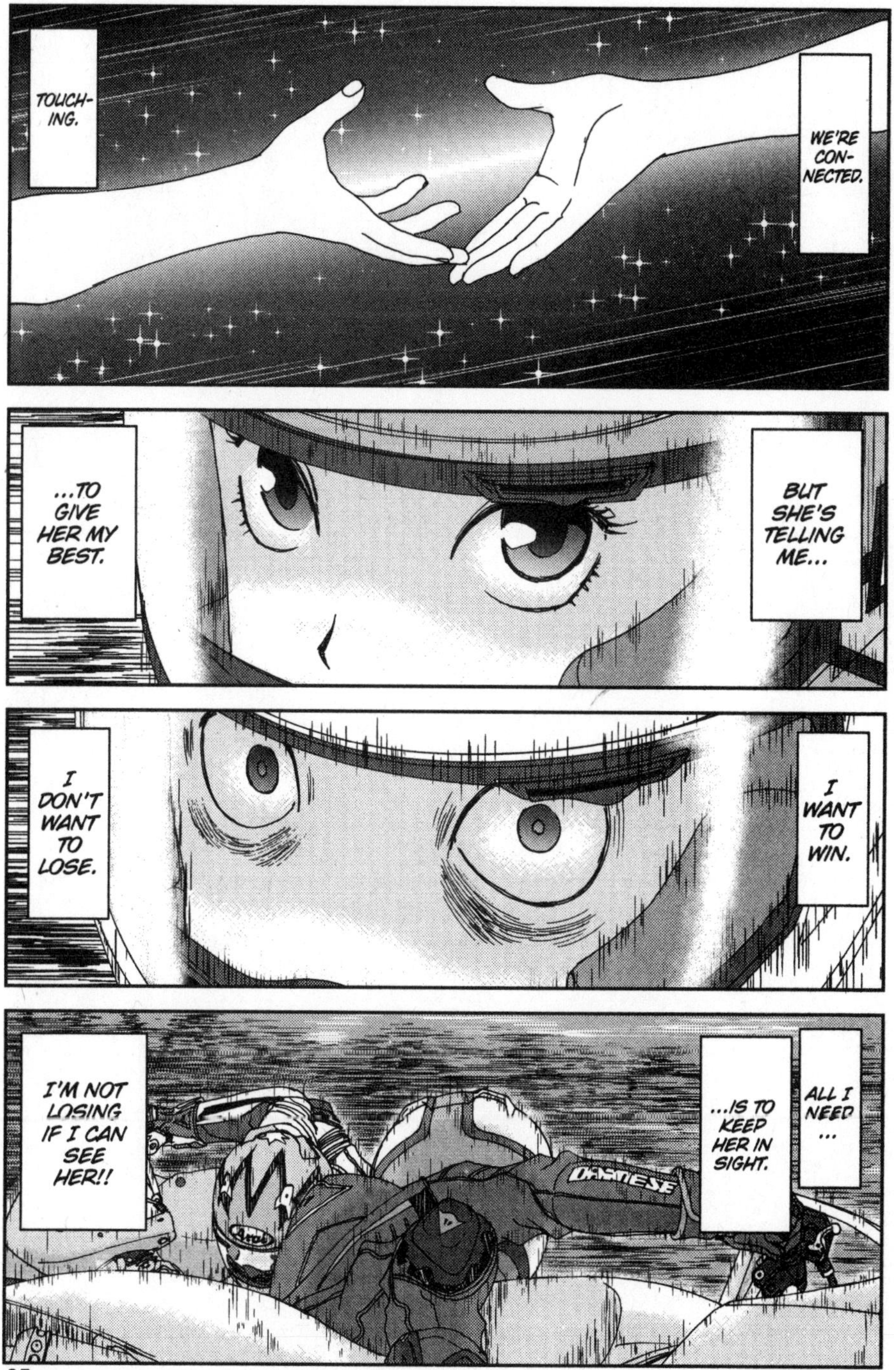
WE'RE CON-NECTED.
TOUCH-ING.
BUT SHE'S TELLING ME...
...TO GIVE HER MY BEST.
I WANT TO WIN.
I DON'T WANT TO LOSE.
ALL I NEED...
...IS TO KEEP HER IN SIGHT.
I'M NOT LOSING IF I CAN SEE HER!!

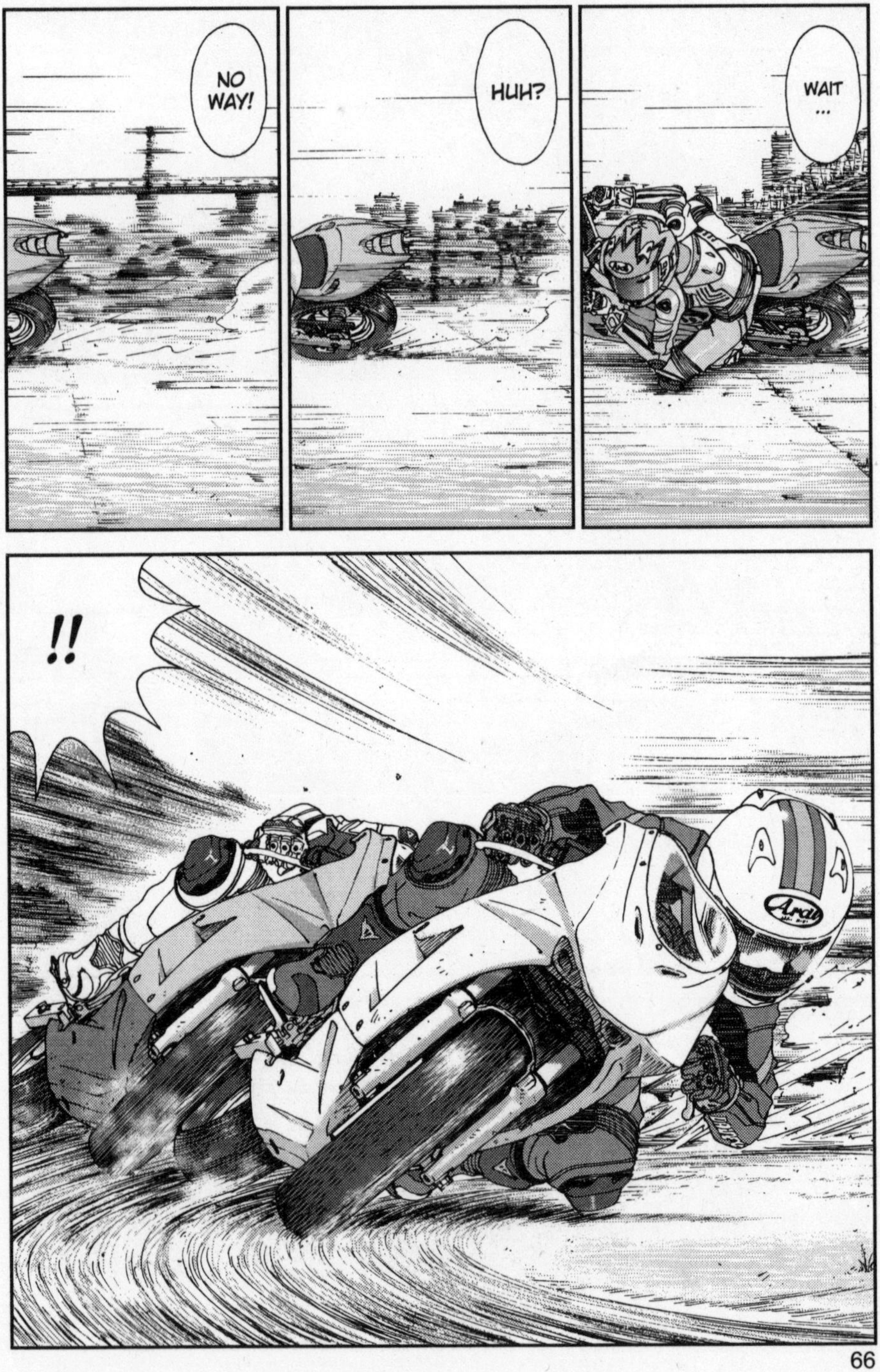
WAIT ...
HUH?
NO WAY!
!!

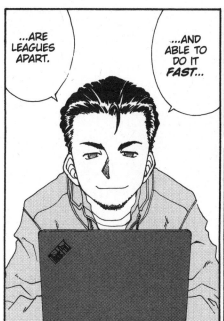

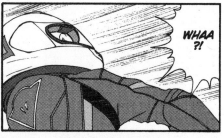

WHAA ?!
BEING ABLE TO DO IT...
...AND ABLE TO DO IT FAST...
...ARE LEAGUES APART.
PARDON ME.
DO YOU HAVE A MOMENT?
YOU NEED TO USE SUBTLER CONTROL, TOPPU.

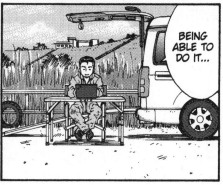

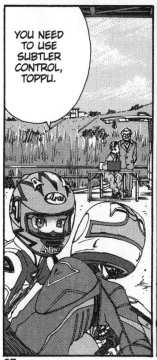

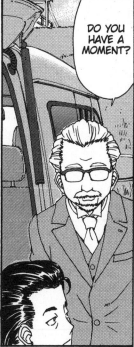

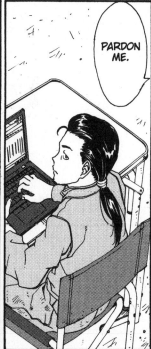

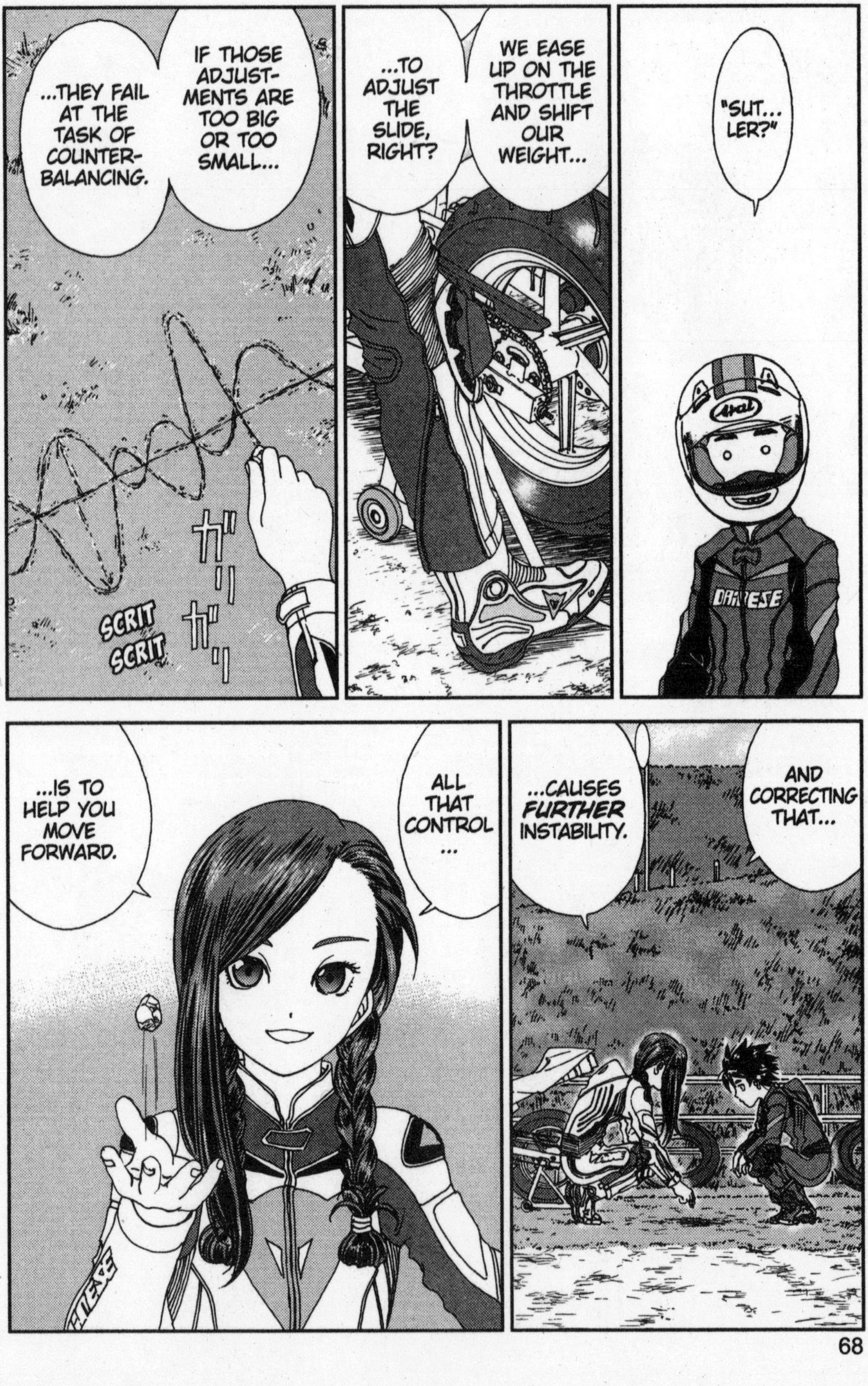
"SUT... LER?"
WE EASE UP ON THE THROTTLE AND SHIFT OUR WEIGHT...
...TO ADJUST THE SLIDE, RIGHT?
IF THOSE ADJUST-MENTS ARE TOO BIG OR TOO SMALL...
...THEY FAIL AT THE TASK OF COUNTER-BALANCING.
ガリガリ
SCRIT SCRIT
AND CORRECTING THAT...
...CAUSES *FURTHER* INSTABILITY.
ALL THAT CONTROL ...
...IS TO HELP YOU MOVE FORWARD.

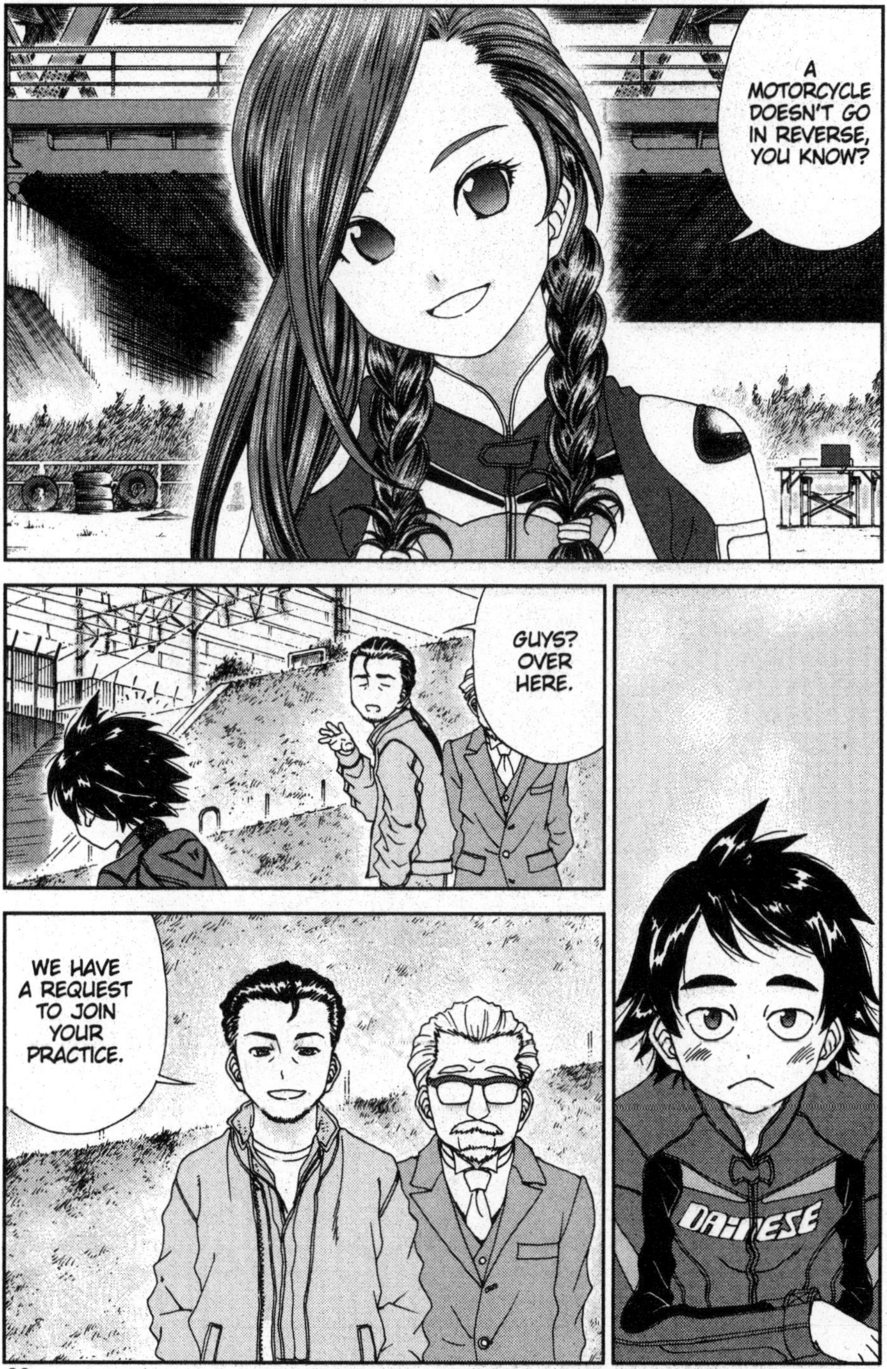
A MOTORCYCLE DOESN'T GO IN REVERSE, YOU KNOW?
GUYS? OVER HERE.
WE HAVE A REQUEST TO JOIN YOUR PRACTICE.
DAINESE

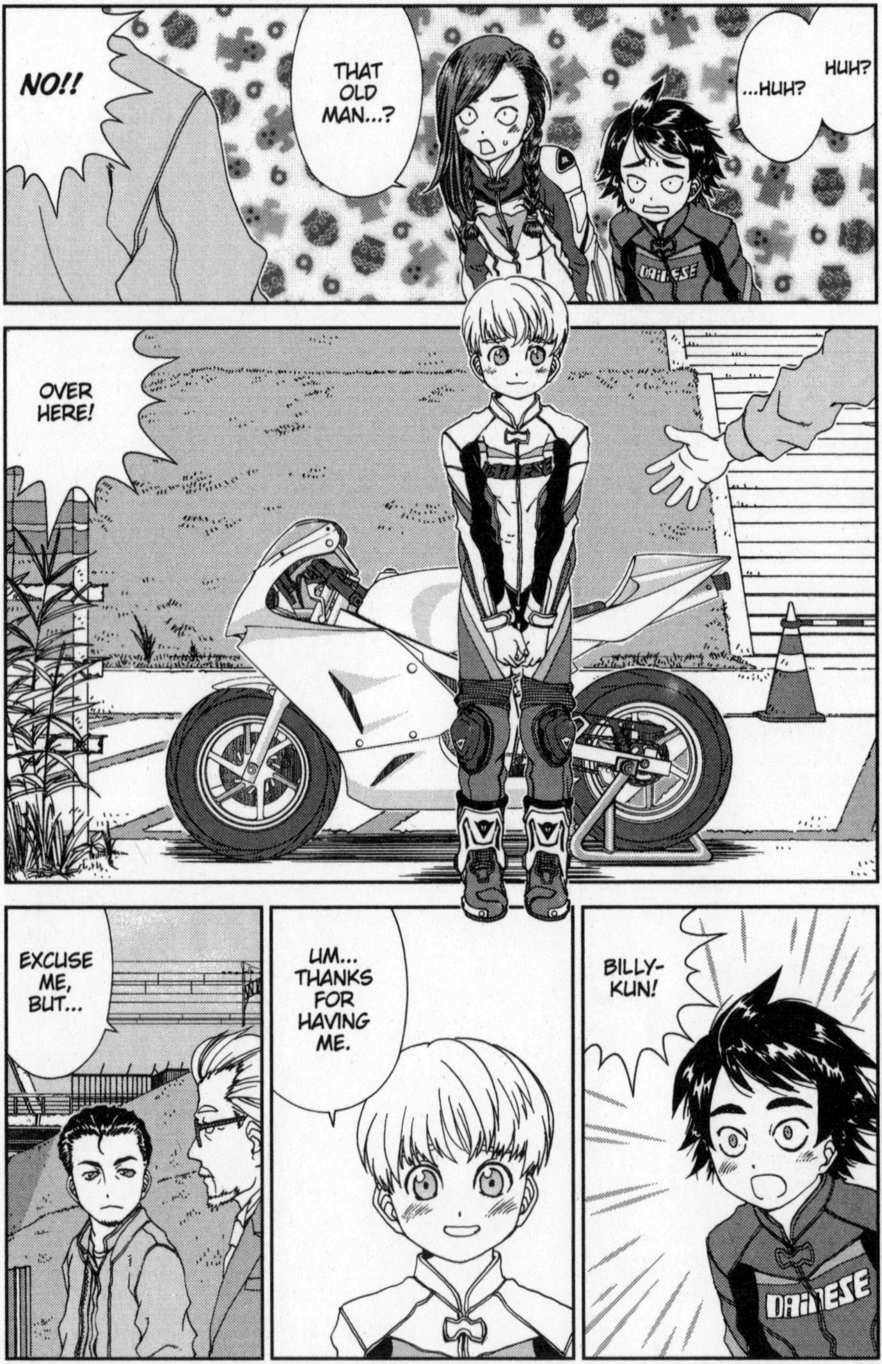
HUH?
...HUH?
THAT OLD MAN...?
NO!!
OVER HERE!
BILLY-KUN!
UM... THANKS FOR HAVING ME.
EXCUSE ME, BUT...

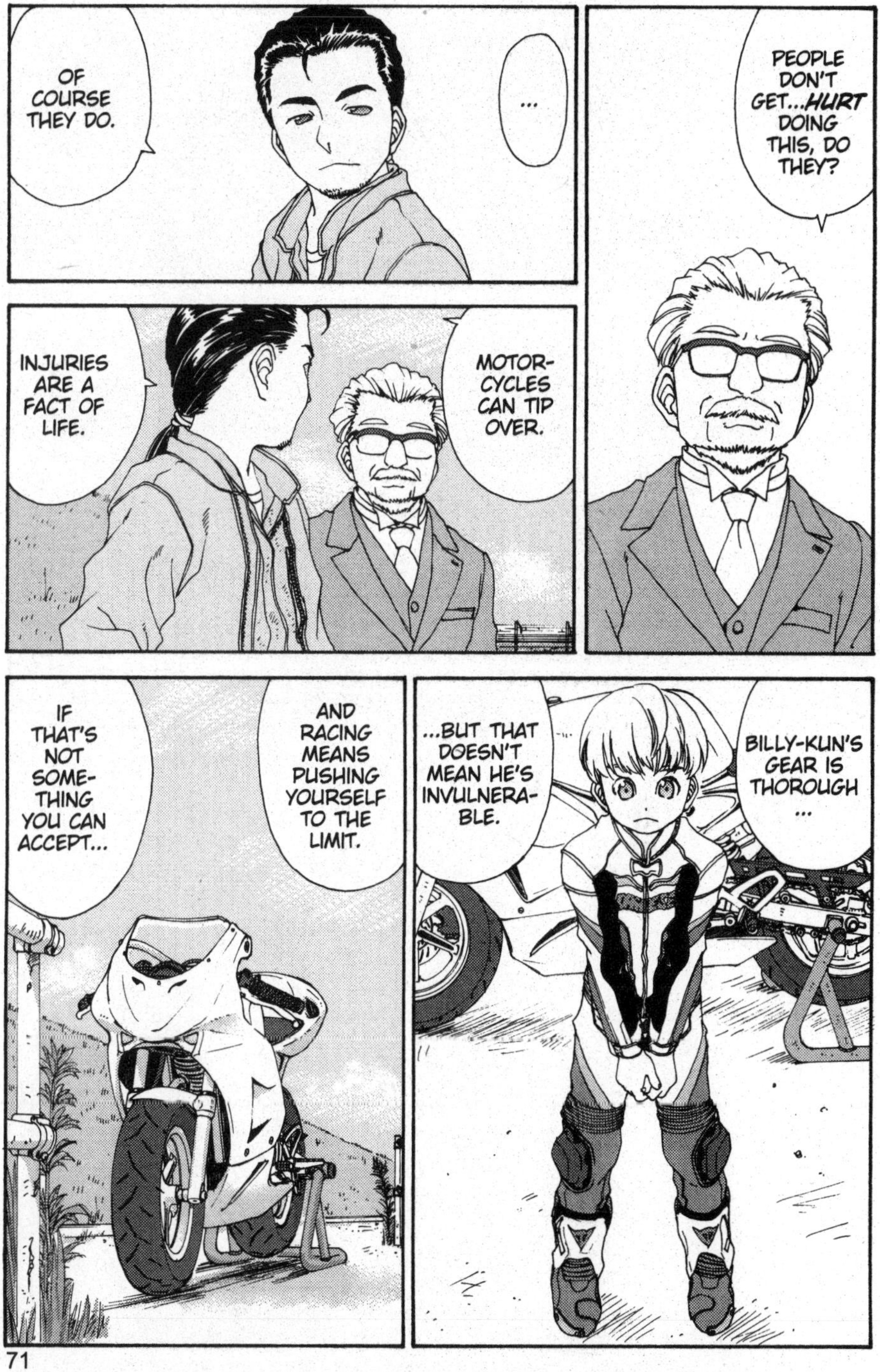
PEOPLE DON'T GET...HURT DOING THIS, DO THEY?
...
OF COURSE THEY DO.
MOTOR-CYCLES CAN TIP OVER.
INJURIES ARE A FACT OF LIFE.
BILLY-KUN'S GEAR IS THOROUGH ...
...BUT THAT DOESN'T MEAN HE'S INVULNERA-BLE.
AND RACING MEANS PUSHING YOURSELF TO THE LIMIT.
IF THAT'S NOT SOME-THING YOU CAN ACCEPT...

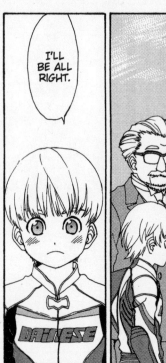

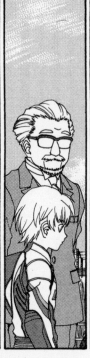

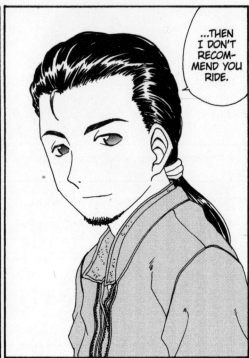

...THEN I DON'T RECOMMEND YOU RIDE.
I'LL BE ALL RIGHT.
I'LL DO MY BEST TO NOT GET HURT...
...EVEN THOUGH IT MIGHT HAPPEN ANYWAY.

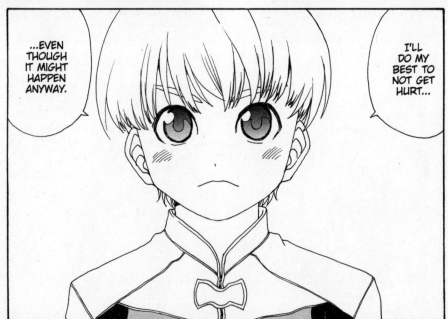

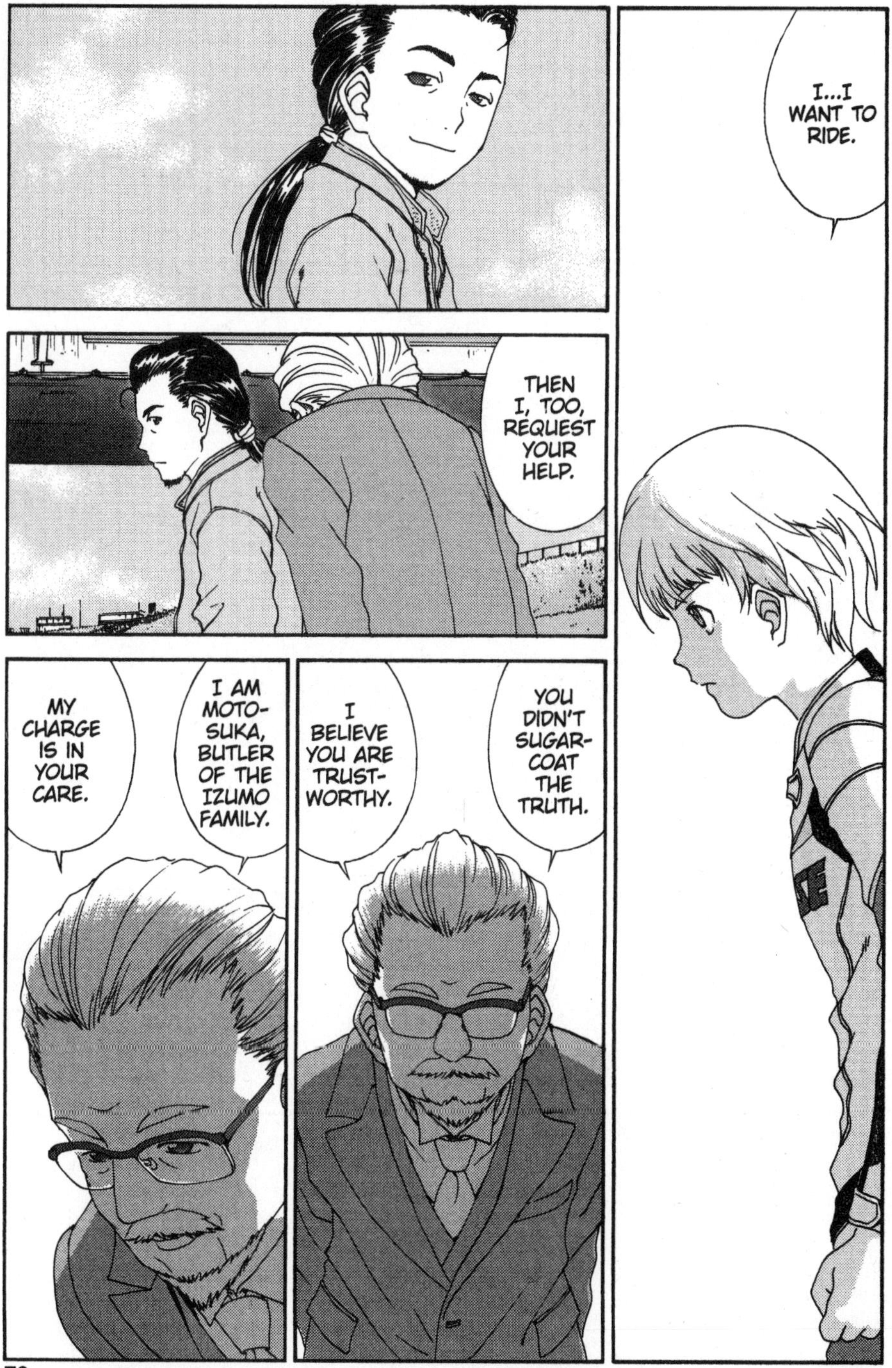

I...I WANT TO RIDE.
THEN I, TOO, REQUEST YOUR HELP.
YOU DIDN'T SUGAR-COAT THE TRUTH.
I BELIEVE YOU ARE TRUST-WORTHY.
I AM MOTO-SUKA, BUTLER OF THE IZUMO FAMILY.
MY CHARGE IS IN YOUR CARE.

HE'S WELCOME TO JOIN.

BUT OF COURSE!

BUTLER?!

YOUR LEFT HAND SHOULD BE ACTING IN CONCERT WITH THE THROTTLE.

BRRUTT

バリリド

UM... BUT...

NICE AND SOFT.

THERE YOU GO.

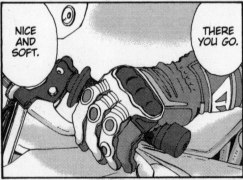

TRY IT AGAIN.

AH.

PFF

スコン

HMM.

JUST WHEN I FINALLY GOT A CHANCE TO RIDE WITH HER.

UGH...

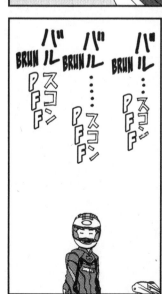

バルル BRUN

バルル BRUN

バルル BRUN

PFF スコン

PFF スコン

PFF スコン

...

PFF

スコン

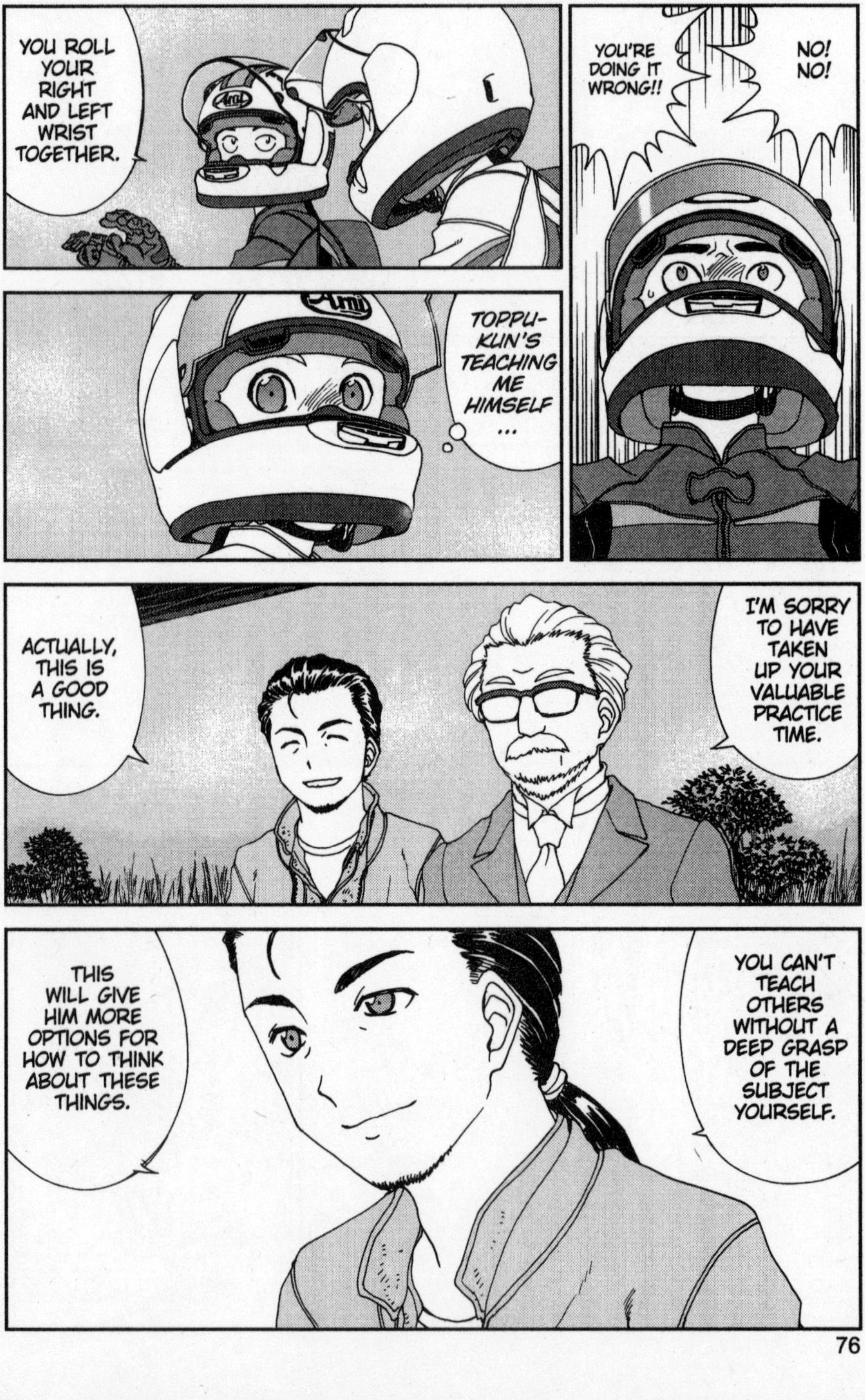
NO! NO!
YOU'RE DOING IT WRONG!!
YOU ROLL YOUR RIGHT AND LEFT WRIST TOGETHER.
TOPPU-KUN'S TEACHING ME HIMSELF ...
I'M SORRY TO HAVE TAKEN UP YOUR VALUABLE PRACTICE TIME.
ACTUALLY, THIS IS A GOOD THING.
YOU CAN'T TEACH OTHERS WITHOUT A DEEP GRASP OF THE SUBJECT YOURSELF.
THIS WILL GIVE HIM MORE OPTIONS FOR HOW TO THINK ABOUT THESE THINGS.

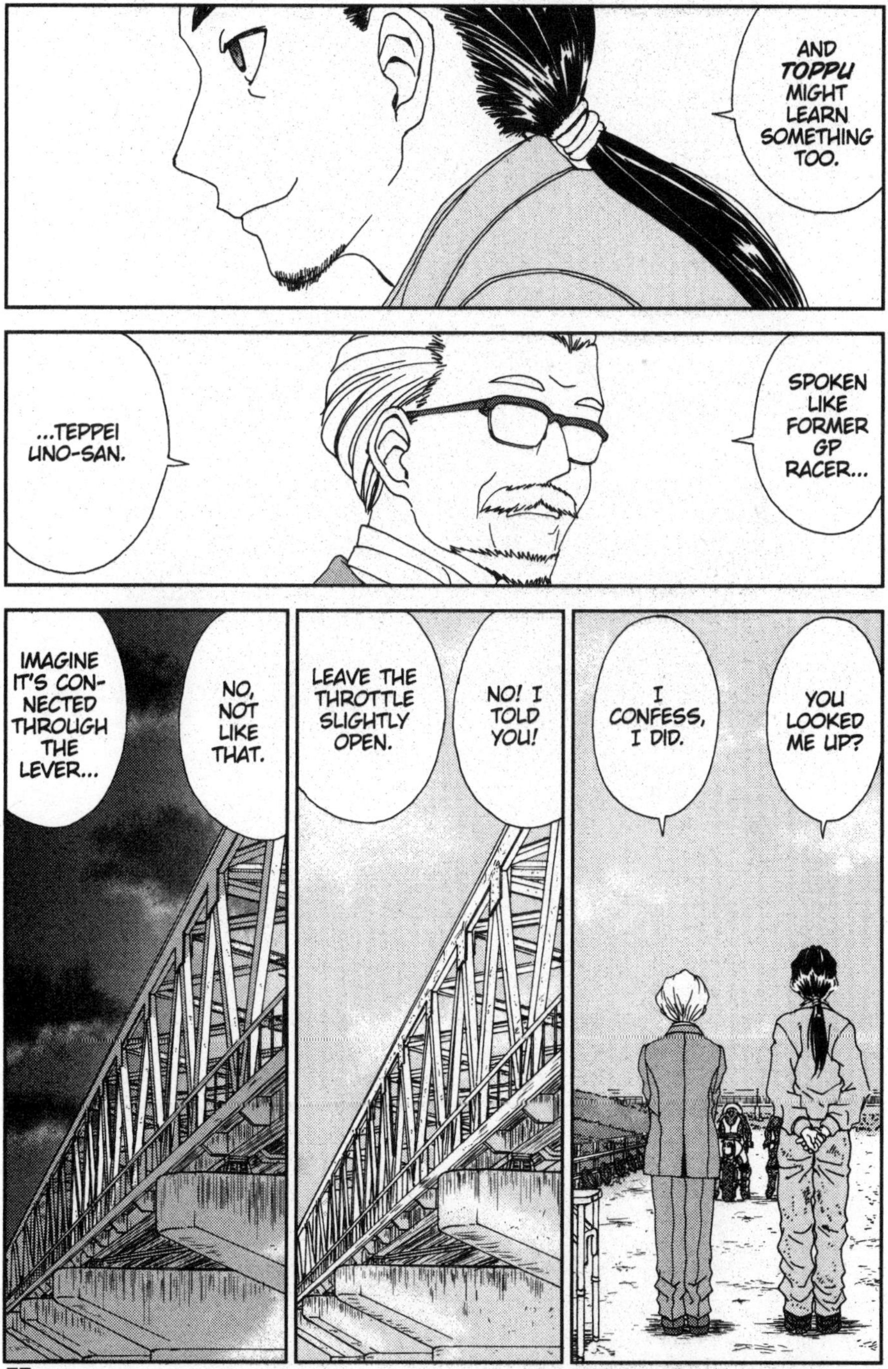
AND *TOPPU* MIGHT LEARN SOMETHING TOO.
SPOKEN LIKE FORMER GP RACER...
...TEPPEI UNO-SAN.
YOU LOOKED ME UP?
I CONFESS, I DID.
NO! I TOLD YOU!
LEAVE THE THROTTLE SLIGHTLY OPEN.
NO, NOT LIKE THAT.
IMAGINE IT'S CONNECTED THROUGH THE LEVER...

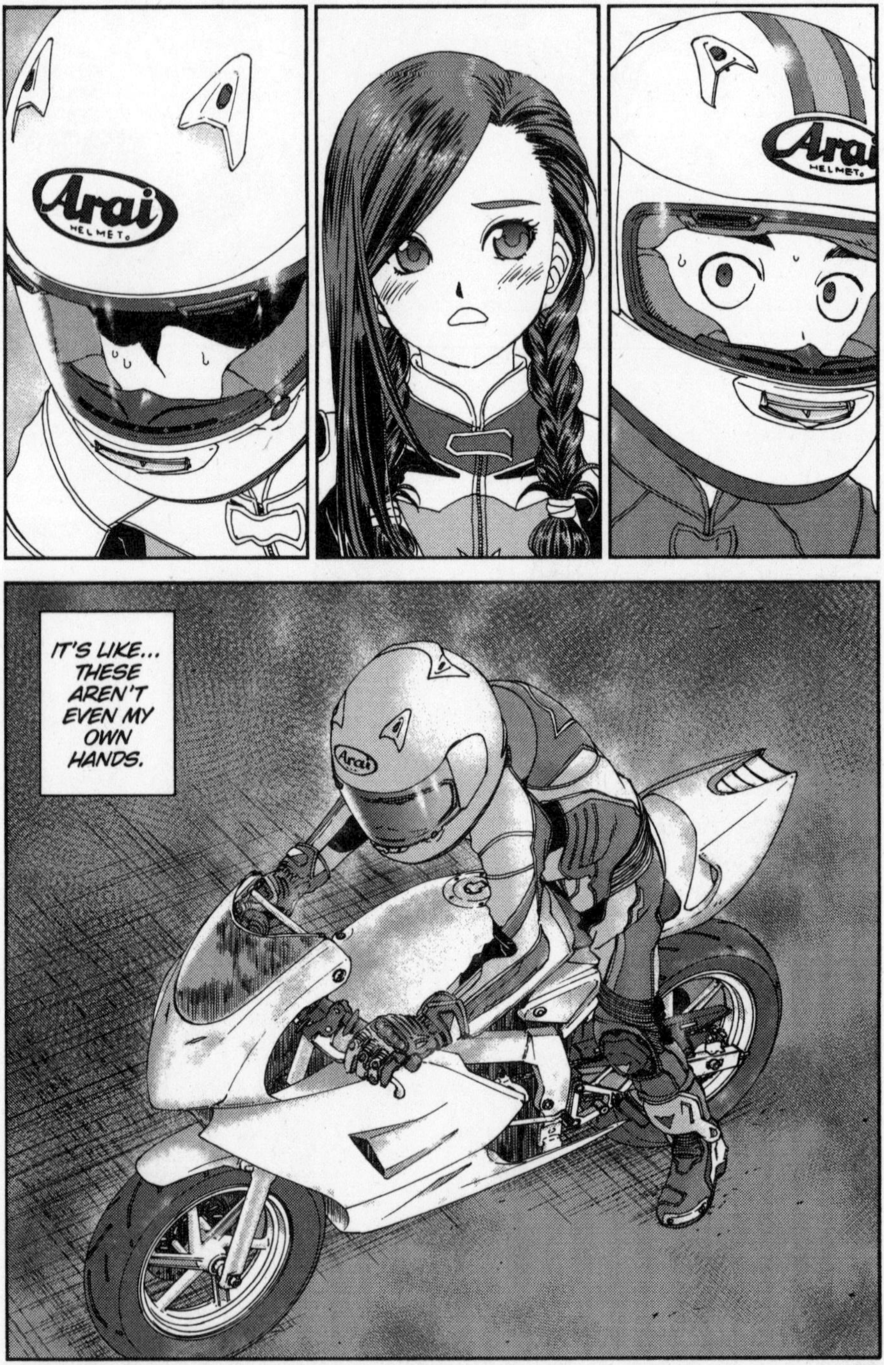
IT'S LIKE... THESE AREN'T EVEN MY OWN HANDS.

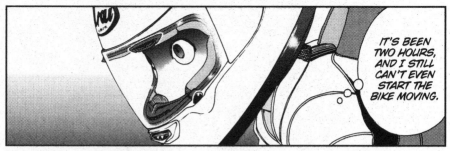

IT'S BEEN TWO HOURS, AND I STILL CAN'T EVEN START THE BIKE MOVING.
THAT'S NOT IT.
HE'S BEEN DOING NOTHING BUT THIS THIS FOR TWO HOURS STRAIGHT.
WHAT KIND OF WILL-POWER...
...MUST THAT TAKE?
JUST GO.
MOVE FORWARD.
SHOW THEM YOU CAN DO IT.

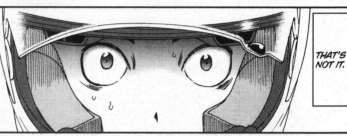

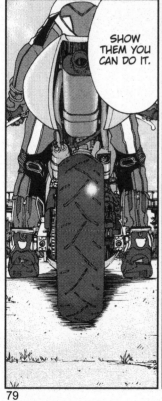

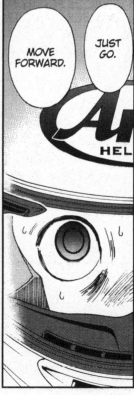

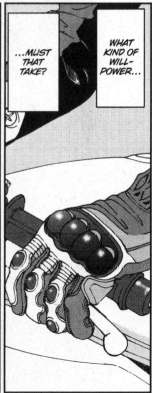

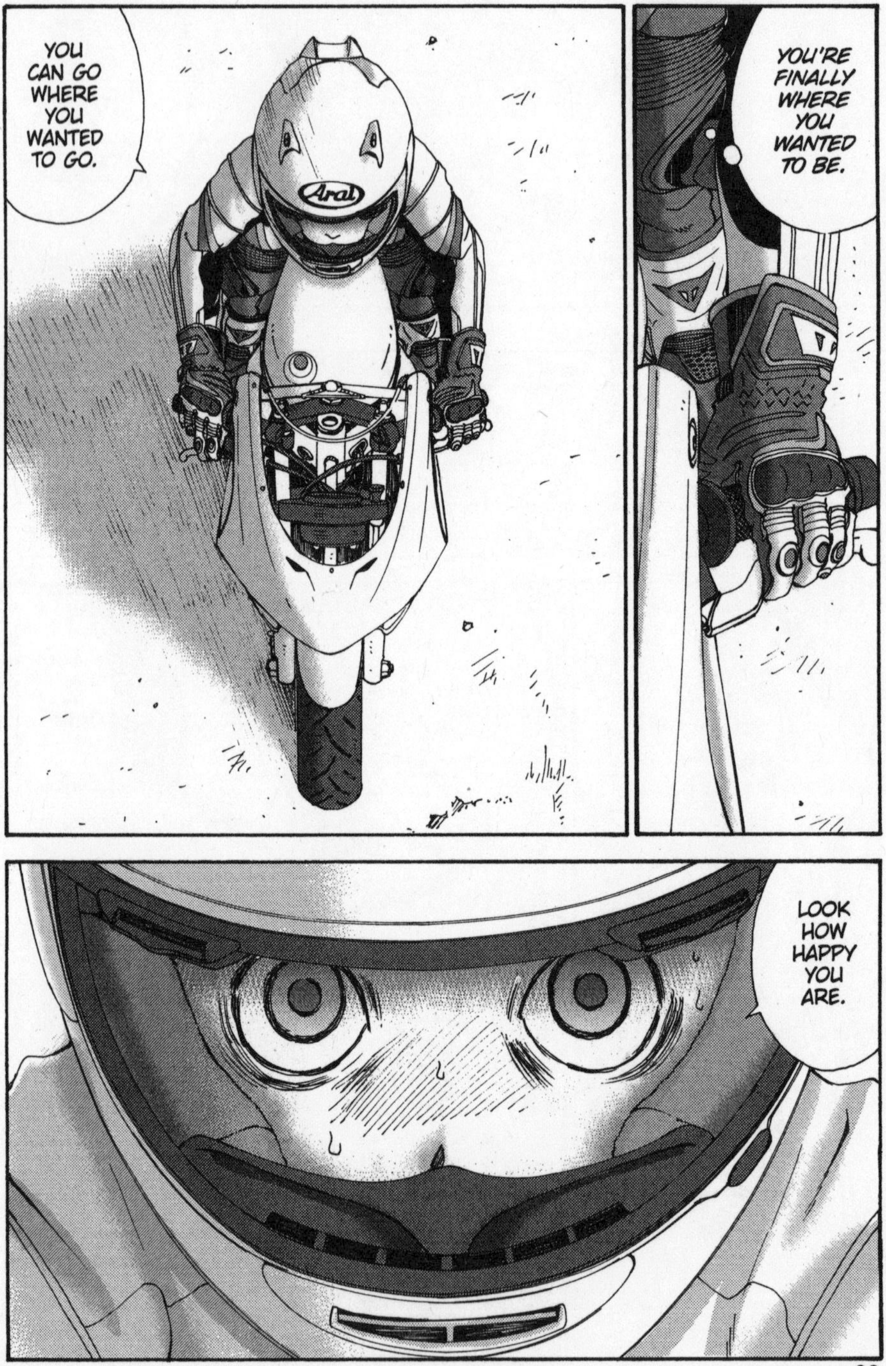

YOU CAN GO WHERE YOU WANTED TO GO.
YOU'RE FINALLY WHERE YOU WANTED TO BE.
LOOK HOW HAPPY YOU ARE.

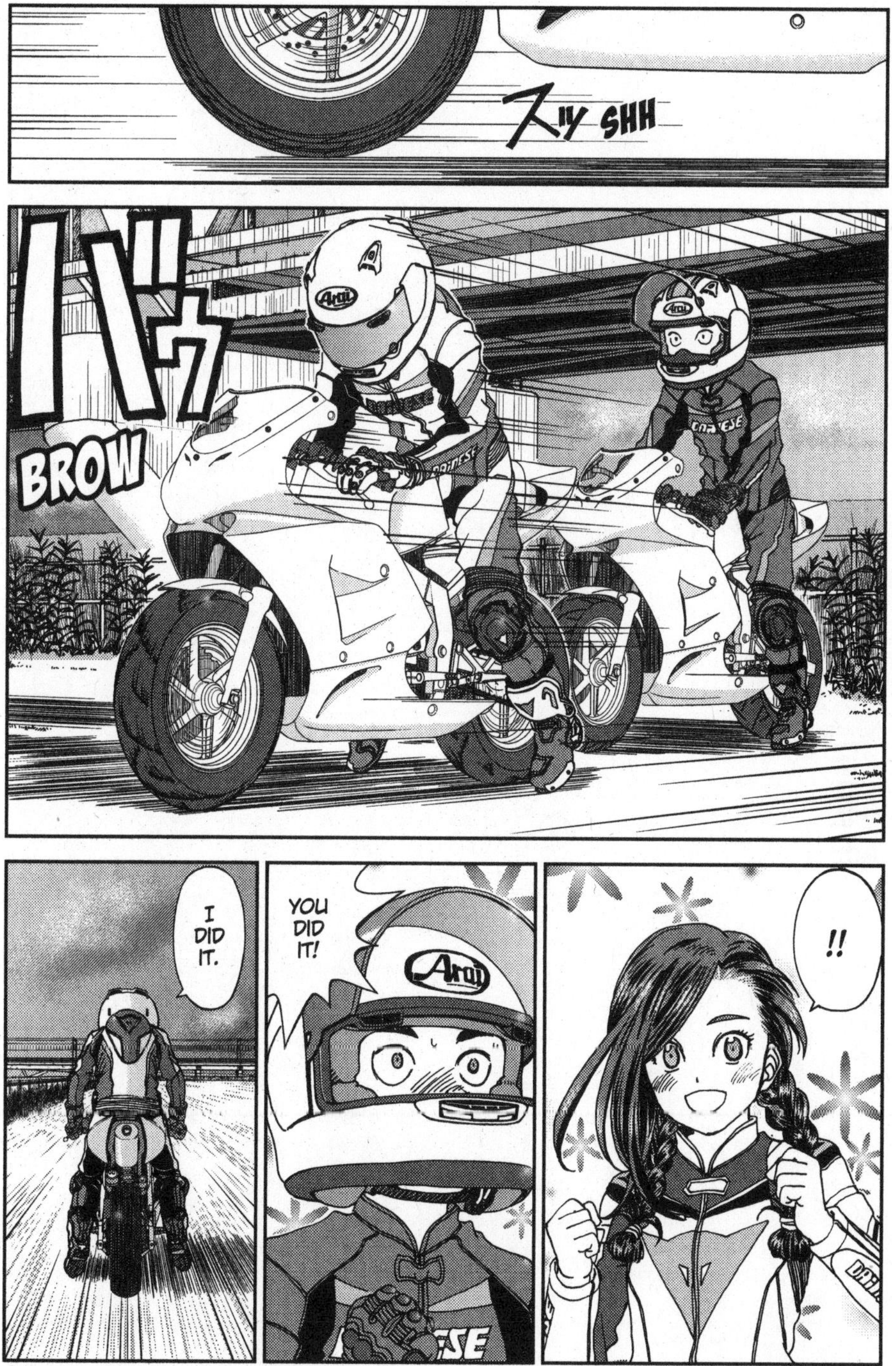
スッ SHH
バウ
BROW
!!
YOU DID IT!
I DID IT.

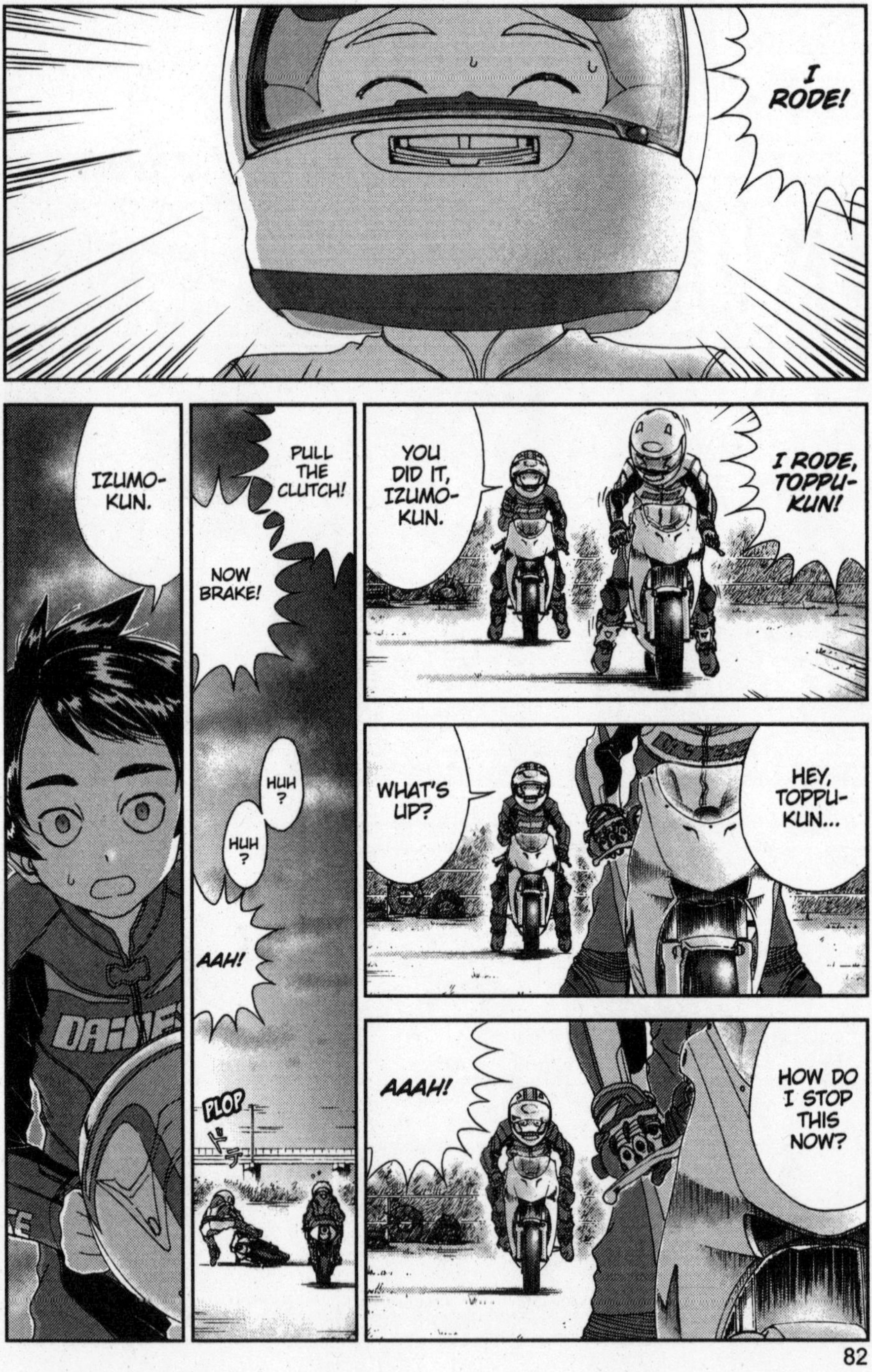
I RODE!
I RODE, TOPPU-KUN!
YOU DID IT, IZUMO-KUN.
HEY, TOPPU-KUN...
WHAT'S UP?
HOW DO I STOP THIS NOW?
AAAH!
PULL THE CLUTCH!
NOW BRAKE!
HUH?
HUH?
AAH!
PLOP
ドテ
IZUMO-KUN.

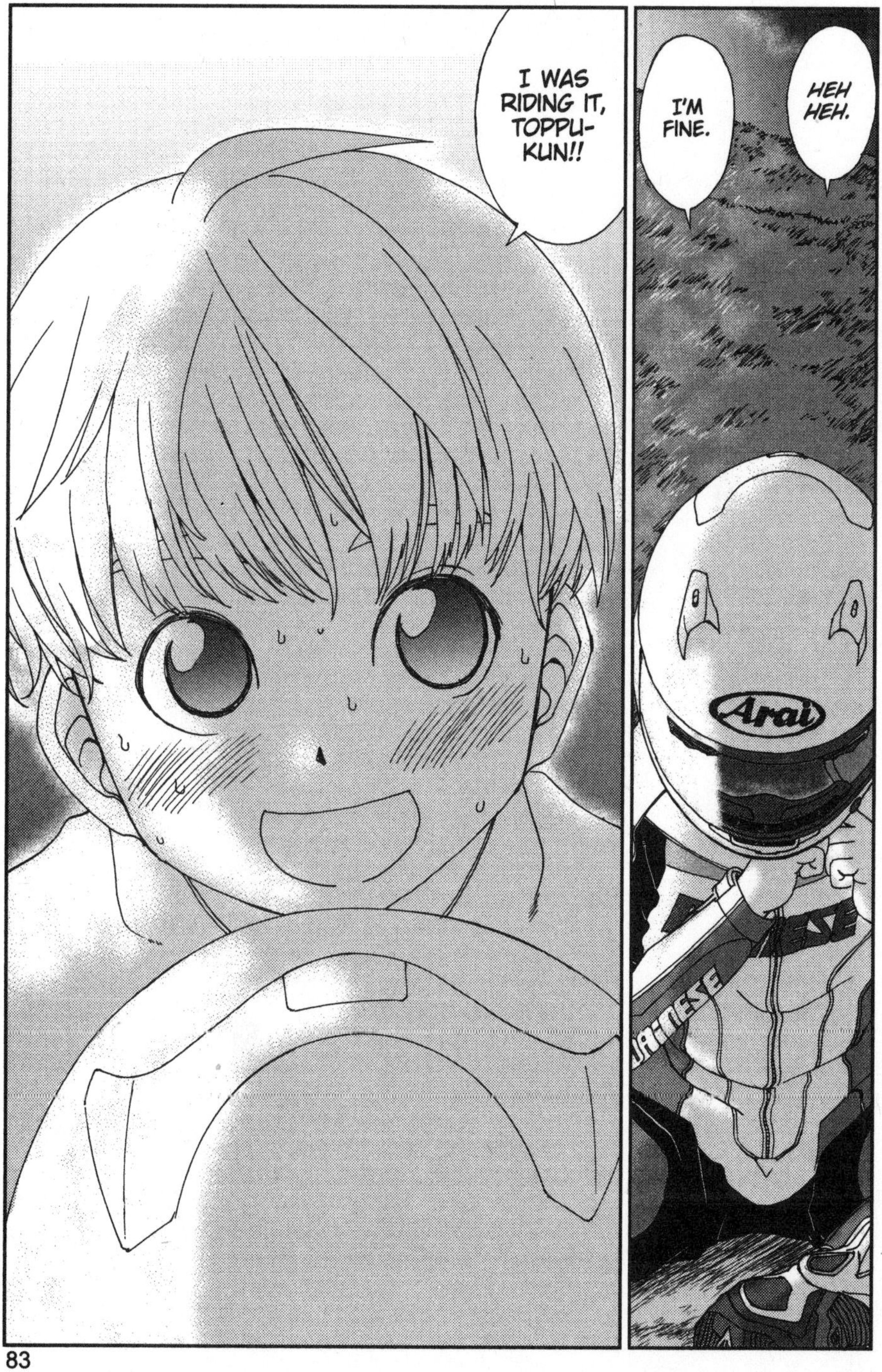
HEH HEH.
I'M FINE.
I WAS RIDING IT, TOPPU-KUN!!
Arai

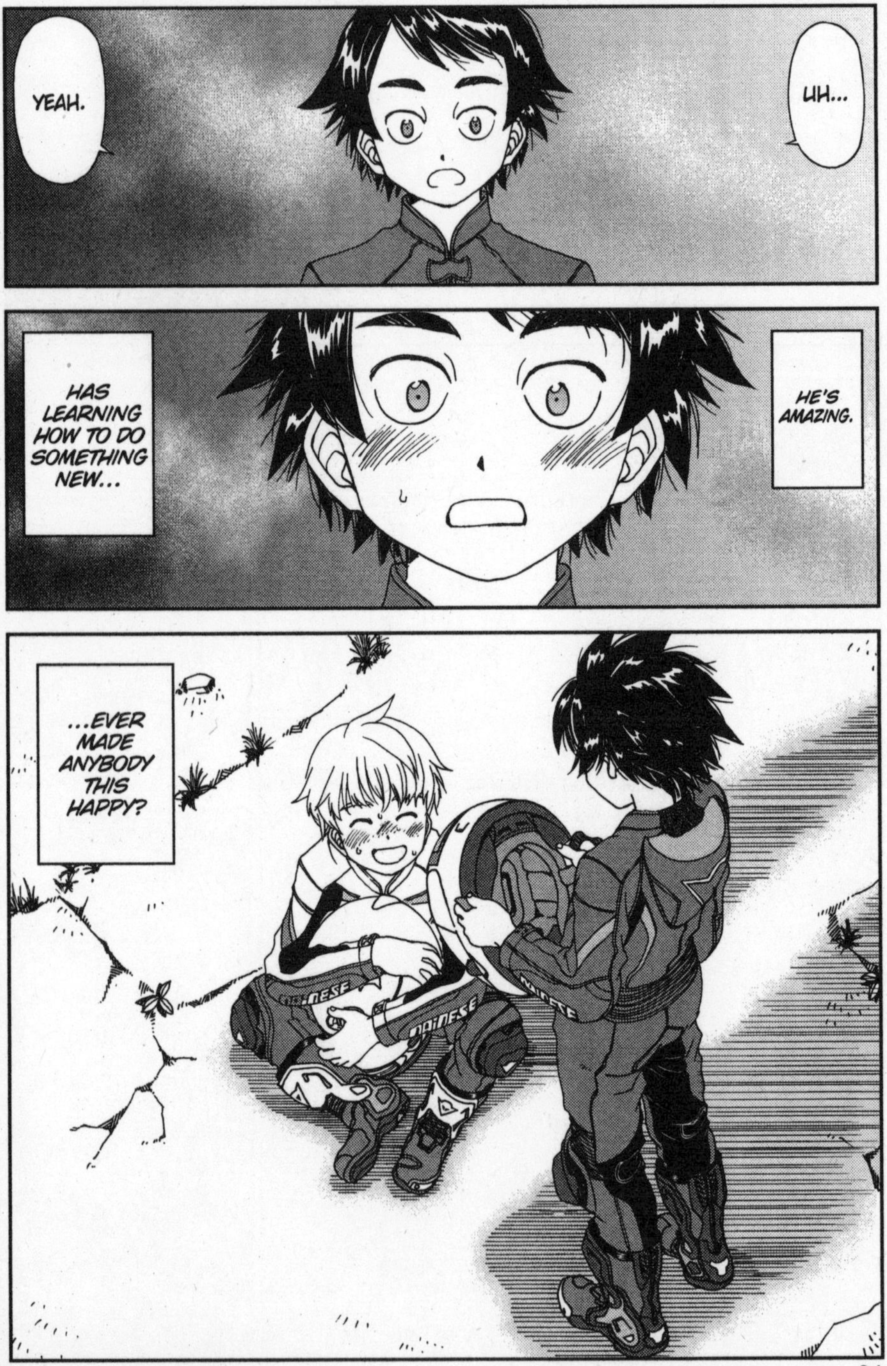
UH...
YEAH.
HE'S AMAZING.
HAS LEARNING HOW TO DO SOMETHING NEW...
...EVER MADE ANYBODY THIS HAPPY?

Lap 17: end

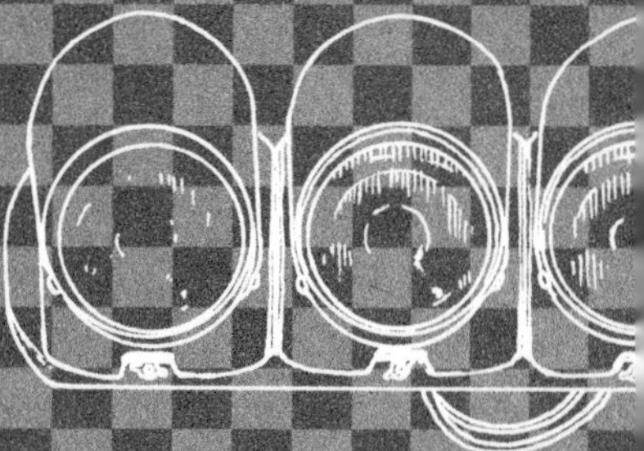

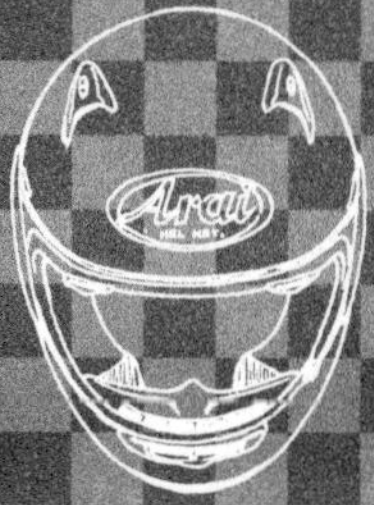
Arai

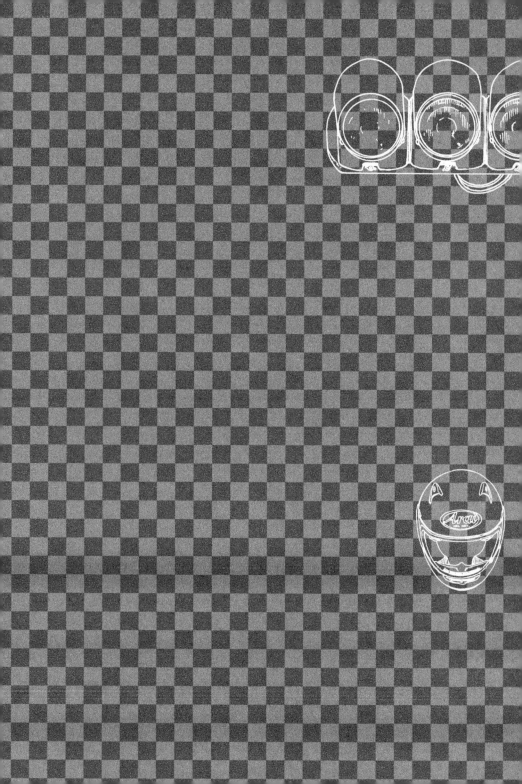

TOPPU
GP

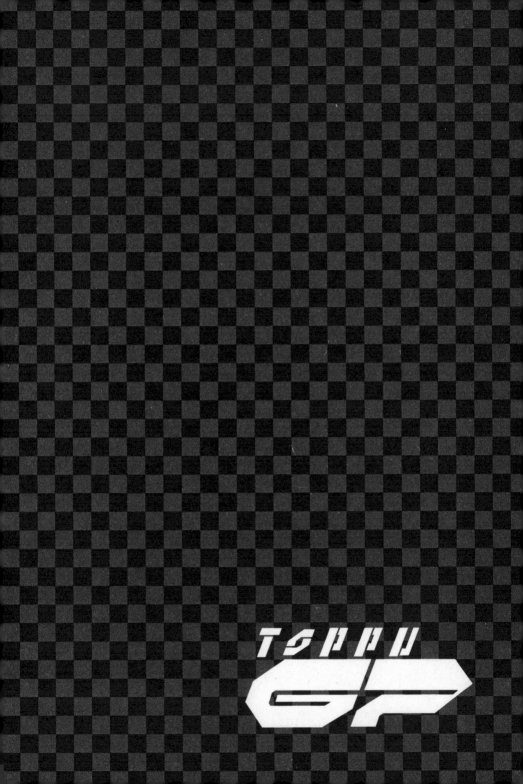

Lap 18: MEMORY

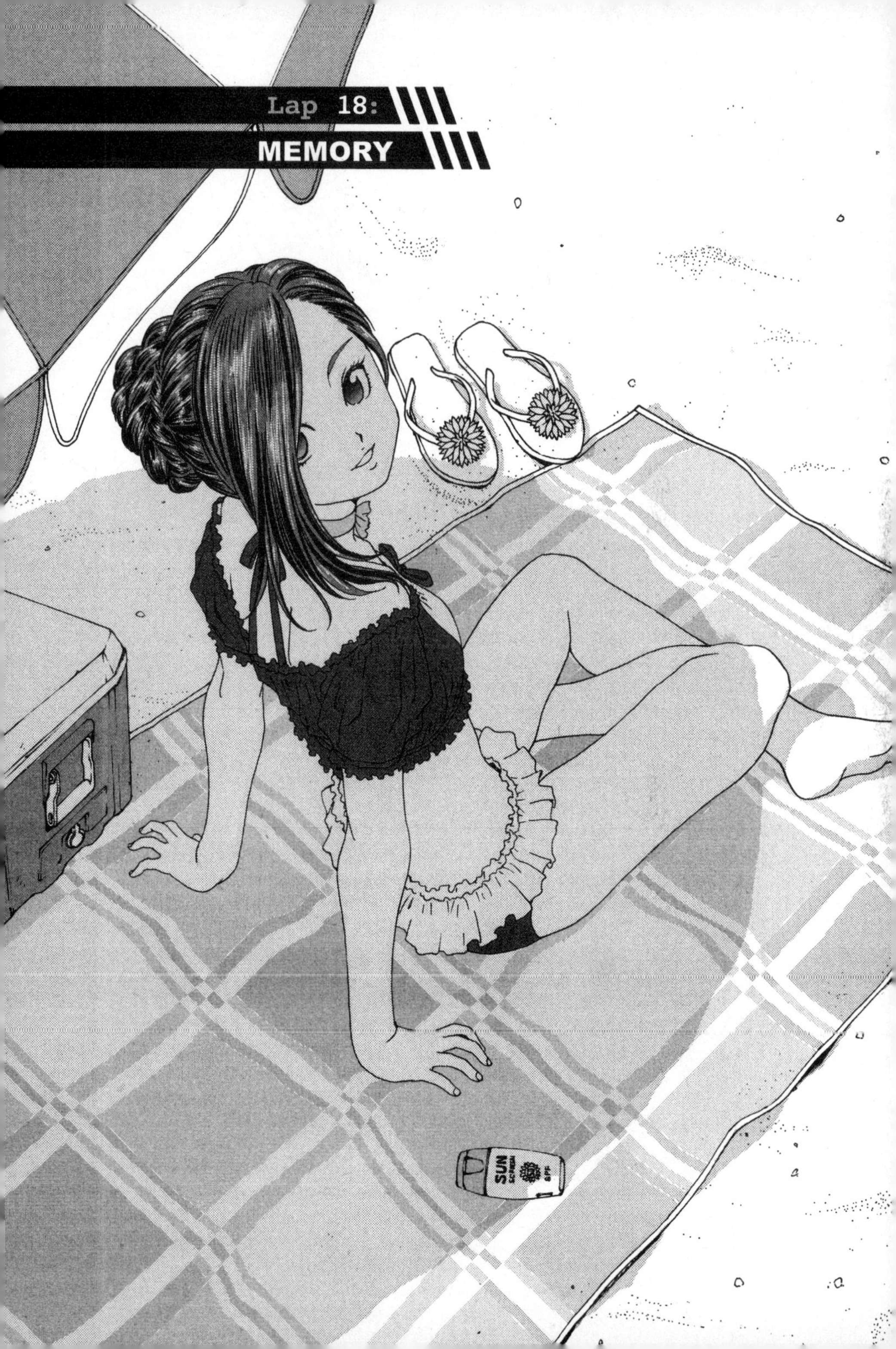
SUN

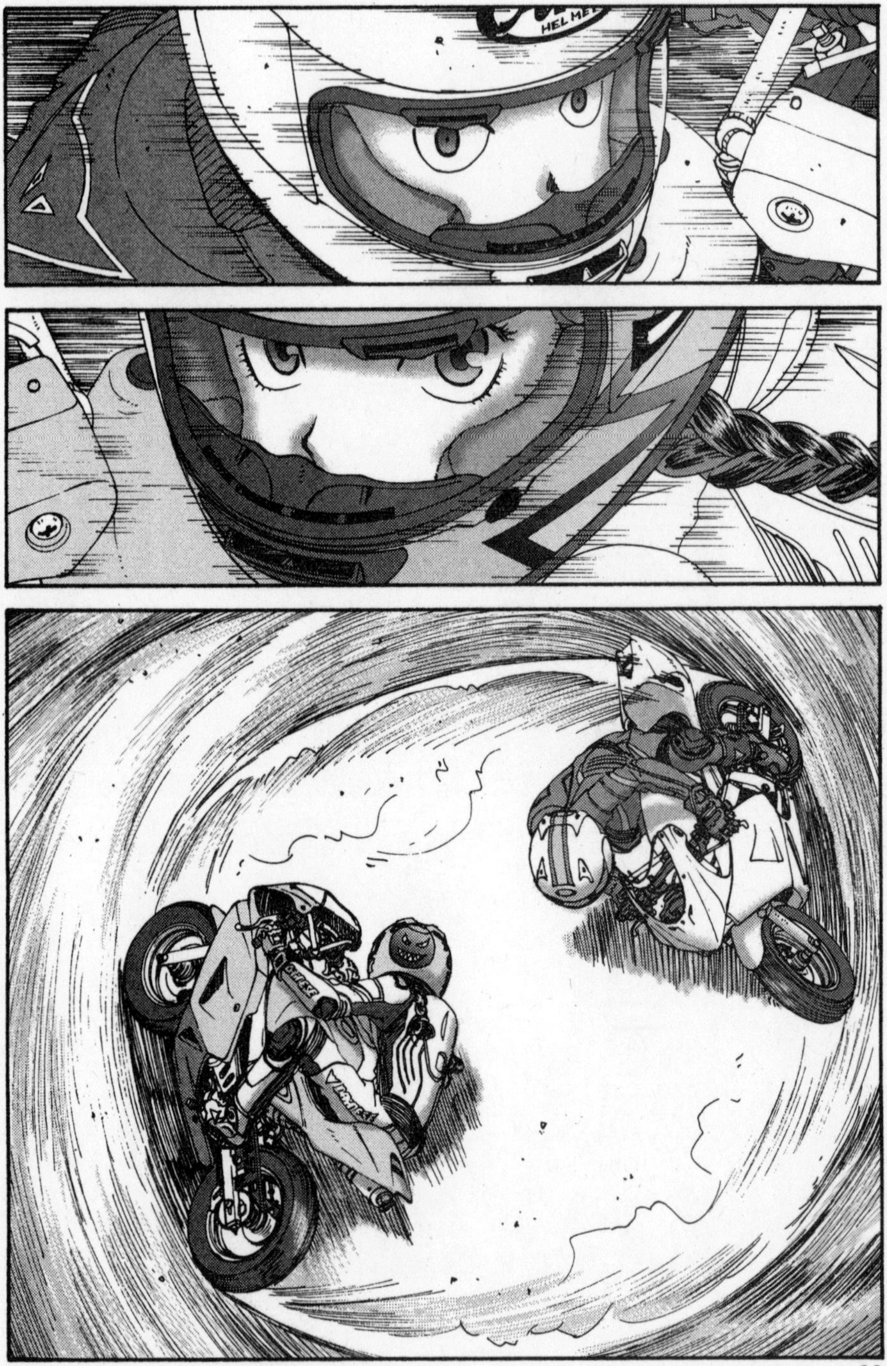

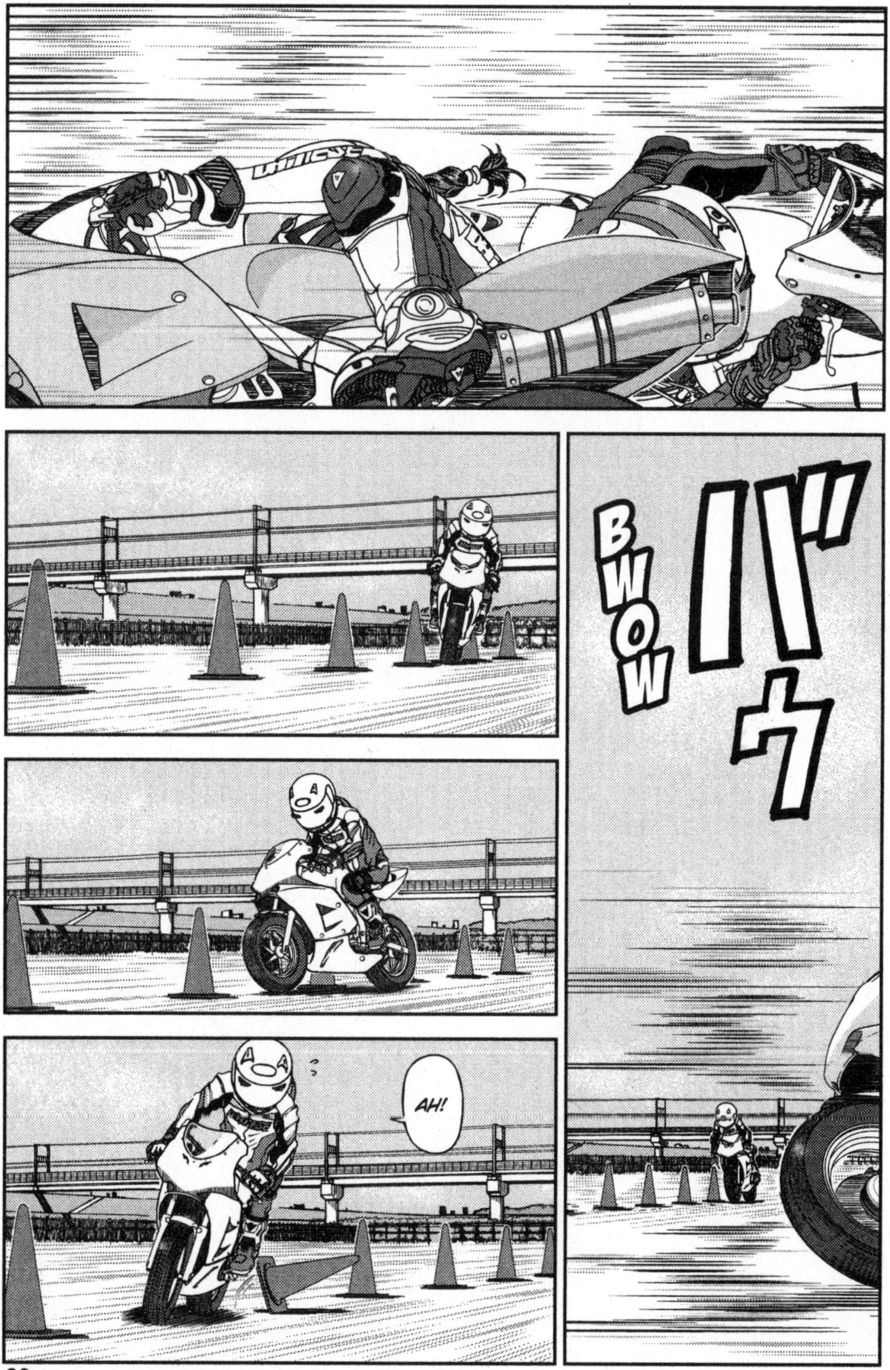
バウ
BWOW
AH!

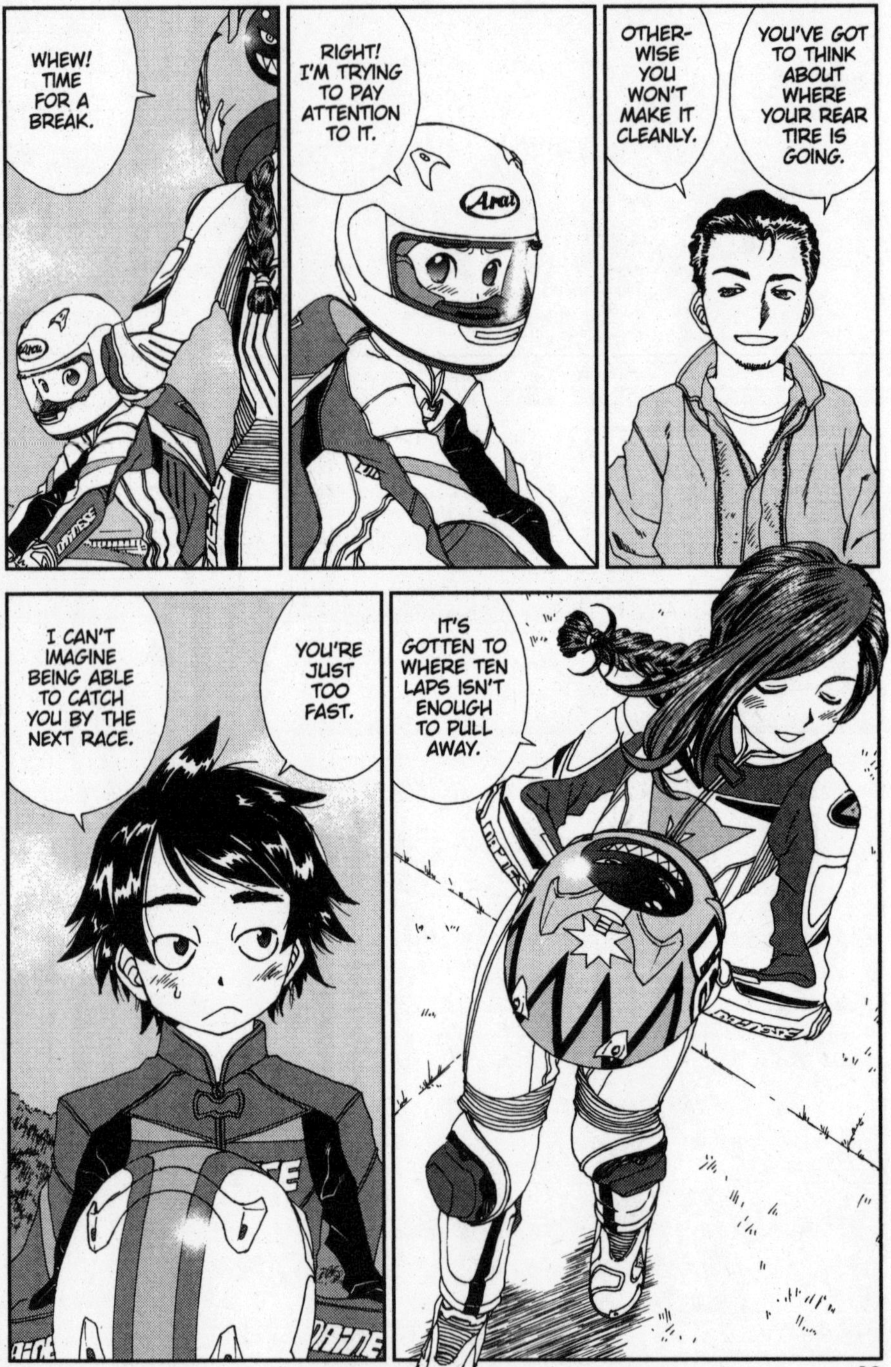
YOU'VE GOT TO THINK ABOUT WHERE YOUR REAR TIRE IS GOING.
OTHER-WISE YOU WON'T MAKE IT CLEANLY.
RIGHT! I'M TRYING TO PAY ATTENTION TO IT.
WHEW! TIME FOR A BREAK.
IT'S GOTTEN TO WHERE TEN LAPS ISN'T ENOUGH TO PULL AWAY.
YOU'RE JUST TOO FAST.
I CAN'T IMAGINE BEING ABLE TO CATCH YOU BY THE NEXT RACE.

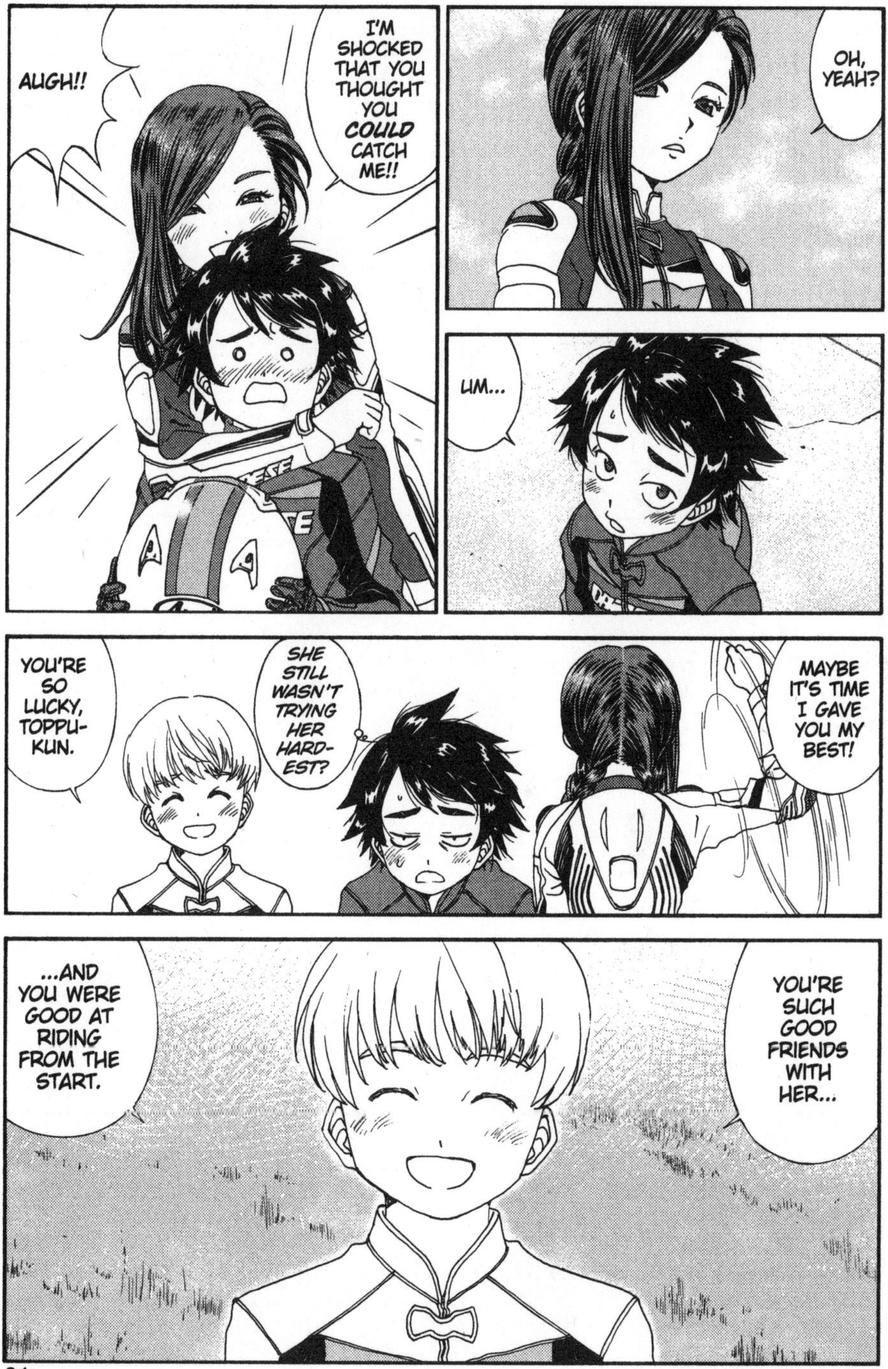
OH, YEAH?
UM...
I'M SHOCKED THAT YOU THOUGHT YOU COULD CATCH ME!!
AUGH!!
MAYBE IT'S TIME I GAVE YOU MY BEST!
SHE STILL WASN'T TRYING HER HARD-EST?
YOU'RE SO LUCKY, TOPPU-KUN.
YOU'RE SUCH GOOD FRIENDS WITH HER...
...AND YOU WERE GOOD AT RIDING FROM THE START.

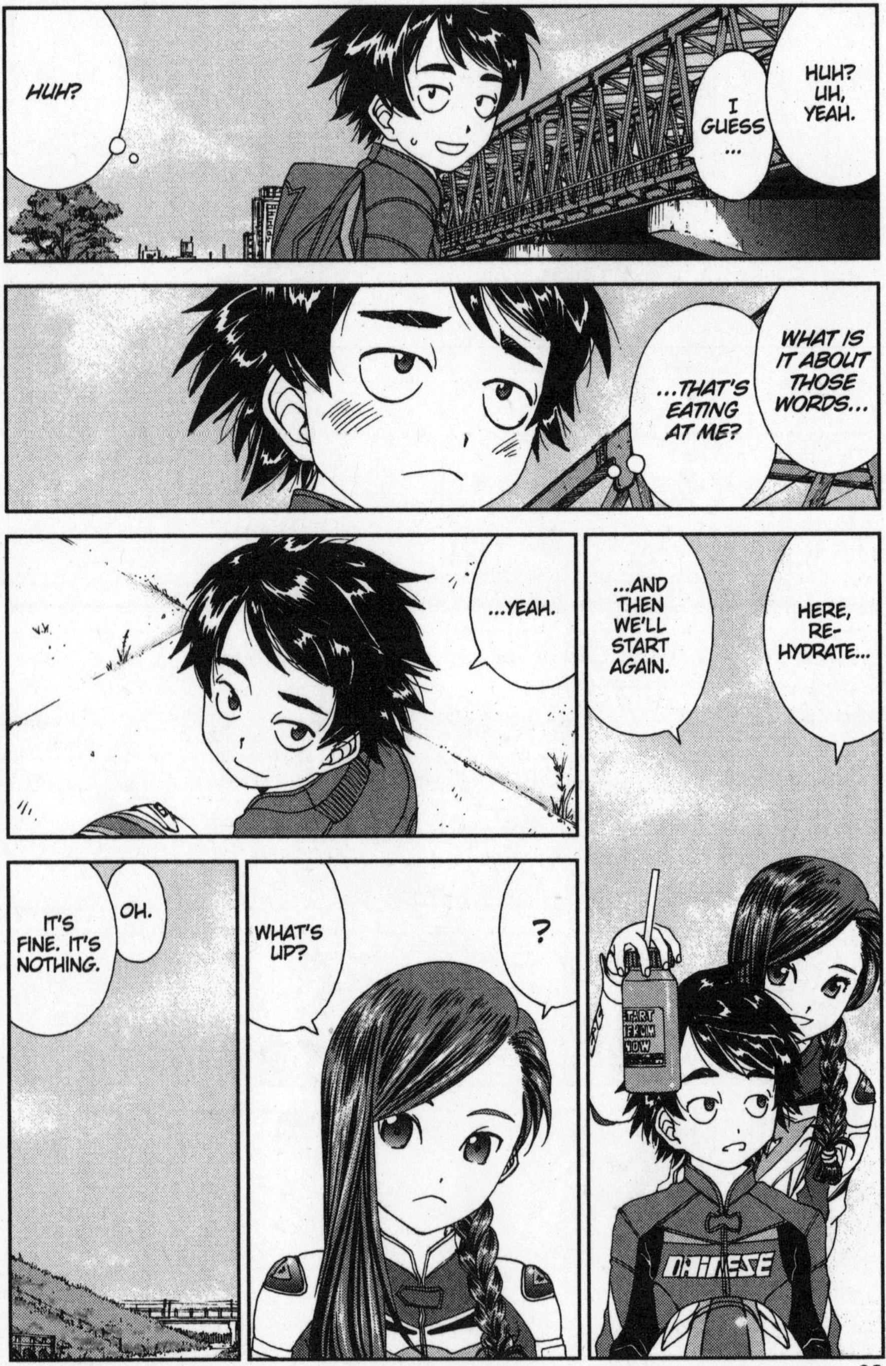
HUH? UH, YEAH.
I GUESS...
HUH?
WHAT IS IT ABOUT THOSE WORDS...
...THAT'S EATING AT ME?
HERE, RE-HYDRATE...
...AND THEN WE'LL START AGAIN.
...YEAH.
?
WHAT'S UP?
OH.
IT'S FINE. IT'S NOTHING.
DAINESE

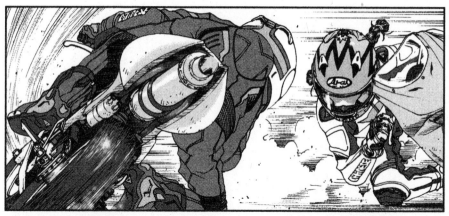

SHE'S PULLING FURTHER AWAY!!

!!

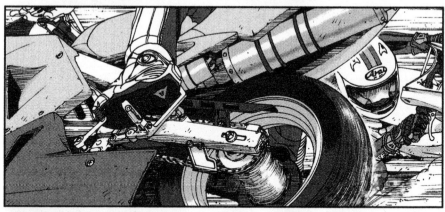

YOUR PROPULSIVE POWER IS STILL TOO WEAK.

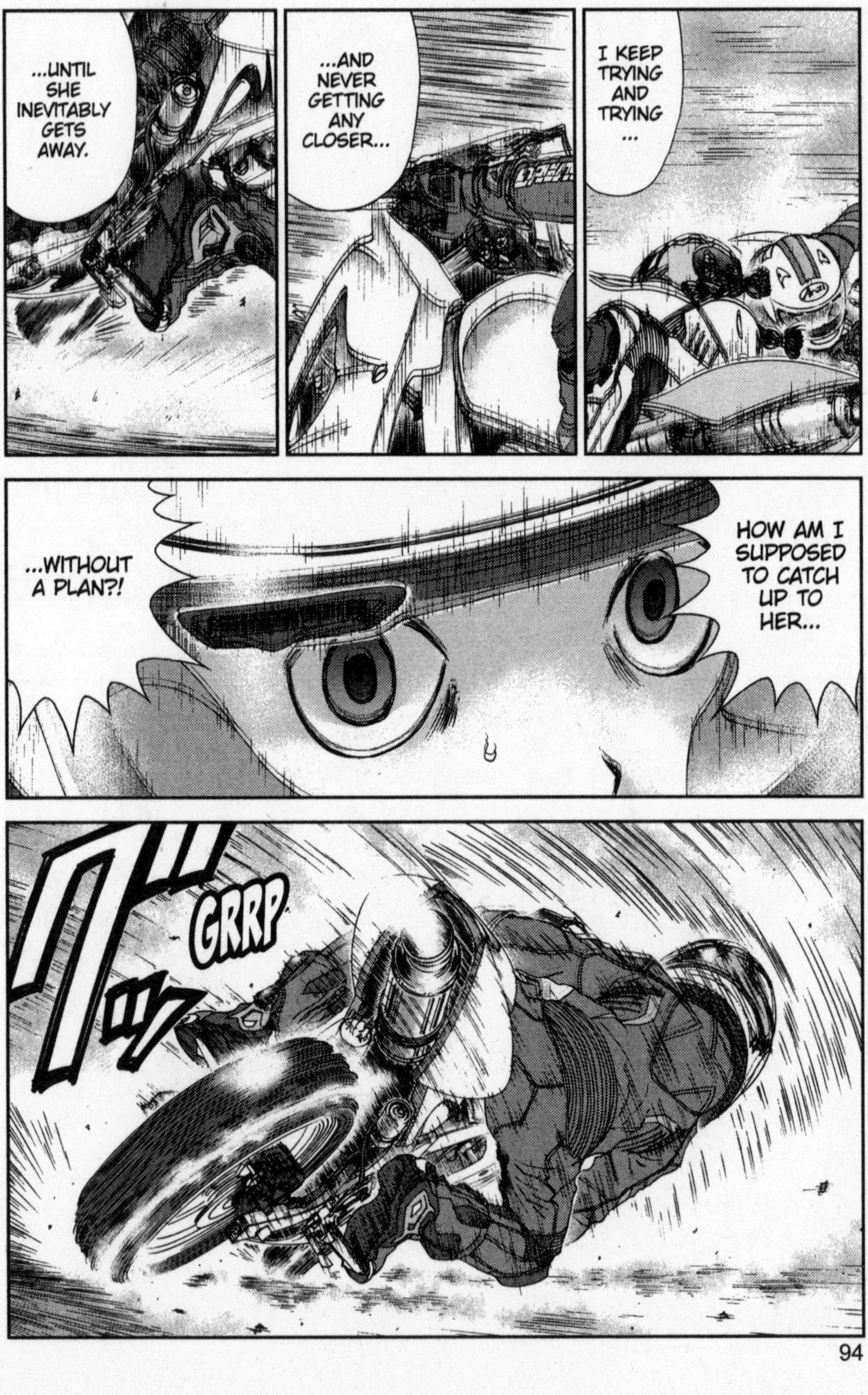
I KEEP TRYING AND TRYING ...
...AND NEVER GETTING ANY CLOSER...
...UNTIL SHE INEVITABLY GETS AWAY.
HOW AM I SUPPOSED TO CATCH UP TO HER...
...WITHOUT A PLAN?!
GRRP

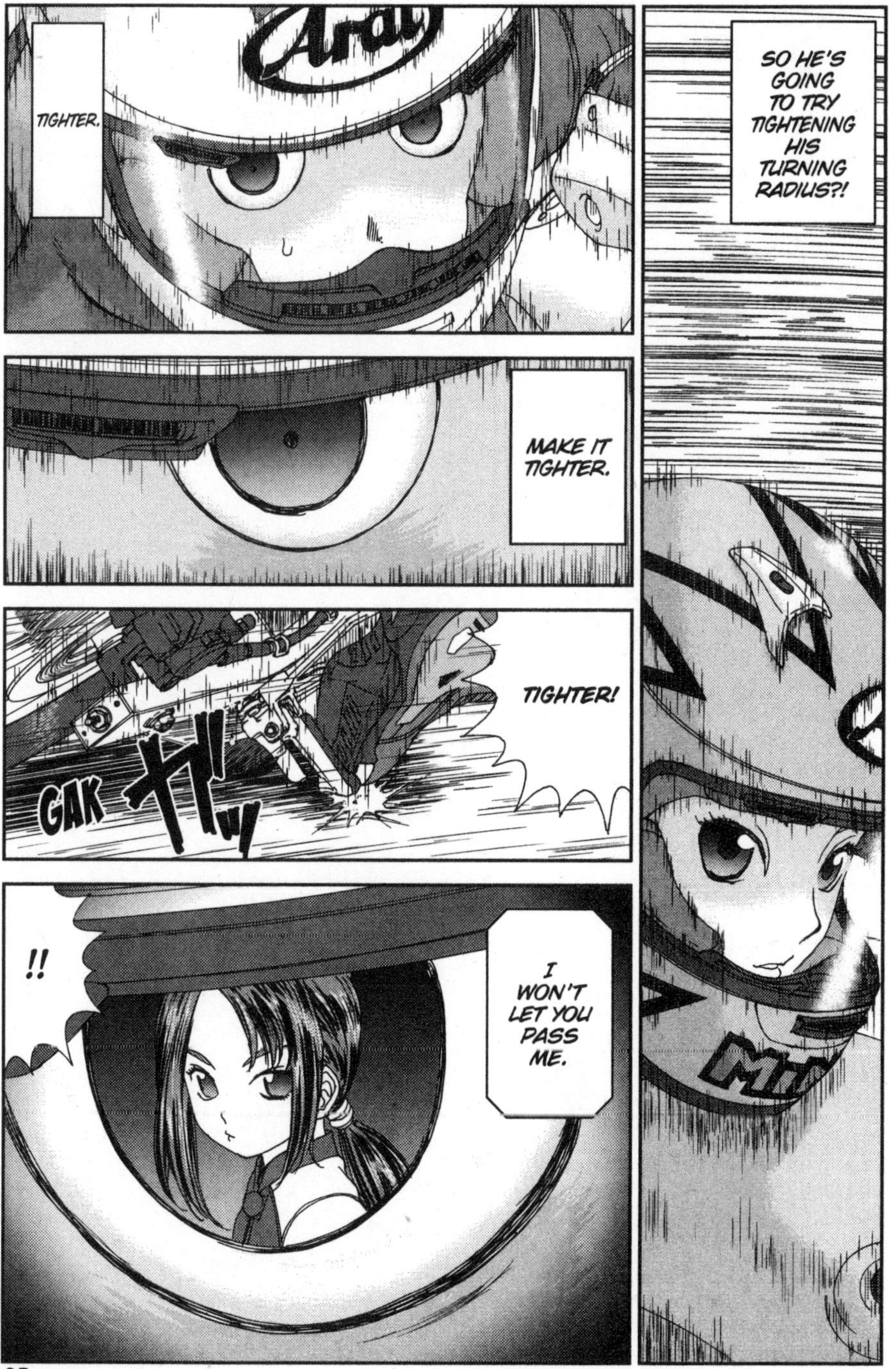
TIGHTER.
MAKE IT TIGHTER.
TIGHTER!
GAK
SO HE'S GOING TO TRY TIGHTENING HIS TURNING RADIUS?!
!!
I WON'T LET YOU PASS ME.

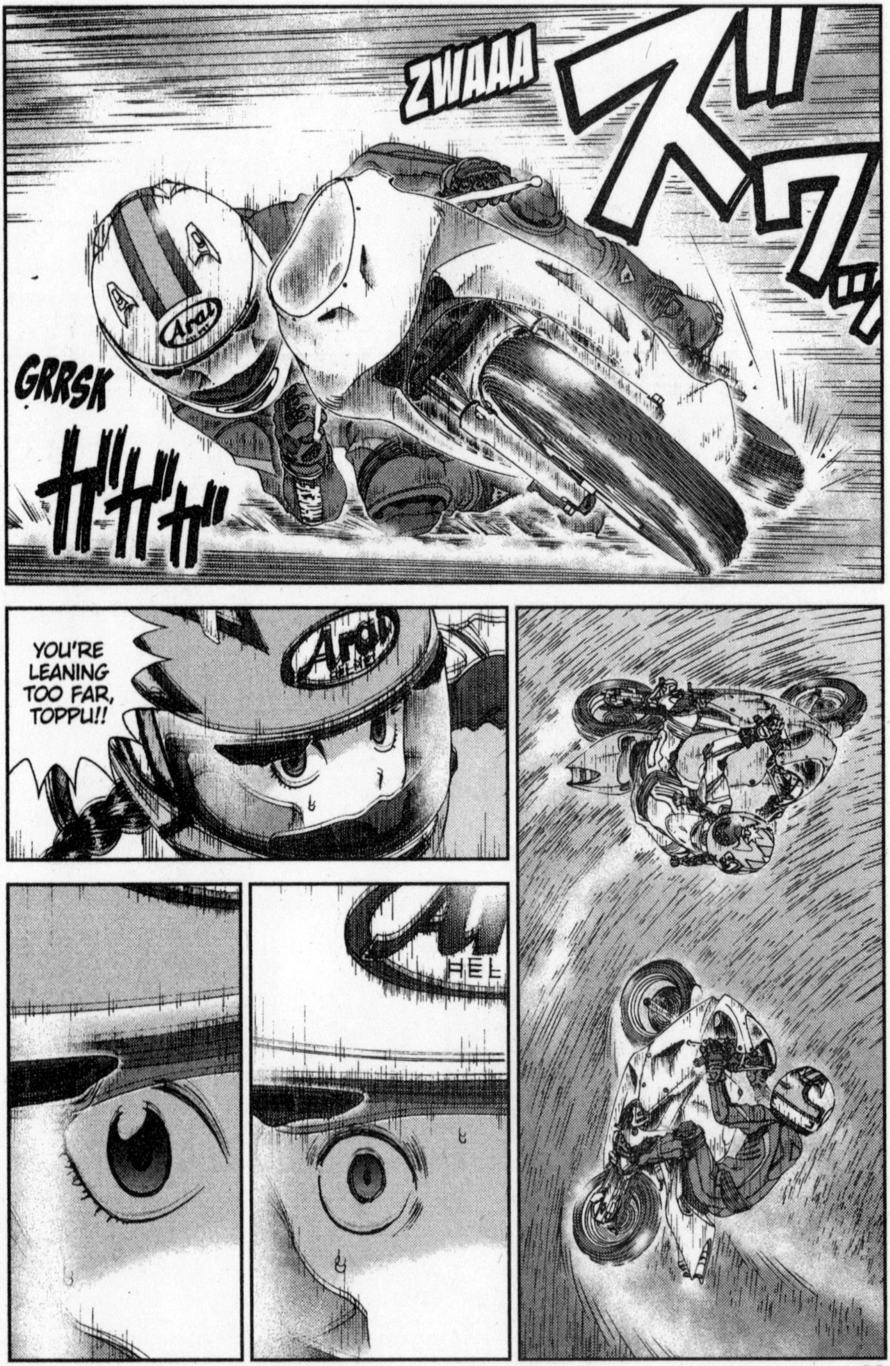
ZWAAA
ズワッ
GRRSK
ガガガ
YOU'RE LEANING TOO FAR, TOPPU!!

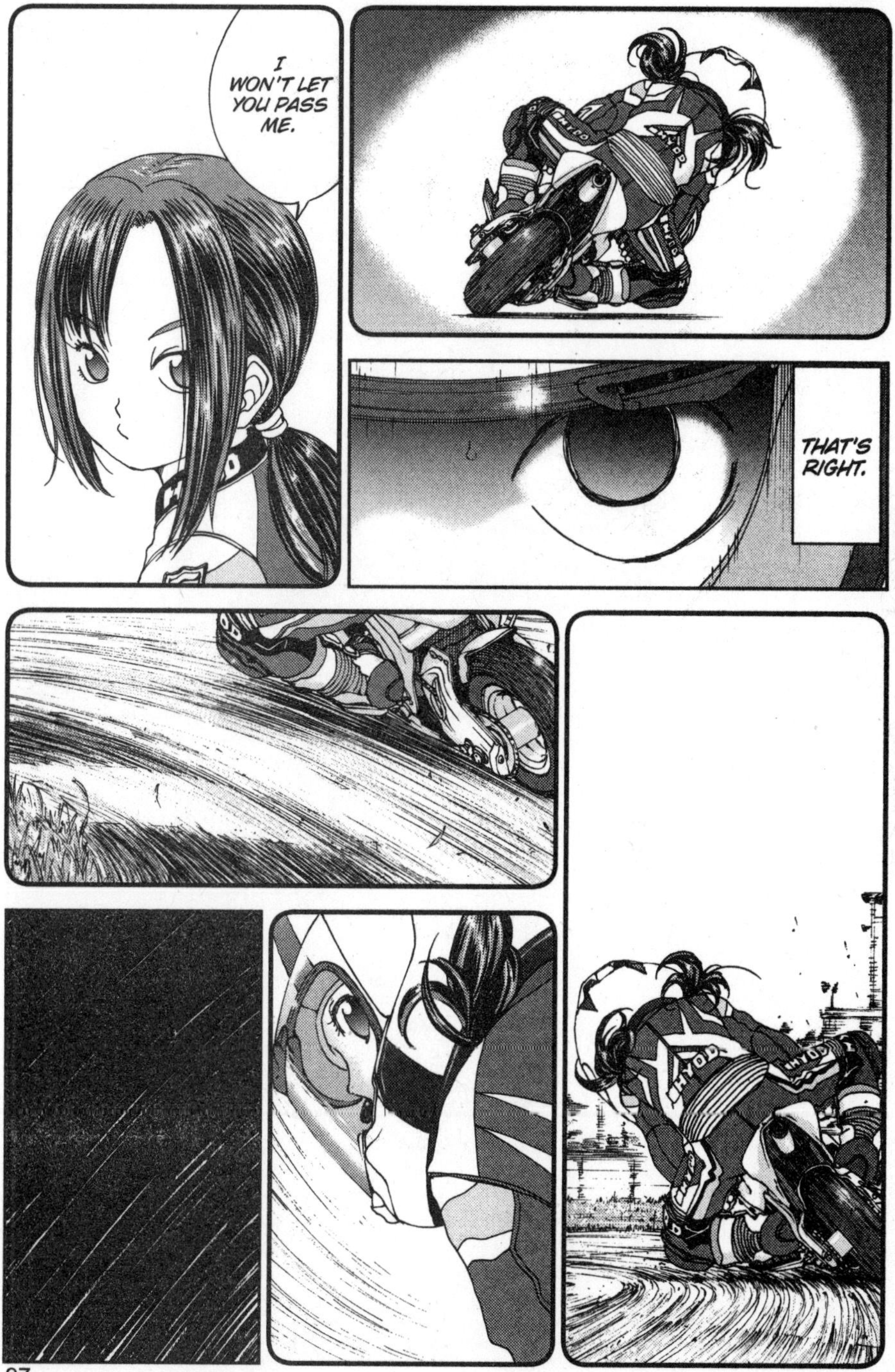
I WON'T LET YOU PASS ME.
THAT'S RIGHT.

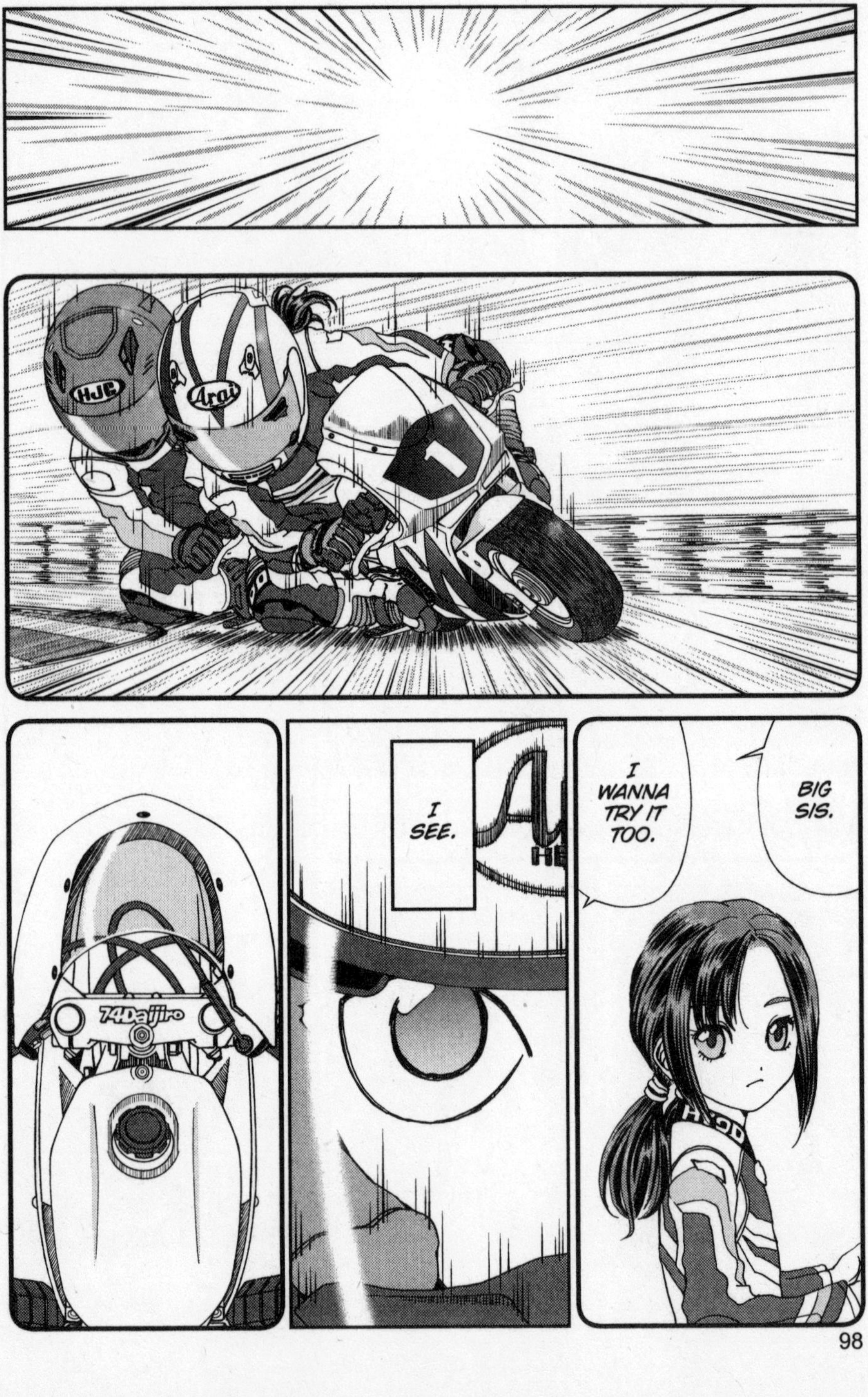
HJC
Arai
BIG SIS.
I WANNA TRY IT TOO.
I SEE.
74Daijiro

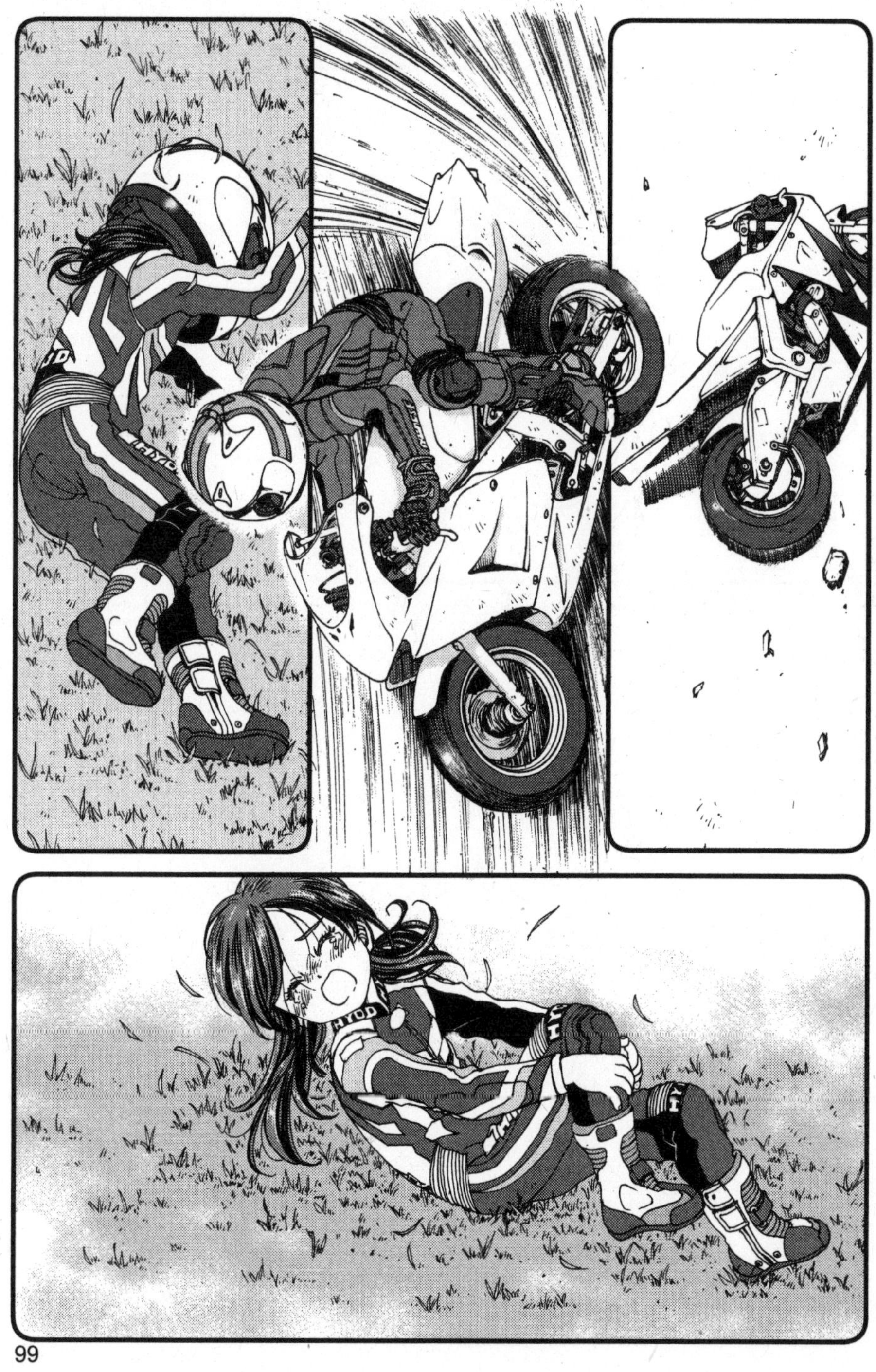
HYOD

...TO HER...

I DID THIS...

OPEN!

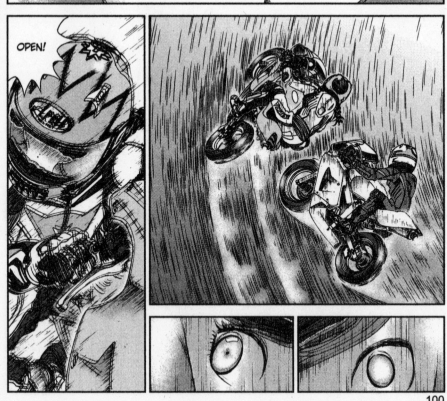

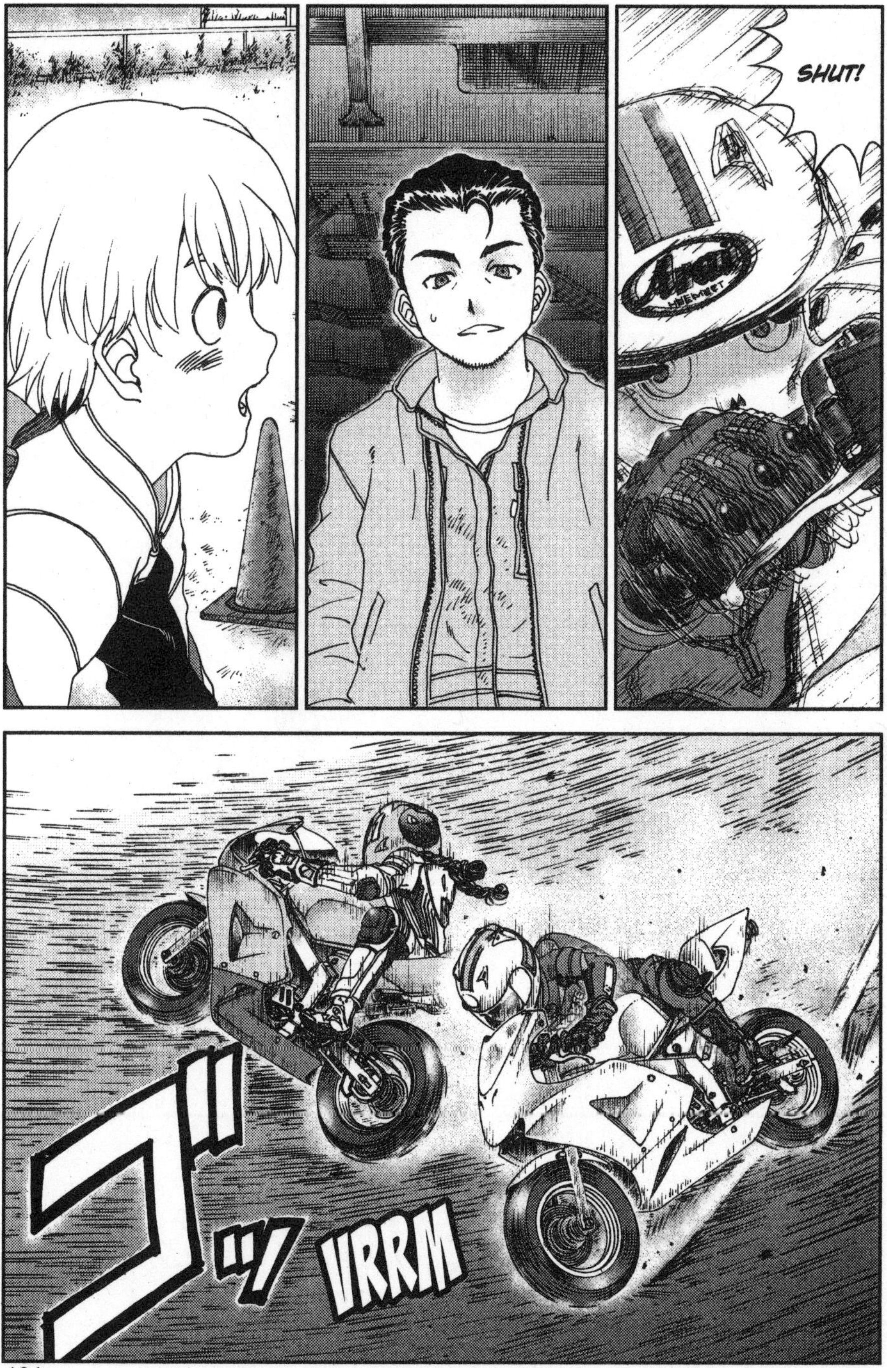
SHUT!
ゴッ
VRRM

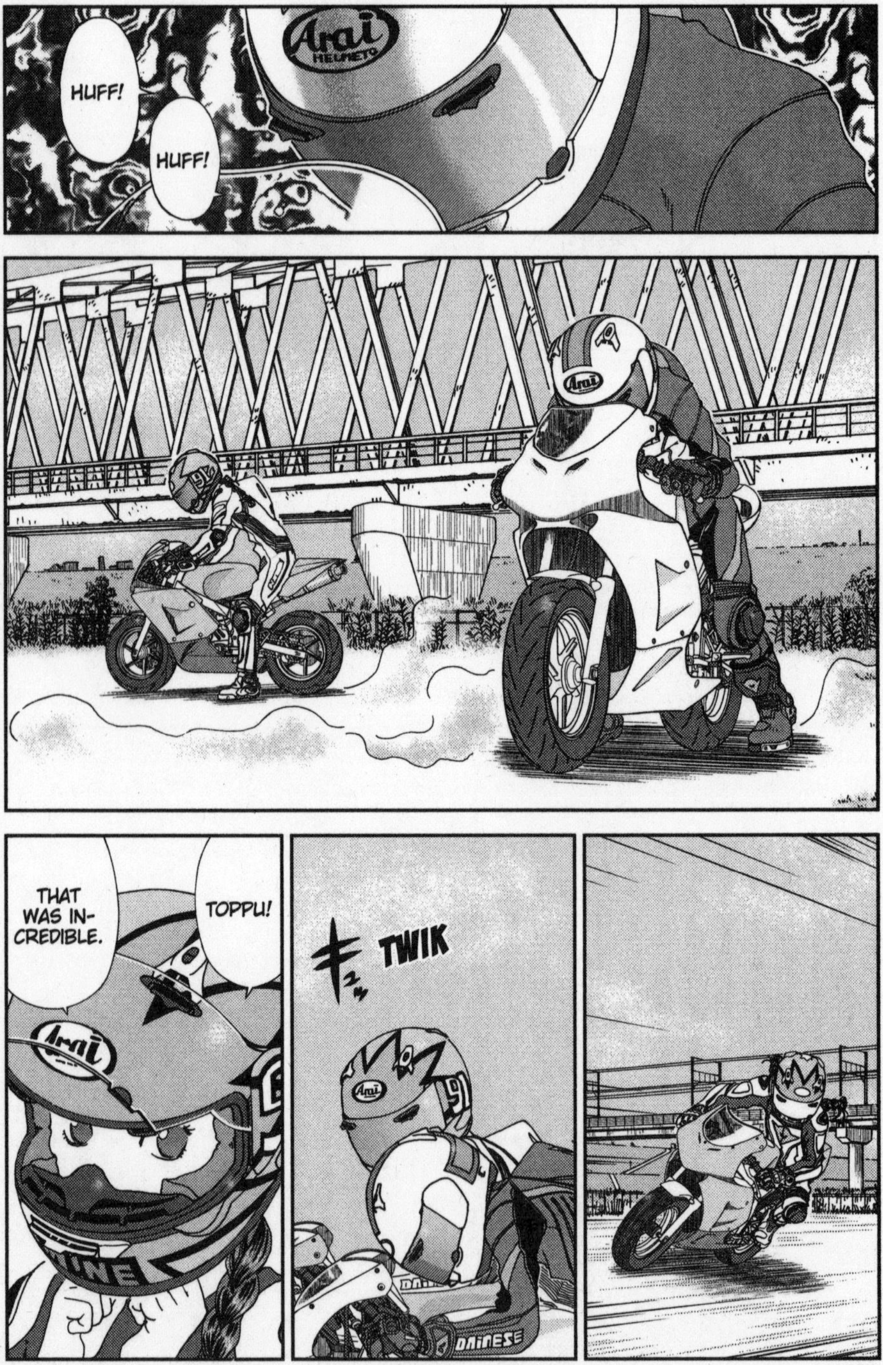
HUFF!
HUFF!
TWIK
TOPPU!
THAT WAS IN-CREDIBLE.

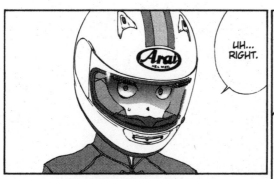

YOU POPPED UP STRAIGHT FROM BEING TOTALLY ON YOUR SIDE!
HOW'D YOU DO THAT?!
UH... RIGHT.
YOU OKAY?
I'M FINE!!

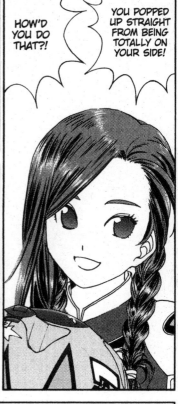

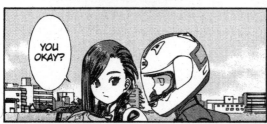

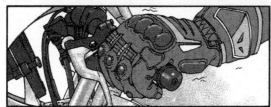

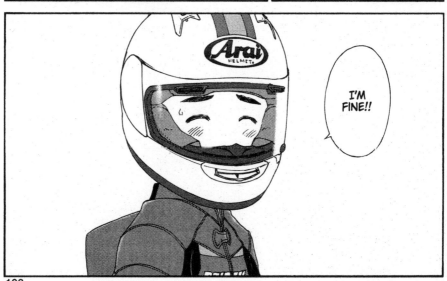

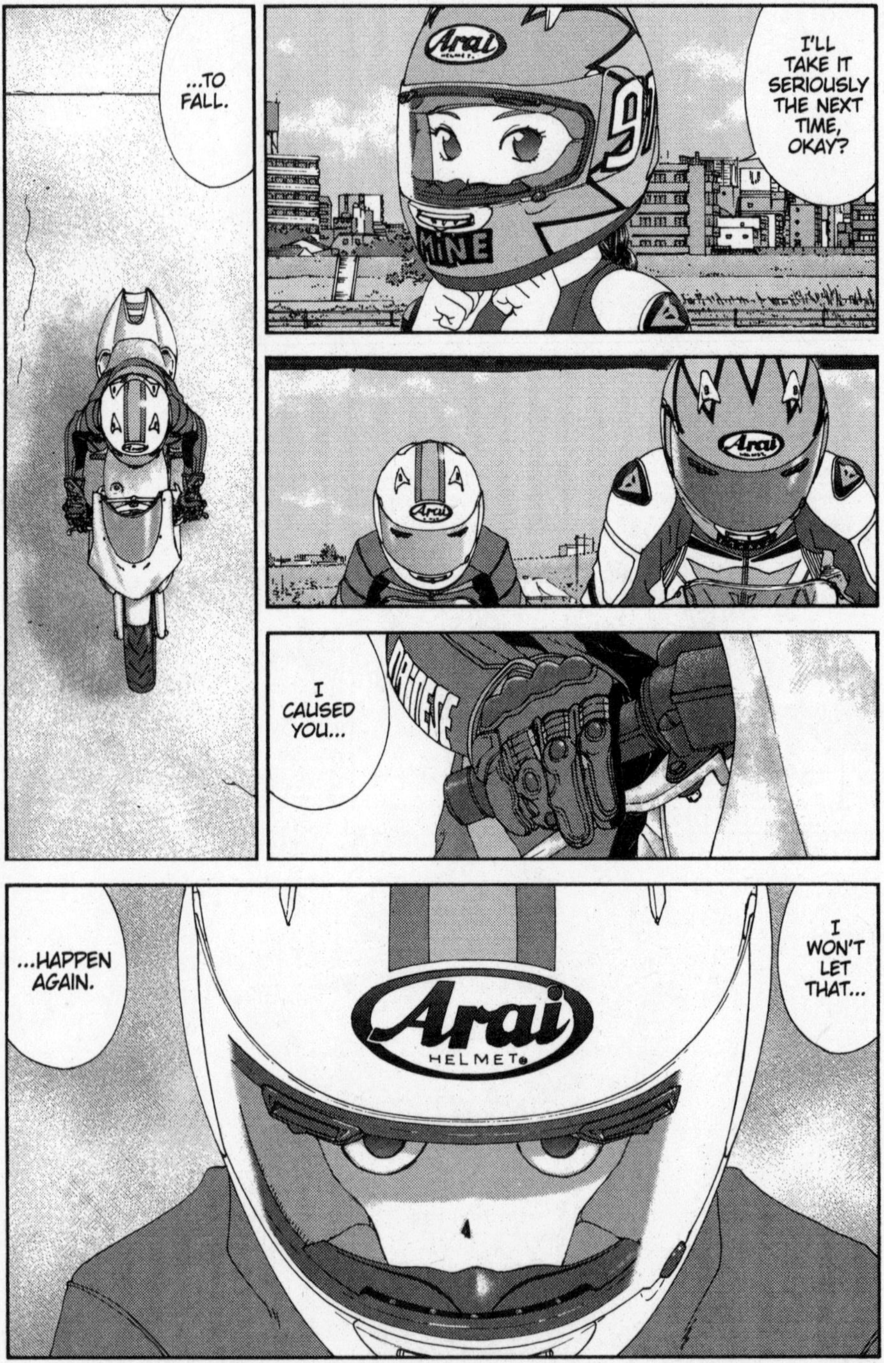
I'LL TAKE IT SERIOUSLY THE NEXT TIME, OKAY?
I CAUSED YOU...
...TO FALL.
I WON'T LET THAT...
...HAPPEN AGAIN.

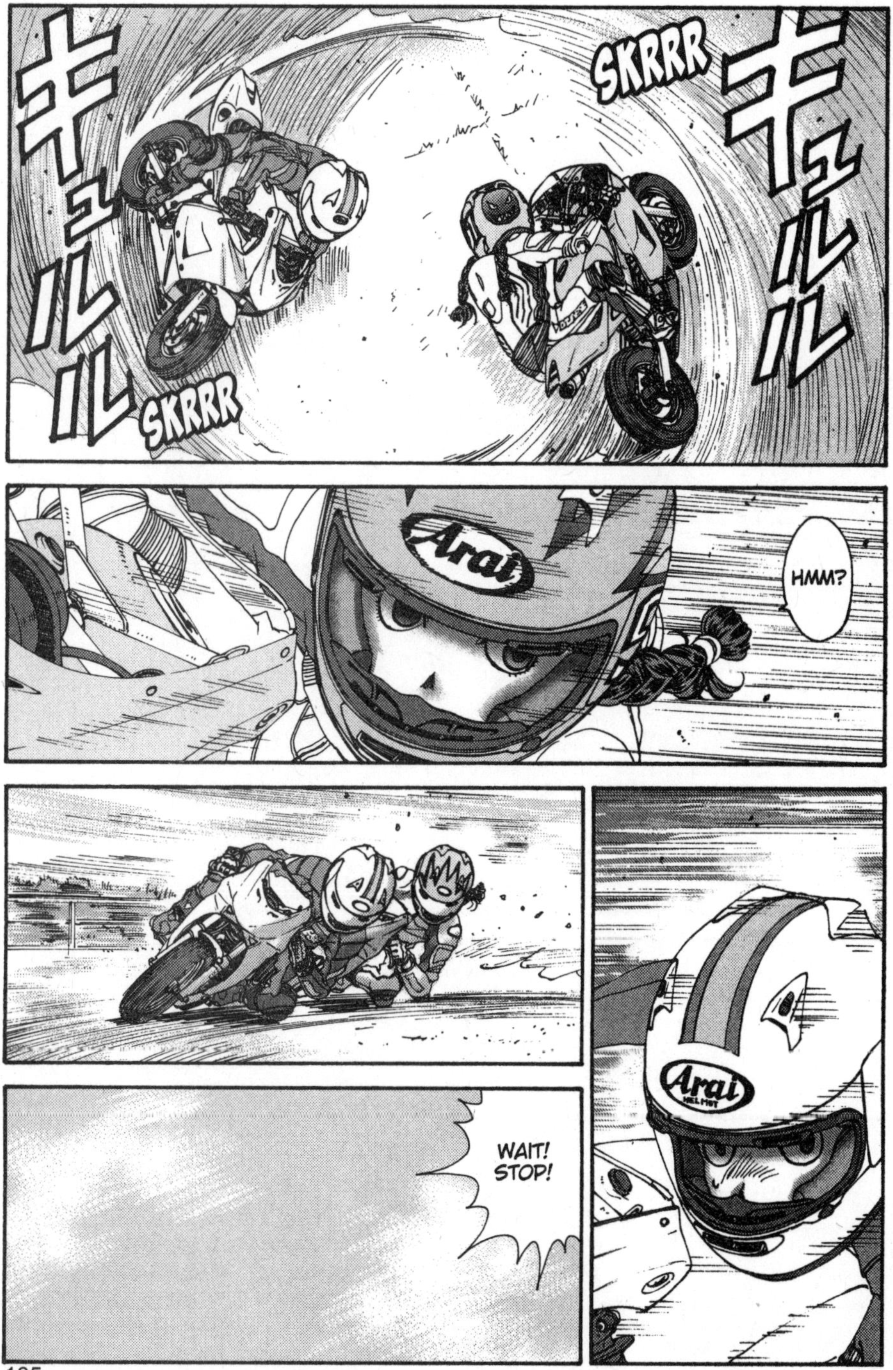

キュルル
SKRRR
キュルル
SKRRR
HMM?
Arai
Arai
WAIT! STOP!

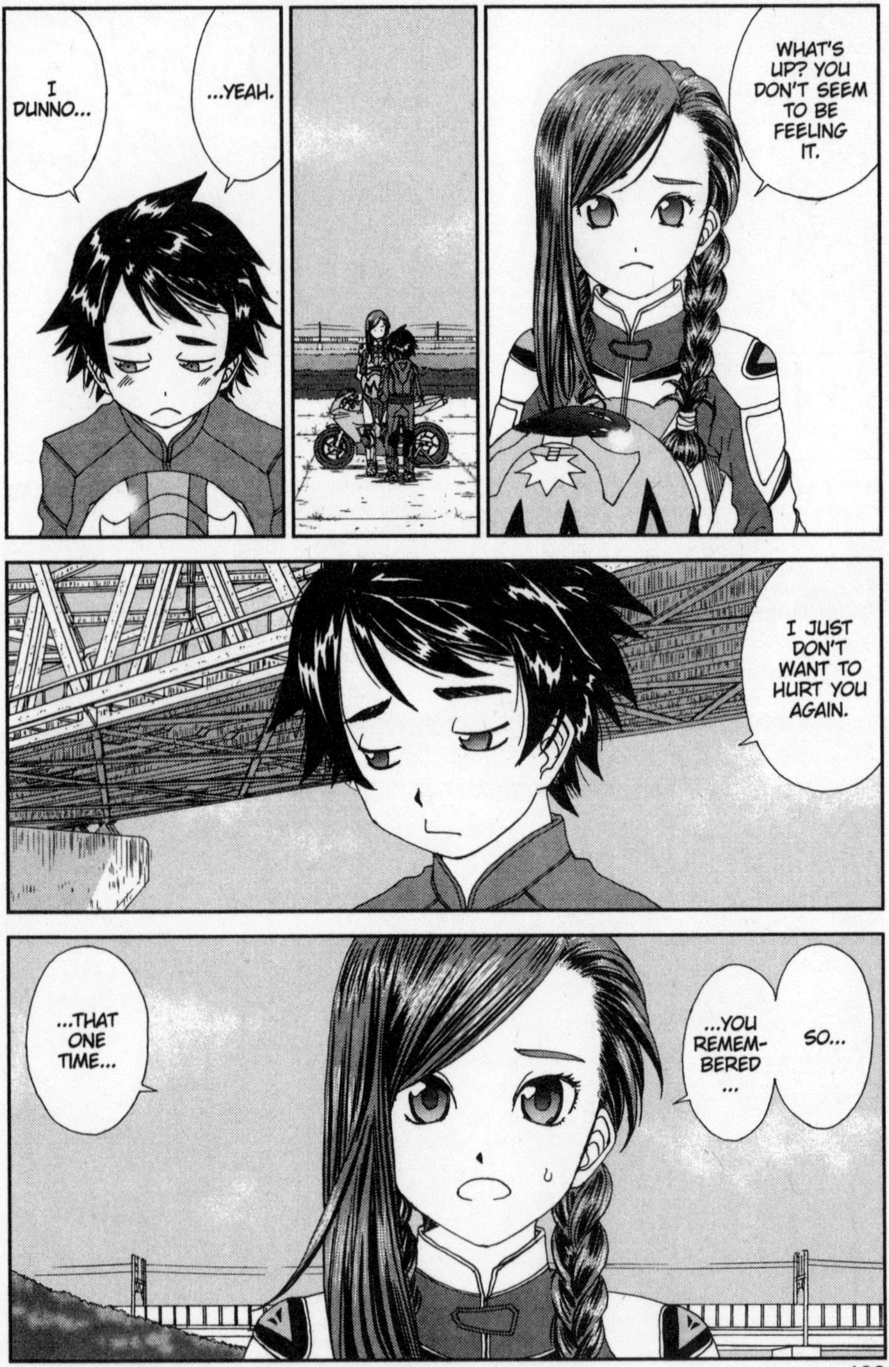
WHAT'S UP? YOU DON'T SEEM TO BE FEELING IT.
...YEAH.
I DUNNO...
I JUST DON'T WANT TO HURT YOU AGAIN.
SO...
...YOU REMEM-BERED ...
...THAT ONE TIME...

HUH?

HUH?

I'M SORRY!!

NO, YOU GO AHEAD.

NO, YOU GO AHEAD.

WHAT?

IT WASN'T YOUR FAULT WE COLLIDED.

HUH? NO WAY!

...AND I COMPLETELY FORGOT ABOUT IT.

SORRY... I REALLY HURT YOU BACK THEN...

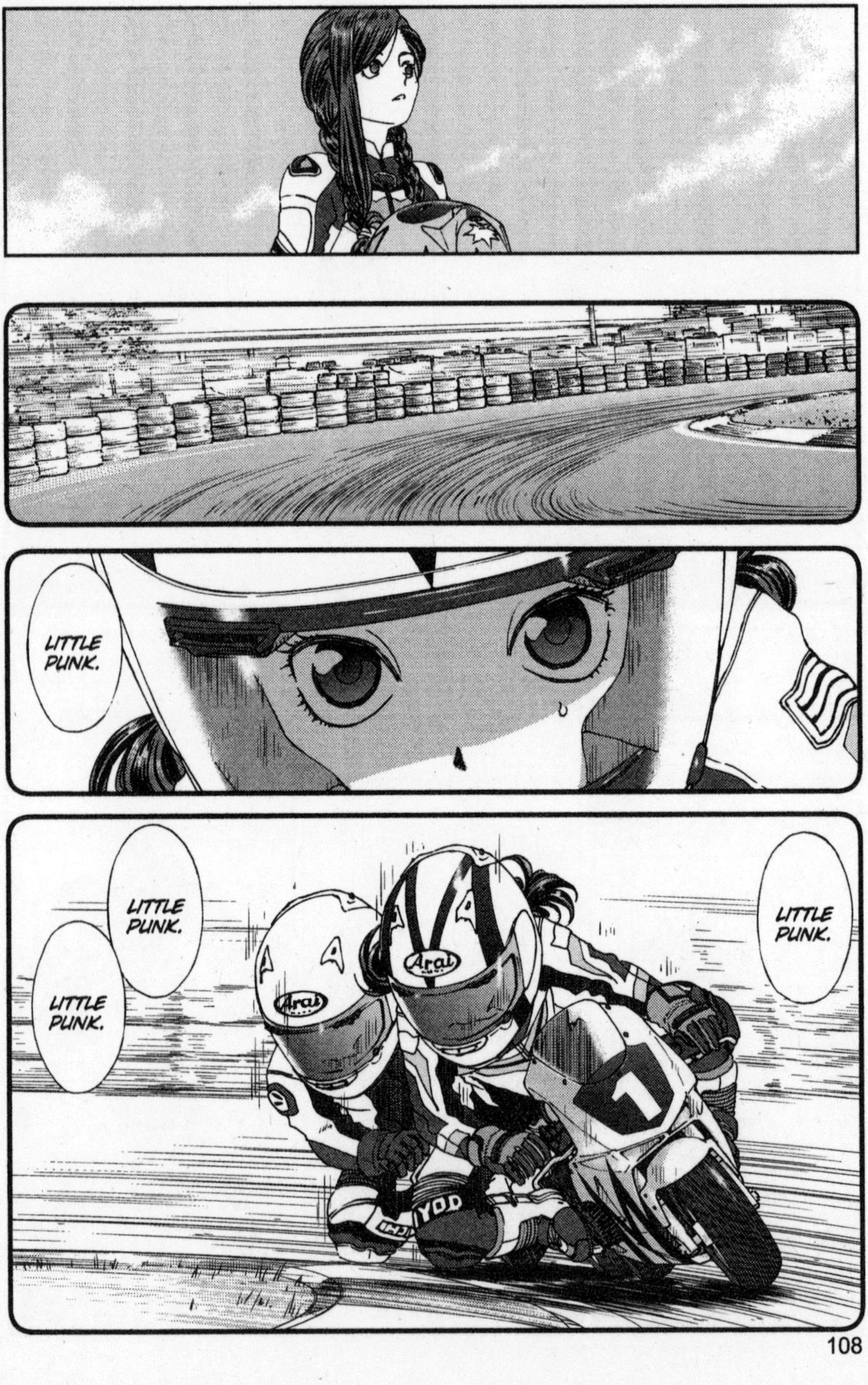
LITTLE PUNK.
LITTLE PUNK.
LITTLE PUNK.
LITTLE PUNK.
Arai
Arai

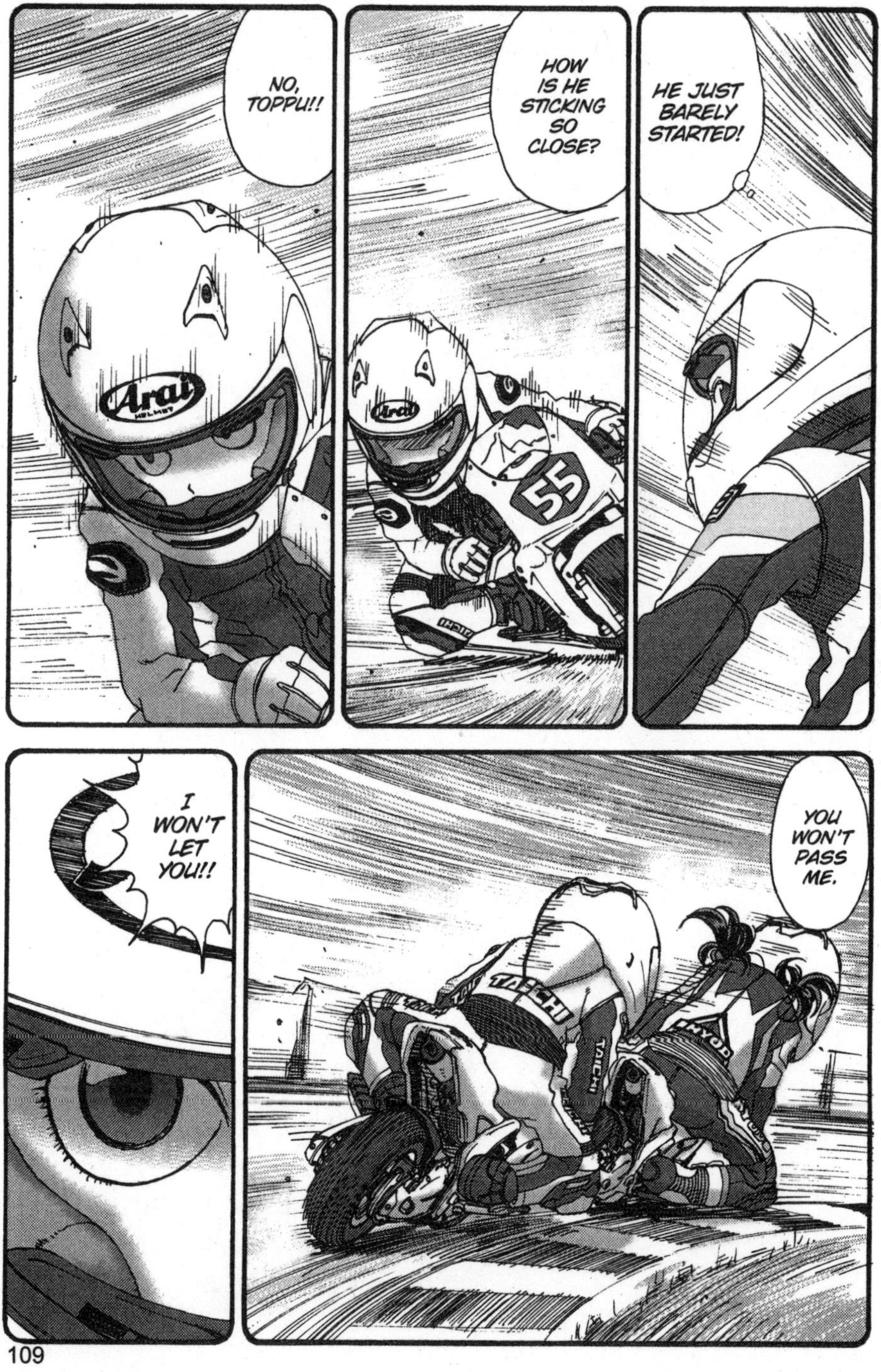
HE JUST BARELY STARTED!
HOW IS HE STICKING SO CLOSE?
NO, TOPPU!!
YOU WON'T PASS ME.
I WON'T LET YOU!!

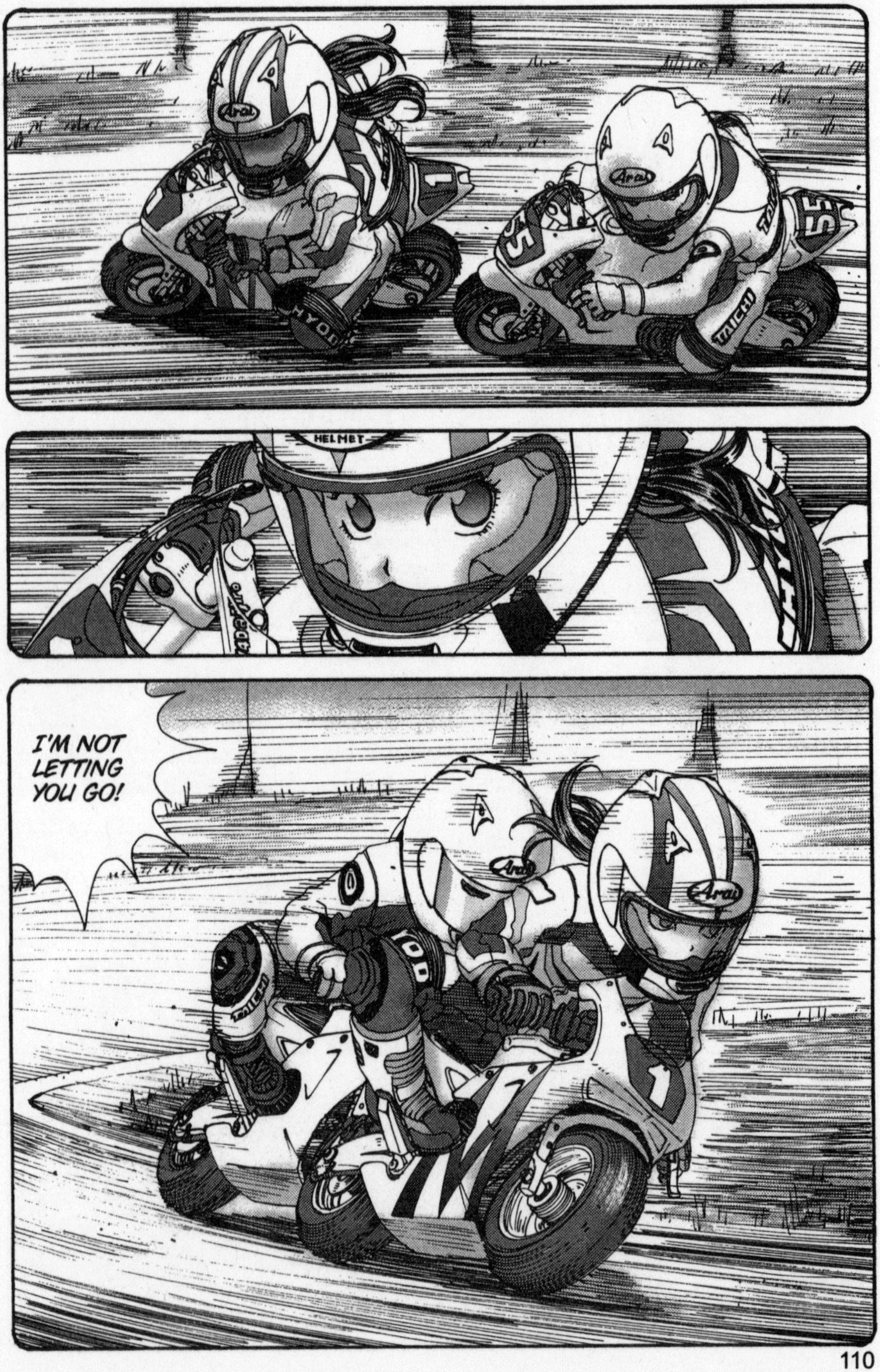
I'M NOT LETTING YOU GO!

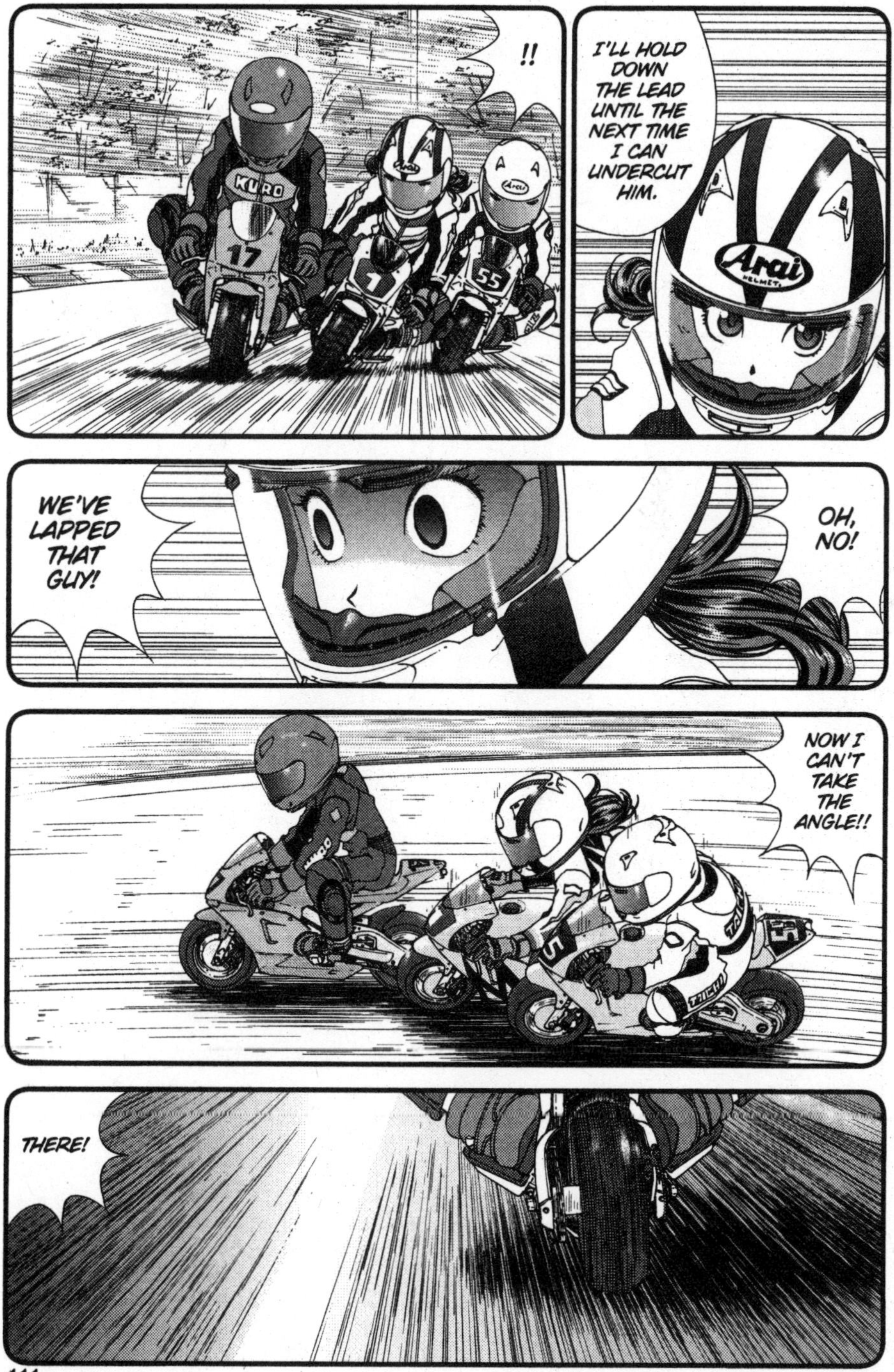
I'LL HOLD DOWN THE LEAD UNTIL THE NEXT TIME I CAN UNDERCUT HIM.
!!
KURO
17
1
55
Arai
OH, NO!
WE'VE LAPPED THAT GUY!
NOW I CAN'T TAKE THE ANGLE!!
THERE!

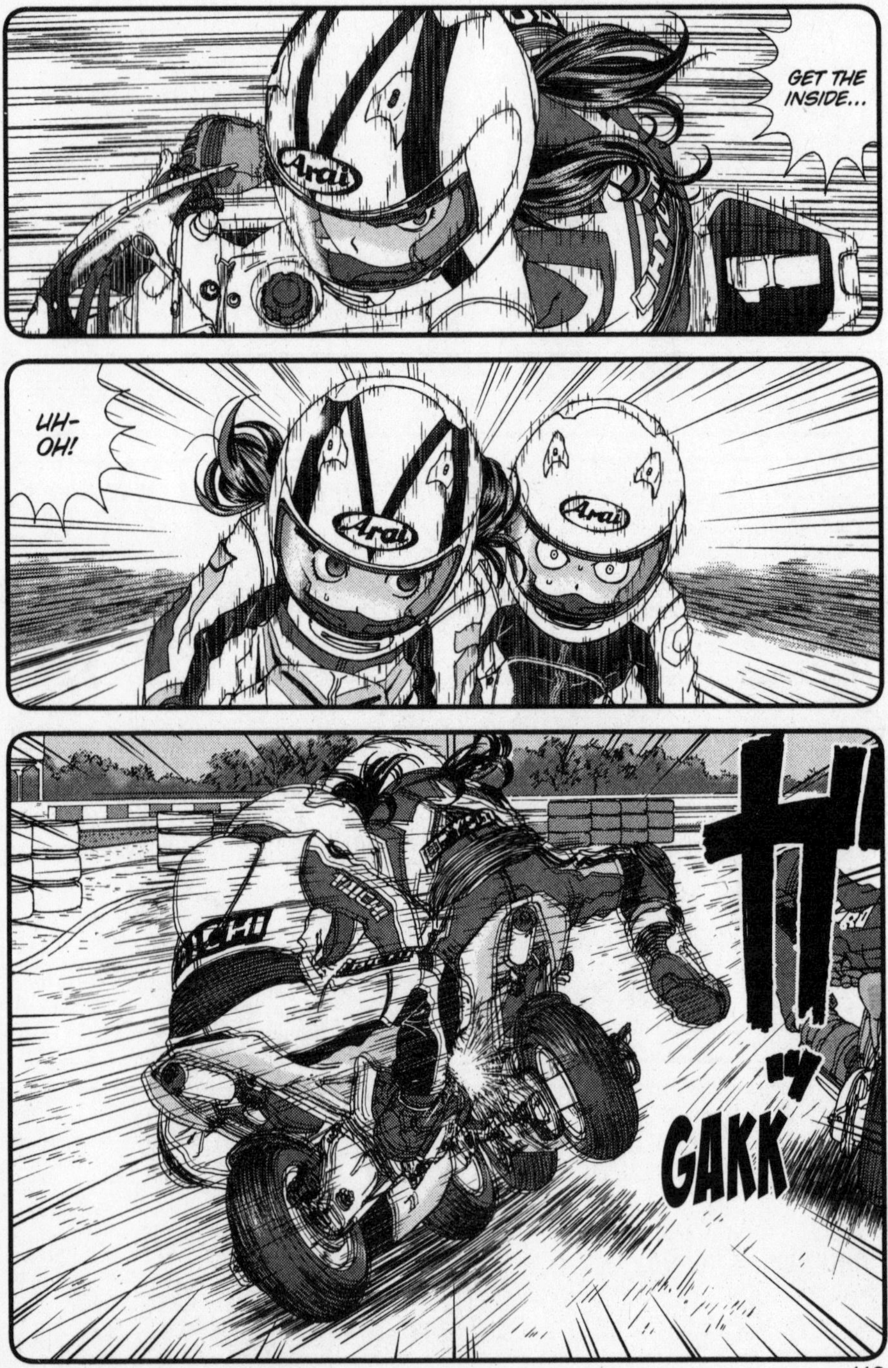
GET THE INSIDE...
UH-OH!
GAKK

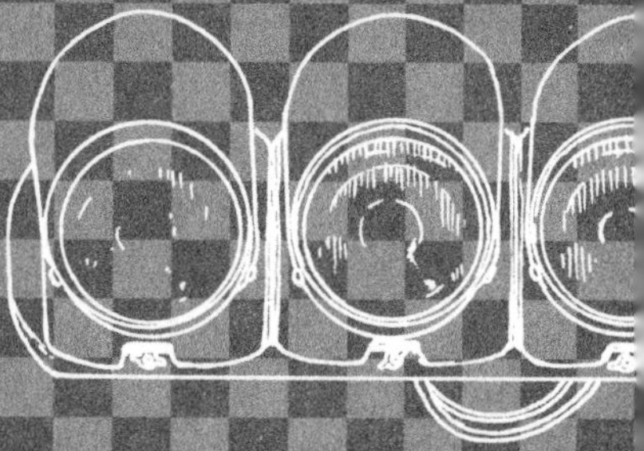

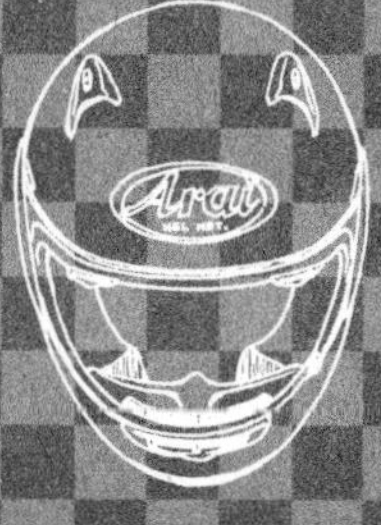
Arai

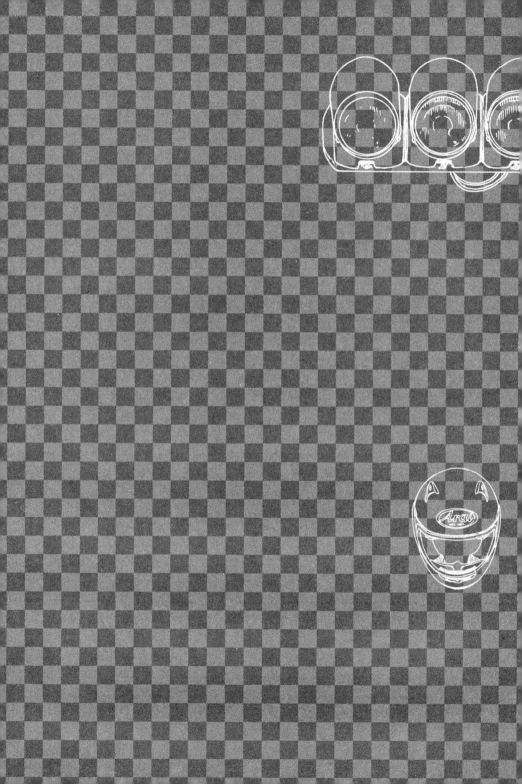

Toppu GP

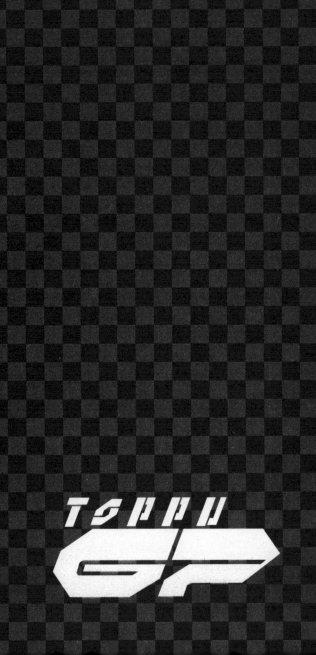

Lap 19: MENTAL BRAKES

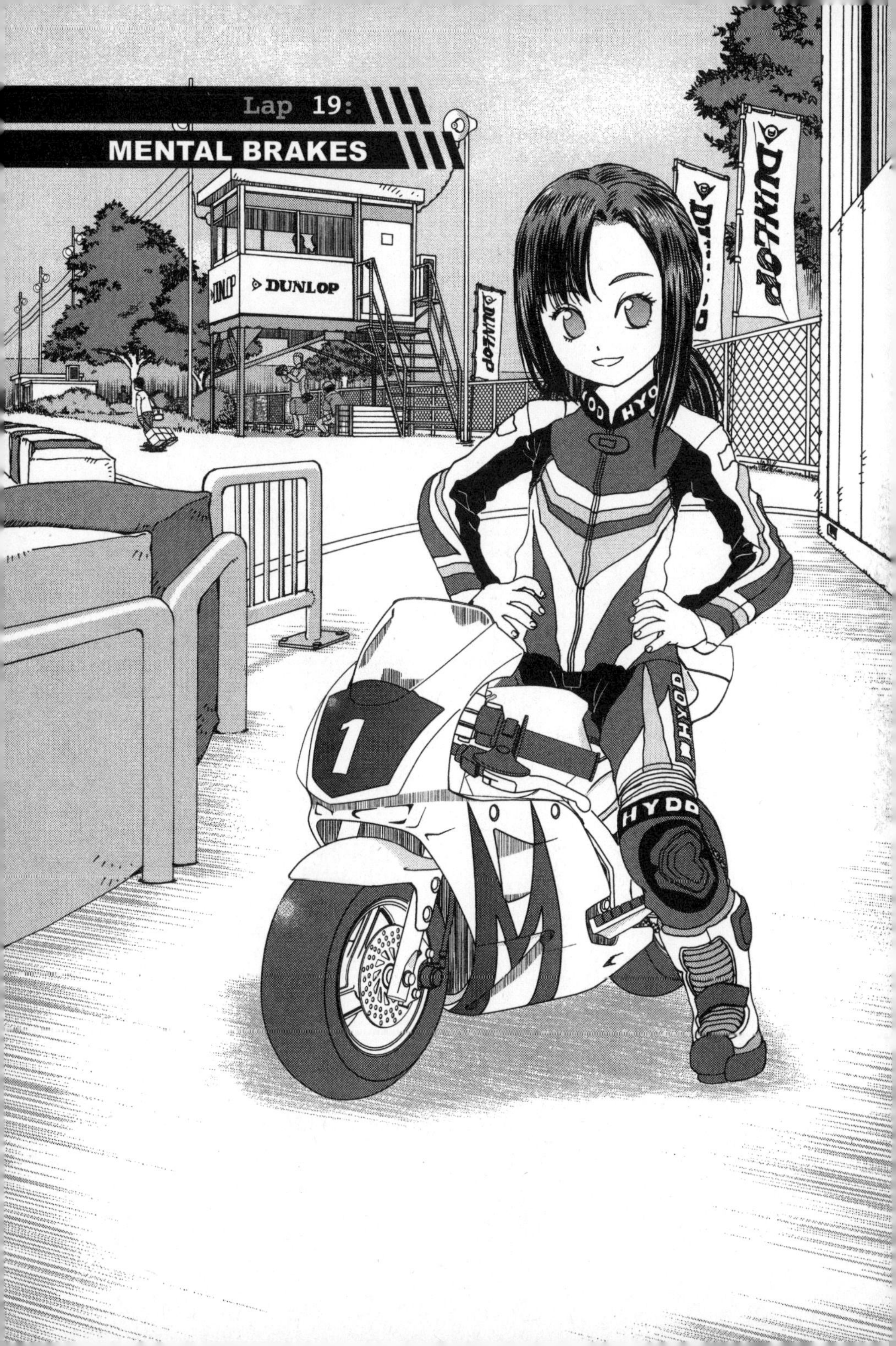
DUNLOP
DUNLOP
DUNLOP
DUNLOP
HYOD
HYOD
HYOD
1

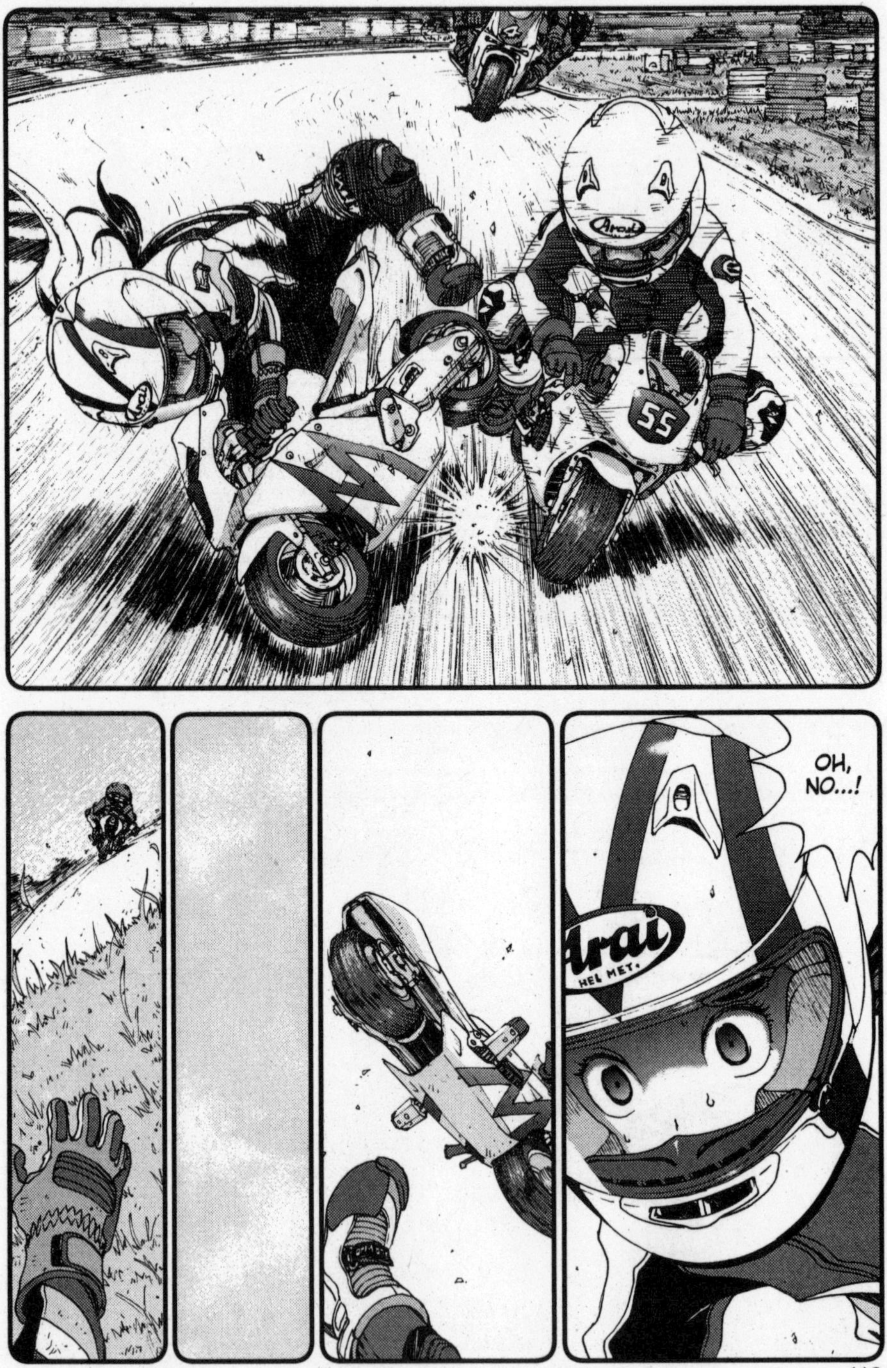
Arai
55
OH, NO...!
Arai
HELMET

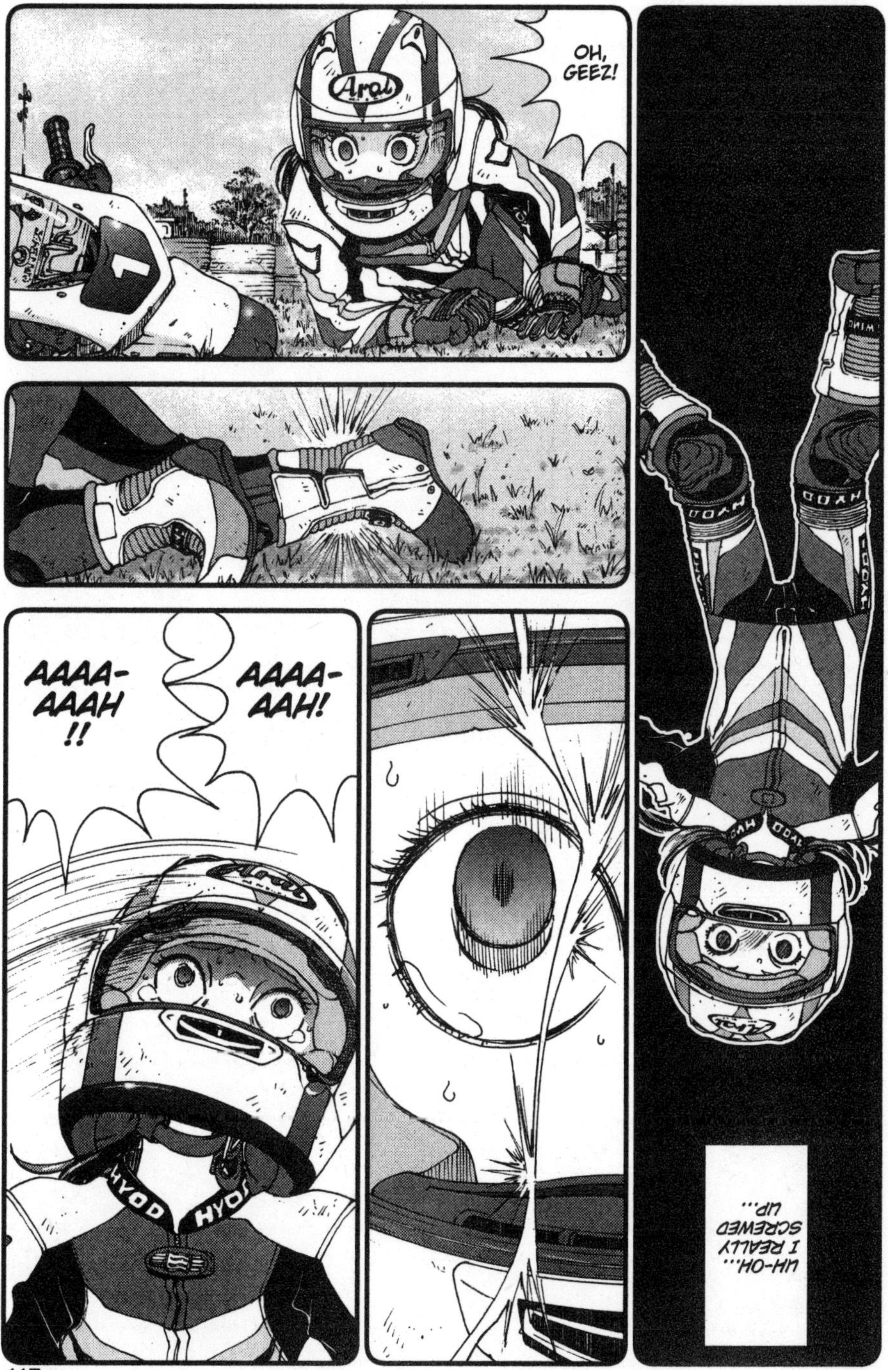
OH, GEEZ!
AAAA-AAAH!!
AAAA-AAH!
UH-OH... I REALLY SCREWED UP...

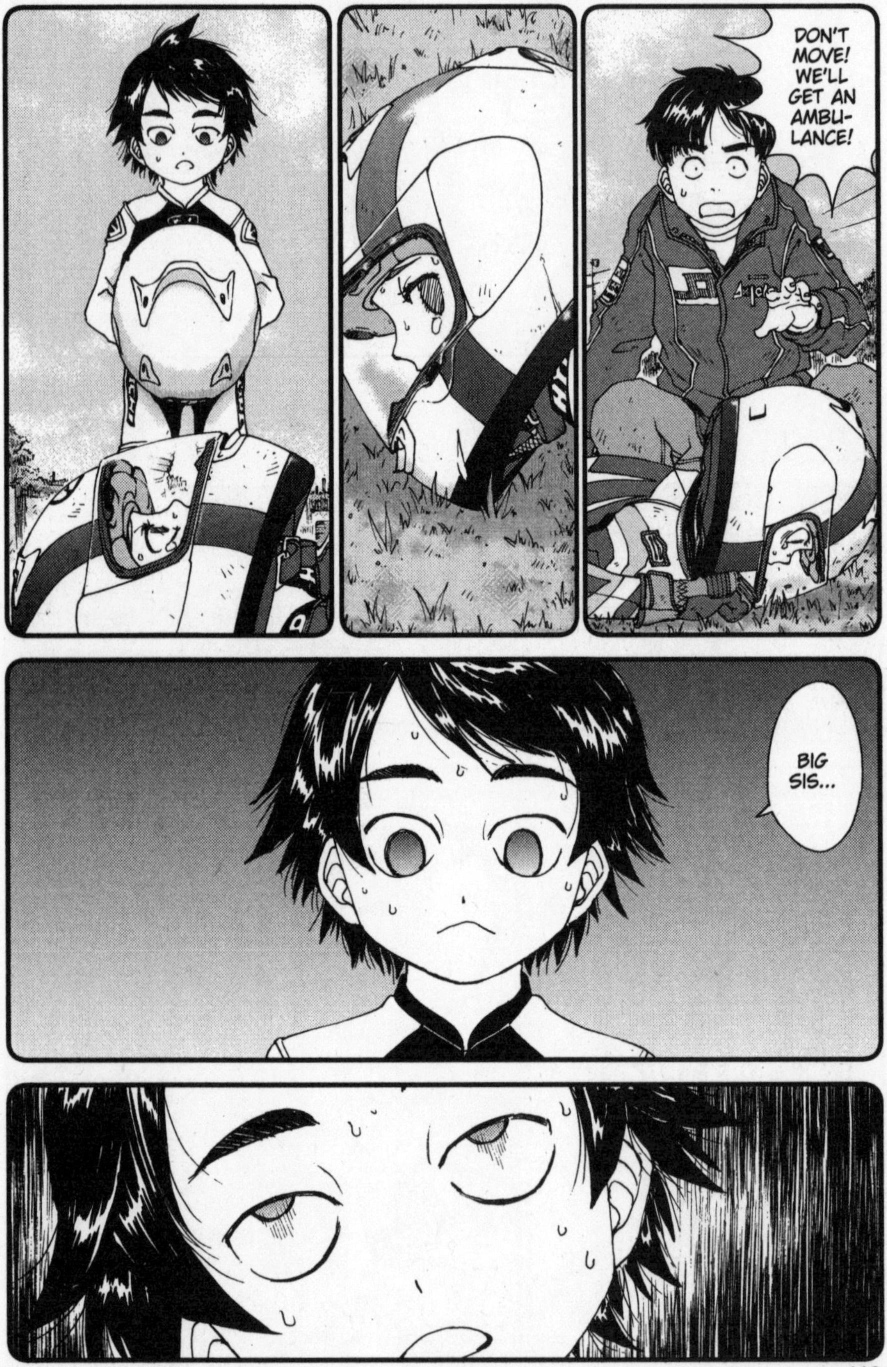
DON'T MOVE! WE'LL GET AN AMBU-LANCE!
BIG SIS...

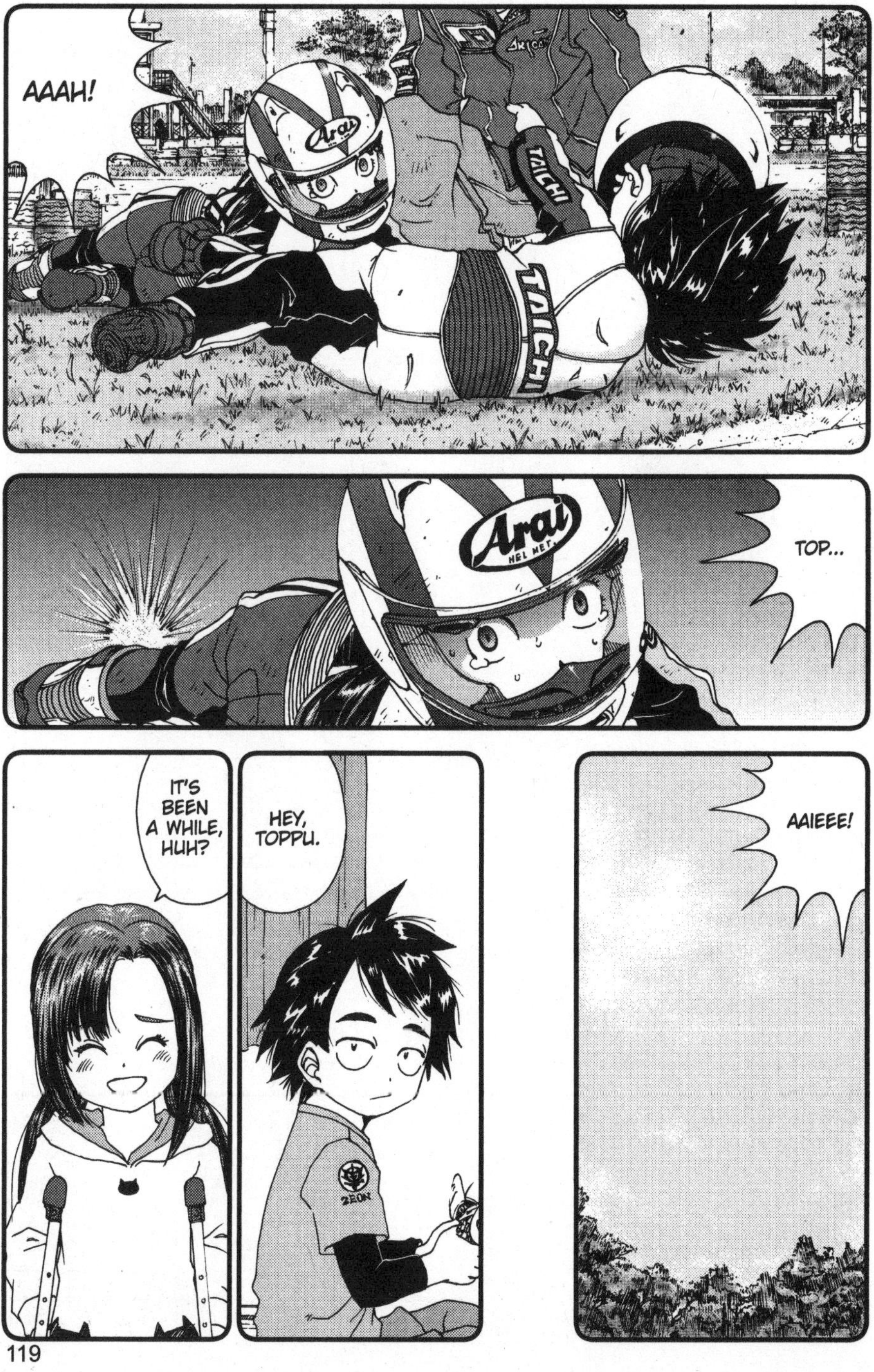
AAAH!
Arai
TAICHI
TAICHI
TOP...
Arai HELMET
AAIEEE!
HEY, TOPPU.
IT'S BEEN A WHILE, HUH?
ZEON

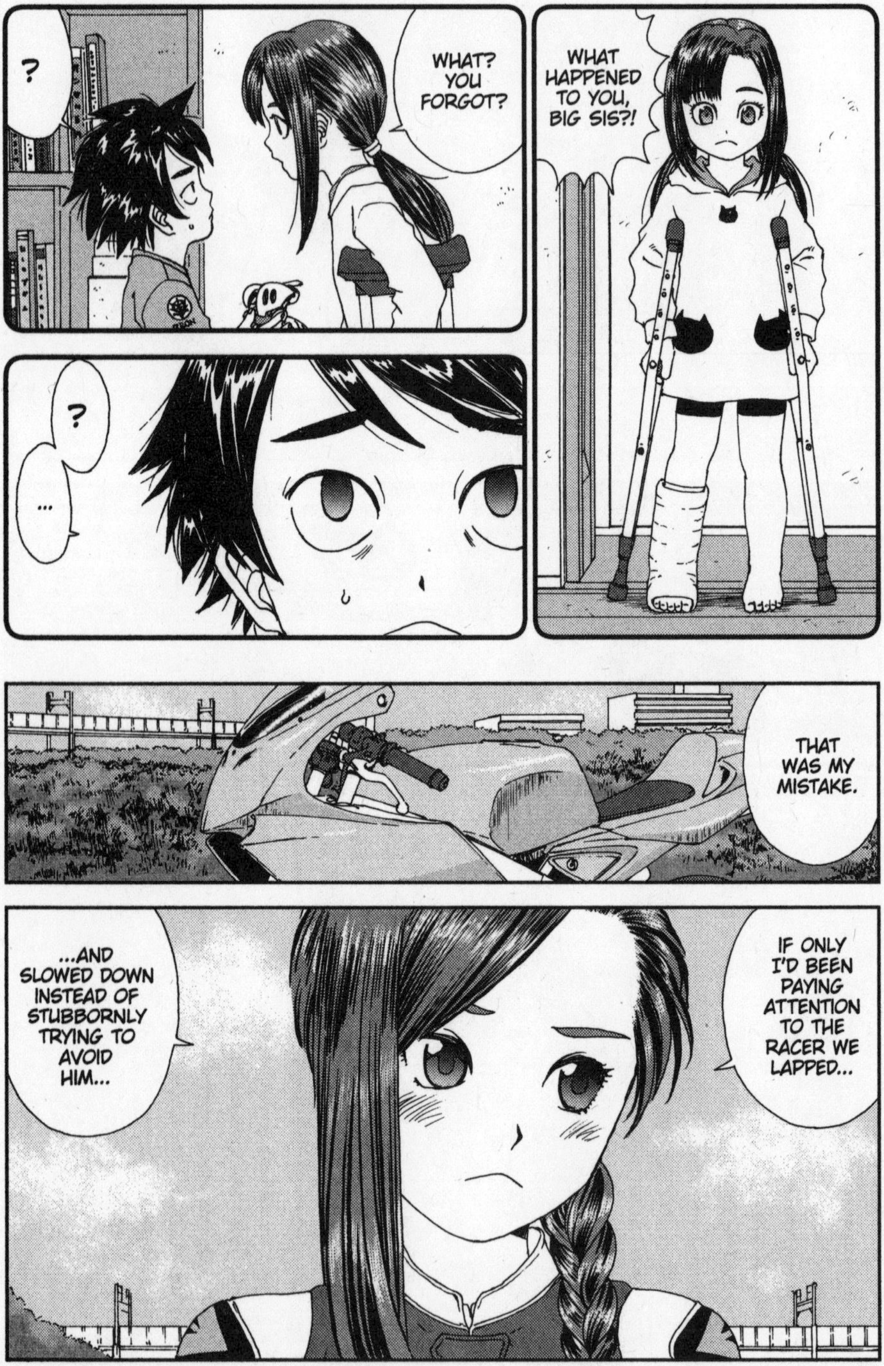
WHAT HAPPENED TO YOU, BIG SIS?!
WHAT? YOU FORGOT?
?
?
...
THAT WAS MY MISTAKE.
IF ONLY I'D BEEN PAYING ATTENTION TO THE RACER WE LAPPED...
...AND SLOWED DOWN INSTEAD OF STUBBORNLY TRYING TO AVOID HIM...

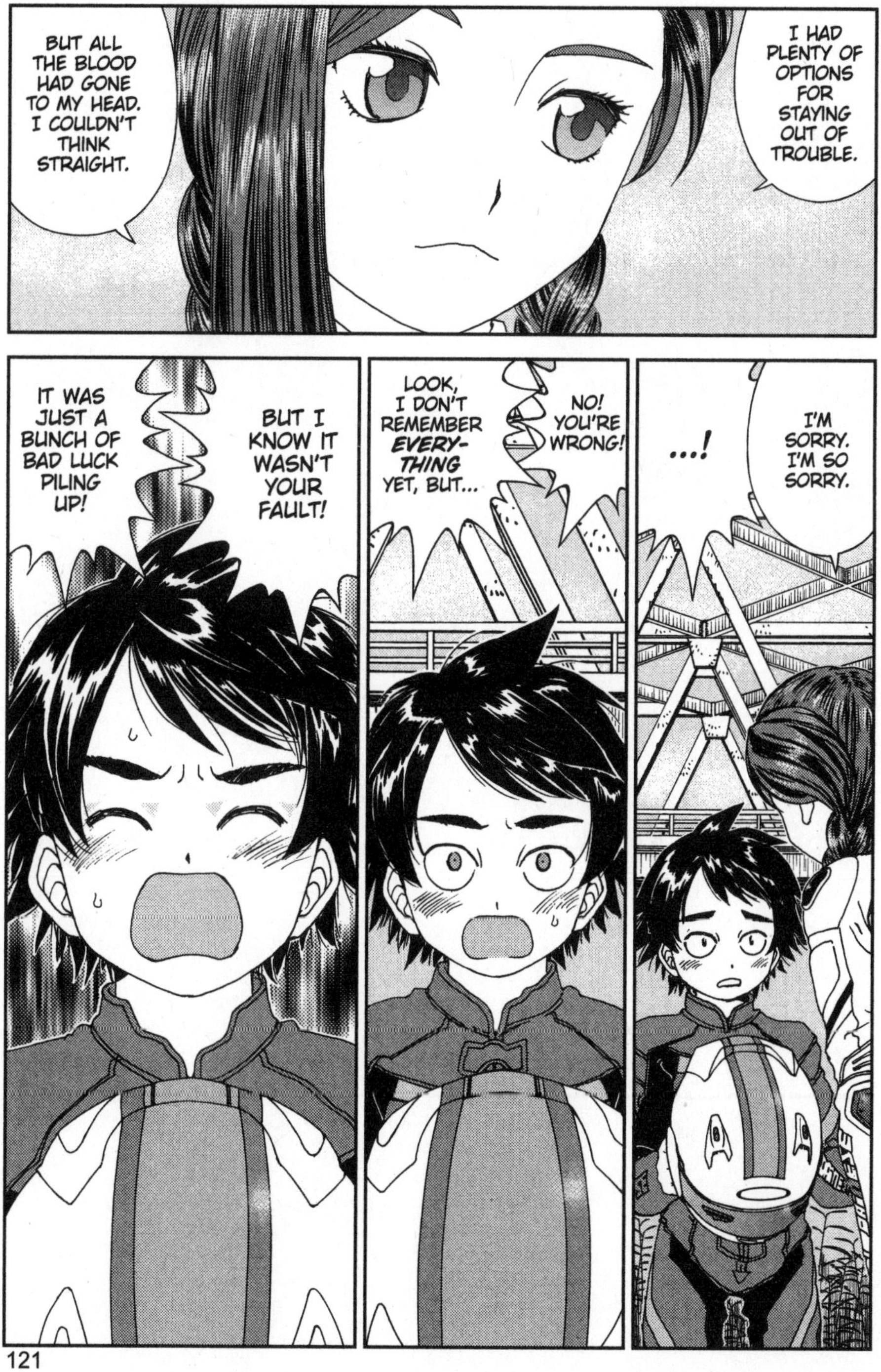
I HAD PLENTY OF OPTIONS FOR STAYING OUT OF TROUBLE.
BUT ALL THE BLOOD HAD GONE TO MY HEAD. I COULDN'T THINK STRAIGHT.
I'M SORRY. I'M SO SORRY.
...!
NO! YOU'RE WRONG!
LOOK, I DON'T REMEMBER *EVERYTHING* YET, BUT...
BUT I KNOW IT WASN'T YOUR FAULT!
IT WAS JUST A BUNCH OF BAD LUCK PILING UP!

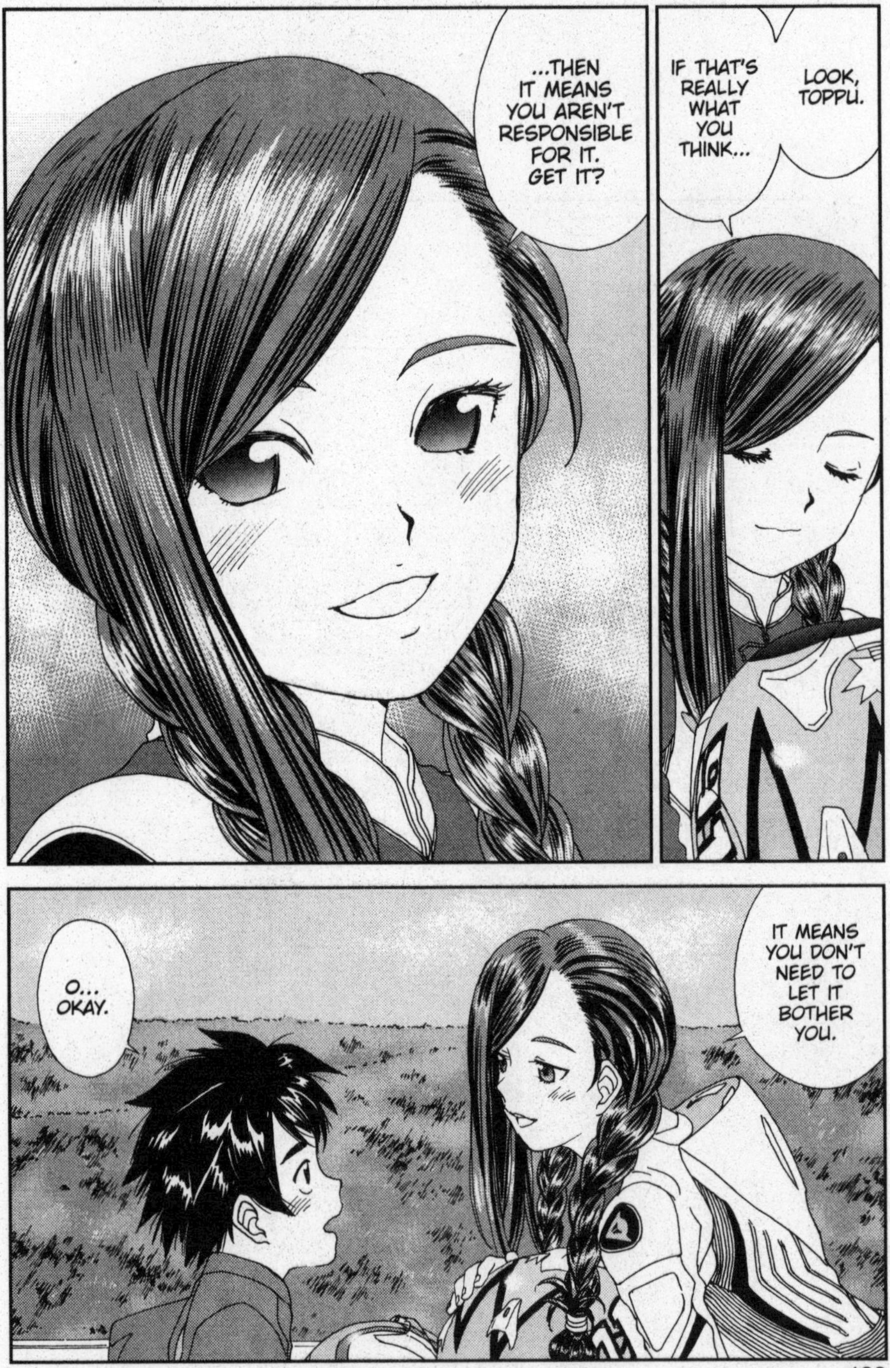
LOOK, TOPPU.
IF THAT'S REALLY WHAT YOU THINK...
...THEN IT MEANS YOU AREN'T RESPONSIBLE FOR IT. GET IT?
IT MEANS YOU DON'T NEED TO LET IT BOTHER YOU.
O... OKAY.

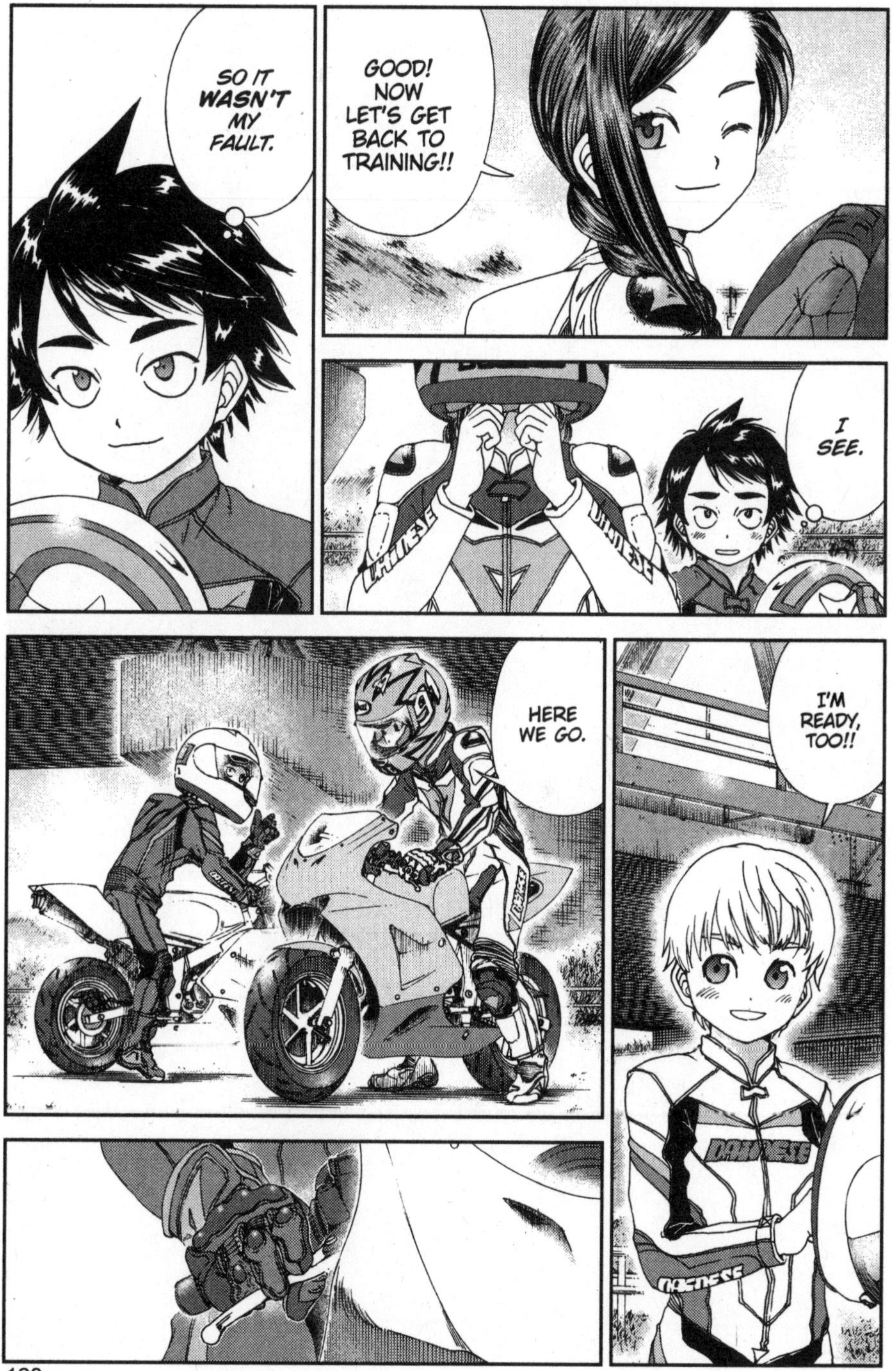
GOOD! NOW LET'S GET BACK TO TRAINING!!
SO IT WASN'T MY FAULT.
I SEE.
I'M READY, TOO!!
HERE WE GO.

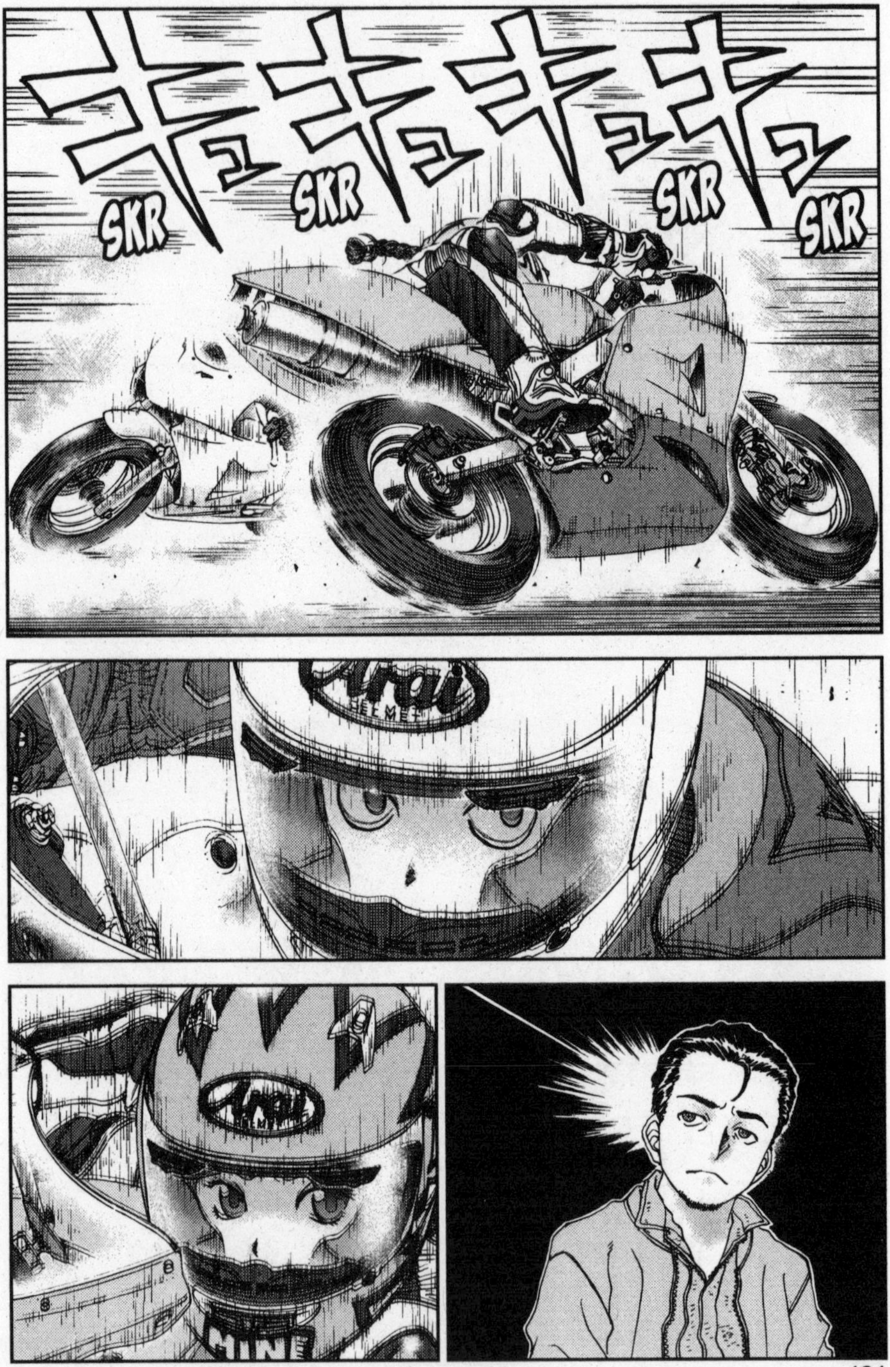
キュキュキュキュ
SKR
SKR
SKR
SKR
Arai

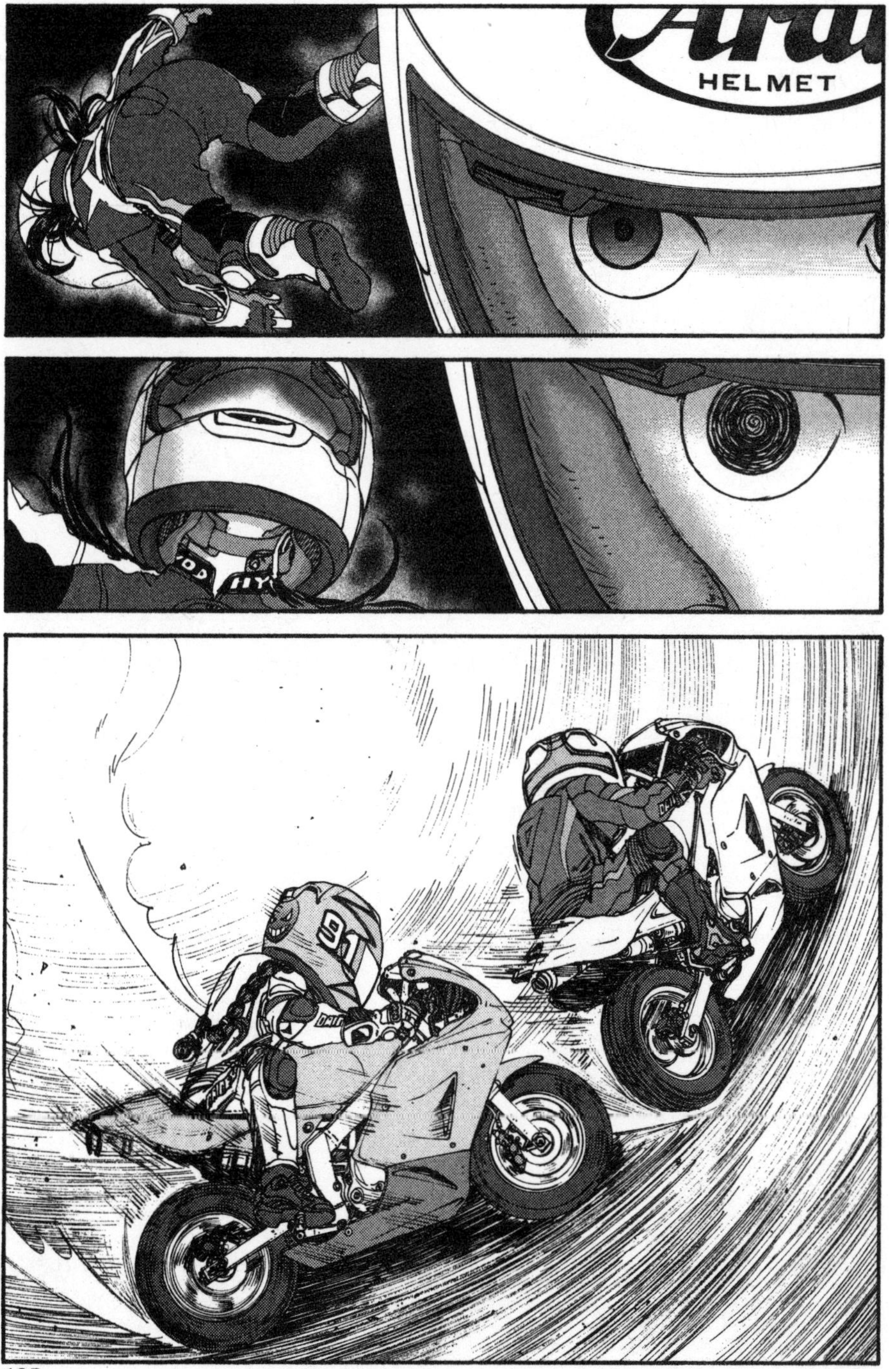
HELMET

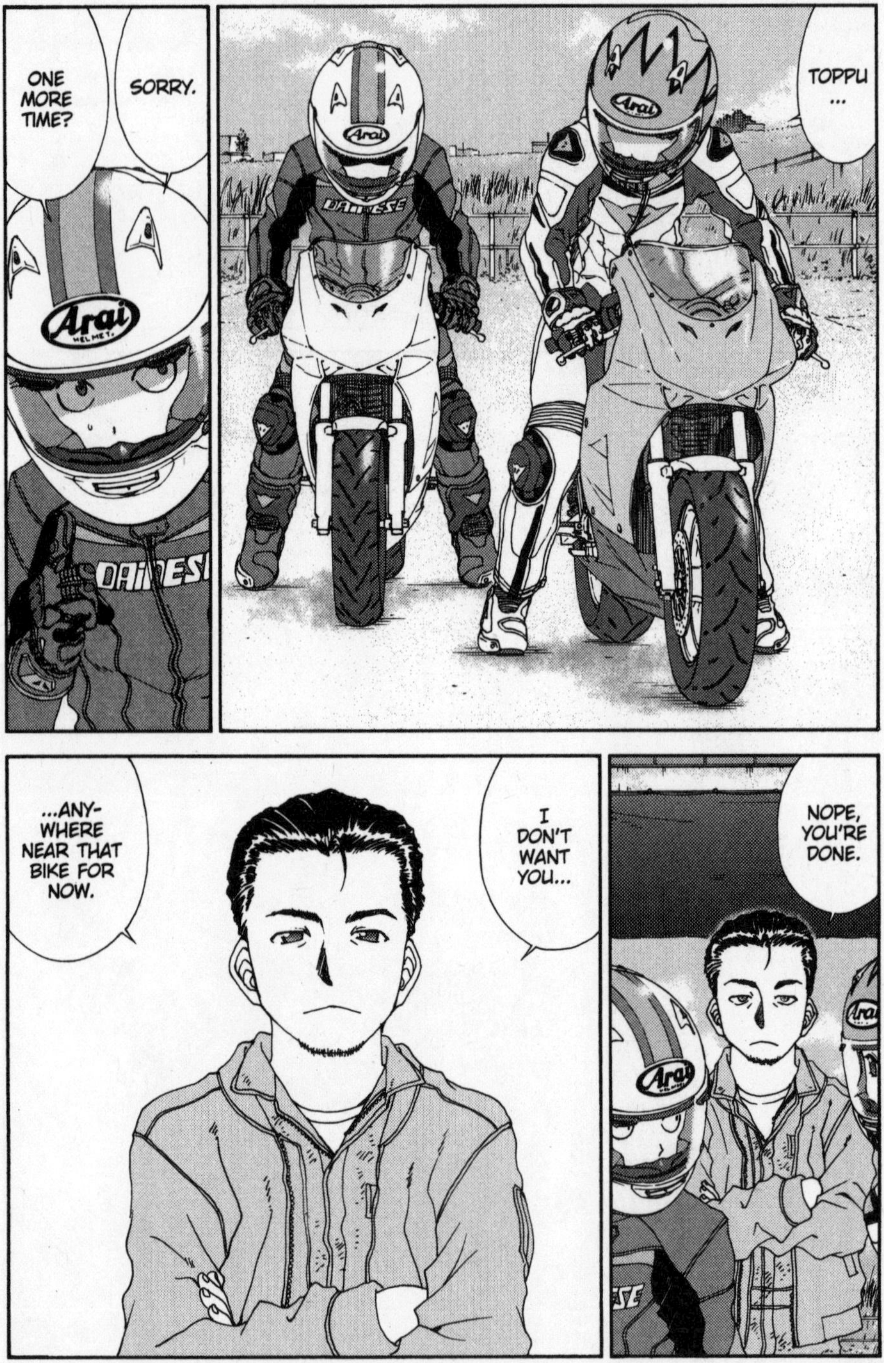
TOPPU ...
SORRY.
ONE MORE TIME?
NOPE, YOU'RE DONE.
I DON'T WANT YOU...
...ANY-WHERE NEAR THAT BIKE FOR NOW.

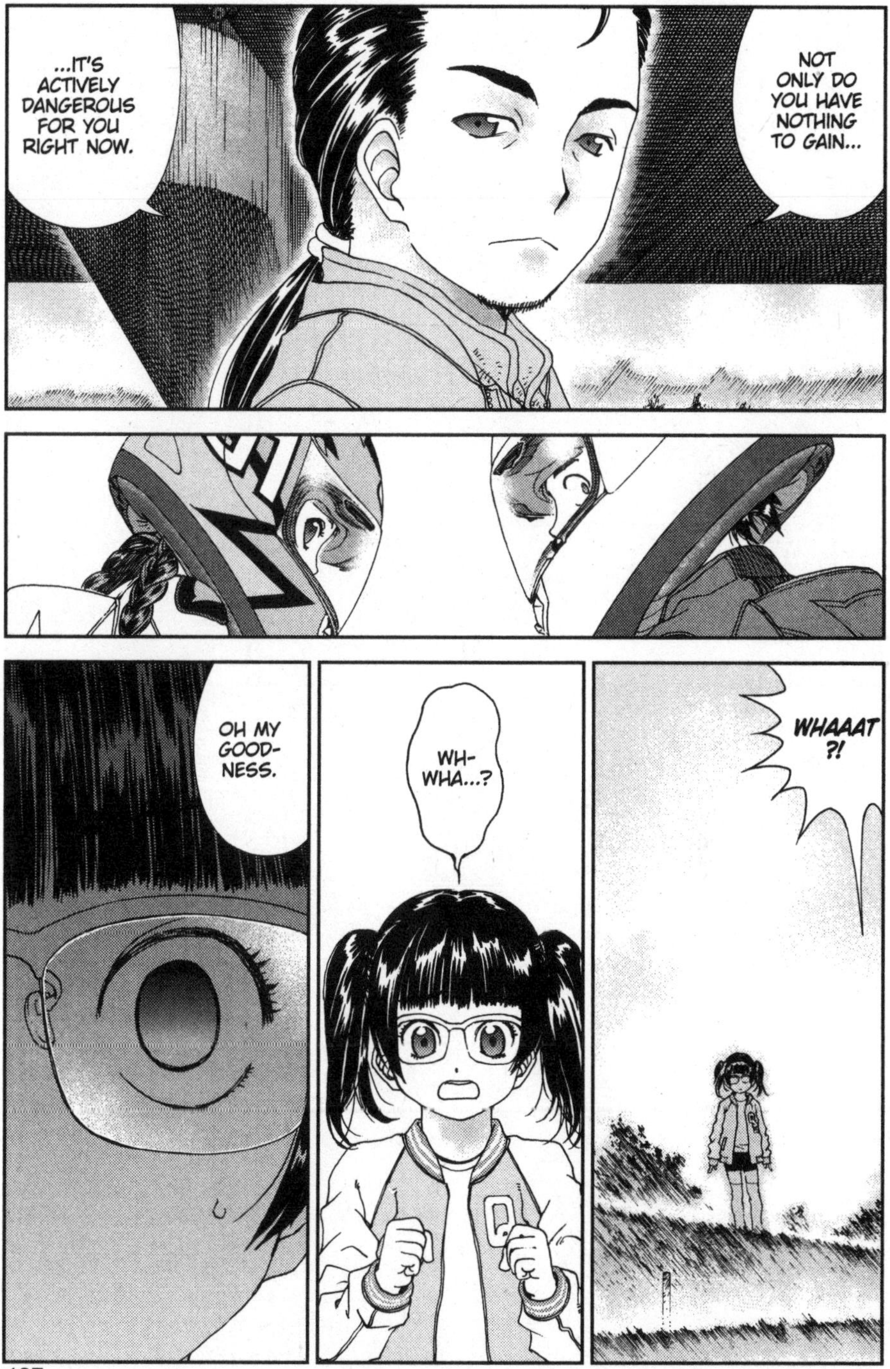
NOT ONLY DO YOU HAVE NOTHING TO GAIN...
...IT'S ACTIVELY DANGEROUS FOR YOU RIGHT NOW.
WHAAAT?!
WH-WHA...?
OH MY GOODNESS.

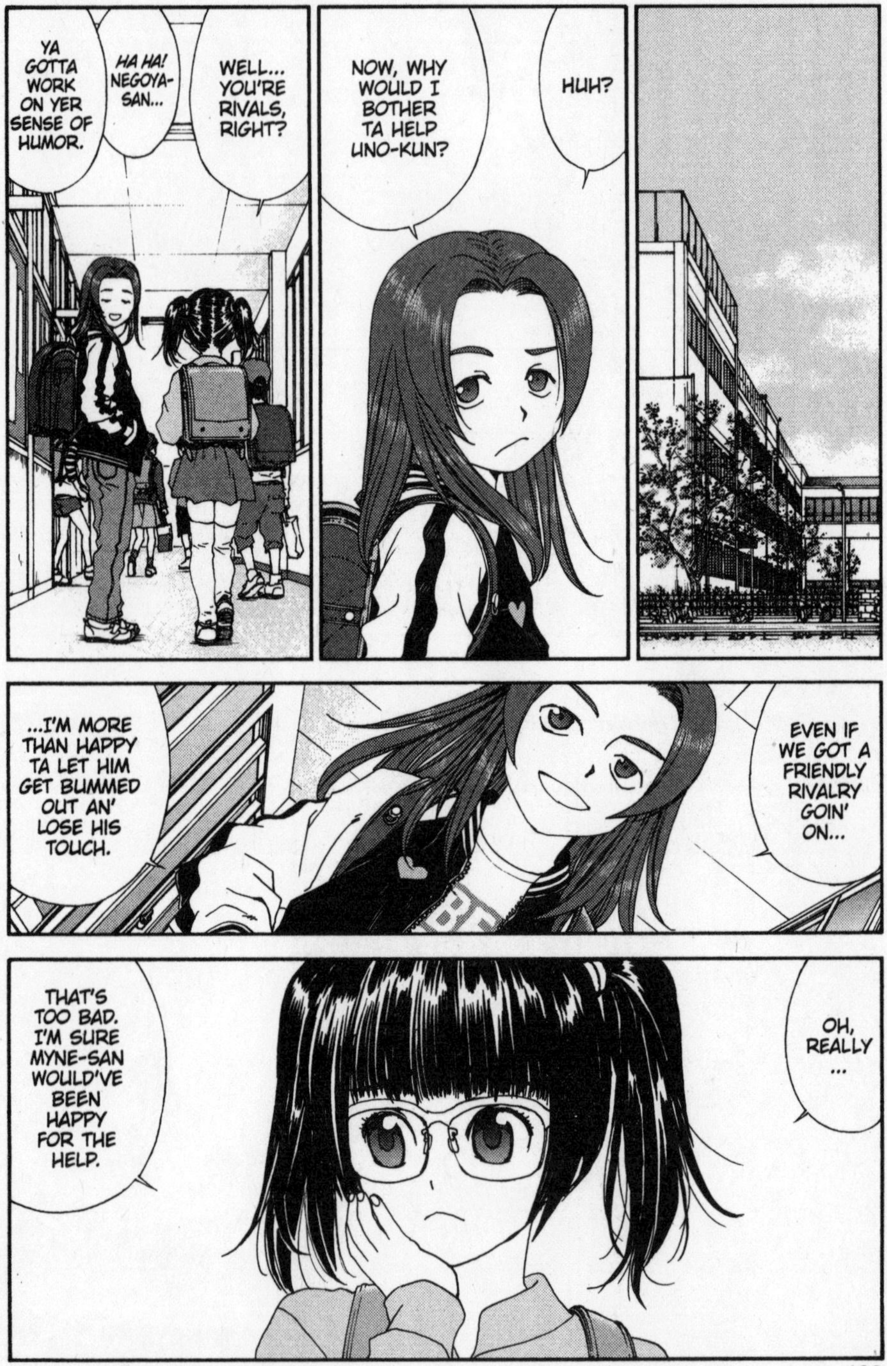
NOW, WHY WOULD I BOTHER TA HELP UNO-KUN?
HUH?
WELL... YOU'RE RIVALS, RIGHT?
HA HA! NEGOYA-SAN...
YA GOTTA WORK ON YER SENSE OF HUMOR.
EVEN IF WE GOT A FRIENDLY RIVALRY GOIN' ON...
...I'M MORE THAN HAPPY TA LET HIM GET BUMMED OUT AN' LOSE HIS TOUCH.
OH, REALLY ...
THAT'S TOO BAD. I'M SURE MYNE-SAN WOULD'VE BEEN HAPPY FOR THE HELP.

SEE, *NOW* YA GOT MY ATTENTION.

COME AGAIN?

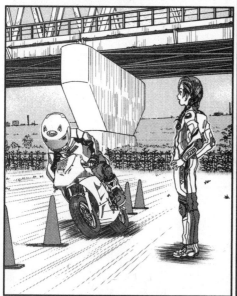

HE'S SO EASY...

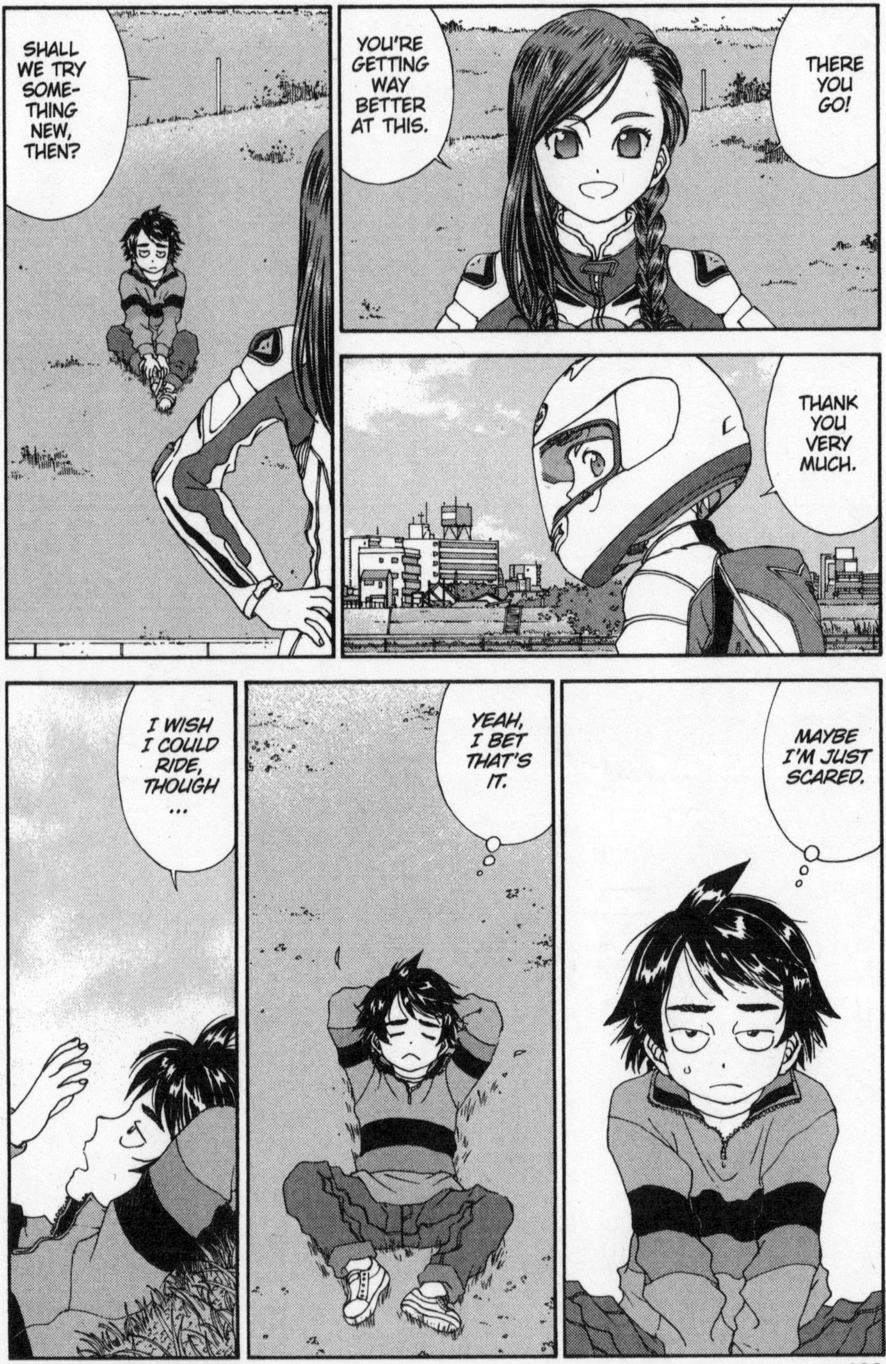
THERE YOU GO!
YOU'RE GETTING WAY BETTER AT THIS.
THANK YOU VERY MUCH.
SHALL WE TRY SOME-THING NEW, THEN?
MAYBE I'M JUST SCARED.
YEAH, I BET THAT'S IT.
I WISH I COULD RIDE, THOUGH ...

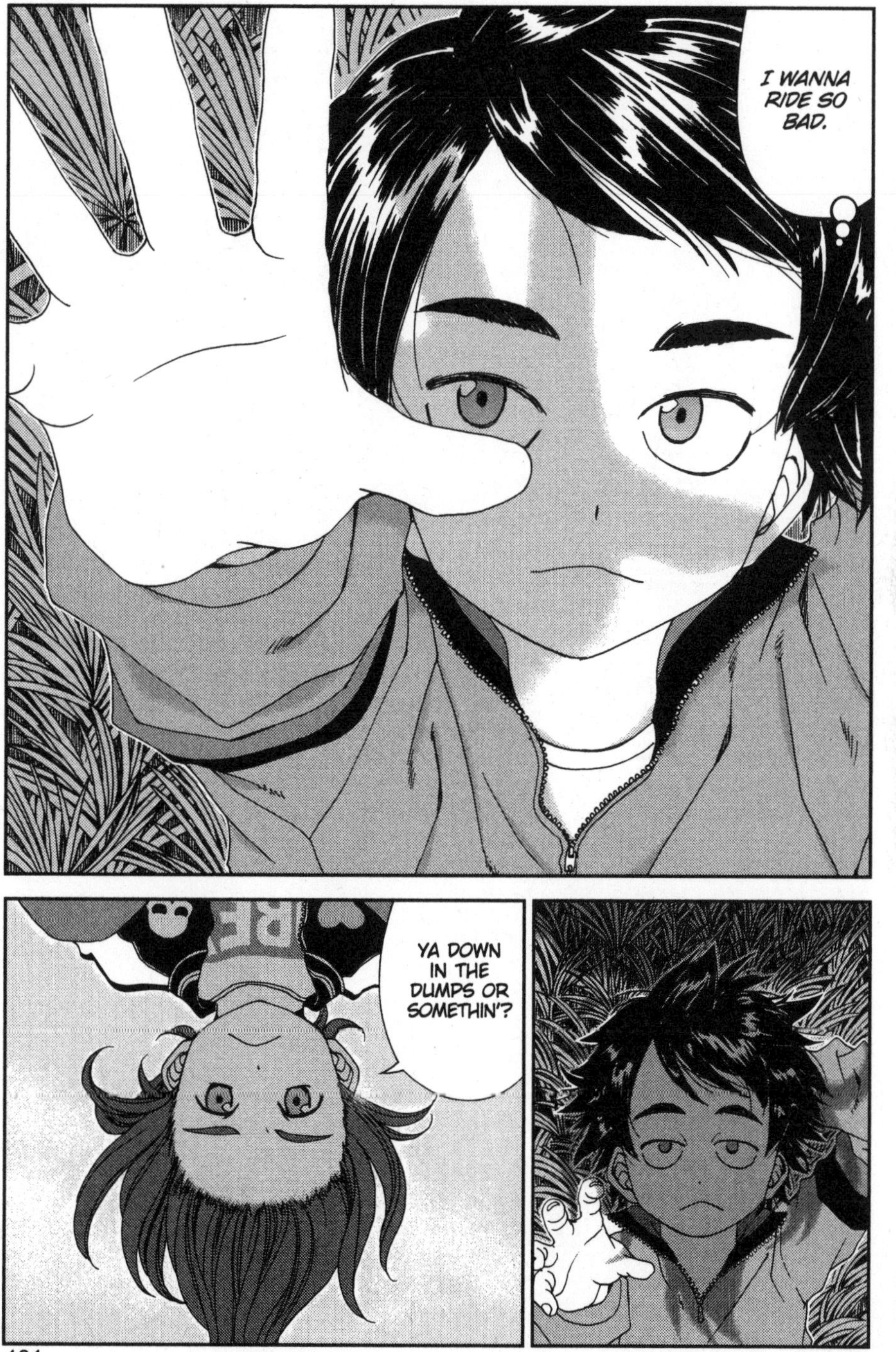
I WANNA RIDE SO BAD.
YA DOWN IN THE DUMPS OR SOMETHIN'?

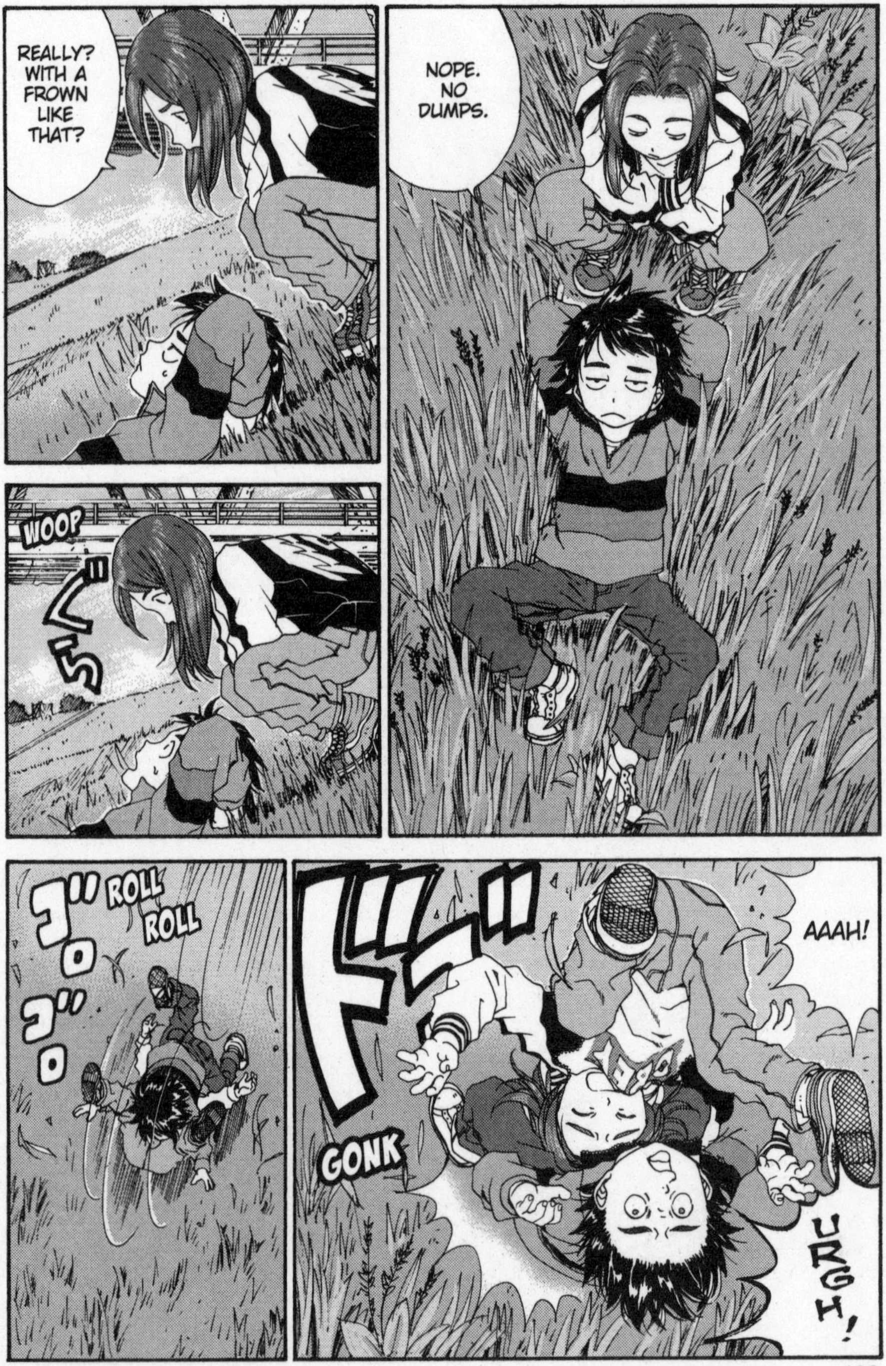
NOPE. NO DUMPS.
REALLY? WITH A FROWN LIKE THAT?
WOOP
AAAH!
GONK
URGH!
ROLL ROLL

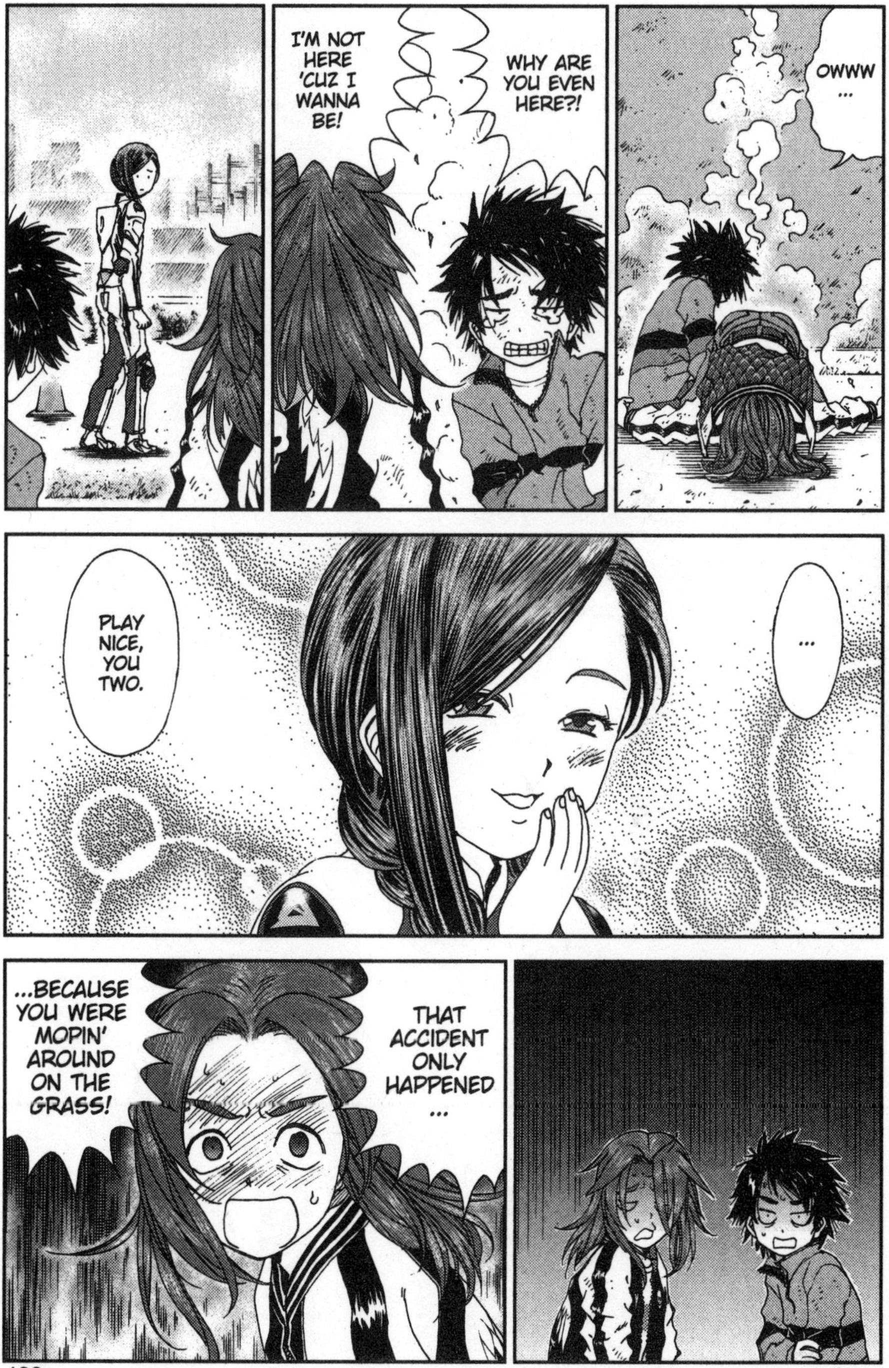
OWWW ...
WHY ARE YOU EVEN HERE?!
I'M NOT HERE 'CUZ I WANNA BE!
...
PLAY NICE, YOU TWO.
THAT ACCIDENT ONLY HAPPENED ...
...BECAUSE YOU WERE MOPIN' AROUND ON THE GRASS!

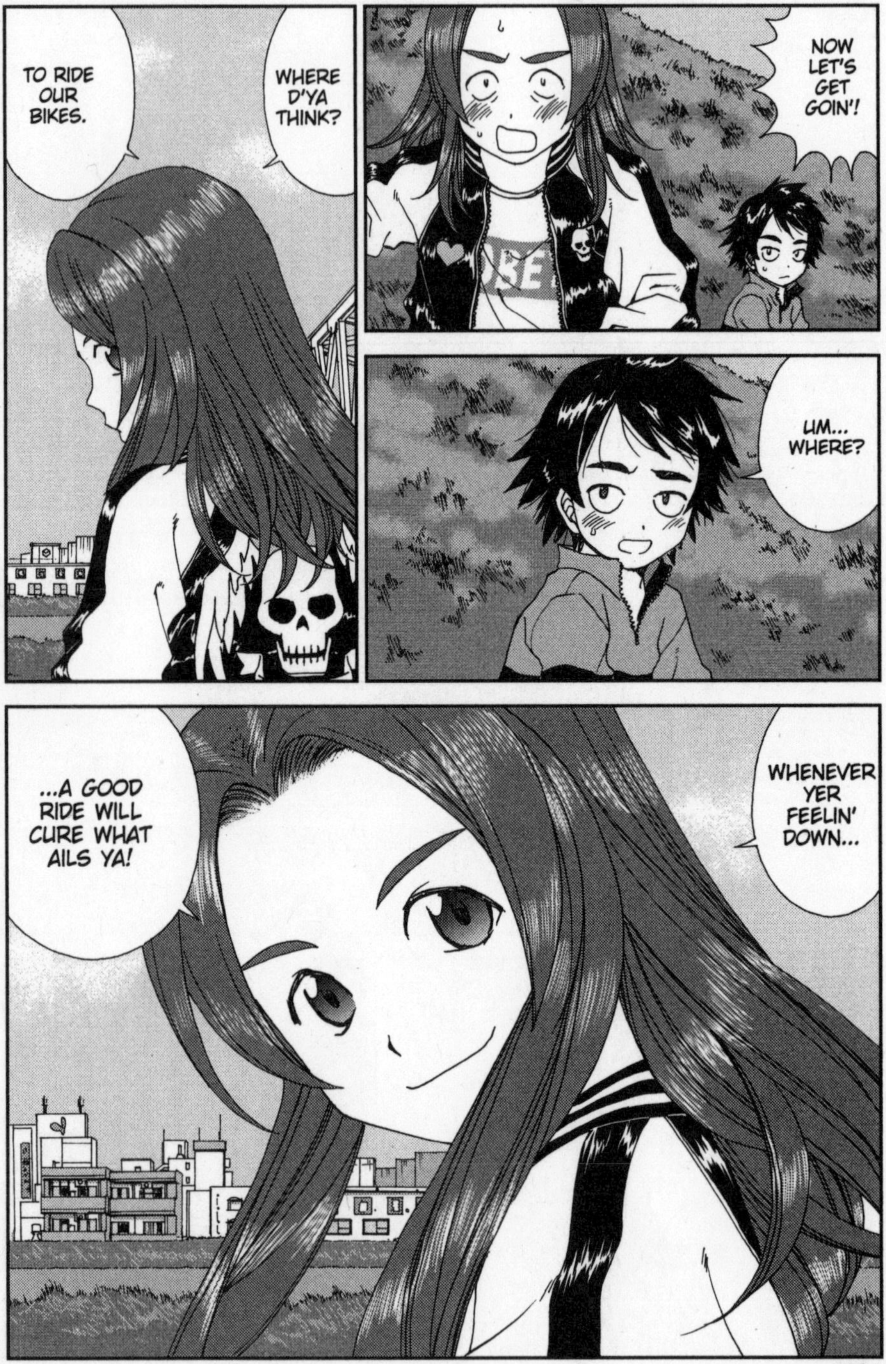
NOW LET'S GET GOIN'!
UM... WHERE?
WHERE D'YA THINK?
TO RIDE OUR BIKES.
WHENEVER YER FEELIN' DOWN...
...A GOOD RIDE WILL CURE WHAT AILS YA!

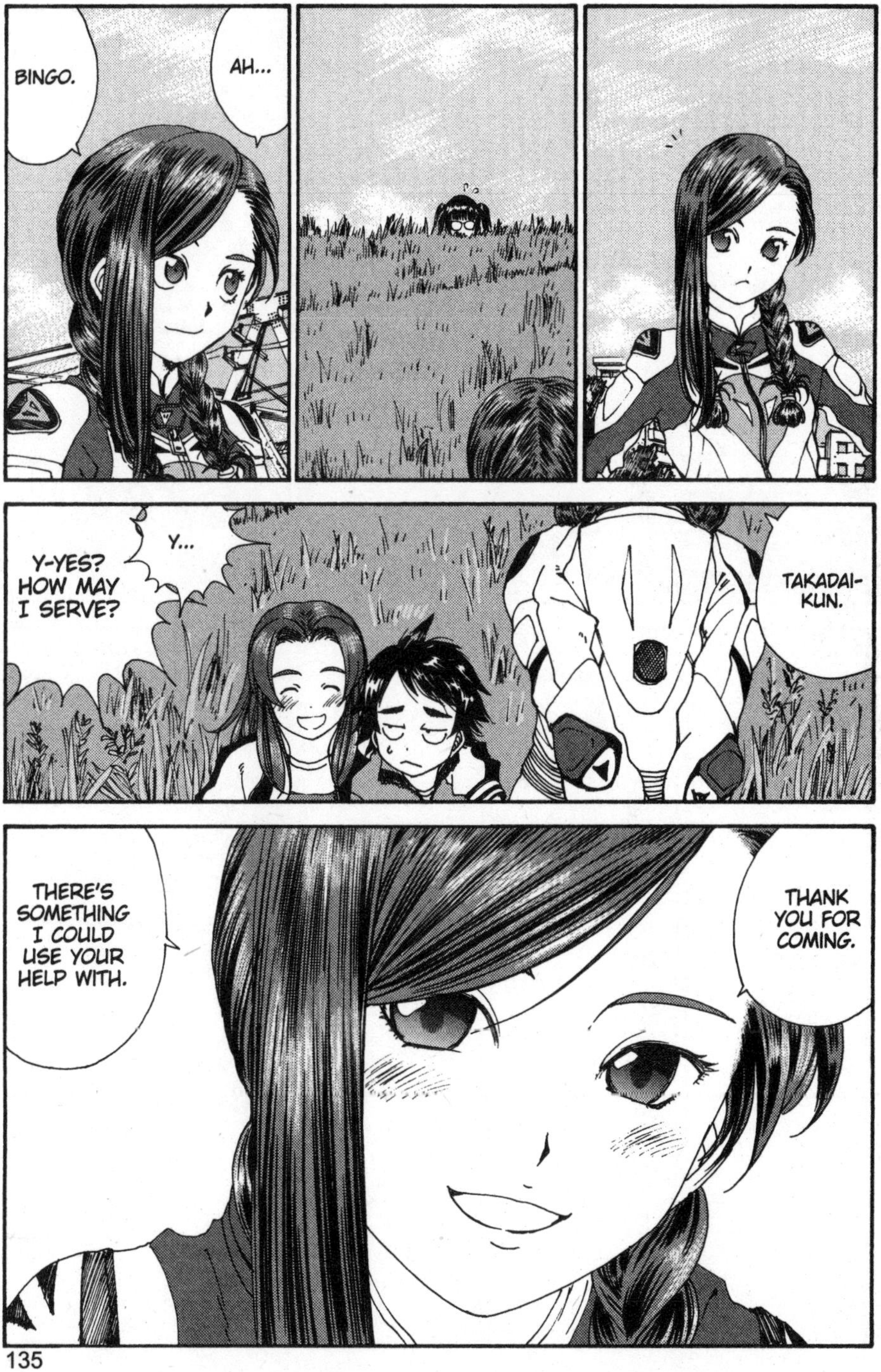
AH...
BINGO.
TAKADAI-KUN.
Y...
Y-YES? HOW MAY I SERVE?
THANK YOU FOR COMING.
THERE'S SOMETHING I COULD USE YOUR HELP WITH.

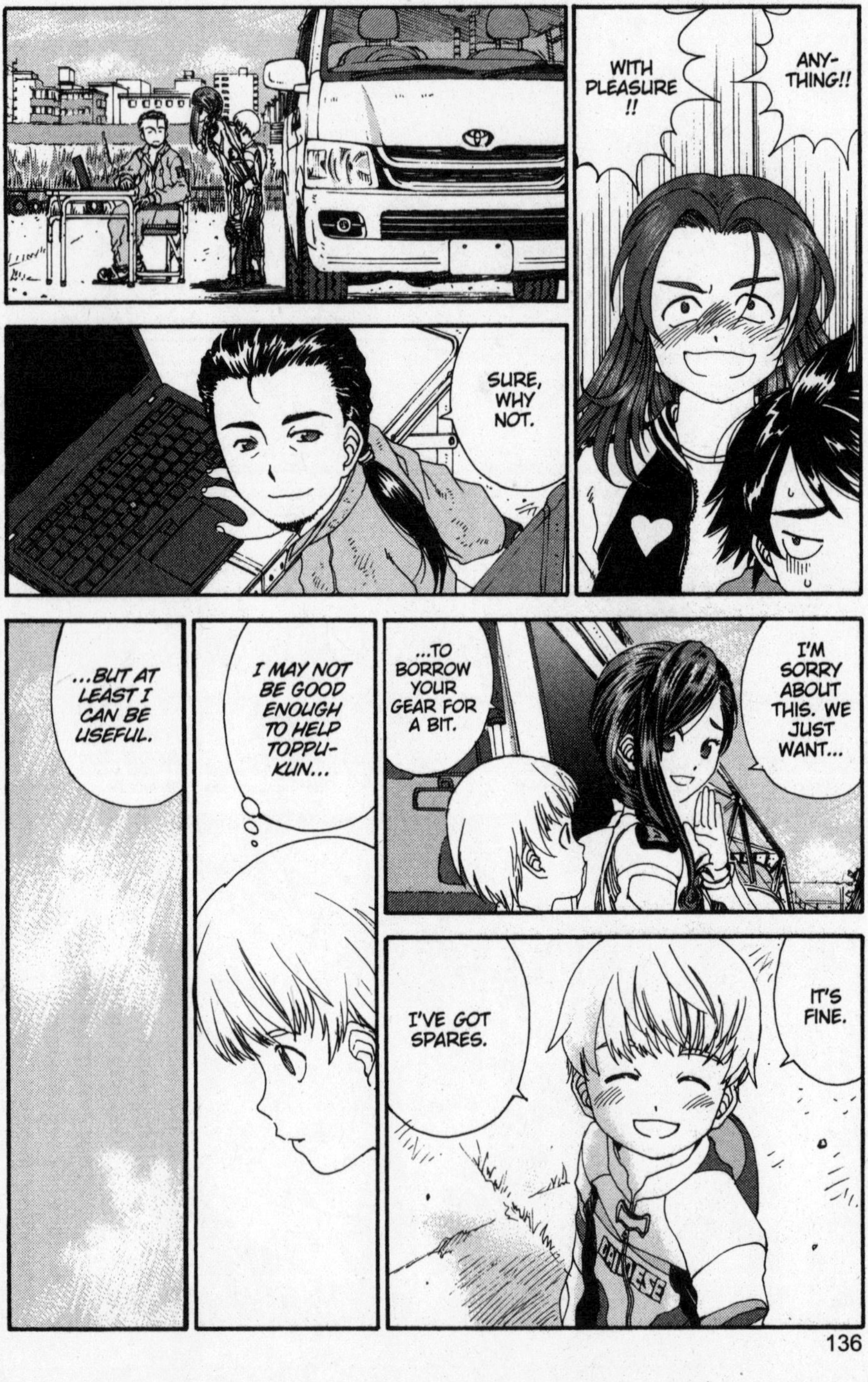
ANY-THING!!
WITH PLEASURE !!
SURE, WHY NOT.
I'M SORRY ABOUT THIS. WE JUST WANT...
...TO BORROW YOUR GEAR FOR A BIT.
IT'S FINE.
I'VE GOT SPARES.
I MAY NOT BE GOOD ENOUGH TO HELP TOPPU-KUN...
...BUT AT LEAST I CAN BE USEFUL.

IT FITS. JUST BARELY.
AS LONG AS I GET TO RIDE...
...I DON'T CARE!!
ALL RIGHT, BOYS!
OVER HERE.

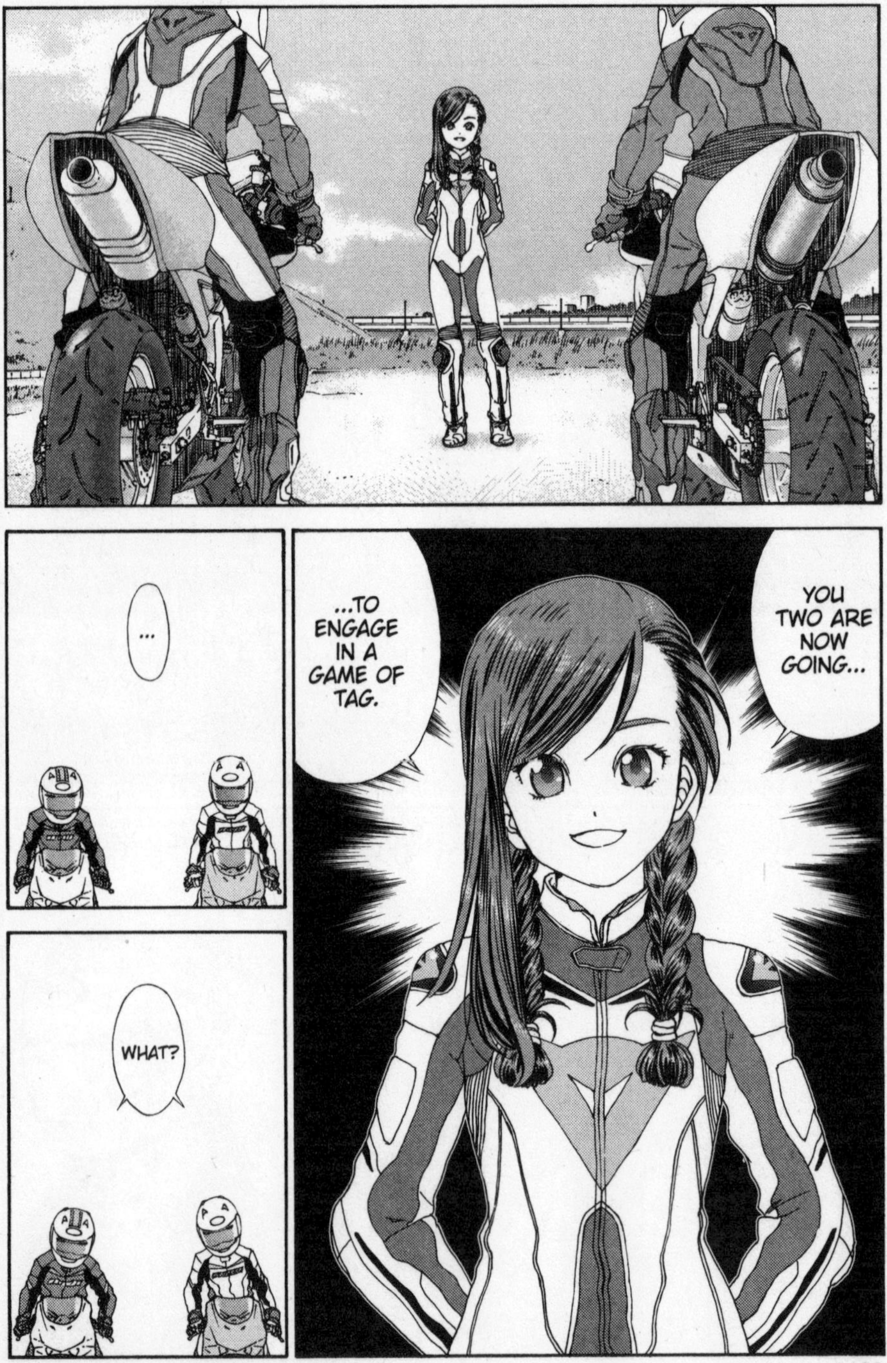
...
YOU TWO ARE NOW GOING...
...TO ENGAGE IN A GAME OF TAG.
...
WHAT?

Lap 19: end

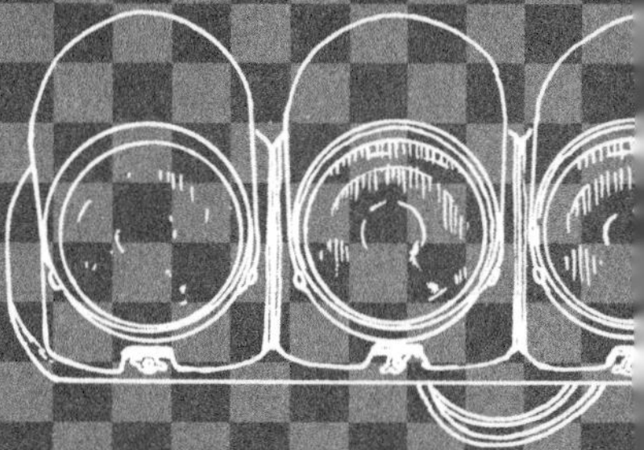

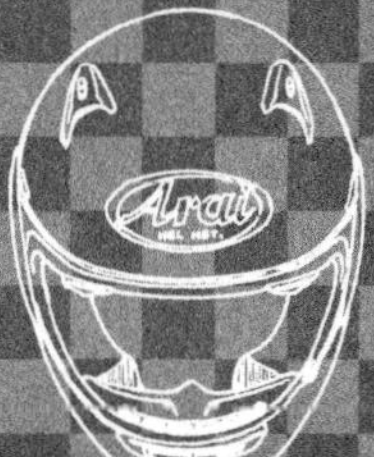
Arai

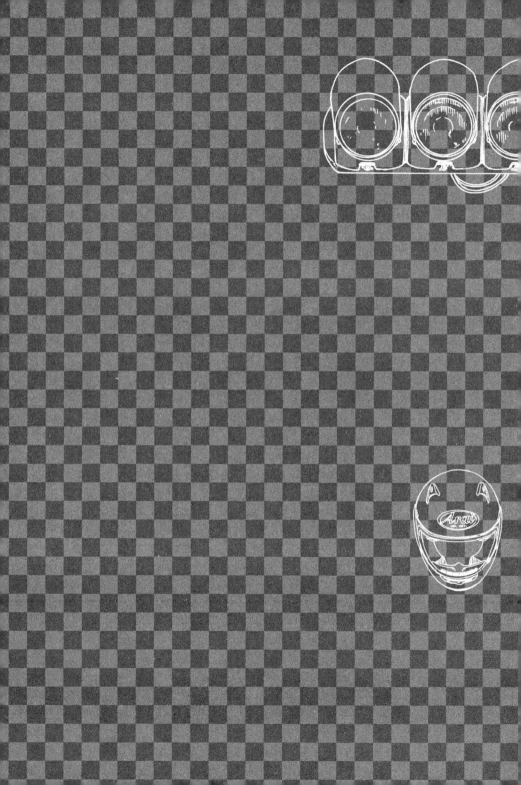

TOPPU GP

Lap 20:

PLAYING TAG

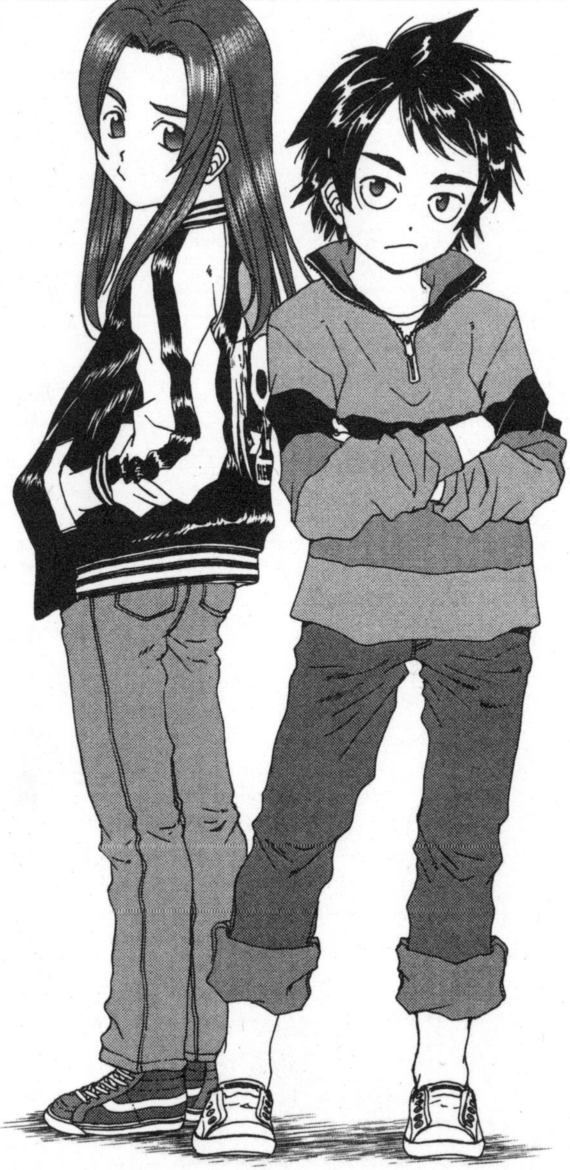

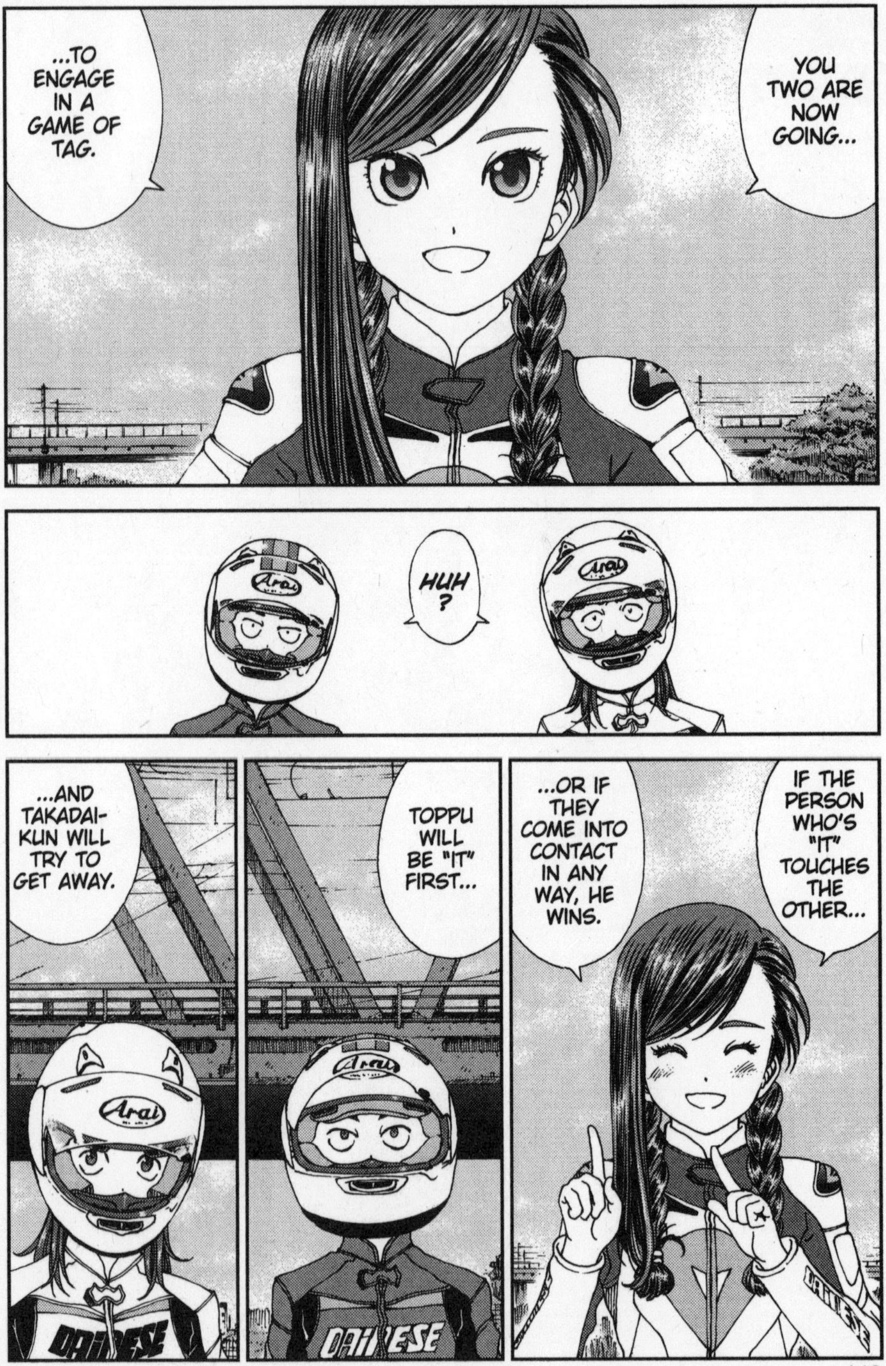
YOU TWO ARE NOW GOING...
...TO ENGAGE IN A GAME OF TAG.
HUH?
IF THE PERSON WHO'S "IT" TOUCHES THE OTHER...
...OR IF THEY COME INTO CONTACT IN ANY WAY, HE WINS.
TOPPU WILL BE "IT" FIRST...
...AND TAKADAI-KUN WILL TRY TO GET AWAY.

HUH?
BUT ISN'T THAT DAN-GEROUS? WE'RE COLLIDING.
WHAT?
YOU'RE CRAZY, PAL.
OH, YEAH?
YOU CAN'T HIT ME. NOT WITH **YOUR** CRAPPY RIDING.

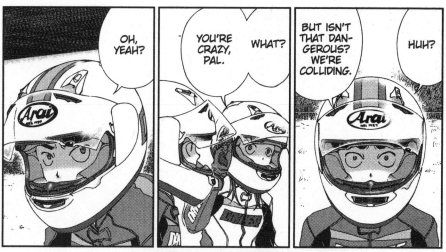

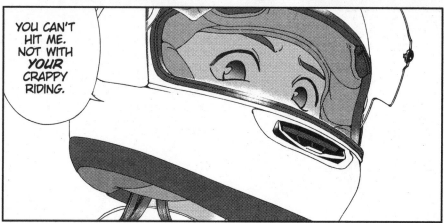

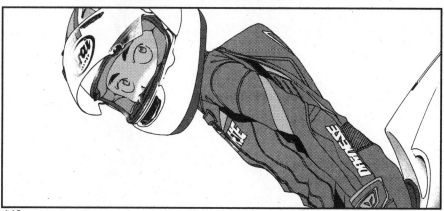

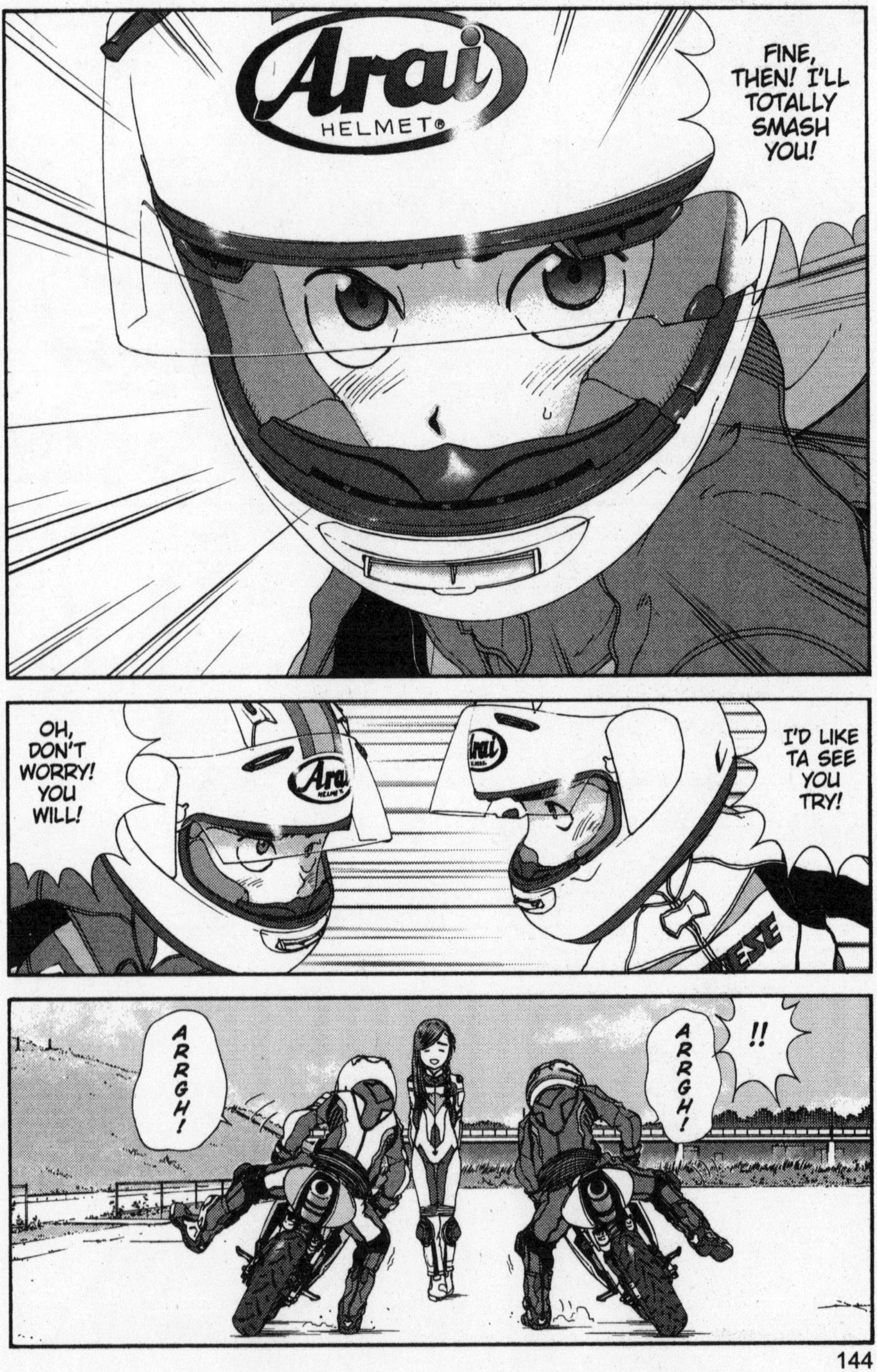
FINE, THEN! I'LL TOTALLY SMASH YOU!
I'D LIKE TA SEE YOU TRY!
OH, DON'T WORRY! YOU WILL!
!!
ARRGH!
ARRGH!

SWITCH AFTER THREE MINUTES!
READY ...
GO!!

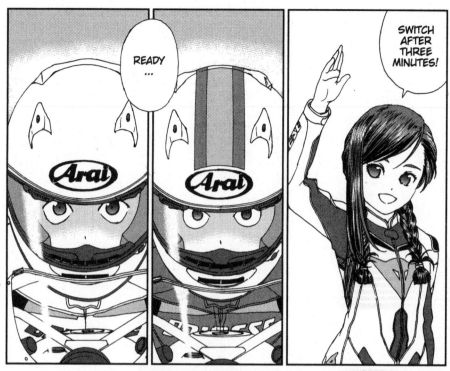

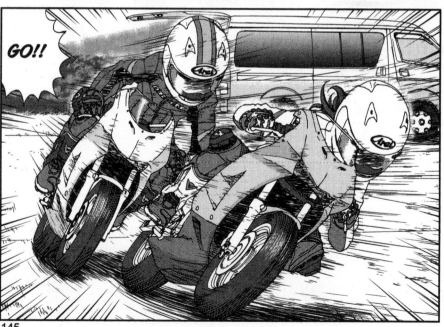

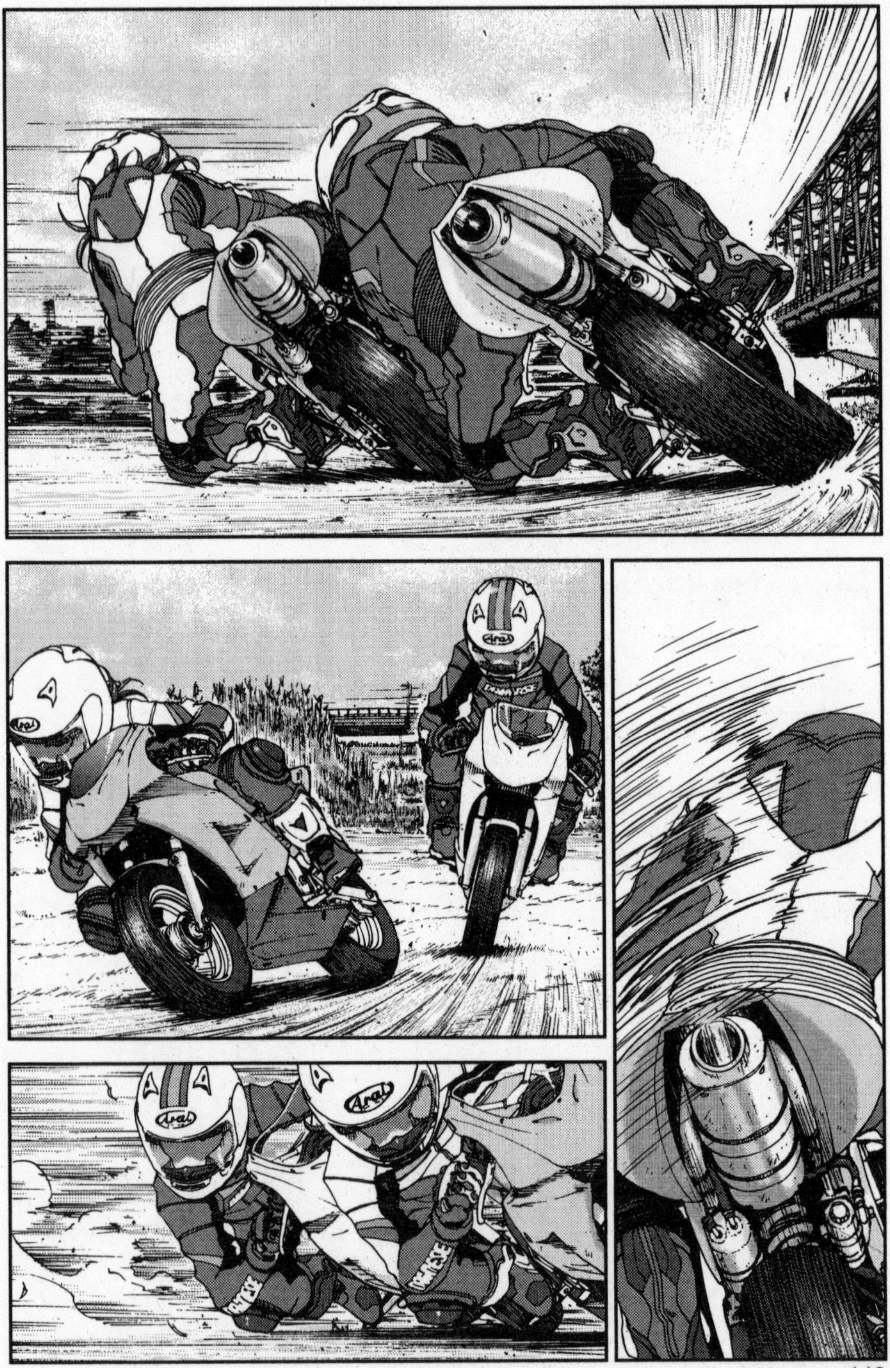

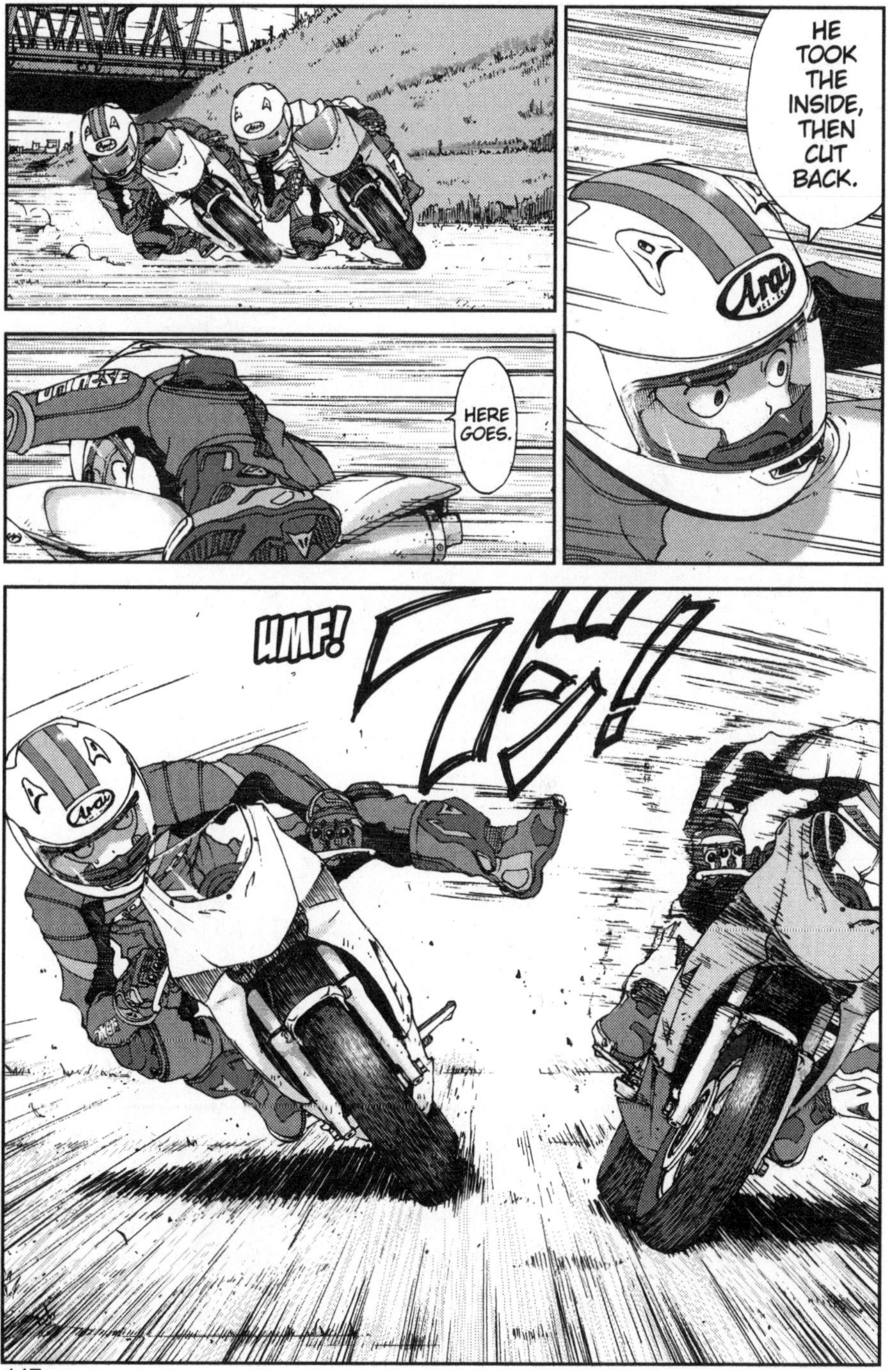
HE TOOK THE INSIDE, THEN CUT BACK.
HERE GOES.
UMF!

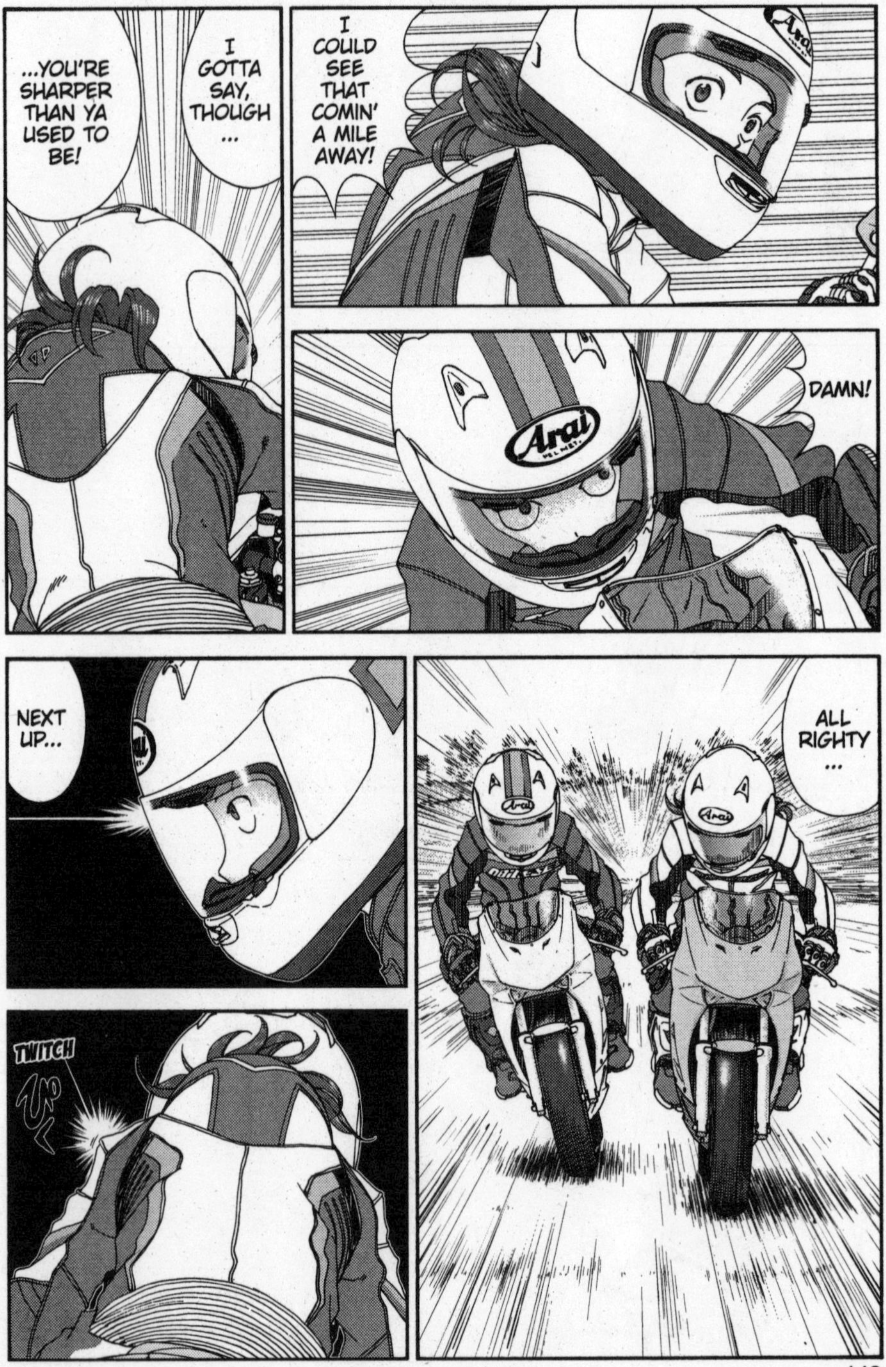
I COULD SEE THAT COMIN' A MILE AWAY!
DAMN!
I GOTTA SAY, THOUGH...
...YOU'RE SHARPER THAN YA USED TO BE!
ALL RIGHTY...
NEXT UP...
TWITCH

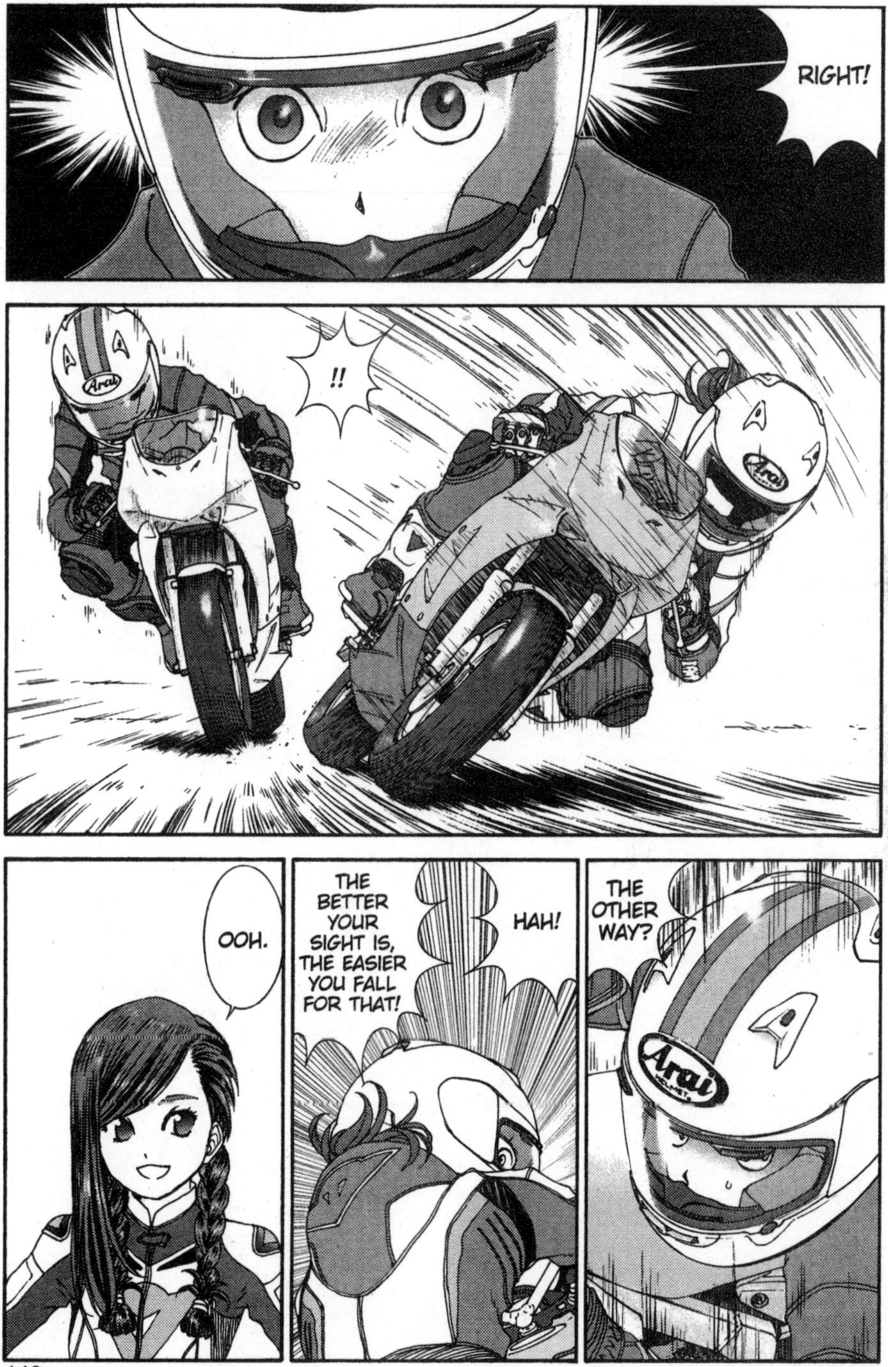
RIGHT!
!!
HAH!
THE BETTER YOUR SIGHT IS, THE EASIER YOU FALL FOR THAT!
THE OTHER WAY?
OOH.

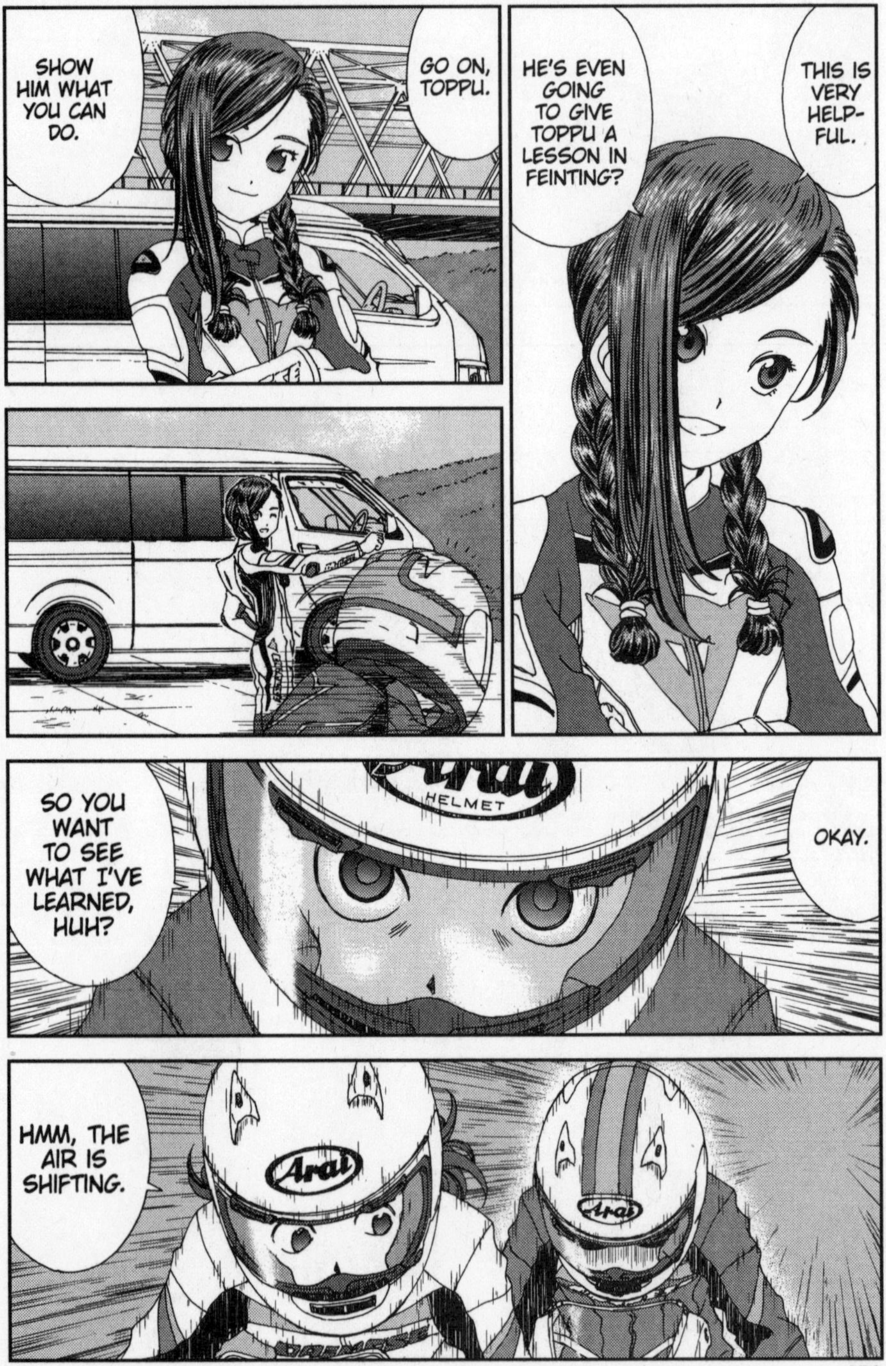
THIS IS VERY HELP-FUL.
HE'S EVEN GOING TO GIVE TOPPU A LESSON IN FEINTING?
GO ON, TOPPU.
SHOW HIM WHAT YOU CAN DO.
Arai HELMET
OKAY.
SO YOU WANT TO SEE WHAT I'VE LEARNED, HUH?
Arai
Arai
HMM, THE AIR IS SHIFTING.

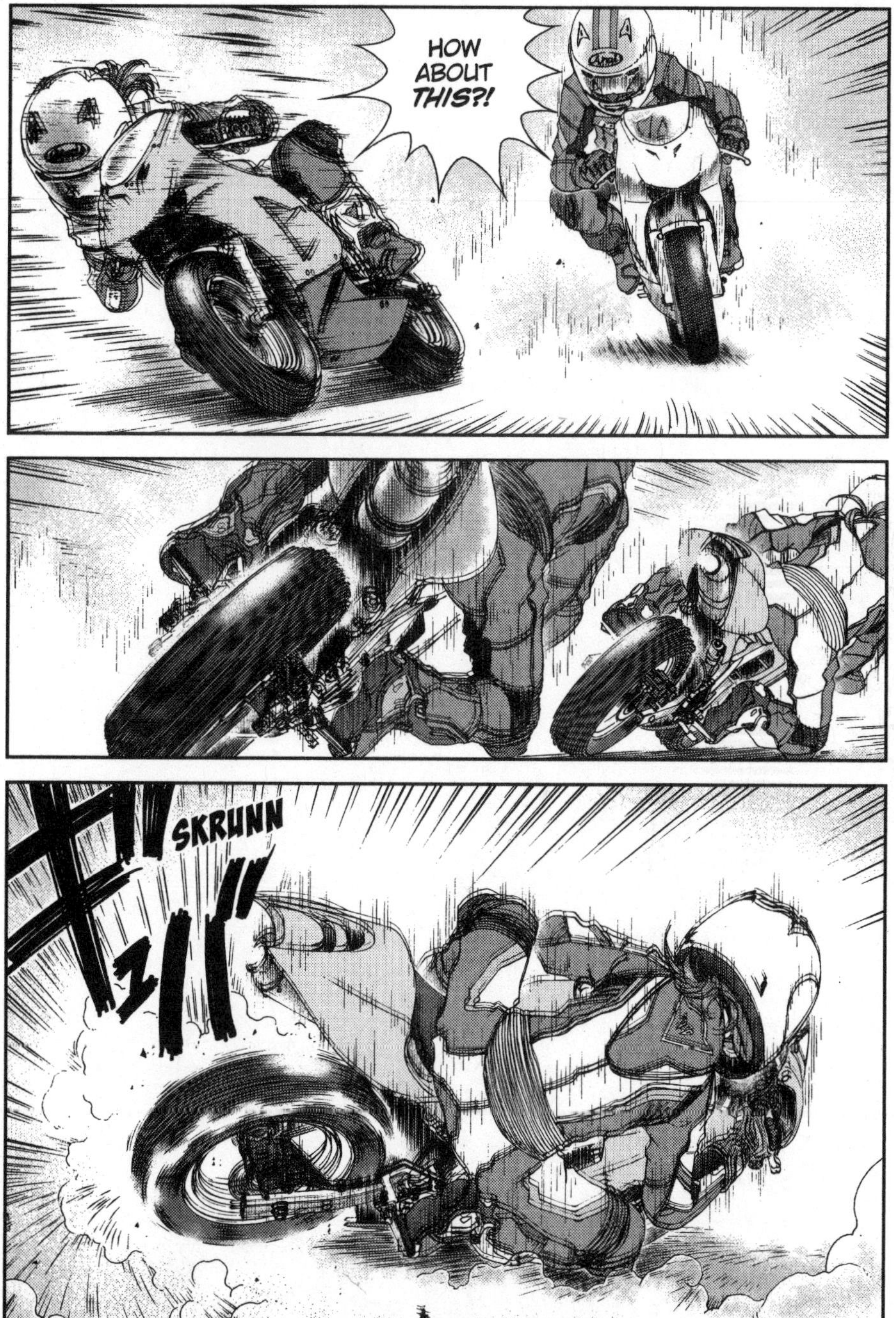
HOW ABOUT THIS?!
SKRUNN

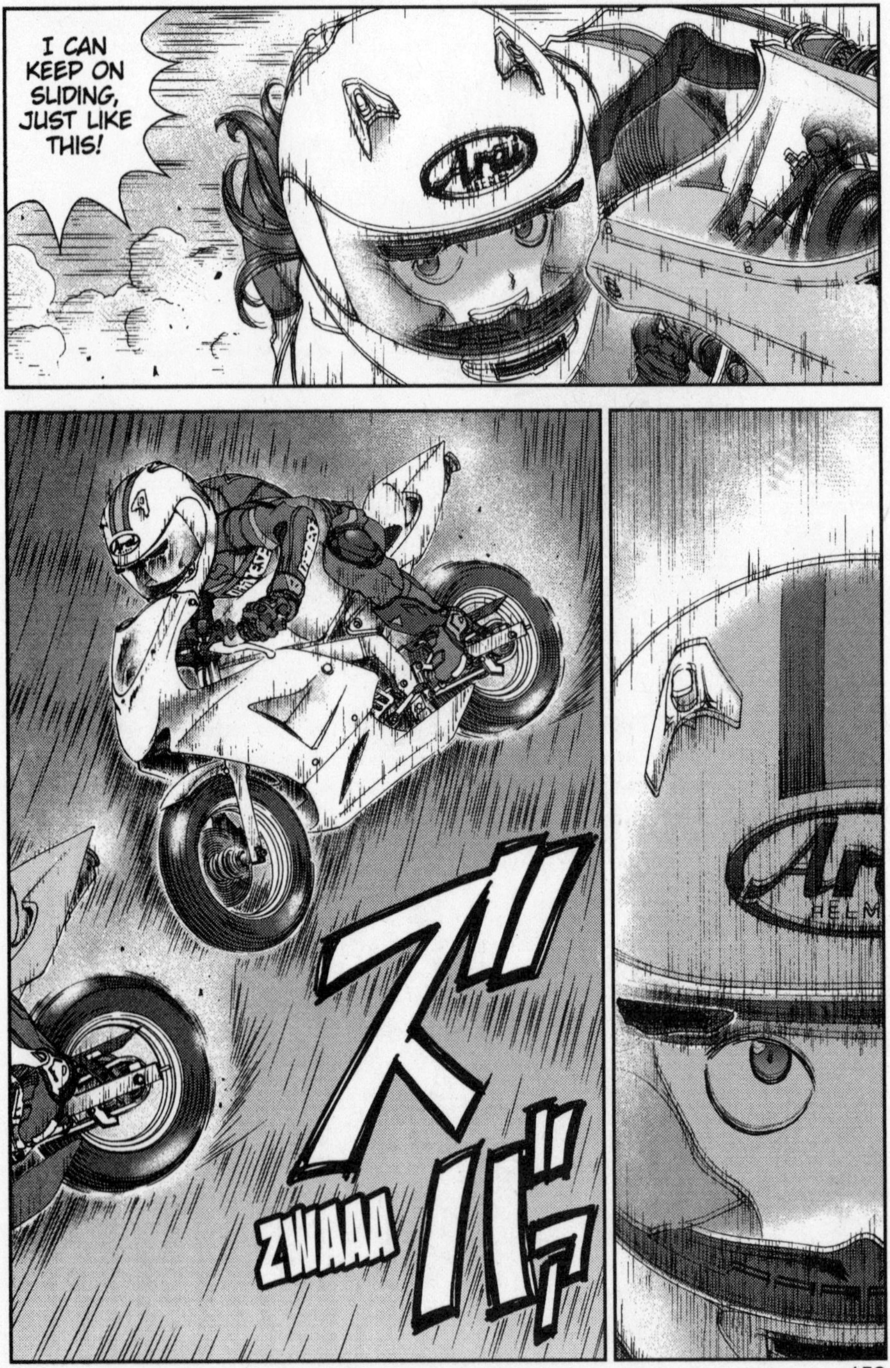
I CAN KEEP ON SLIDING, JUST LIKE THIS!
ズバッ
ZWAAA

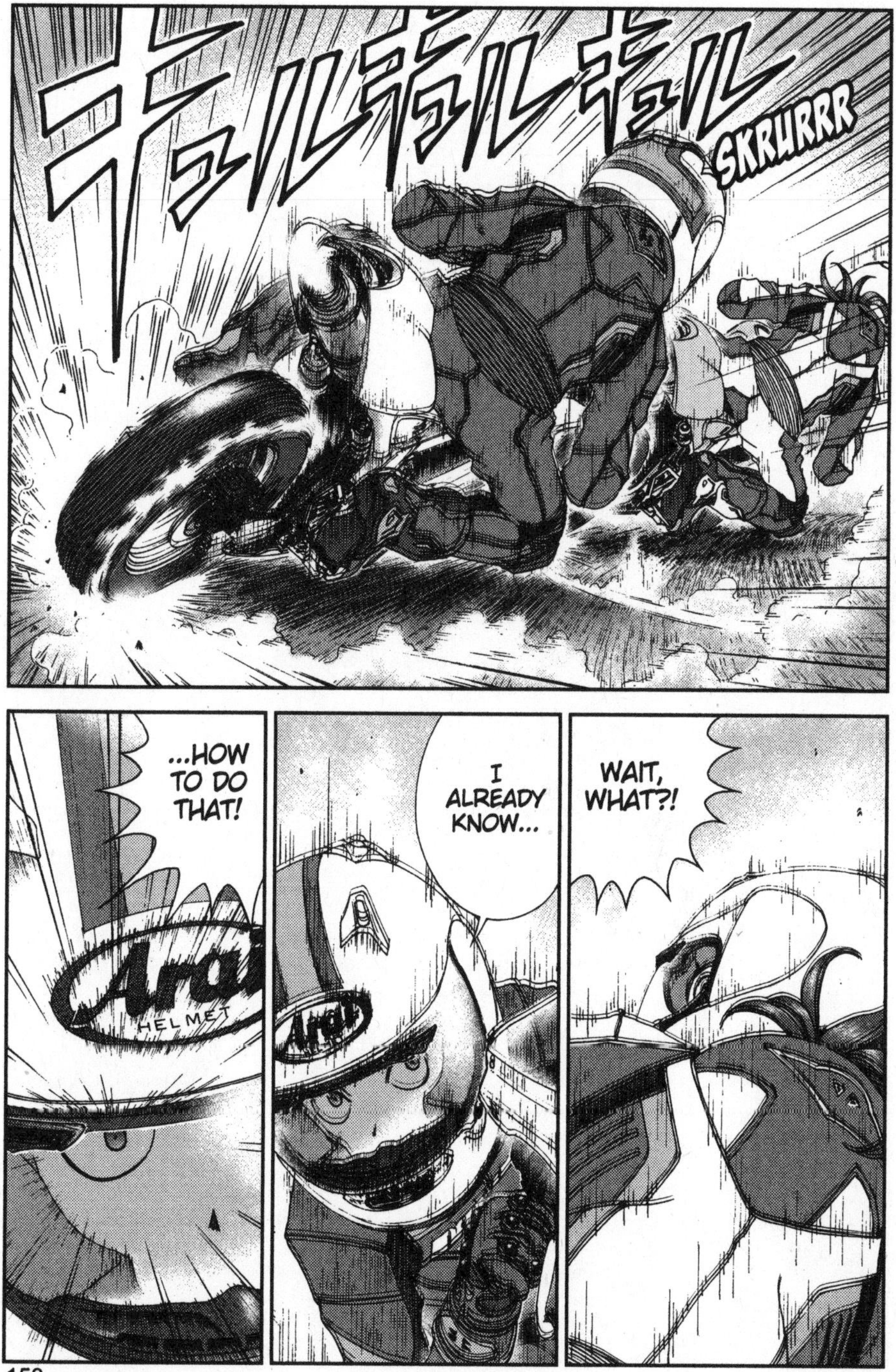
キュルキュルキュル
SKRURRR
WAIT, WHAT?!
I ALREADY KNOW...
Arai
...HOW TO DO THAT!
Arai
HELMET

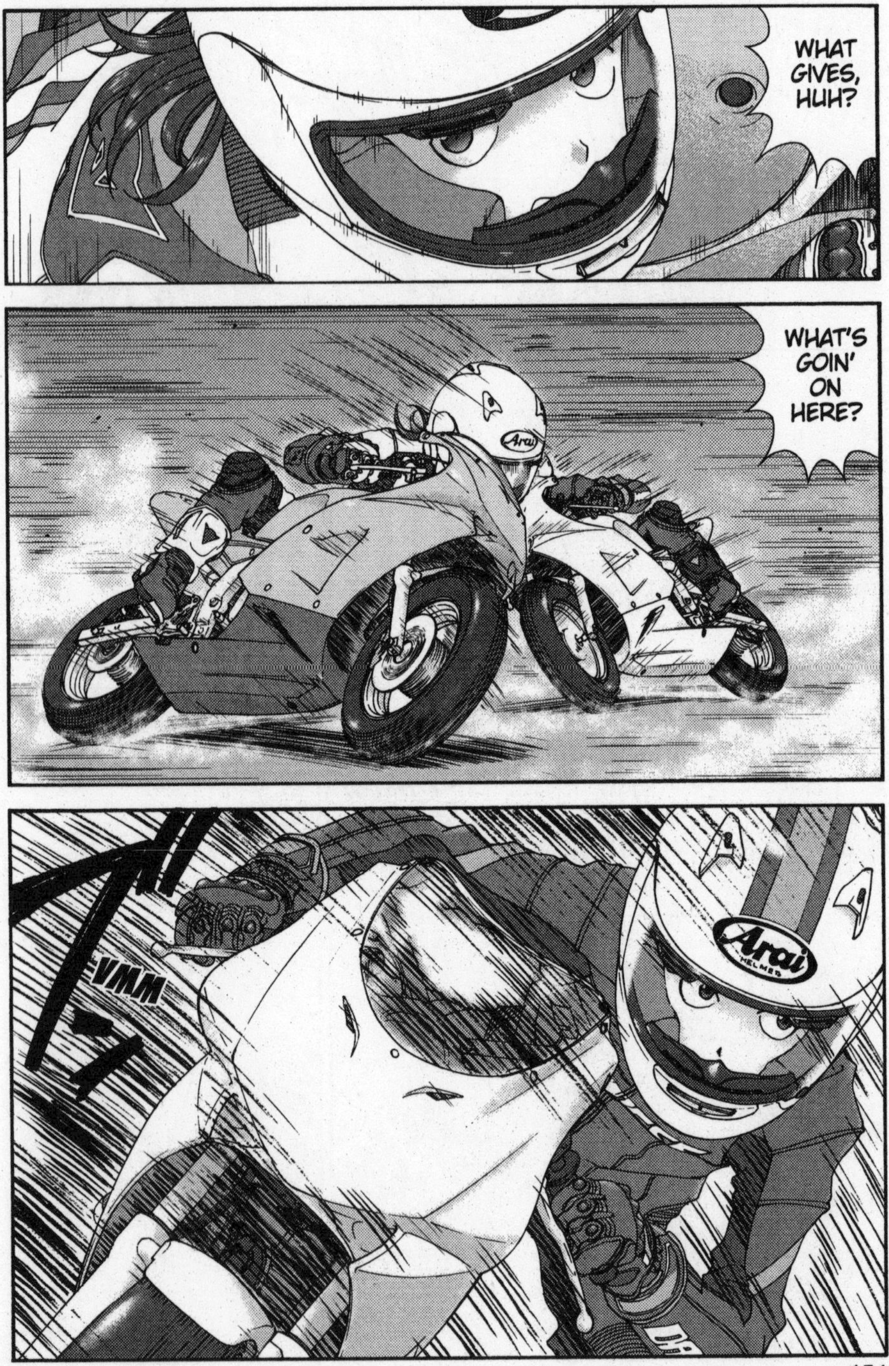
WHAT GIVES, HUH?
WHAT'S GOIN' ON HERE?
VMM

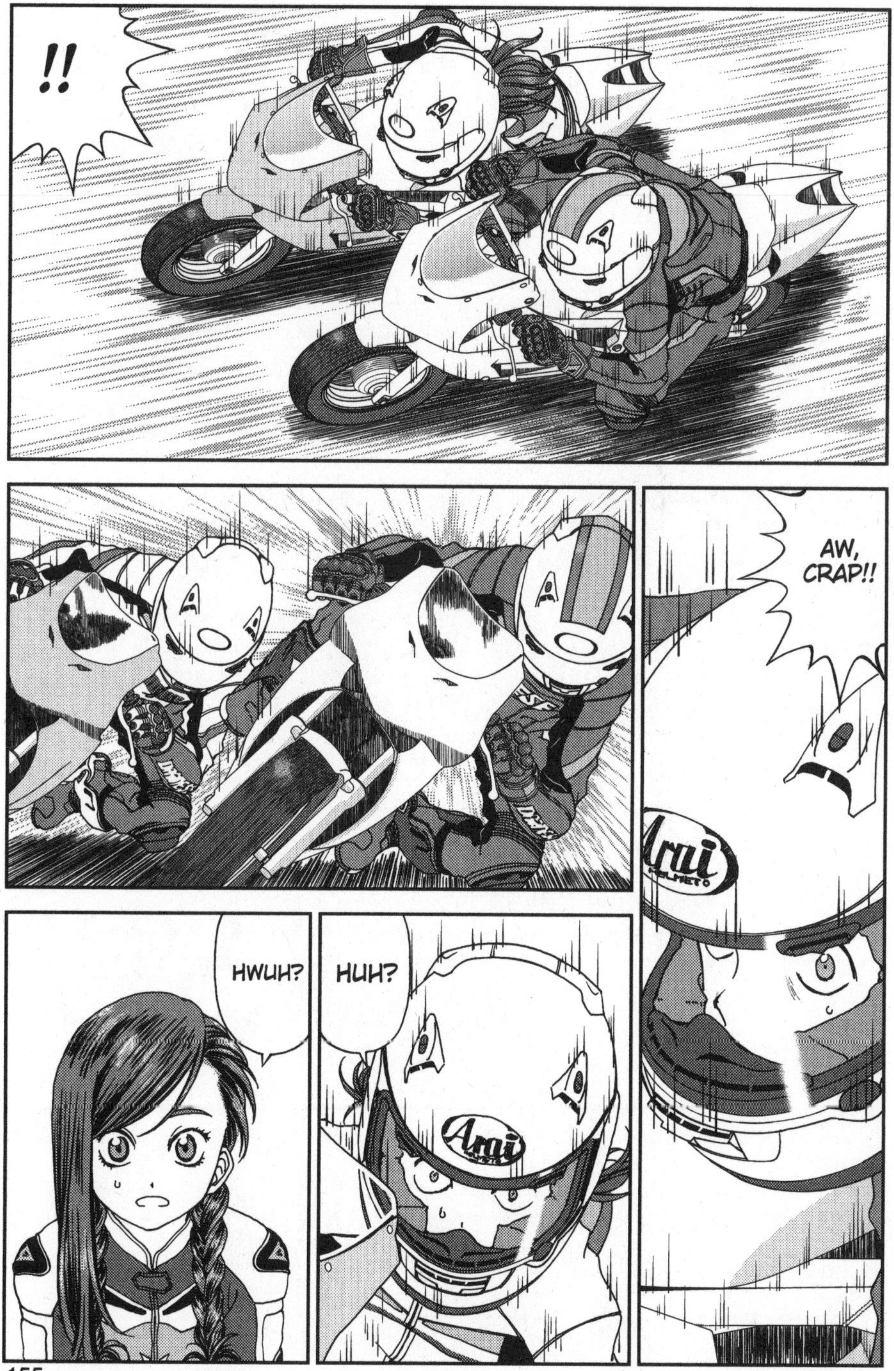
!!
AW, CRAP!!
HUH?
HWUH?

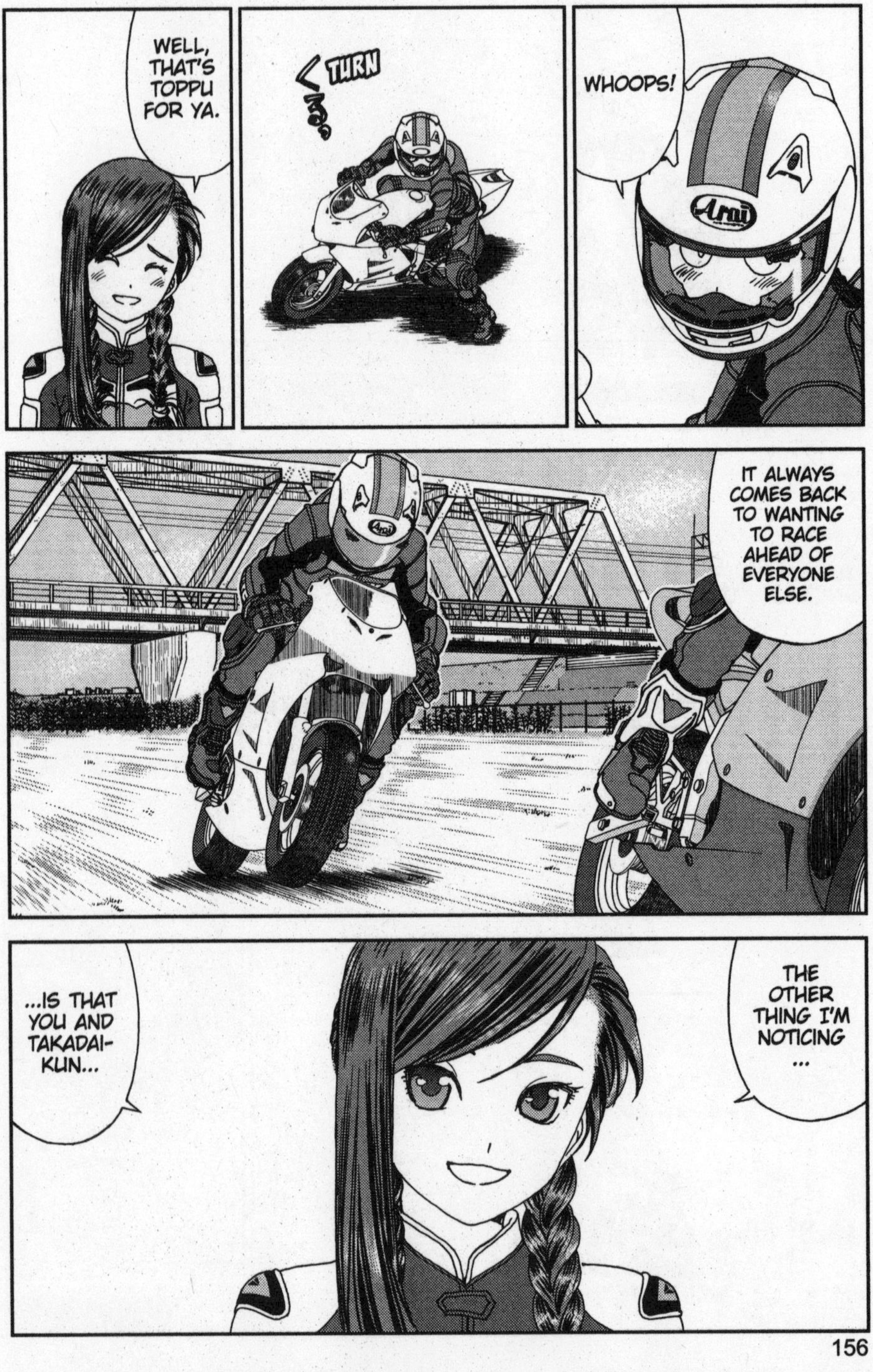
WHOOPS!
TURN
WELL, THAT'S TOPPU FOR YA.
IT ALWAYS COMES BACK TO WANTING TO RACE AHEAD OF EVERYONE ELSE.
THE OTHER THING I'M NOTICING ...
...IS THAT YOU AND TAKADAI-KUN...

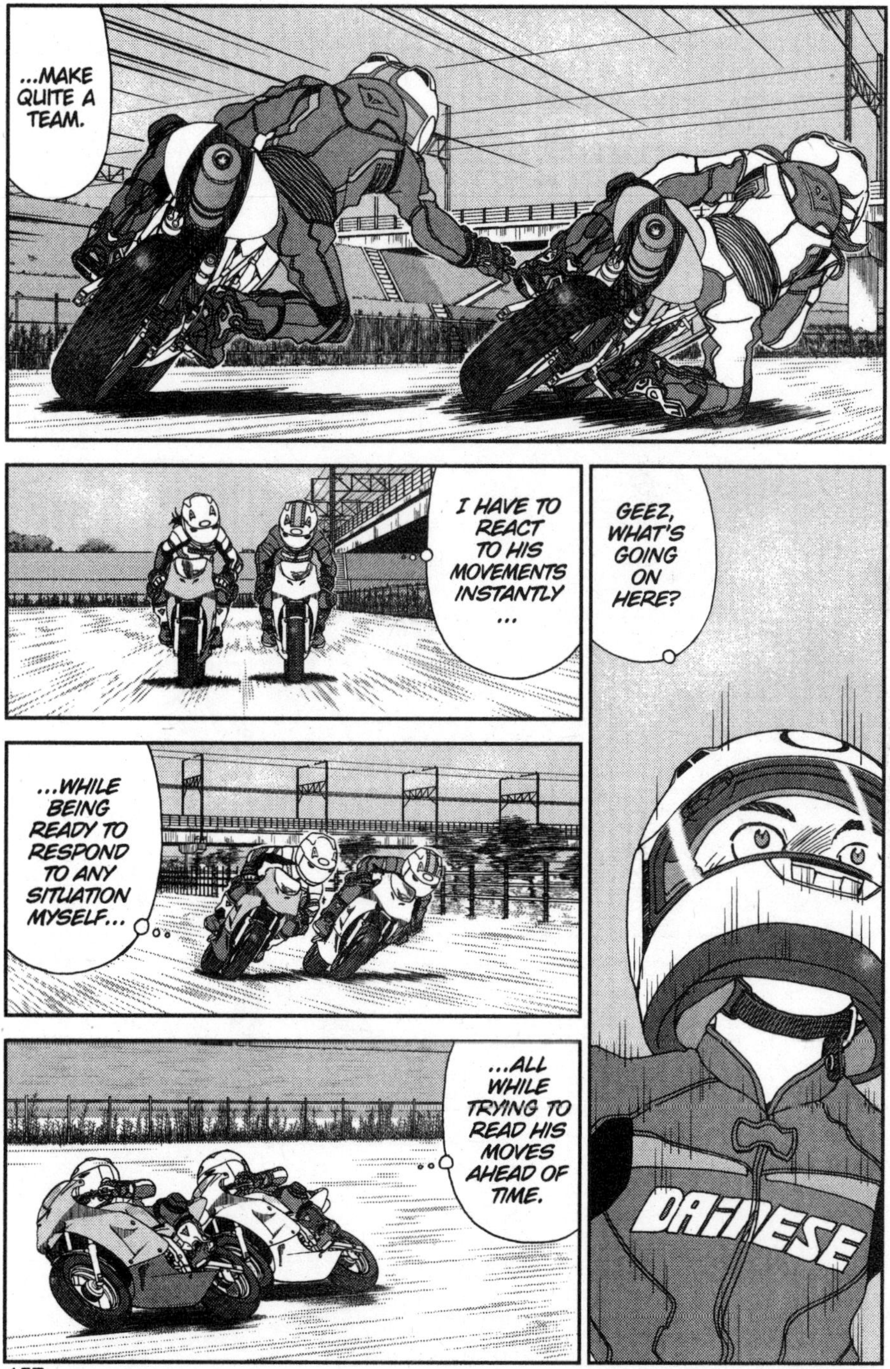
...MAKE QUITE A TEAM.
GEEZ, WHAT'S GOING ON HERE?
I HAVE TO REACT TO HIS MOVEMENTS INSTANTLY ...
...WHILE BEING READY TO RESPOND TO ANY SITUATION MYSELF...
...ALL WHILE TRYING TO READ HIS MOVES AHEAD OF TIME.
DAINESE

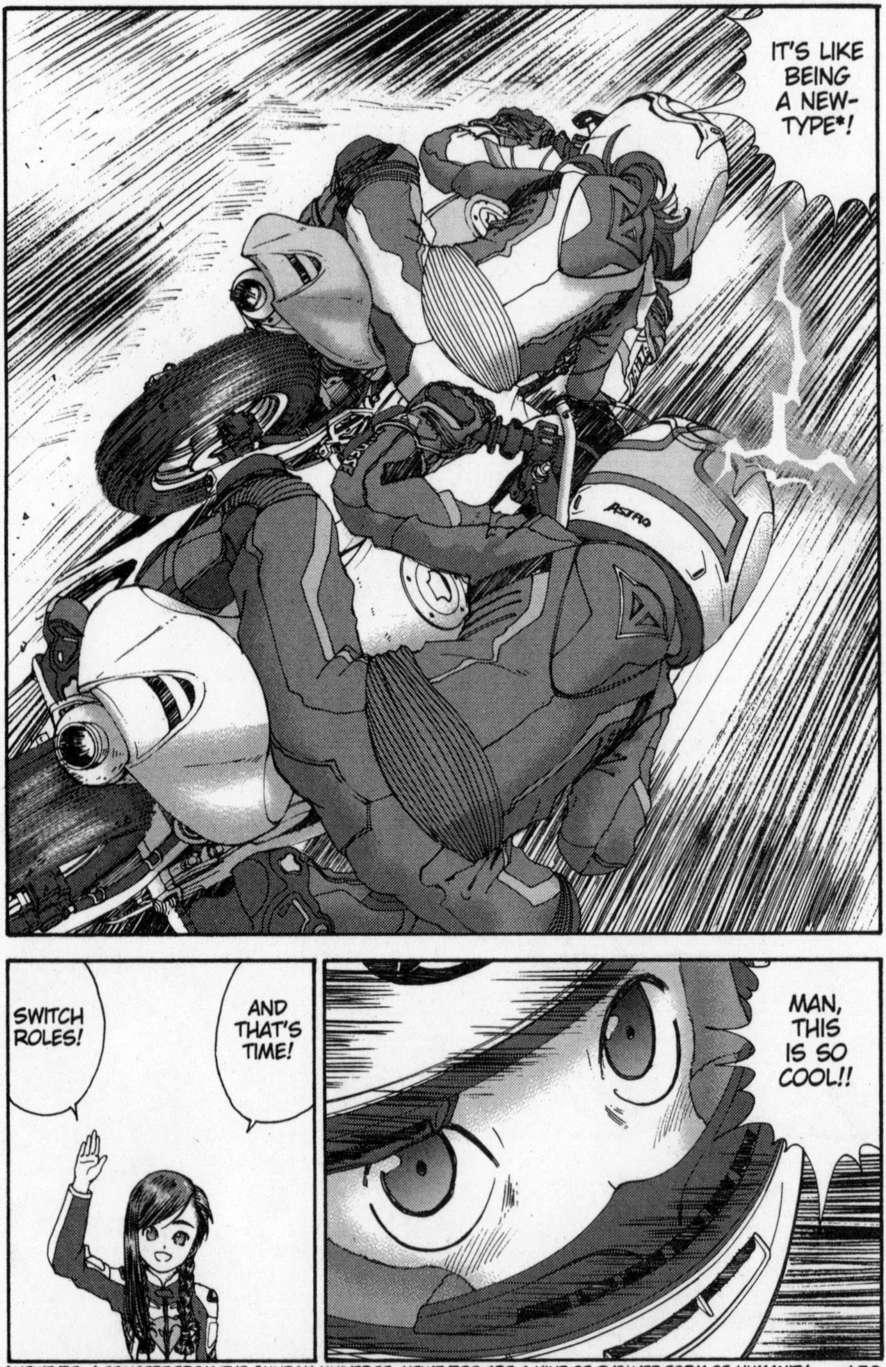
IT'S LIKE BEING A NEW-TYPE*!
MAN, THIS IS SO COOL!!
AND THAT'S TIME!
SWITCH ROLES!

*NEWTYPE: A CONCEPT FROM THE GUNDAM UNIVERSE. NEWTYPES ARE A KIND OF EVOLVED FORM OF HUMANITY THAT IS BETTER SUITED TO LIFE IN SPACE. THEIR SENSES ARE EXTREMELY SHARP AND INTUITIVE, SUCH THAT THEY HAVE SOMETHING OF A SIXTH SENSE ATTUNED TO PEOPLE AROUND THEM, POTENTIAL DANGER, AND SO ON.

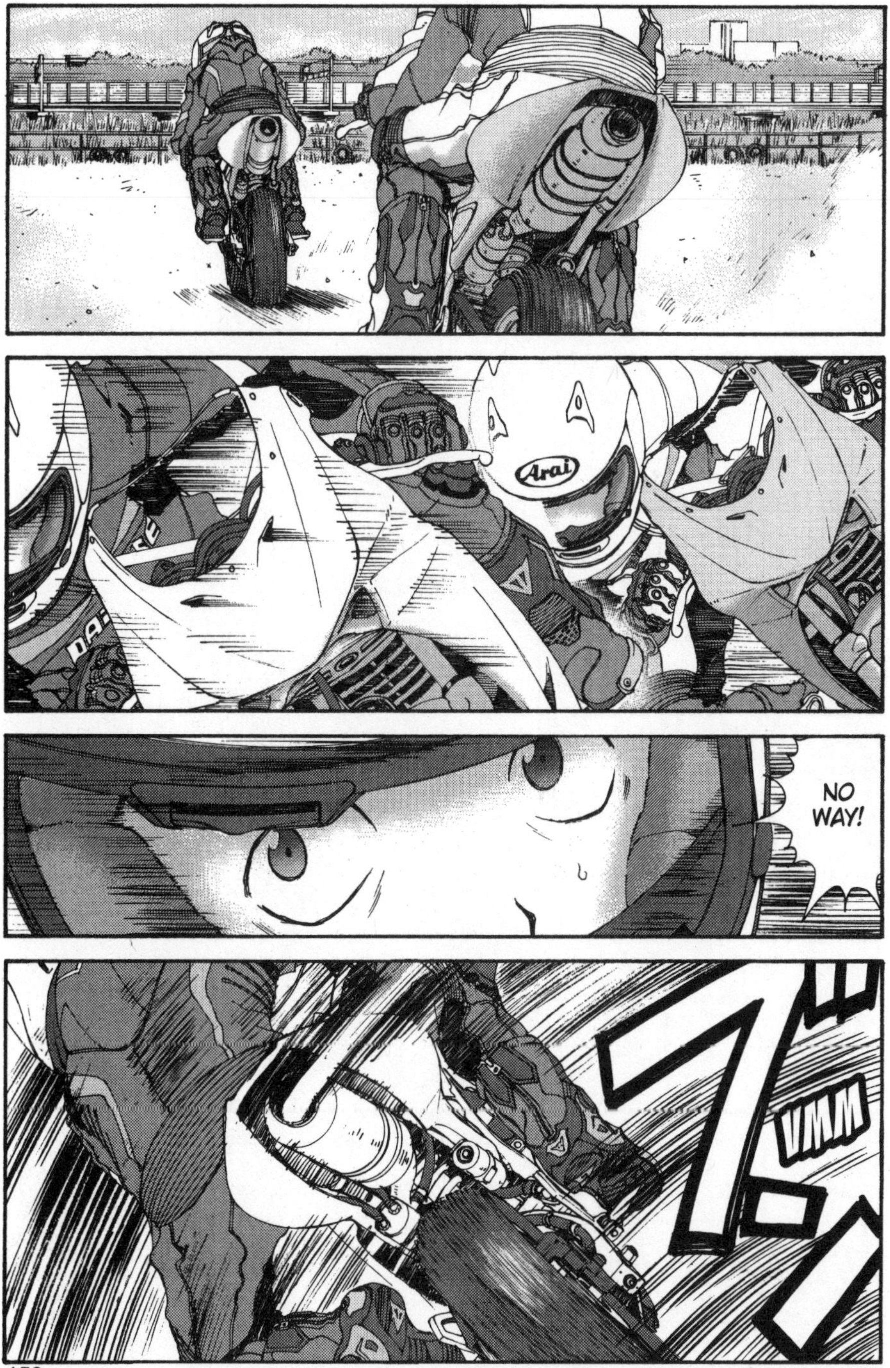
Arai
NO WAY!
VMM

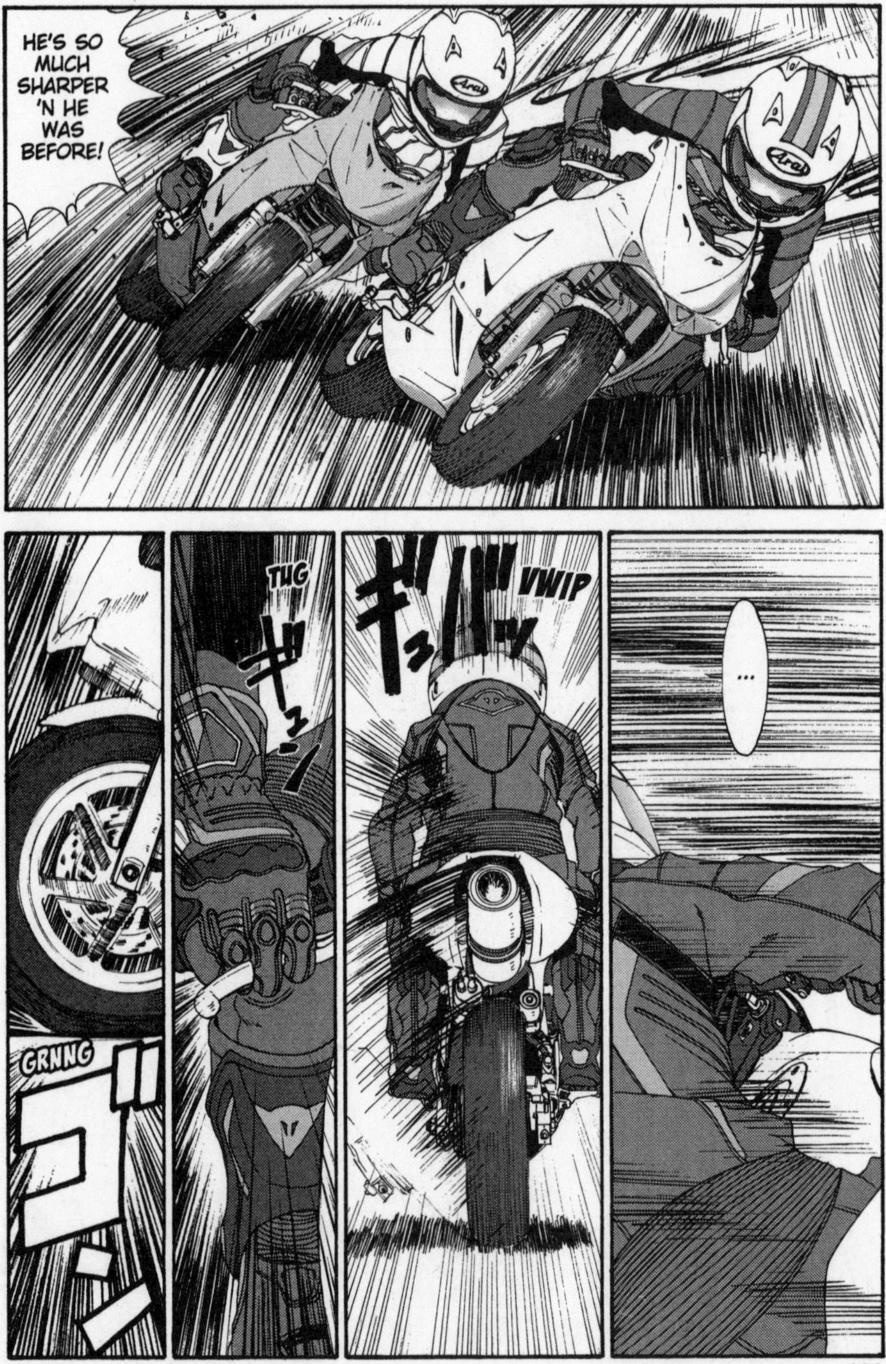
HE'S SO MUCH SHARPER 'N HE WAS BEFORE!
...
VWIP
TUG
GRNNG

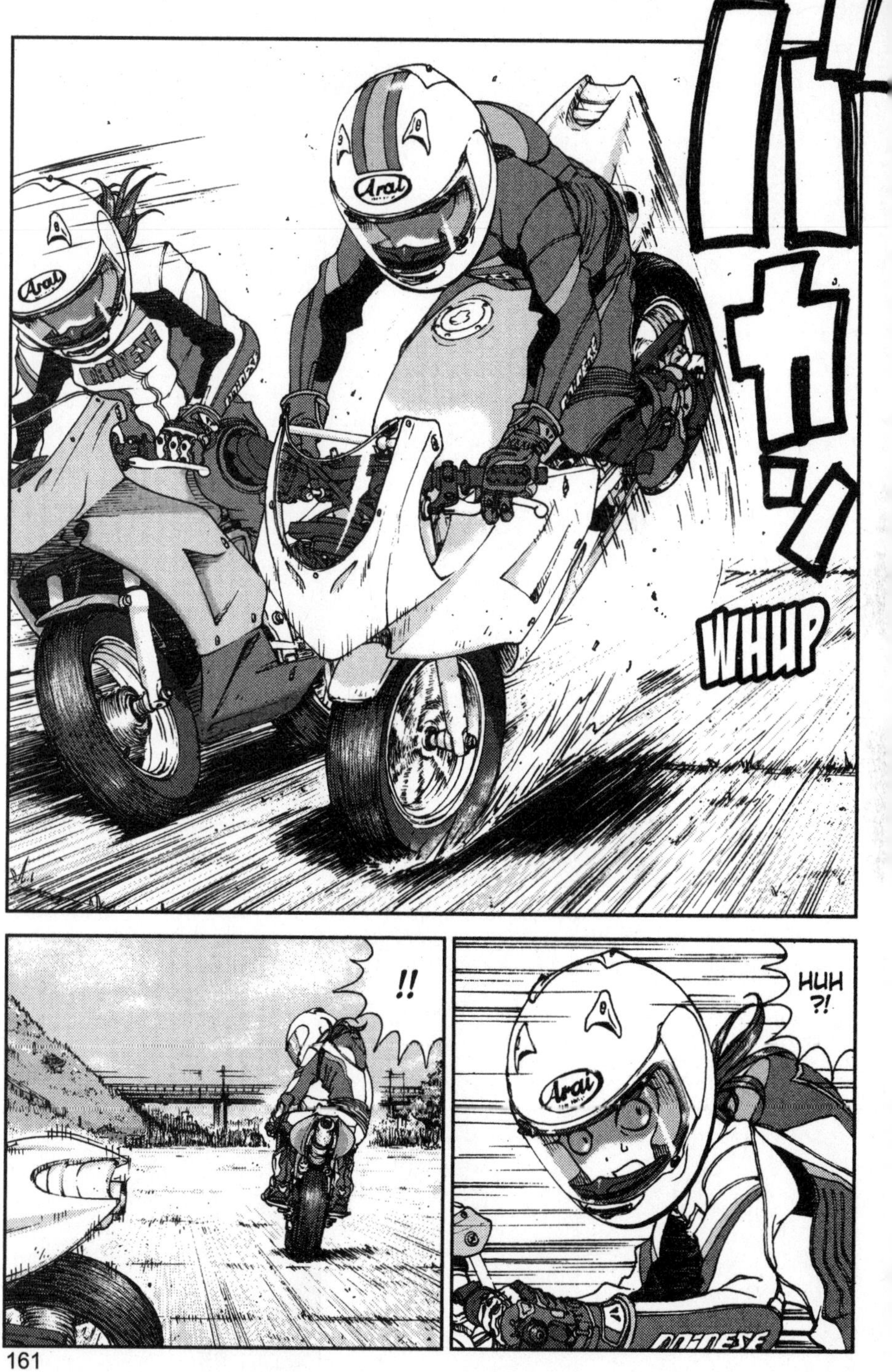
バカッ
WHUP
HUH ?!
!!

YOU CAN'T BE SERIOUS!

ONE DAY...

...I'LL BE ABLE TO DO THAT, TOO!!

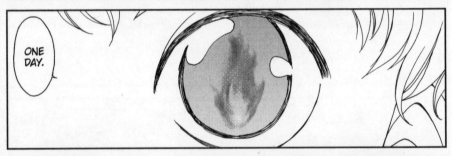

ONE DAY.

LET'S WRAP IT UP!

ALL RIGHT!

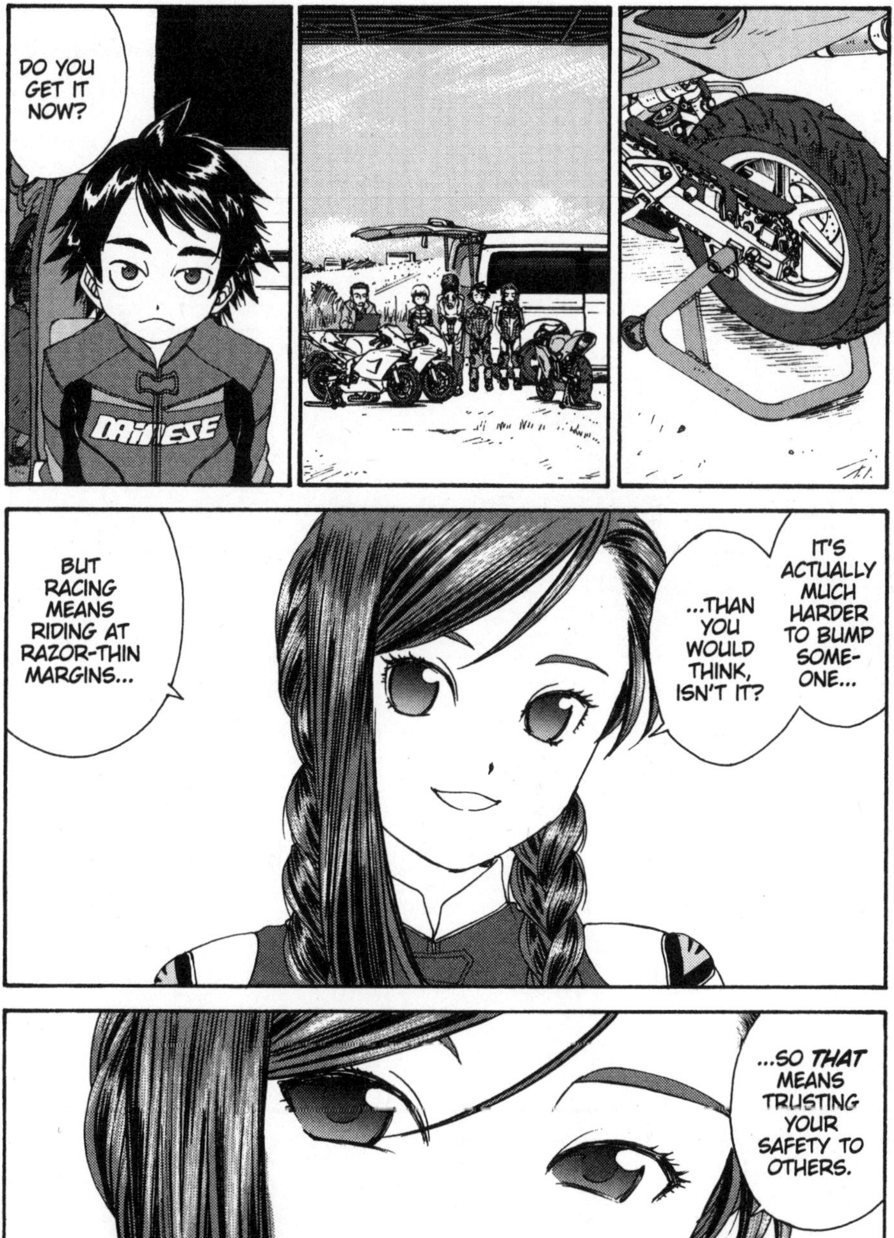

DO YOU GET IT NOW?
IT'S ACTUALLY MUCH HARDER TO BUMP SOME-ONE...
...THAN YOU WOULD THINK, ISN'T IT?
BUT RACING MEANS RIDING AT RAZOR-THIN MARGINS...
...SO *THAT* MEANS TRUSTING YOUR SAFETY TO OTHERS.

JUST LIKE YOU TWO.
SO...
WITH THAT OUT OF THE WAY...
HOW ABOUT THREE MORE SETS WITH *ME* THIS TIME?
REALLY?
IT LOOKS LIKE SO MUCH FUN!
...
NO WAY.

Lap 20: end

Arai

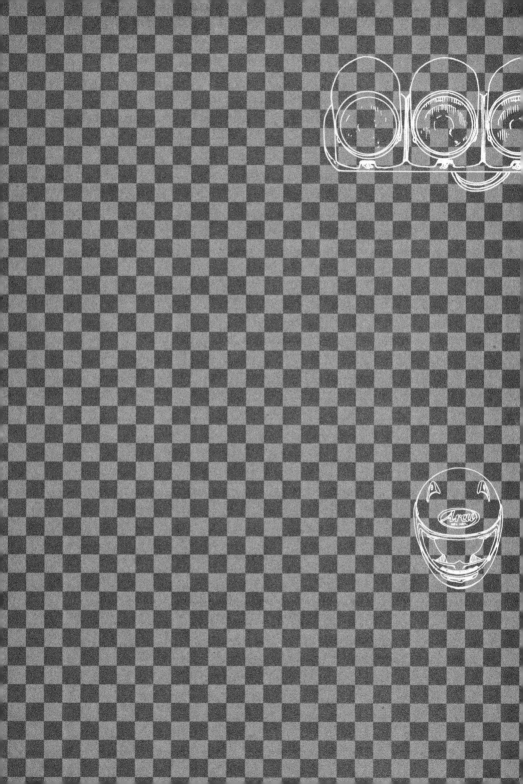

TOPPU GP

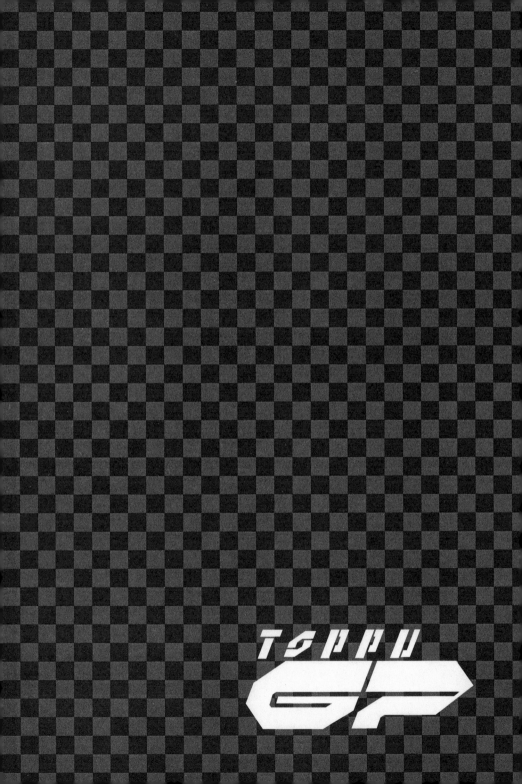

Lap 21:

RAIN

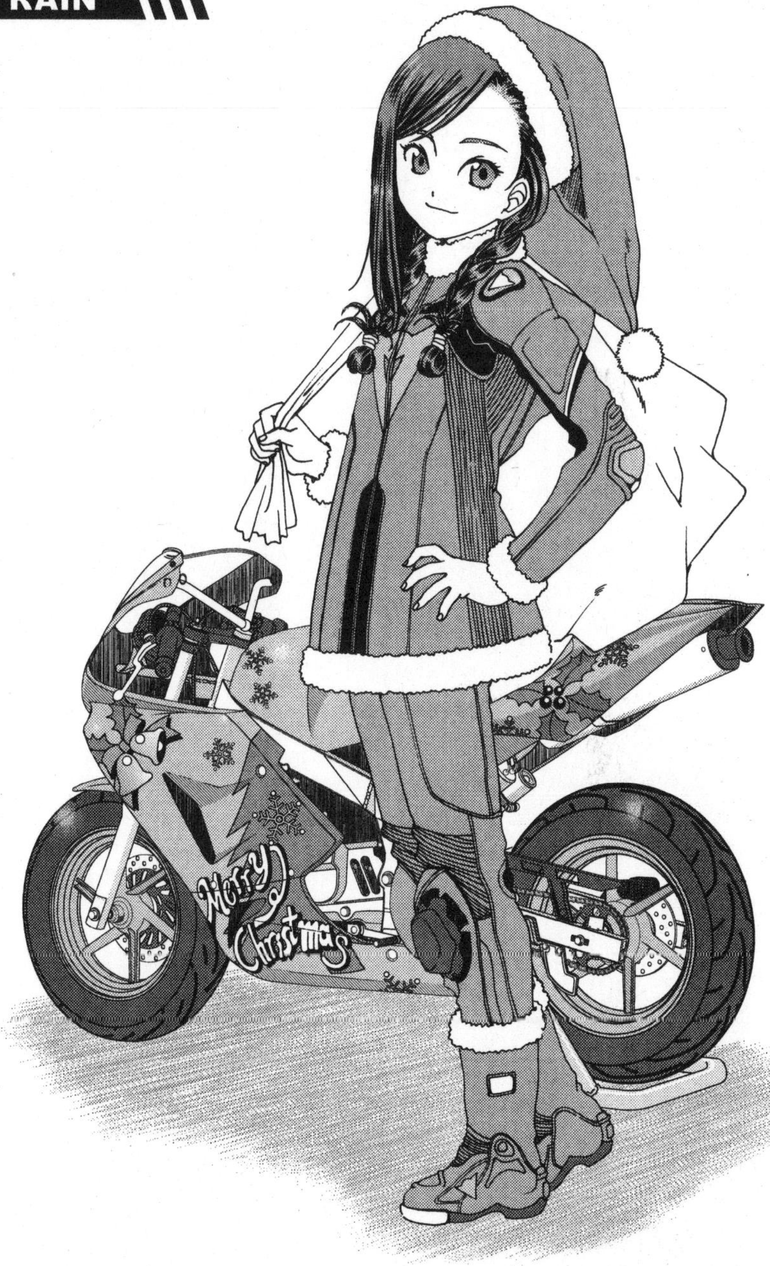

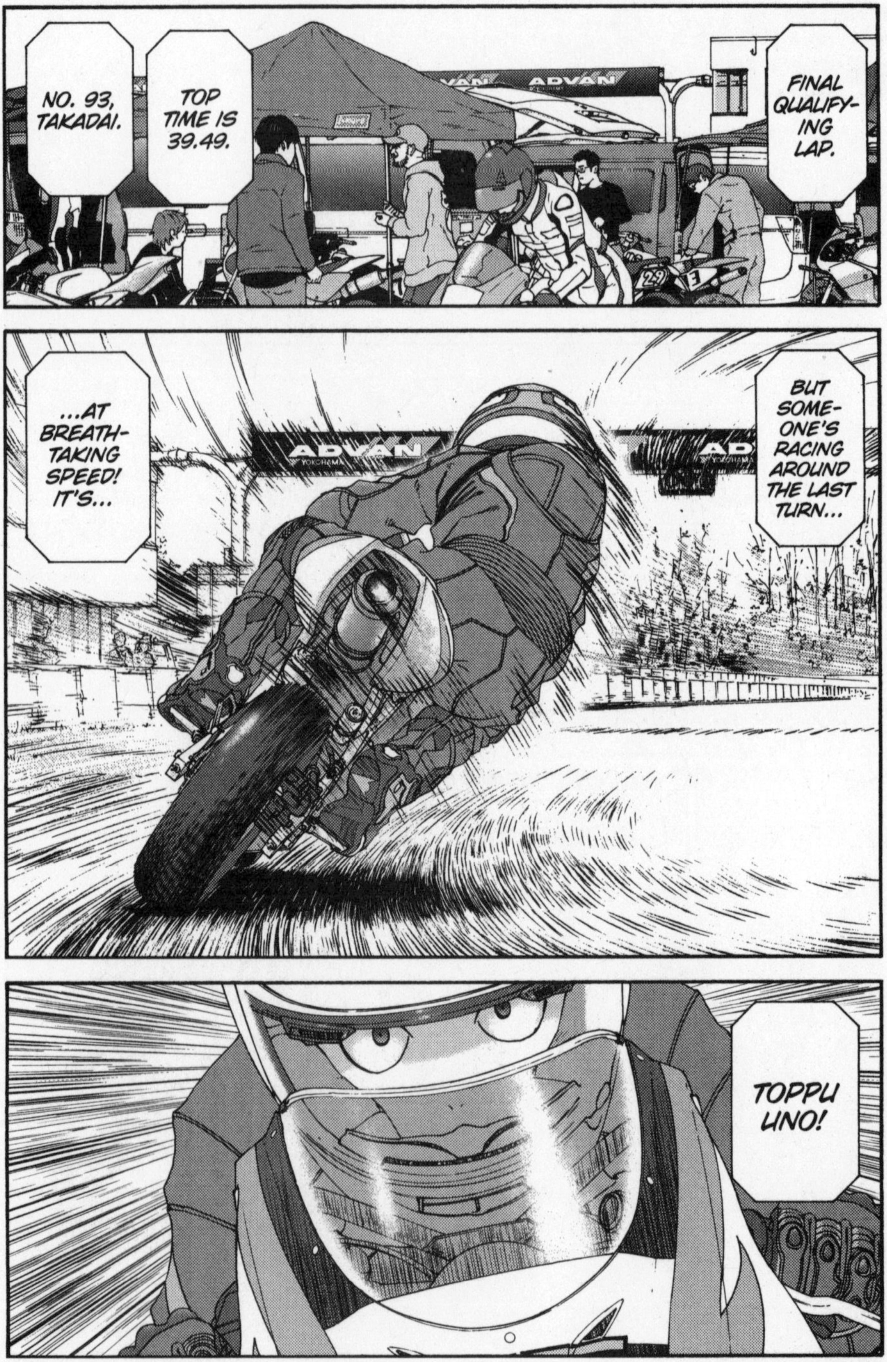
FINAL QUALIFY-ING LAP.
TOP TIME IS 39.49.
NO. 93, TAKADAI.
ADVAN
BUT SOME-ONE'S RACING AROUND THE LAST TURN...
...AT BREATH-TAKING SPEED! IT'S...
TOPPU UNO!

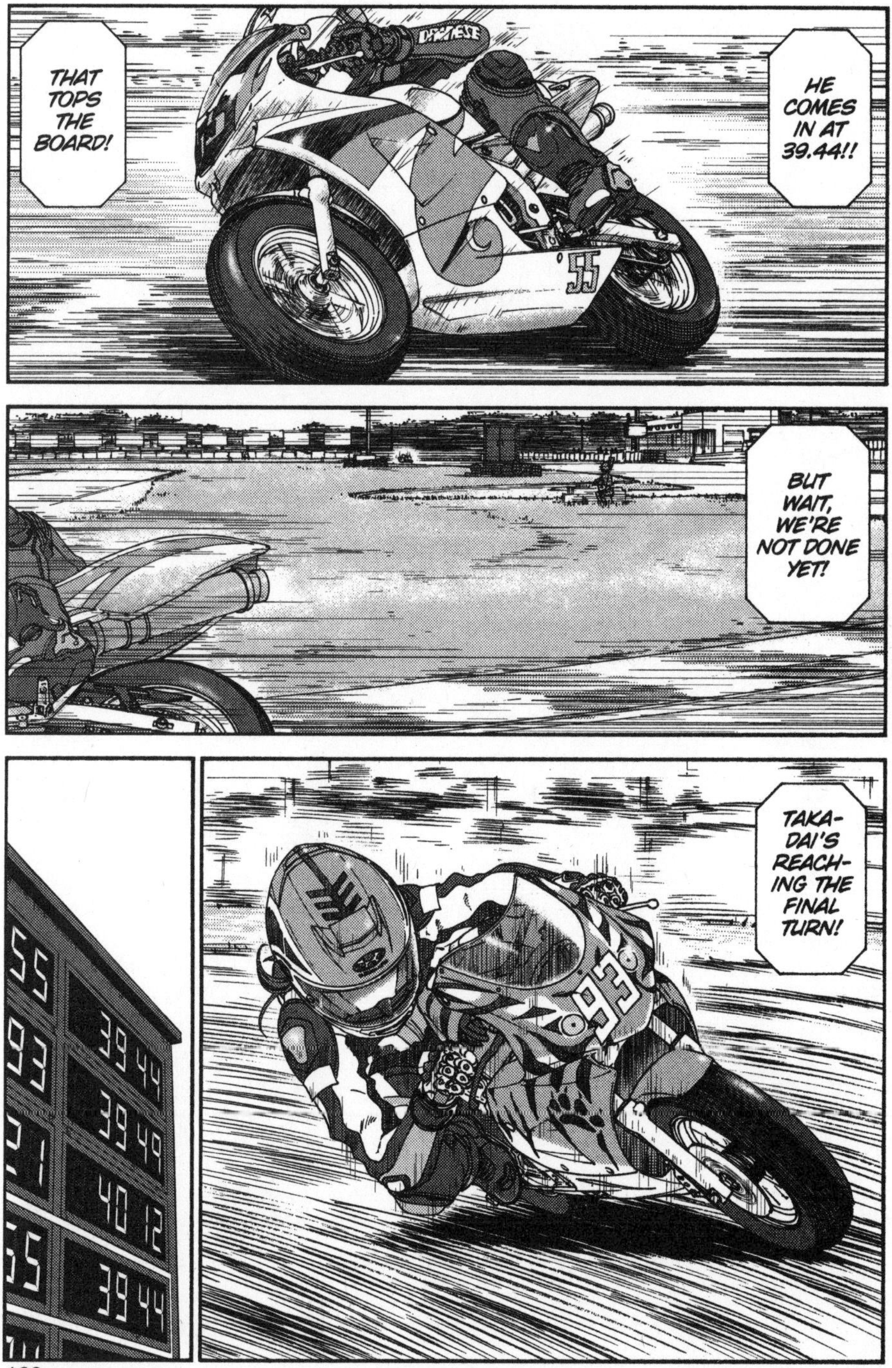
HE COMES IN AT 39.44!!
THAT TOPS THE BOARD!
BUT WAIT, WE'RE NOT DONE YET!
TAKA-DAI'S REACH-ING THE FINAL TURN!

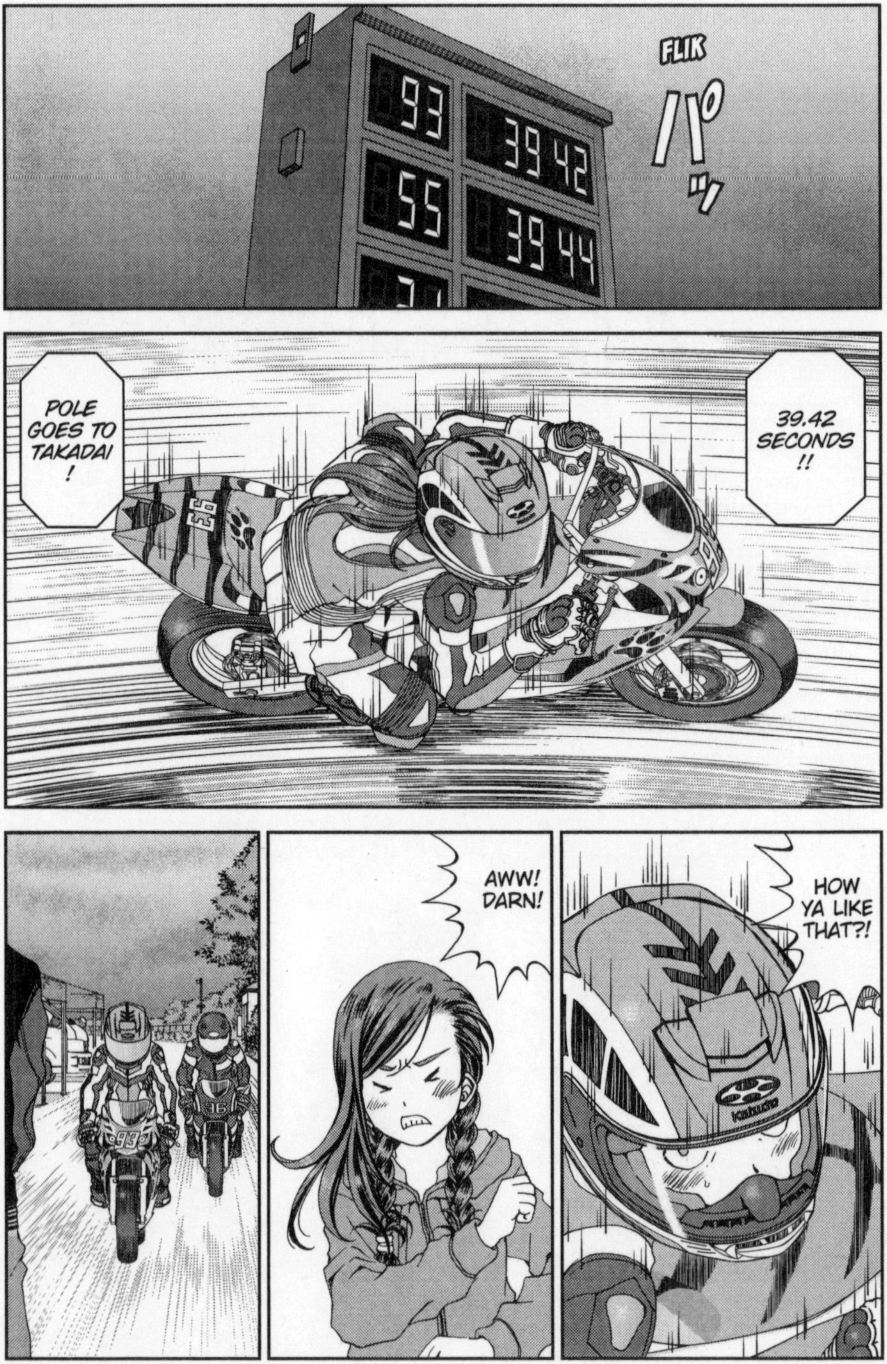
93 39 42
55 39 44
FLIK
パッ
39.42 SECONDS !!
POLE GOES TO TAKADAI !
HOW YA LIKE THAT?!
AWW! DARN!

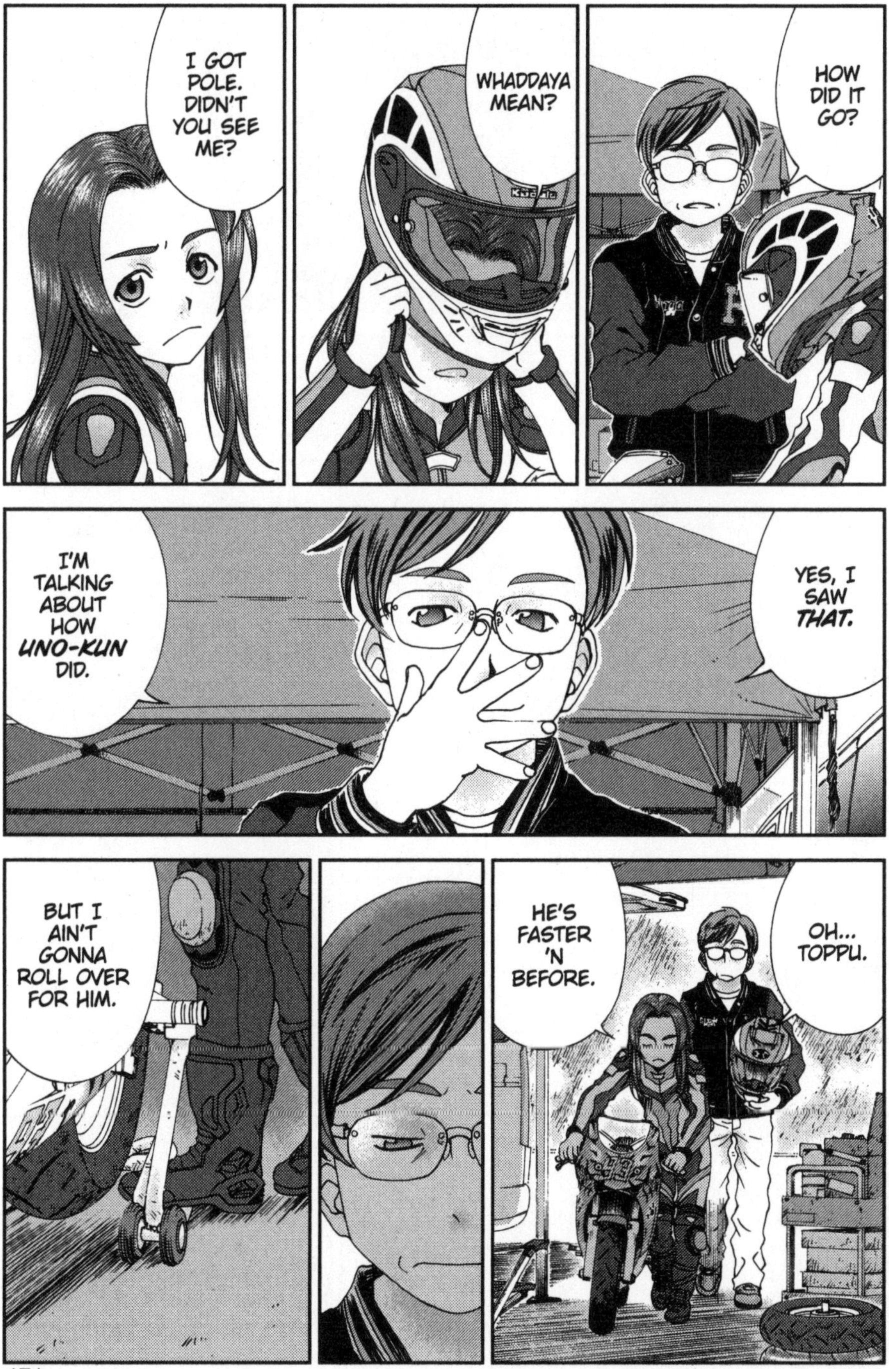
HOW DID IT GO?
WHADDAYA MEAN?
I GOT POLE. DIDN'T YOU SEE ME?
YES, I SAW *THAT.*
I'M TALKING ABOUT HOW *UNO-KUN* DID.
OH... TOPPU.
HE'S FASTER 'N BEFORE.
BUT I AIN'T GONNA ROLL OVER FOR HIM.

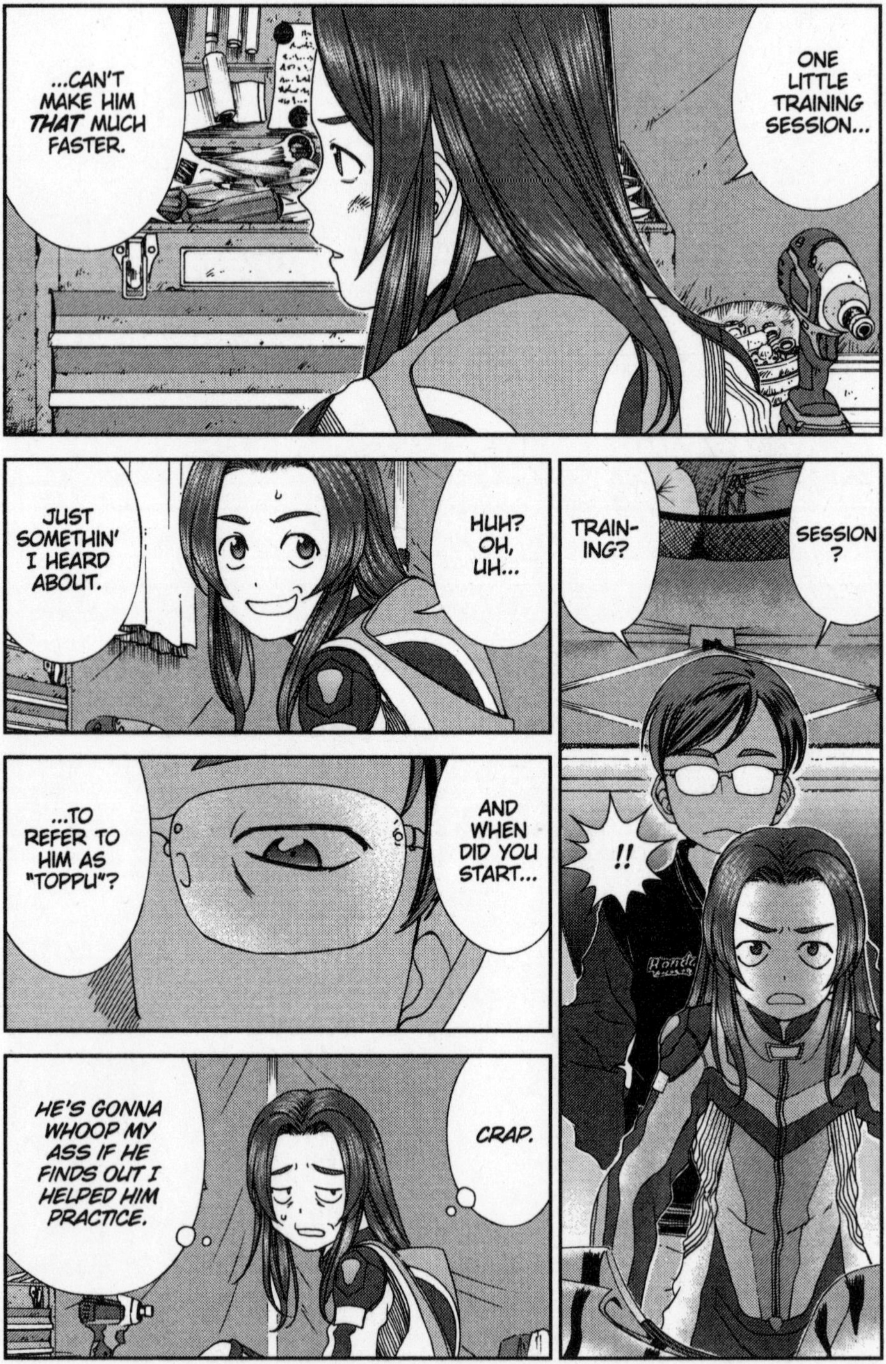

ONE LITTLE TRAINING SESSION...
...CAN'T MAKE HIM *THAT* MUCH FASTER.
SESSION ?
TRAIN-ING?
HUH? OH, UH...
JUST SOMETHIN' I HEARD ABOUT.
!!
AND WHEN DID YOU START...
...TO REFER TO HIM AS "TOPPU"?
CRAP.
HE'S GONNA WHOOP MY ASS IF HE FINDS OUT I HELPED HIM PRACTICE.

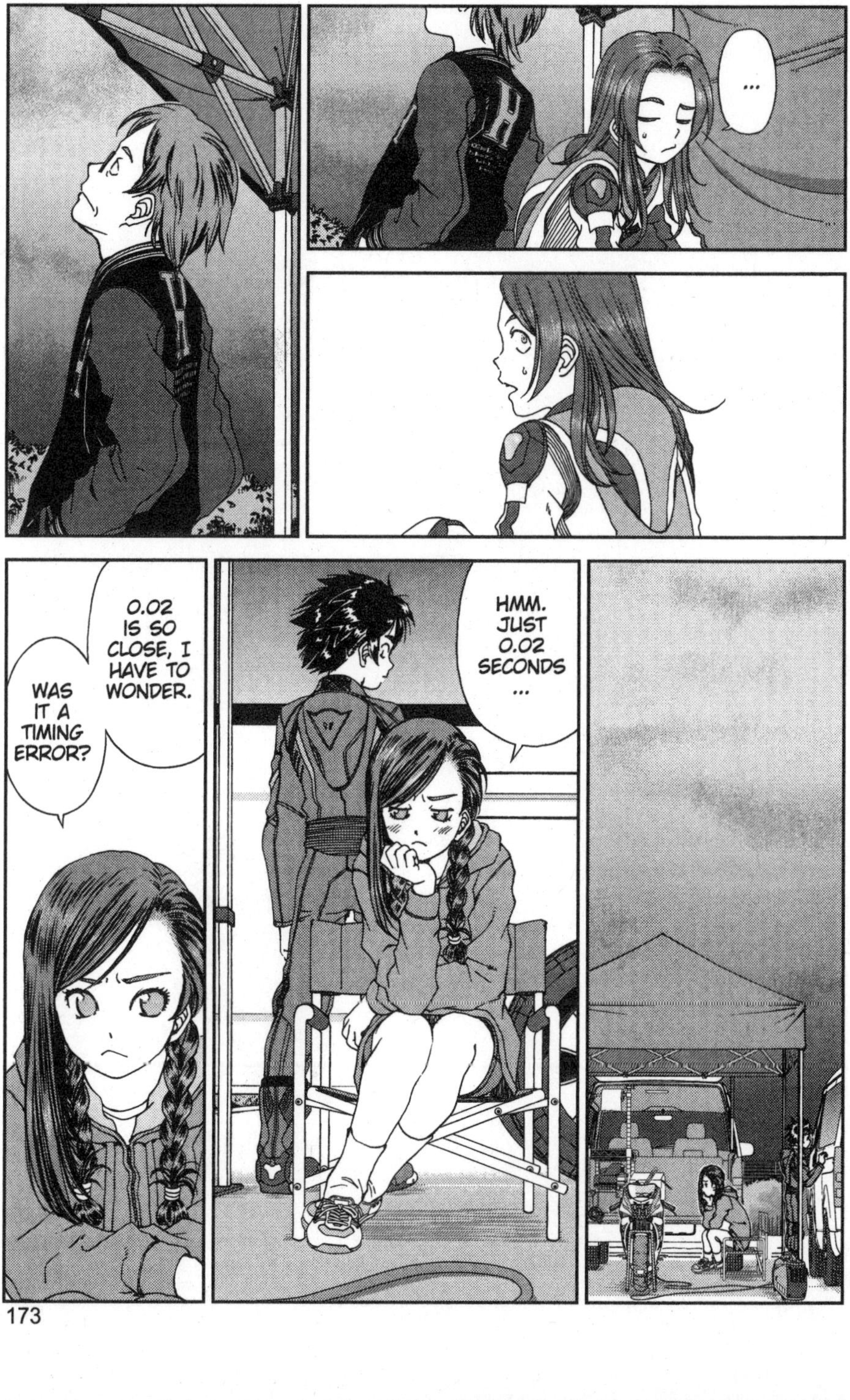
...
HMM. JUST 0.02 SECONDS ...
0.02 IS SO CLOSE, I HAVE TO WONDER.
WAS IT A TIMING ERROR?

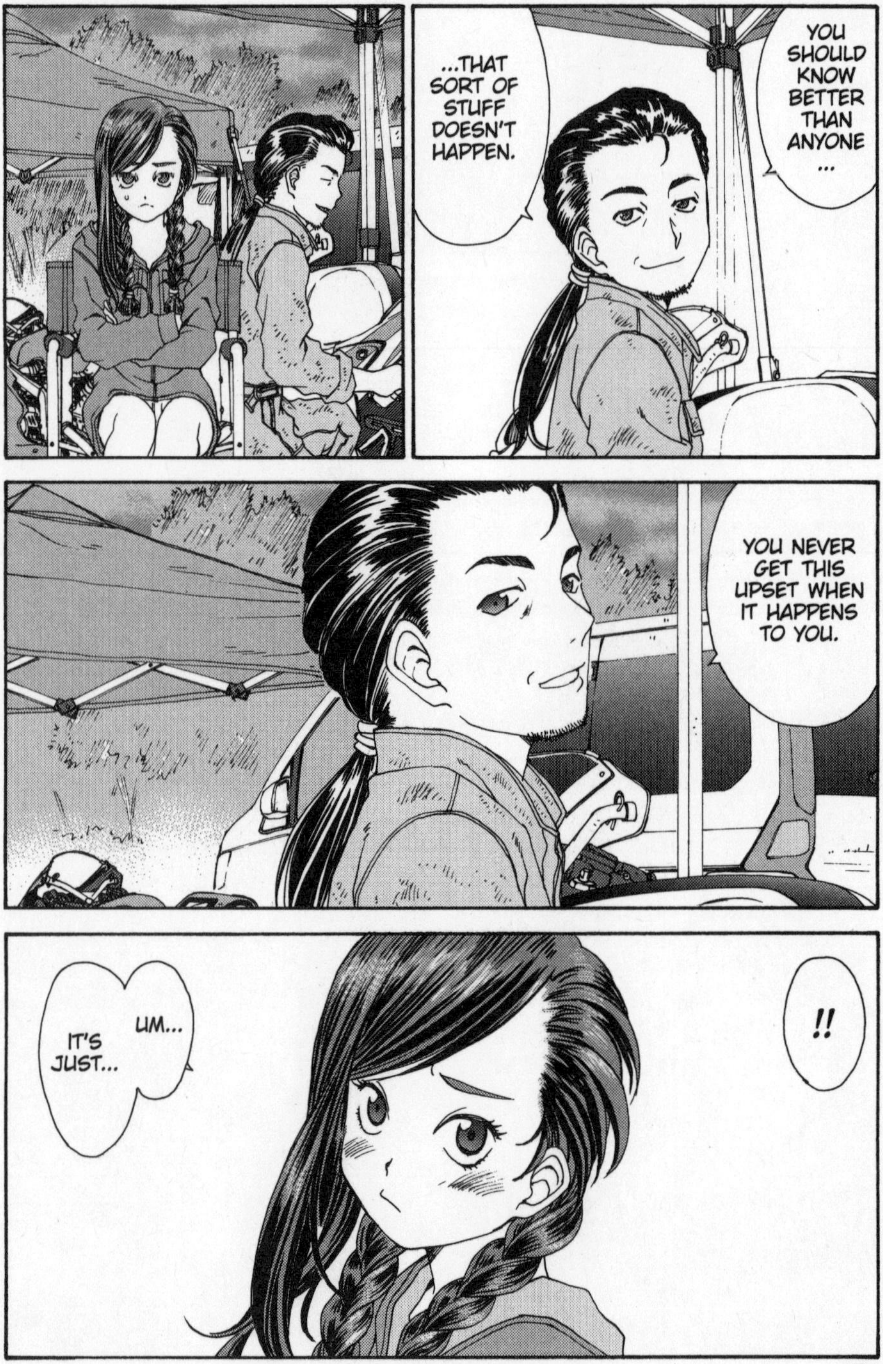
YOU SHOULD KNOW BETTER THAN ANYONE ...
...THAT SORT OF STUFF DOESN'T HAPPEN.
YOU NEVER GET THIS UPSET WHEN IT HAPPENS TO YOU.
!!
UM... IT'S JUST...

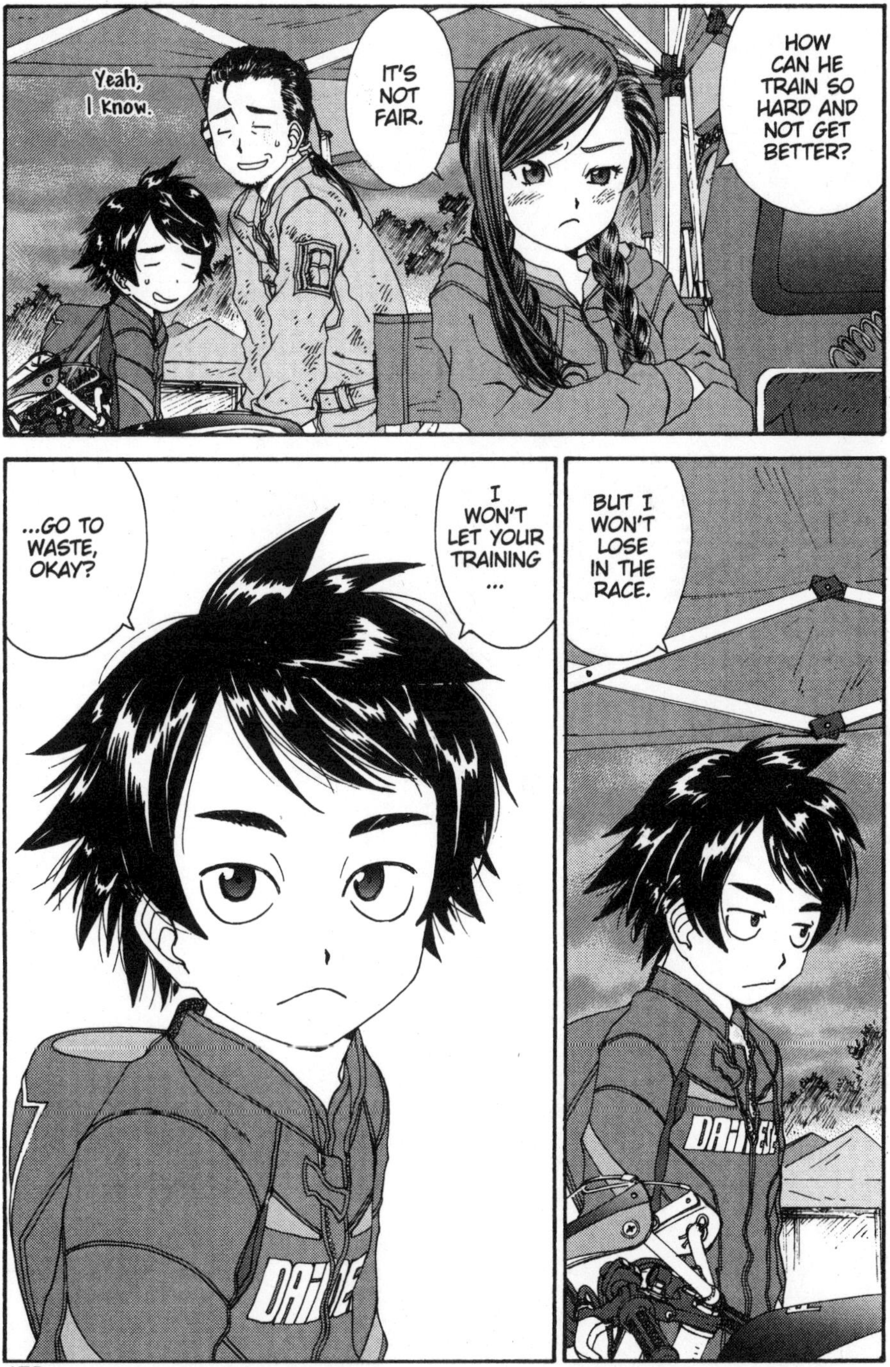
HOW CAN HE TRAIN SO HARD AND NOT GET BETTER?
IT'S NOT FAIR.
Yeah, I know.
BUT I WON'T LOSE IN THE RACE.
I WON'T LET YOUR TRAINING ...
...GO TO WASTE, OKAY?

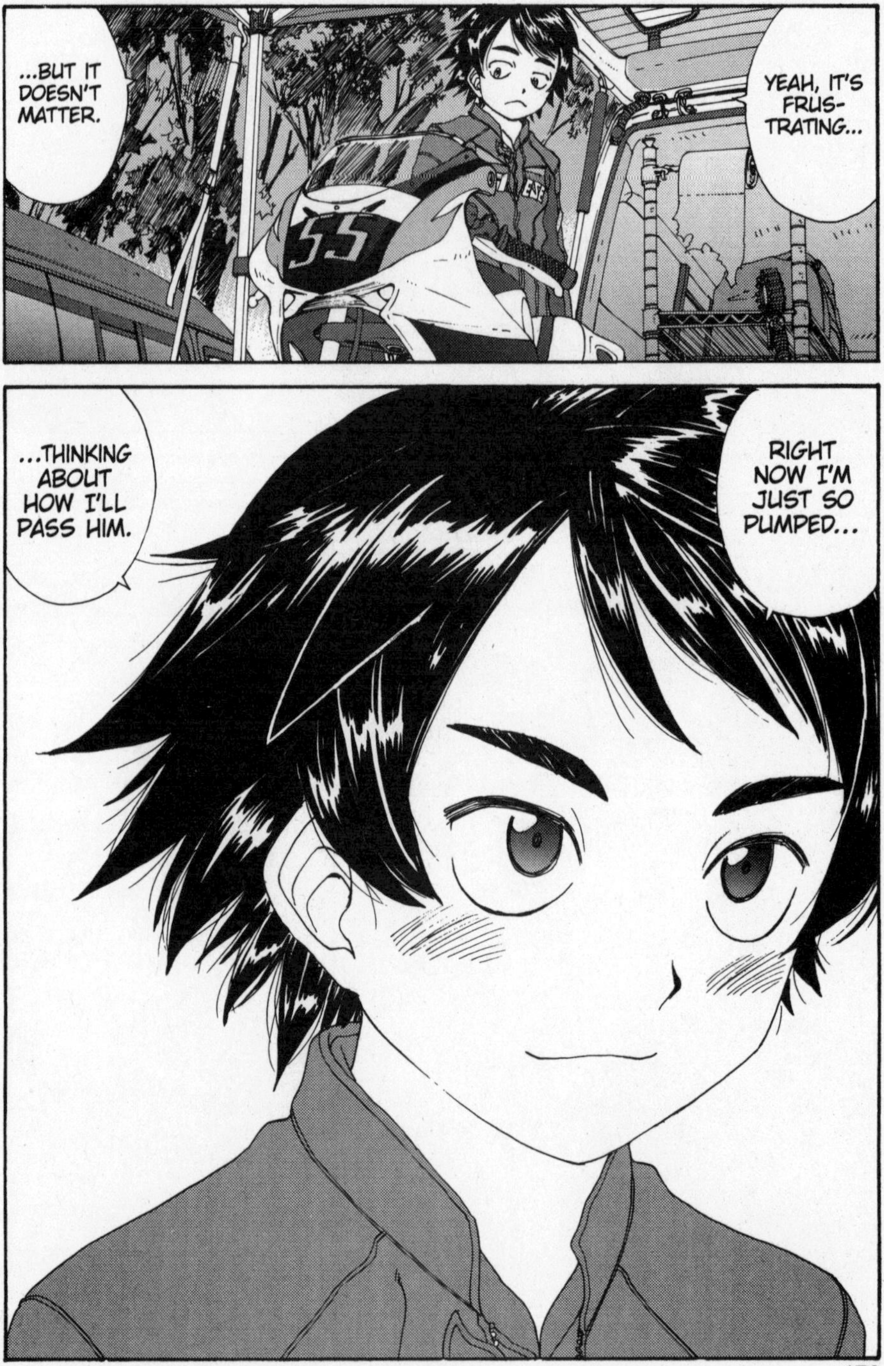
YEAH, IT'S FRUS-TRATING...
...BUT IT DOESN'T MATTER.
RIGHT NOW I'M JUST SO PUMPED...
...THINKING ABOUT HOW I'LL PASS HIM.

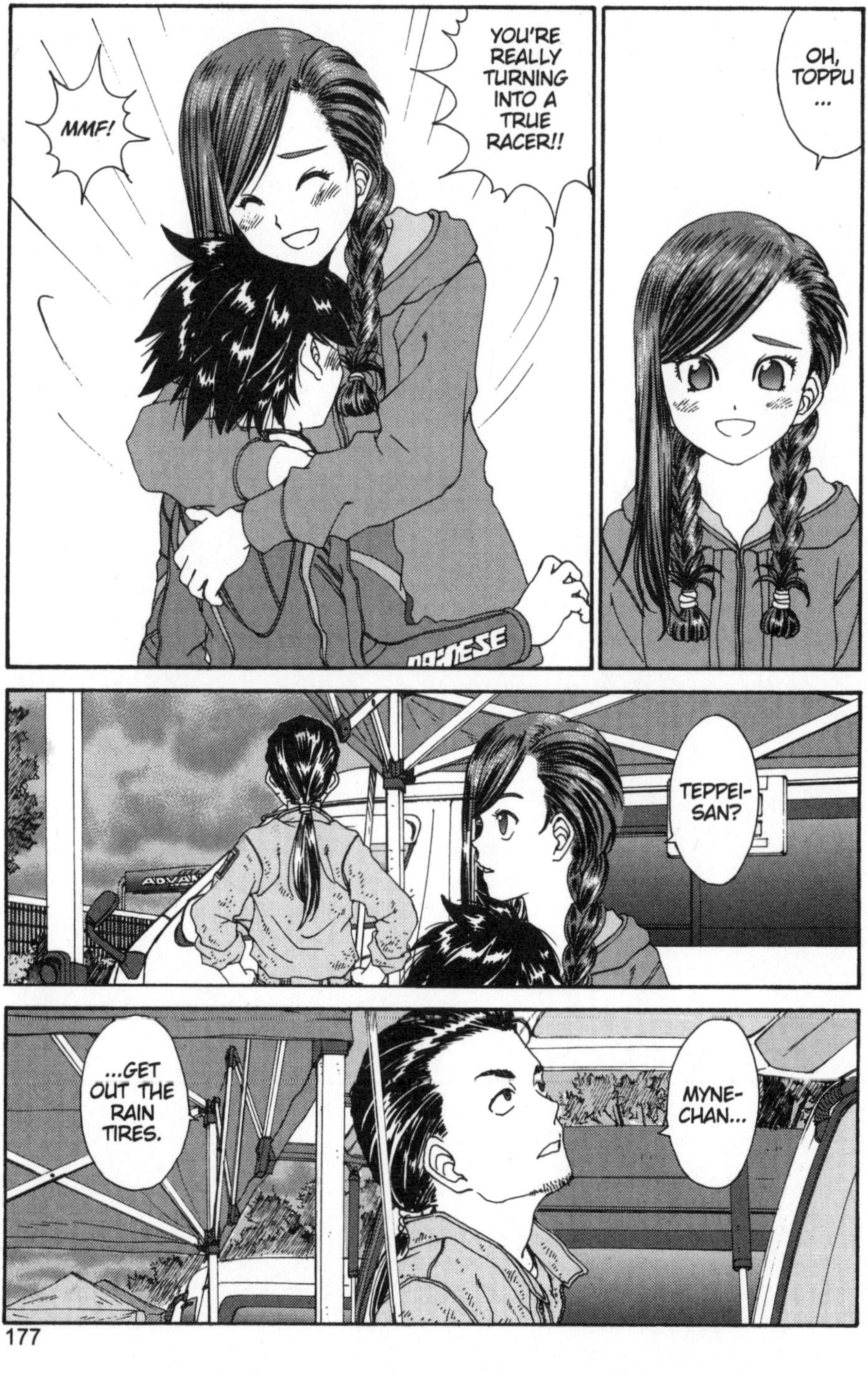
OH, TOPPU ...
YOU'RE REALLY TURNING INTO A TRUE RACER!!
MMF!
TEPPEI-SAN?
MYNE-CHAN...
...GET OUT THE RAIN TIRES.

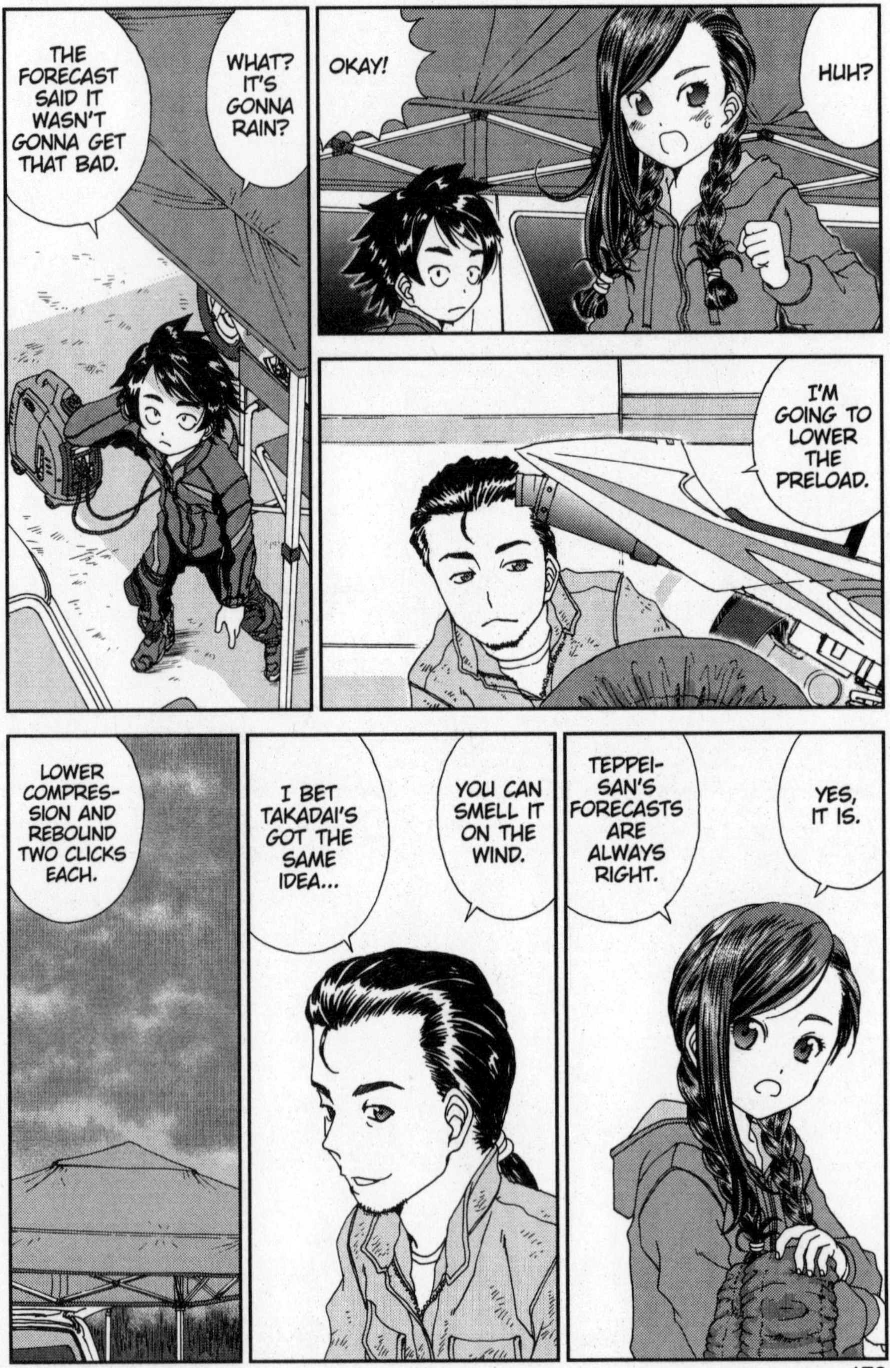
HUH?
OKAY!
WHAT? IT'S GONNA RAIN?
THE FORECAST SAID IT WASN'T GONNA GET THAT BAD.
I'M GOING TO LOWER THE PRELOAD.
YES, IT IS.
TEPPEI-SAN'S FORECASTS ARE ALWAYS RIGHT.
YOU CAN SMELL IT ON THE WIND.
I BET TAKADAI'S GOT THE SAME IDEA...
LOWER COMPRESSION AND REBOUND TWO CLICKS EACH.

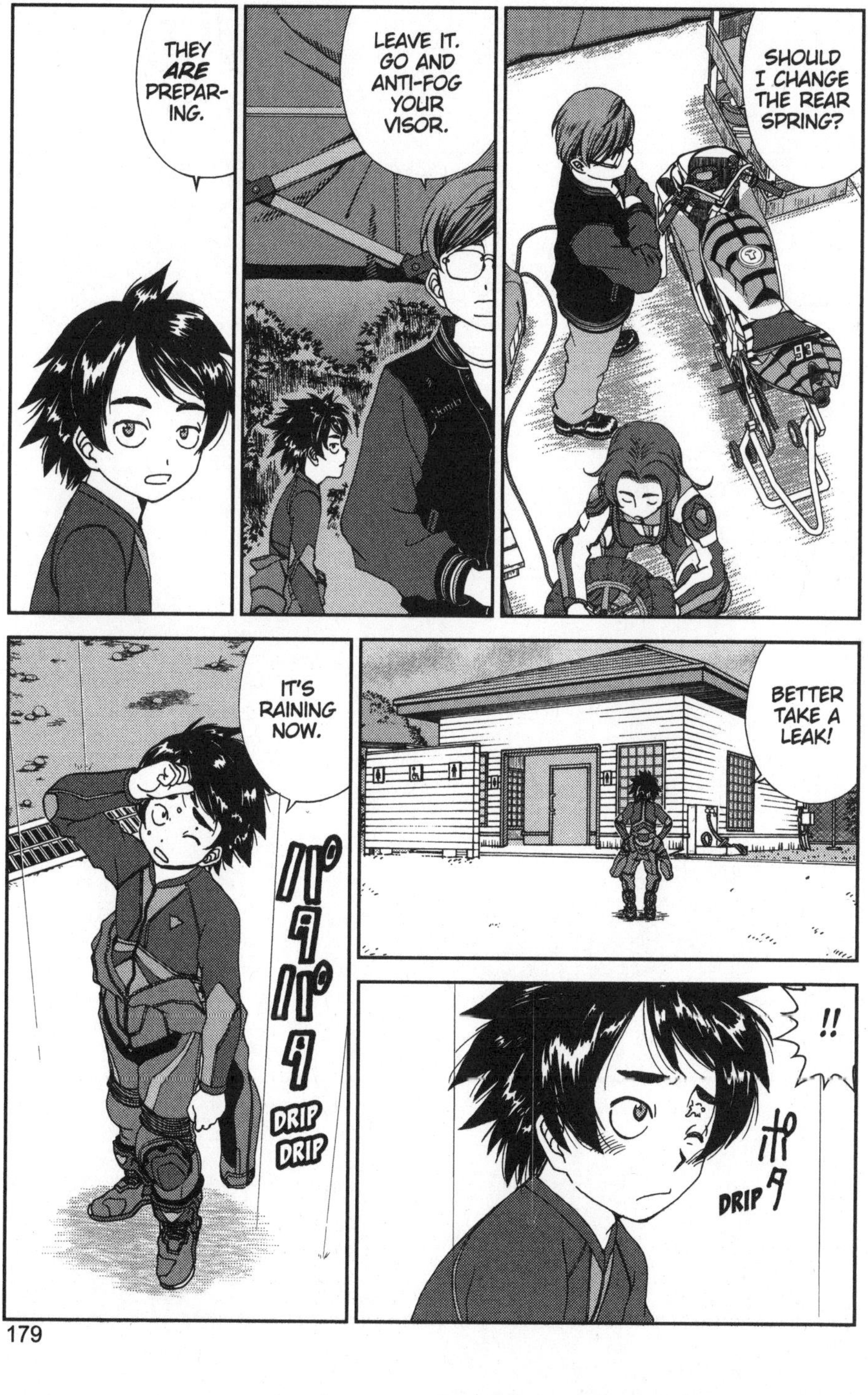
SHOULD I CHANGE THE REAR SPRING?
LEAVE IT. GO AND ANTI-FOG YOUR VISOR.
THEY *ARE* PREPARING.
BETTER TAKE A LEAK!
IT'S RAINING NOW.
パタパタ
DRIP DRIP
!!
ポタ
DRIP

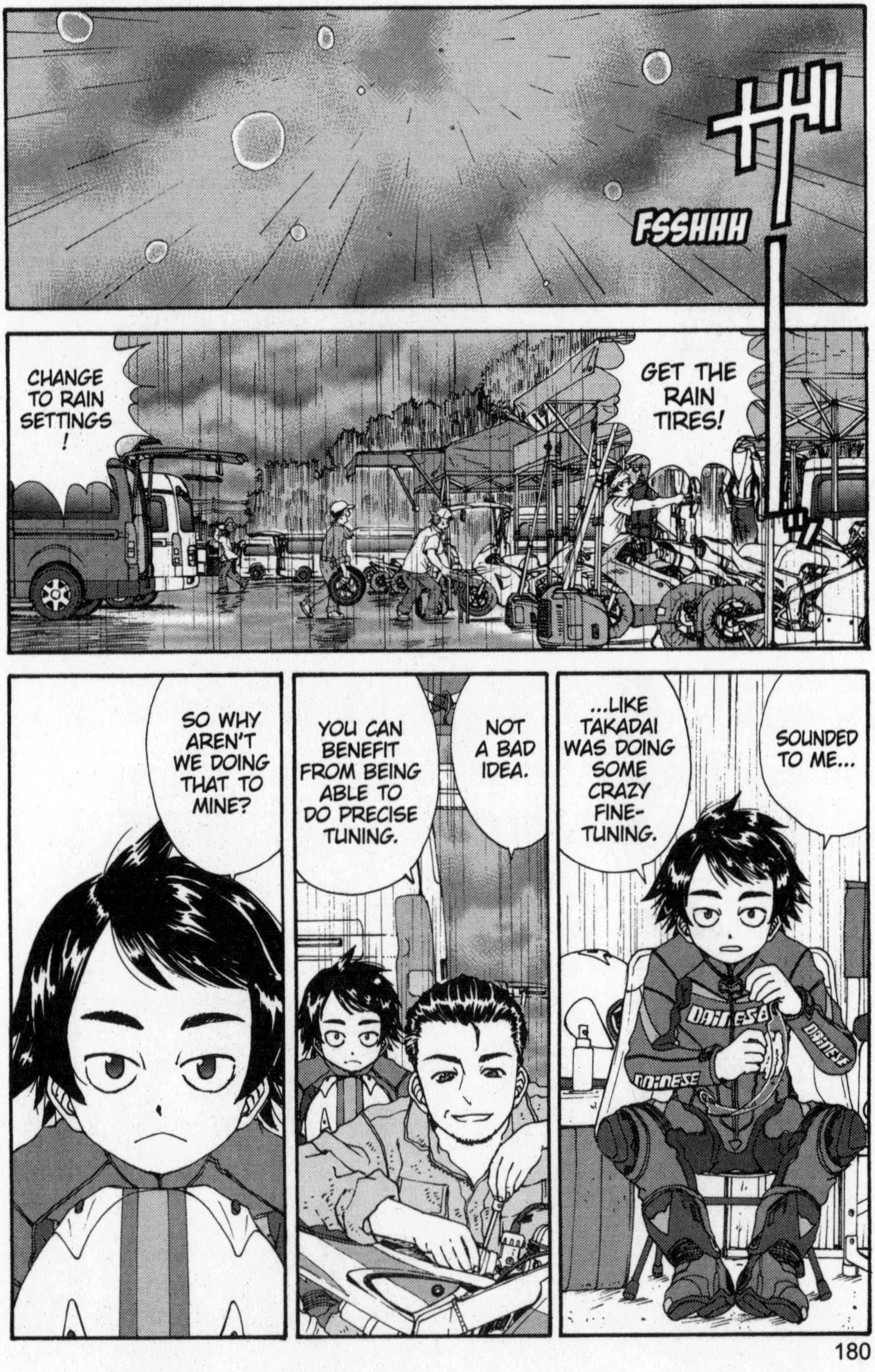
FSSHHH
GET THE RAIN TIRES!
CHANGE TO RAIN SETTINGS!
SOUNDED TO ME...
...LIKE TAKADAI WAS DOING SOME CRAZY FINE-TUNING.
NOT A BAD IDEA.
YOU CAN BENEFIT FROM BEING ABLE TO DO PRECISE TUNING.
SO WHY AREN'T WE DOING THAT TO MINE?

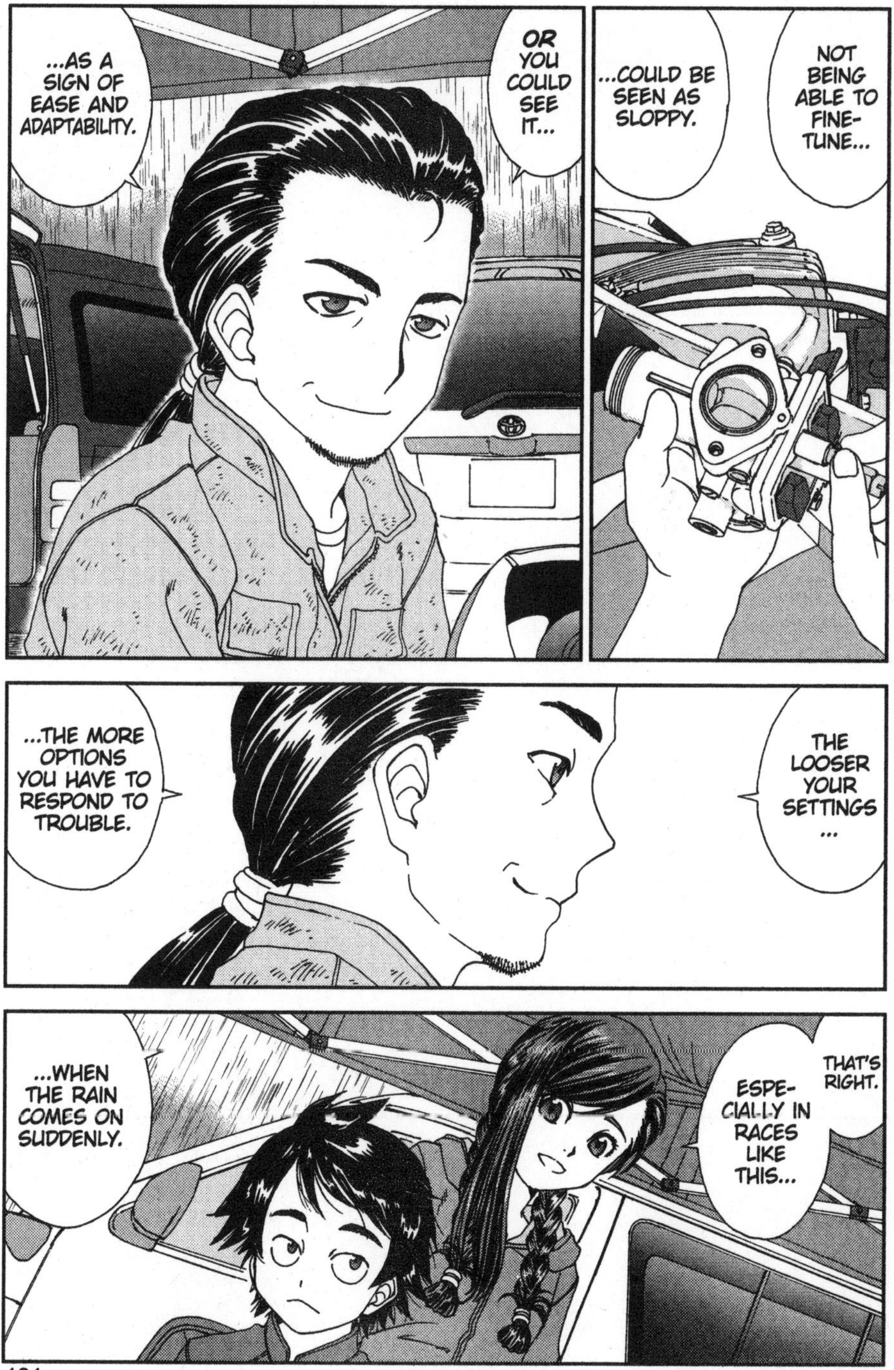
NOT BEING ABLE TO FINE-TUNE...
...COULD BE SEEN AS SLOPPY.
OR YOU COULD SEE IT...
...AS A SIGN OF EASE AND ADAPTABILITY.
THE LOOSER YOUR SETTINGS...
...THE MORE OPTIONS YOU HAVE TO RESPOND TO TROUBLE.
THAT'S RIGHT.
ESPE-CIALLY IN RACES LIKE THIS...
...WHEN THE RAIN COMES ON SUDDENLY.

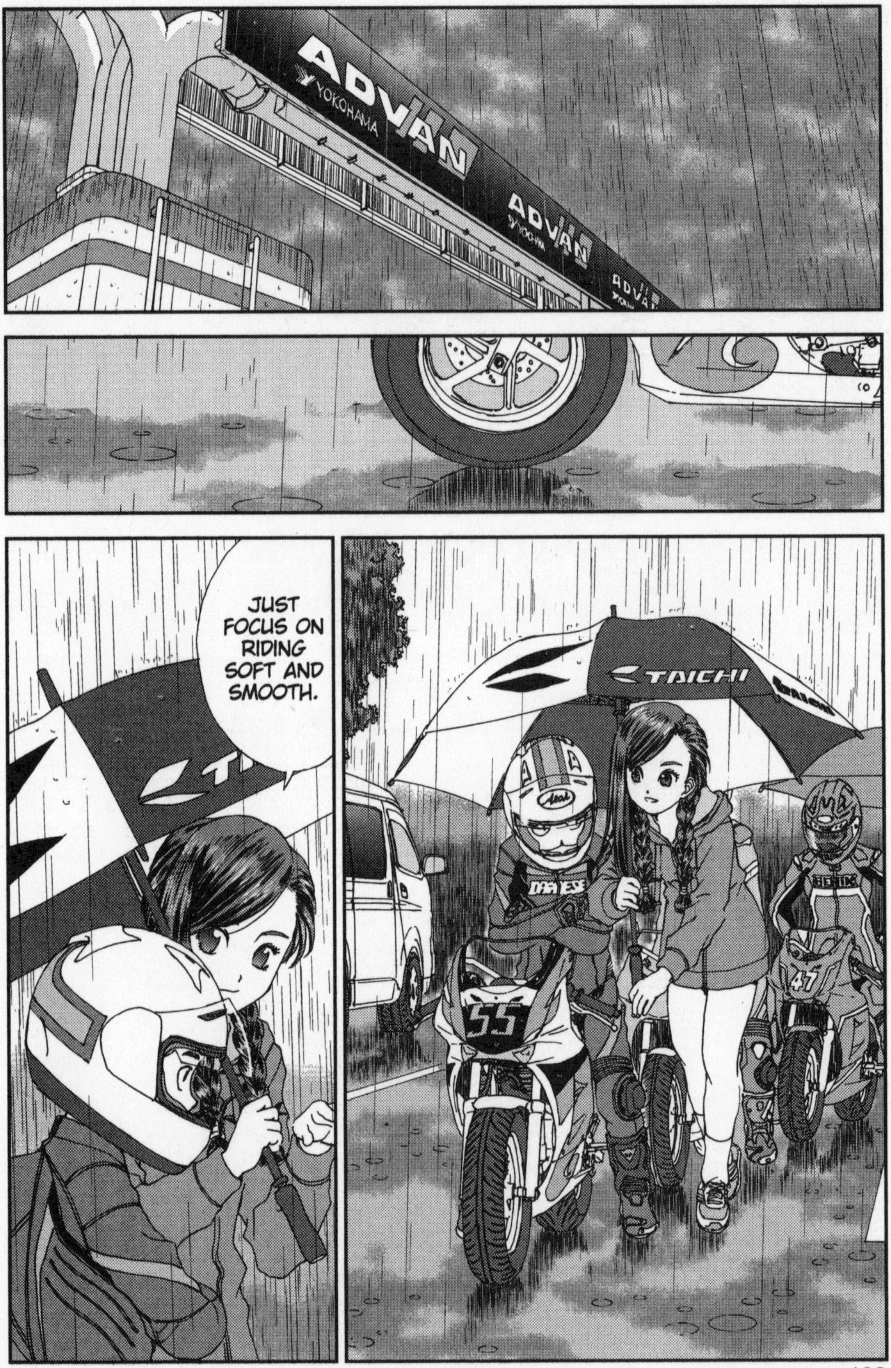
ADVAN
YOKOHAMA
ADVAN
ADVAN
JUST FOCUS ON RIDING SOFT AND SMOOTH.
TAICHI
55
47

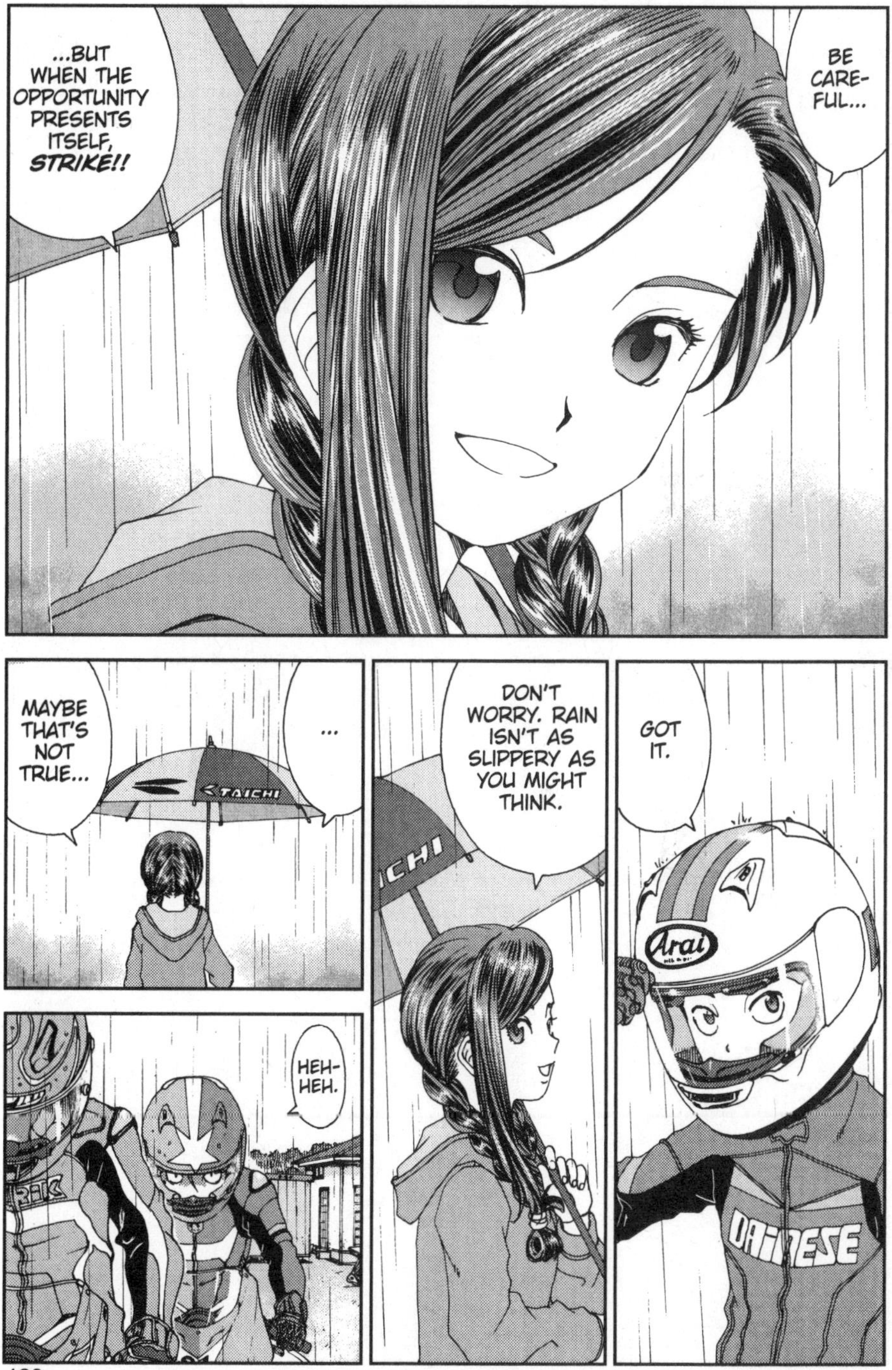
BE CARE-FUL...
...BUT WHEN THE OPPORTUNITY PRESENTS ITSELF, STRIKE!!
GOT IT.
DON'T WORRY. RAIN ISN'T AS SLIPPERY AS YOU MIGHT THINK.
Arai
...
MAYBE THAT'S NOT TRUE...
TAICHI
HEH-HEH.

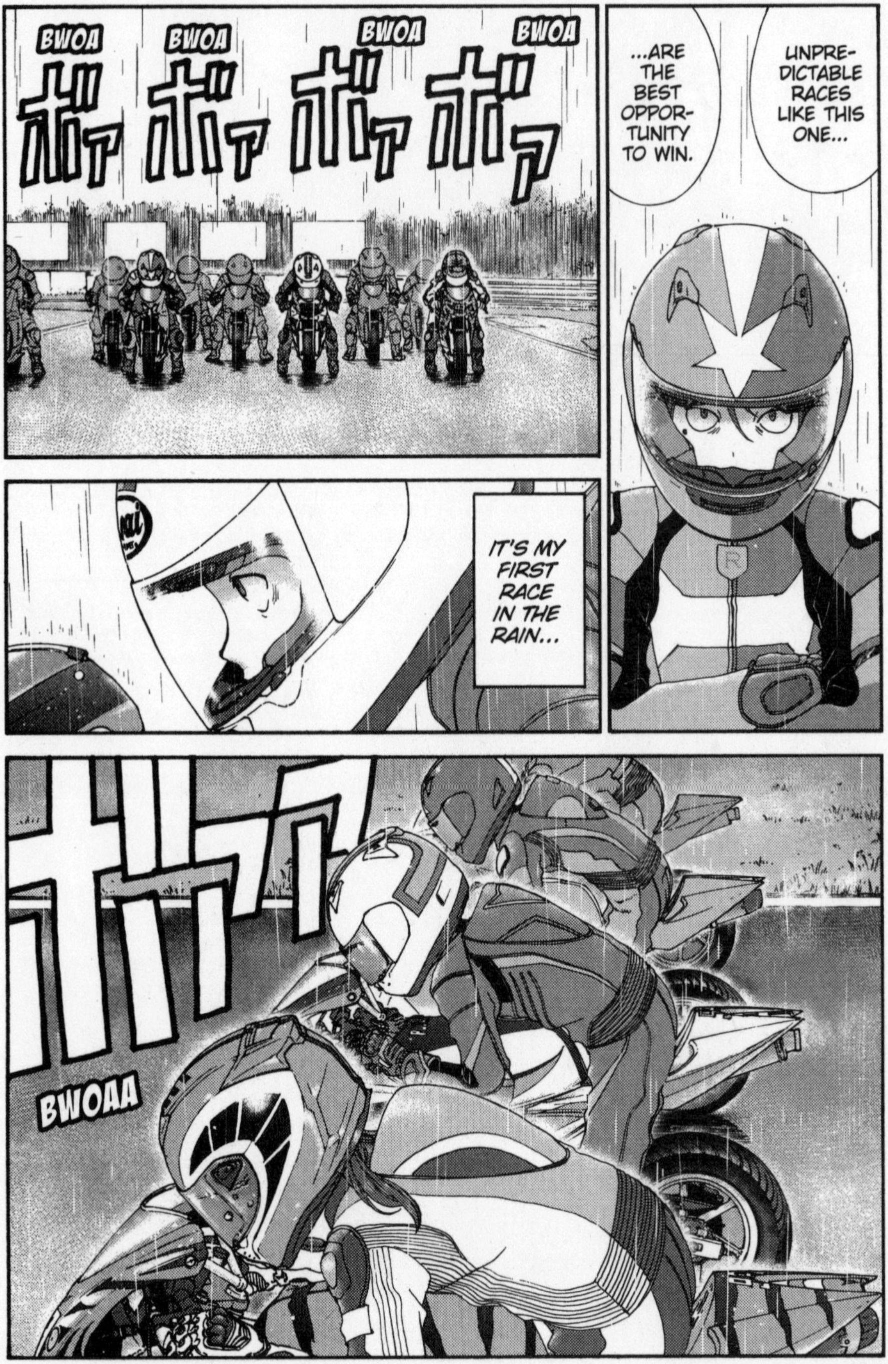
UNPREDICTABLE RACES LIKE THIS ONE...
...ARE THE BEST OPPORTUNITY TO WIN.
BWOA
ボァ
BWOA
ボァ
BWOA
ボァ
BWOA
ボァ
IT'S MY FIRST RACE IN THE RAIN...
ボァァ
BWOAA

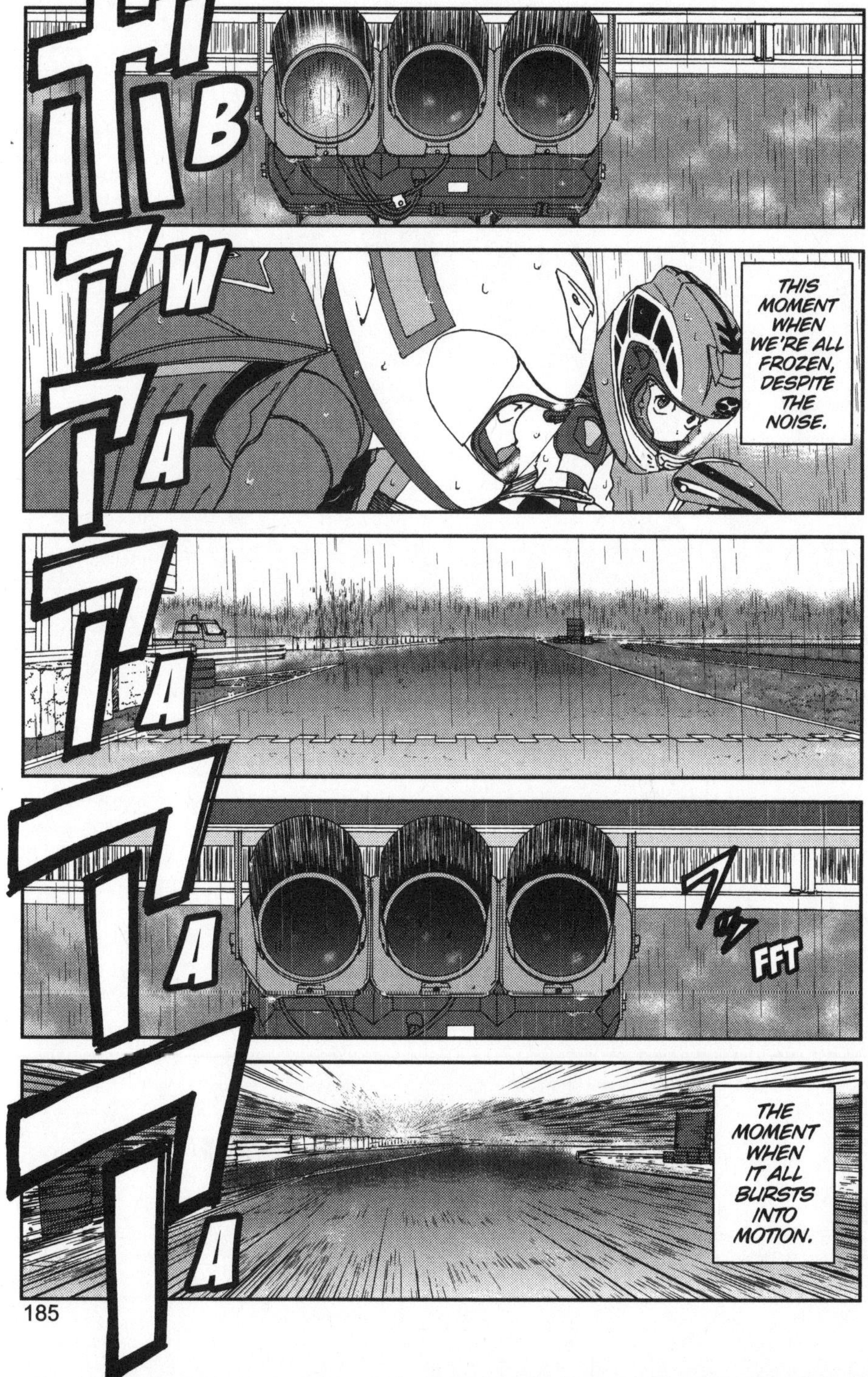
BWAAAAA
THIS MOMENT WHEN WE'RE ALL FROZEN, DESPITE THE NOISE.
FFT
THE MOMENT WHEN IT ALL BURSTS INTO MOTION.

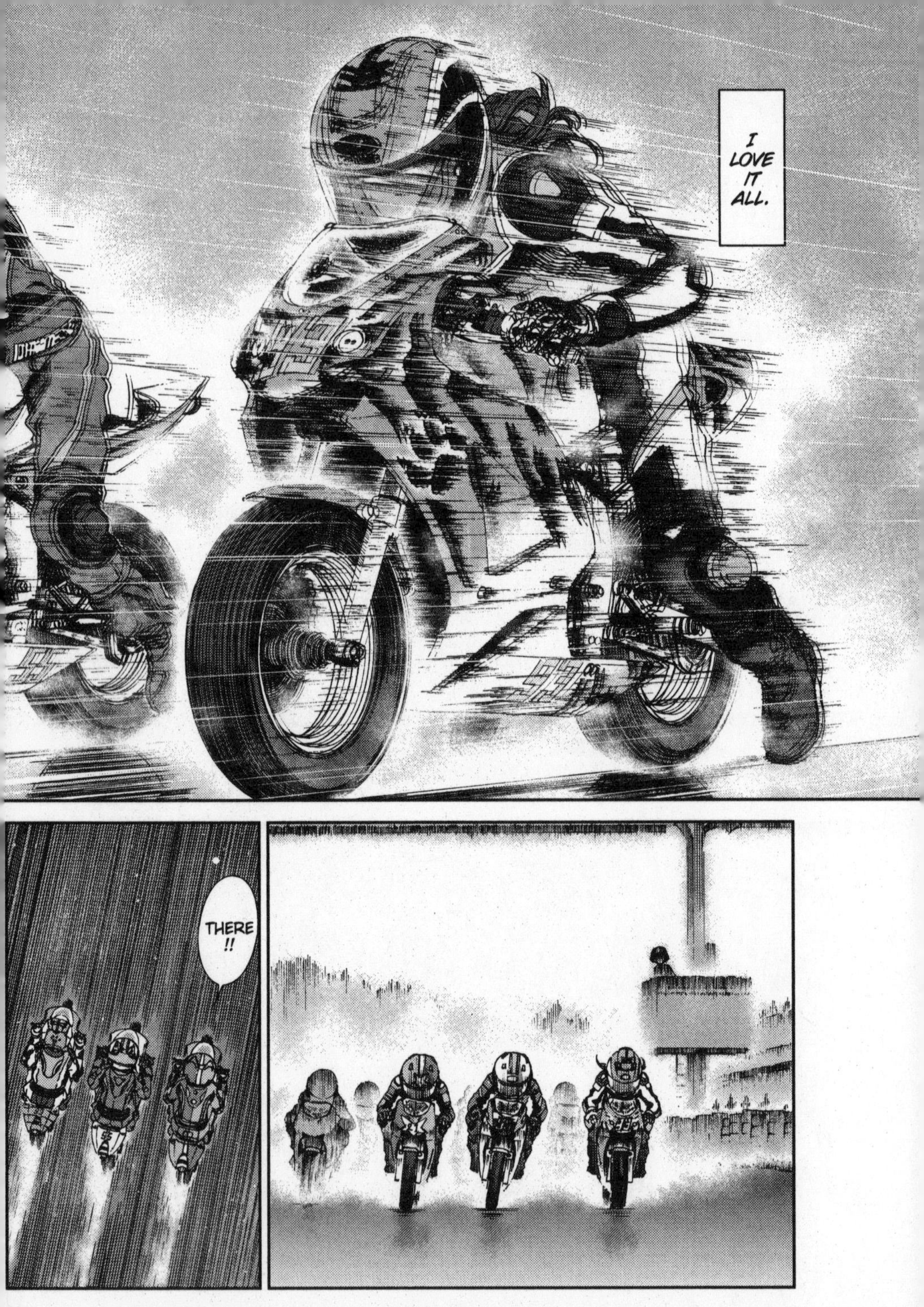
I LOVE IT ALL.
THERE !!

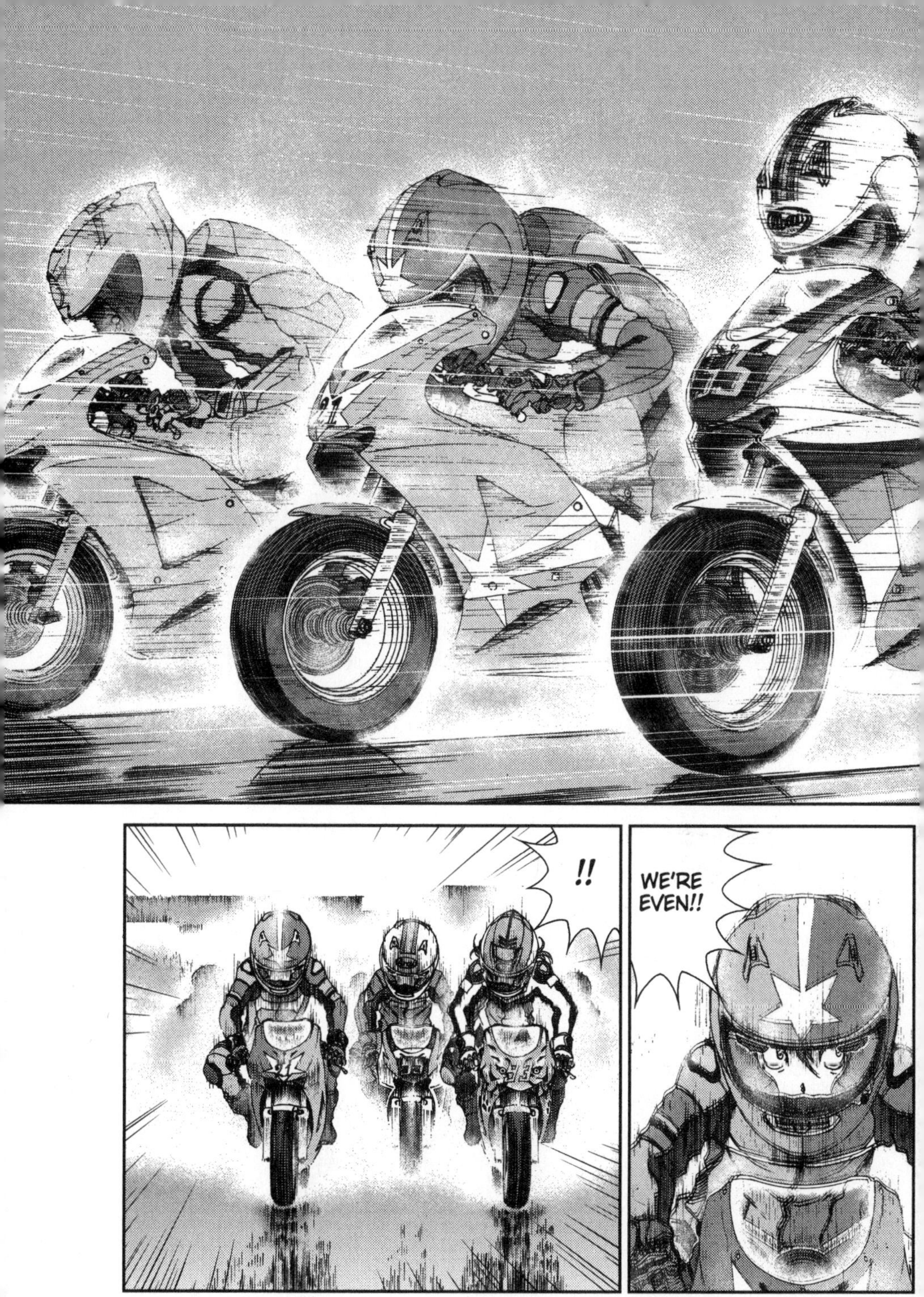
!!
WE'RE EVEN!!

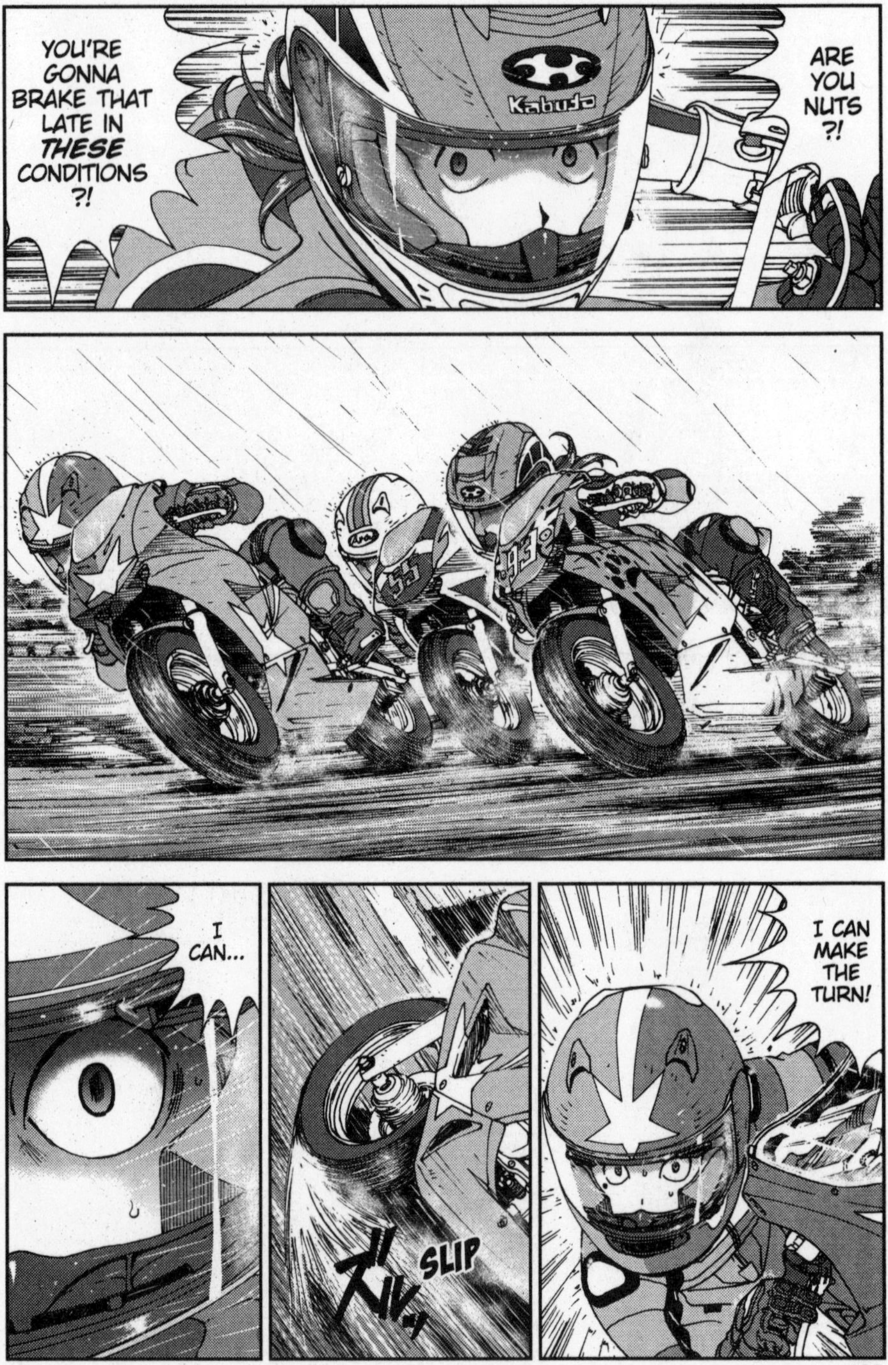
YOU'RE GONNA BRAKE THAT LATE IN *THESE* CONDITIONS ?!
ARE YOU NUTS ?!
I CAN...
SLIP
I CAN MAKE THE TURN!

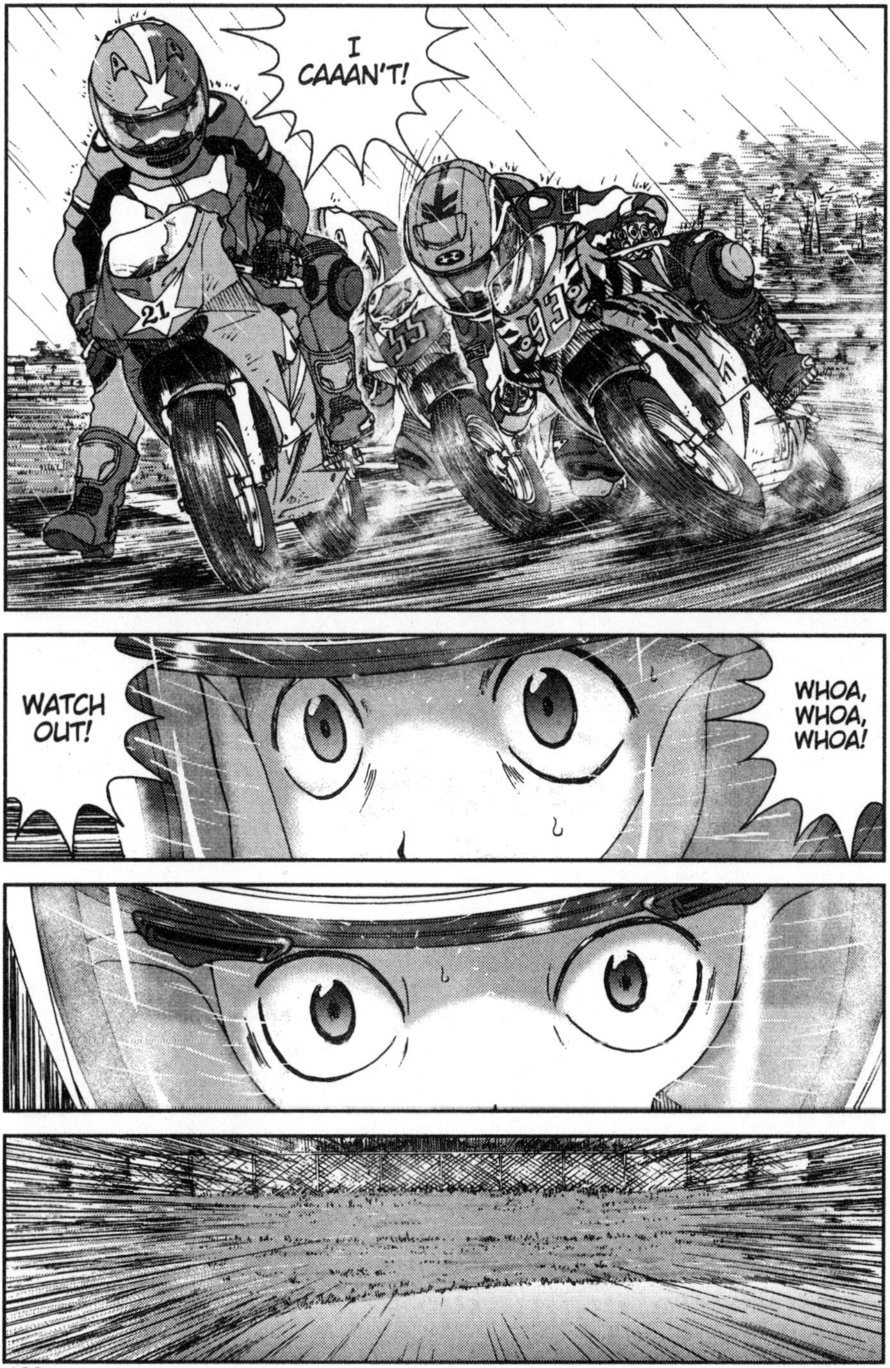
I CAAAN'T!
WHOA, WHOA, WHOA!
WATCH OUT!

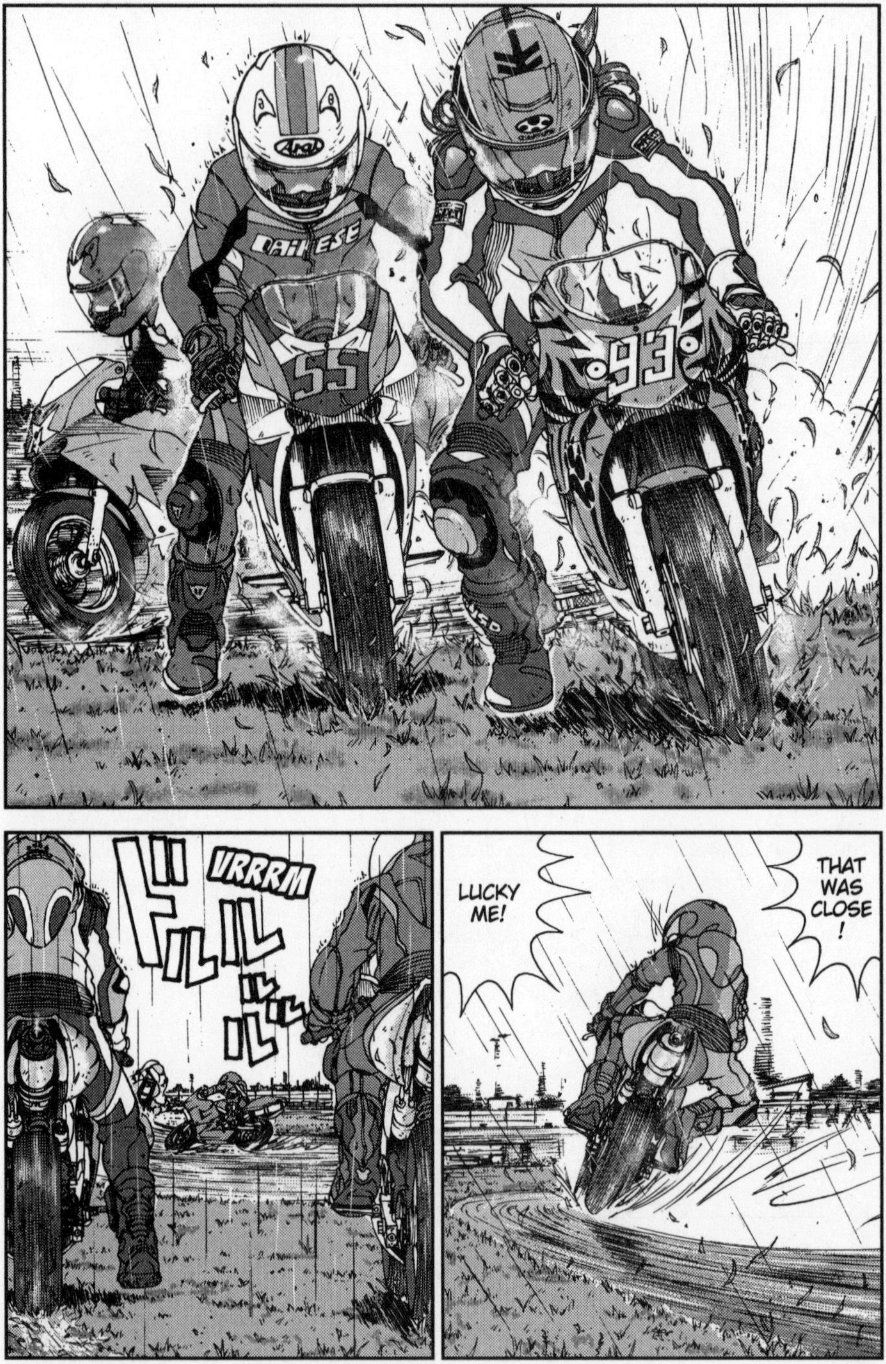
THAT WAS CLOSE!
LUCKY ME!
VRRRM